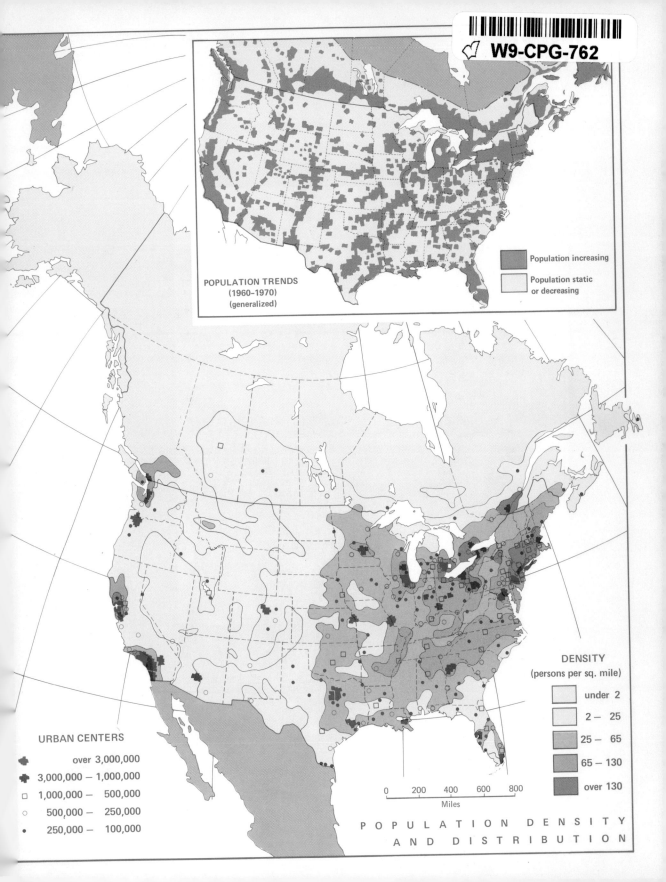

W9-CPG-762

POPULATION TRENDS
(1960–1970)
(generalized)

Population increasing

Population static
or decreasing

DENSITY
(persons per sq. mile)

under 2

2 – 25

25 – 65

65 – 130

over 130

URBAN CENTERS

over 3,000,000

3,000,000 – 1,000,000

1,000,000 – 500,000

500,000 – 250,000

250,000 – 100,000

0   200   400   600   800
Miles

POPULATION DENSITY
AND DISTRIBUTION

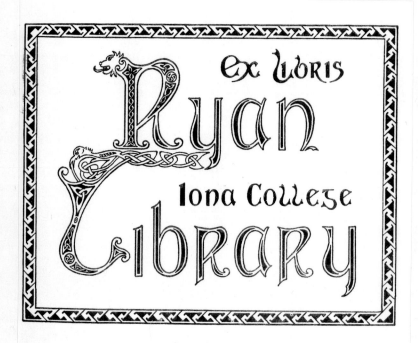

THE ANGLO-AMERICAN REALM

McGRAW-HILL SERIES IN GEOGRAPHY

EDWARD J. TAAFFE AND JOHN W. WEBB
Consulting Editors

Broek and Webb   A Geography of Mankind

Carlson   Africa's Lands and Nations

Cressey   Asia's Lands and Peoples

Cressey   Land of the 500 Million: A Geography of China

Demko, Rose, and Schnell   Population Geography: A Reader

Detwyler   Man's Impact on Environment

Eliot Hurst   Transportation Geography: Comments and Readings

Fryer   Emerging Southeast Asia: A Study in Growth and Stagnation

Fryer   World Economic Development

Kolars and Nystuen   Geography: The Study of Location, Culture, and Environment

Kolars and Nystuen   Human Geography: Spatial Design in World Society

Lanegran and Palm   An Invitation to Geography

Mather   Climatology: Fundamentals and Applications

Murphy   The American City: An Urban Geography

Pounds   Europe and the Soviet Union

Pounds   Political Geography

Raisz   General Cartography

Raisz   Principles of Cartography

Starkey, Robinson, and Miller   The Anglo-American Realm

Thoman and Corbin   The Geography of Economic Activity

Trewartha   An Introduction to Climate

Trewartha, Robinson, and Hammond   Fundamentals of Physical Geography

Trewartha, Robinson, and Hammond   Elements of Geography: Physical and Cultural

Trewartha, Robinson, and Hammond   Physical Elements of Geography (A republication of Part I of the above)

Van Riper   Man's Physical World

Watts   Principles of Biogeography: An Introduction to the Functional Mechanisms of Ecosystems

Yeates   An Introduction to Quantitative Analysis in Human Geography

THE ANGLO-AMERICAN REALM

OTIS P. STARKEY
Professor Emeritus of Geography
Indiana University

J. LEWIS ROBINSON
Professor of Geography
University of British Columbia

CRANE S. MILLER
Associate Professor of Geography
California State Polytechnic University, Pomona

SECOND EDITION

McGRAW-HILL BOOK COMPANY

New York   St. Louis   San Francisco   Auckland
Düsseldorf   Johannesburg   Kuala Lumpur   London
Mexico   Montreal   New Delhi   Panama   Paris
São Paulo   Singapore   Sydney   Tokyo   Toronto

The Montana–Alberta border shown on the title page indicates how the boundary between two political regions may be reflected in the landscape. The soil, relief, and climate are the same on both sides of the 49th parallel, but United States laws make the Montana land profitable for the dry farming of wheat. (*Photo from Air Photo Library, Lands and Forests, Alberta Government.*)

Library of Congress Cataloging in Publication Data

Starkey, Otis Paul, date
    The Anglo-American realm.

    (McGraw-Hill series in geography)
    Bibliography: p.
    1. United States—Economic conditions—1961–
2. Canada—Economic conditions—1945–   3. United
States—Description and travel—1960–   4. Canada—
Description and travel—1951–   I. Robinson, John
Lewis, date   joint author. II. Miller, Crane S.,
joint author. III. Title.
HC106.6.S75 1975   330.9′73′092   74-18410
ISBN 0-07-060872-5

THE ANGLO-AMERICAN REALM

 2 3 4 5 6 7 8 9 0   VHVH   7 9 8 7 6

This book was set in Helvetica Light by York Graphic Services, Inc.
The editors were Janis M. Yates and David Dunham;
the designer was Nicholas Krenitsky;
the production supervisor was Sam Ratkewitch.
New drawings were done by Andrew Mudryk.
Von Hoffmann Press, Inc., was printer and binder.

CONTENTS

Preface

1 TWO WEALTHY COUNTRIES
WITH PROBLEMS   3
A wealthy area   4
Problems and limitations   6
Geographic tools in regional
analysis   9

2 THE LANDS AND THE
SETTLERS   19
The settlers encounter aboriginal
America   19
Anglo-American counterparts of
European homelands   23
Settlement penetrates the water-
deficient lands   35

3 URBANIZATION AND URBAN
CRISES, 1860–1970   47
The growth of American cities   49
The economic evolution of
Canada, 1867–1970   56
Evolving patterns and urban crises   59

4 THE ATLANTIC MEGALOPOLIS
AND THE ADJACENT
NORTHEAST   69
The physical setting   72
The New York gateway   77
The New England gateway   86
The Delaware-Chesapeake
gateways   96
The future   106

5 THE CENTRAL LOWLAND   109
The Ohio Basin   113
The Great Lakes region   124
The Midwest   138
The American heartland   151

6 THE SOUTH   153
The Southern Uplands   157
The Southeastern Plain   167
The Gulf South   176
The future of the South   187

7 THE INTERIOR WEST   191
Environment and resources   192
The Southwest   202
The sparsely settled High West   208
Looking ahead   219

8 THE PACIFIC STATES   225
Physical landscapes and climates   227
The developing Southern
  California megalopolis   231
Focus on San Francisco Bay   241
The Hawaiian Islands   250
The Pacific Northwest   251

Alaska   262
Regional prospect: decelerating
  growth   264

9 EASTERN CANADA   267
Canada as a separate nation   267
Eastern Canada   270
The Atlantic Provinces   272
The heartland of Canada   278
The Canadian shield   294

10 WESTERN CANADA AND THE
NORTHLANDS   303
The Prairie Provinces   305
British Columbia   319
The Northlands   327

11 THE FUTURE OF
ANGLO-AMERICA   341
Growth problems in a finite world 342
Land shortage—nationally and
  regionally?   349
The clouded crystal ball   353

Index   357

PREFACE

Like the first edition, this second edition of *The Anglo-American Realm* is organized into regions which are urban-centered. This is appropriate since both Canadians and Americans are predominantly city people. The cities occupy less than 1 percent of the land area, but urban employment, income, and homes far outnumber those in the rural areas. Although urbanization has been significant in Anglo-America for at least a century, metropolitan dominance has been politically recognized for only a few decades. In the past decade, many urgent social and economic problems seemed to be related to geographic changes resulting from urbanization. These problems include rural-to-urban shifts in employment opportunities, suburban expansion, increasing environmental pollution, threats of resource exhaustion, and overcrowding in the central cities.

In a broader context, these changes involve geographical concepts of areal relationships and man-environment relationships which are relevant to solving a large proportion of our current problems. Even the more conservative (and optimistic) of our citizens now recognize that drastic changes in human values, in resource use, and in applied ecology will be required. In the first edition, we noted that "Within the present century a severe shortage of raw materials seems likely only in two re-sources; ironically these are the two that have long been considered free goods: fresh air and pure water.'' Our conclusions in this edition will not be so optimistic!

To understand our homelands—whether the purpose is to consider pressing national or regional problems or merely to adjust our life-styles to the geographical setting—we need a conceptual framework that recognizes Anglo-America as a working organism. This frame-work would include:

1   The quantity and quality of the land re-source—not only for its agricultural value but for its contribution to wealth production for recreational, industrial, and urban uses.

2   Those past events which still significantly affect our present use of, and attitudes toward, the land and its resources.

3   The inhabitants of the lands and their rela-tionships to the lands from which they earn a living.

4   The accumulations of structures, route-ways, technologies, skills, and cultural habits which have made our present physical produc-tion much higher than was possible for the aborigines on the same land.

5   Local cultural patterns which may aid or impede optimum use of the land. At present the outstanding cultural syndrome is related to urban problems which grow more rapidly than urban governments can cure them.

6   The concept that regions are interrelated and often interdependent.

All the preceding topics cannot be covered exhaustively in a volume of this size and scope. It is possible to present major themes on Anglo-America as a whole and on each of its major regions. The text stresses broad pat-terns, adding selected details where illustration seems required.

Features of the Second Edition

1   We have eliminated many statistics, techni-cal terms, and some descriptive details in the interests of brevity and clarity. For more details,

the reader should consult the Selected Refer-ences ending each chapter. The reader should become especially familiar with such basic ref-erence works as the *National Atlas of the United States of America,* the *Atlas of Canada,* the *Canada Yearbook,* and the *Statistical Ab-stract of the United States.* The colored maps on the endpapers and the maps and graphs in the book should be consulted while one is reading the text, and one should have at hand an atlas, such as *Goode's World Atlas* or the *Oxford World Atlas.*

2   As examples of geographic data obtainable by remote sensing, images taken by unmanned satellites have been included. Three of these are individual images of areas 115 miles square; two are parts of a mosaic of the United States prepared by the Soil Conservation Service and NASA from selected cloud-free images transmitted by the ERTS-1 satellite.

3   Although the regional divisions of the first edition have been retained, the number of re-gional chapters has been reduced to bring related regions together into larger units. Thus Chapter 4, The Atlantic Megalopolis and the Adjacent Northeast, combines the New Eng-land, New York, and Delaware-Chesapeake gateways, which together form the major Anglo-American concentrations of population, commerce, manufacturing, and services. With better transportation and communications, the former boundaries between the major subdivi-sions of the Atlantic Megalopolis are becoming increasingly blurred. It is thus more realistic to discuss the unity of the entire megalopolis and to use its subdivisions to show internal differ-ences. Throughout the book, each major re-gion is introduced by a broad descriptive char-acterization before the major subregions are analyzed.

4   The number of deviation (location quotient) graphs has been reduced. A better format has been adopted which will make the graphs more valuable and understandable to the student.

5   The Basic Data tables have been eliminated except for a summary table of the regions and subregions in the last chapter.

6 New materials on current problems have been added to each section. The student should realize that newspapers and magazines must be consulted to get contemporary data.

Acknowledgments

Each of us has made contributions to each part of the book. J. Lewis Robinson assumed primary responsibility for the Canadian sections; Crane Miller for the western United States; and Otis Starkey for the other sections. Many useful suggestions on facts, concepts, and phrasing have been received from the consulting editors and from a number of critics whose names are unknown to us. Although we made some changes in response to many suggestions received, we take final responsibility for any errors in the text. The patient, friendly, and stimulating help of the editorial staff of McGraw-Hill has done much to improve the readability, format, and beauty of the present work. Many of the maps and graphs retained from the first edition were the work of Dr. Gerald Ruth of Indiana University; maps and graphs especially drawn for this edition are the work of Andrew Mudryk. Finally, we thank teachers and students who have passed on to us their suggestions and reactions to the first edition.

Otis P. Starkey
J. Lewis Robinson
Crane S. Miller

THE ANGLO-AMERICAN REALM

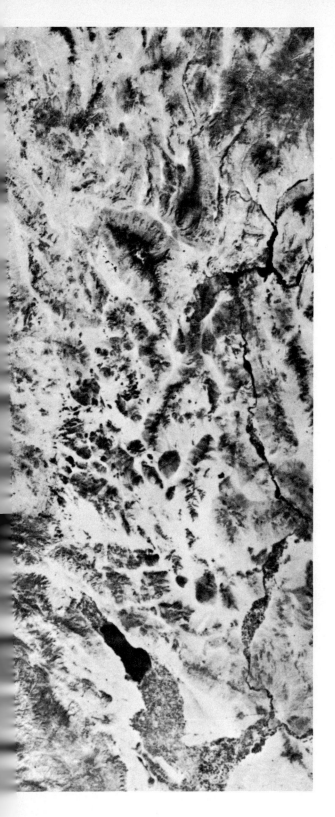

1

TWO WEALTHY COUNTRIES WITH PROBLEMS

The United States, Canada, and Greenland constitute Anglo-America, a region of more than 8 million square miles unevenly occupied by some quarter of a billion people. The unifying factor of the region is the dominance of a modified British culture—hence the name Anglo-America. Although almost all of the settled areas show considerable British influence, the nature of the cultural background varies from place to place. In Canada the French-Canadians represent a distinctive group, especially in the province of Quebec and in neighboring provinces. In northern Canada small groups of Indians and Eskimos still retain some traits of the aboriginal culture. In the United States, minorities such as the blacks, the Chicanos (of Mexican-American heritage), and the Indians maintain distinctive non-Anglo traits. In sparsely settled Greenland, which is politically Danish, Eskimo and Danish influences are strong in the older settlements, while American influences dominate in military and scientific stations. Thus the use of the convenient term Anglo-America does not imply that this culture region is absolutely uniform. A study of Anglo-

A mosaic of images taken by an Earth Resources Technology Satellite (ERTS) 560 statute miles (905 kilometers) above the earth. The area covered extends from San Diego to San Francisco Bay, California. (NASA)

American history and geography soon demonstrates that French, Spanish, German, Scandinavian, aboriginal, African, Oriental, Polynesian, and other cultures have made important contributions to the Anglo-American region.

Anglo-America encompasses an area more than twice that of Europe; yet about half of the region is unsettled or very sparsely settled. The undeveloped, and perhaps undevelopable, areas are mostly in Canada, Alaska, and Greenland. Throughout almost all of the settled area, English language and institutions prevail, and thus an Anglo-American manner of living is widespread with only minor local modification. Within recent decades minority groups, especially Indians, blacks, Chicanos, and French-Canadians, have become increasingly vocal concerning their disadvantageous position within the Anglo-American economy and society. On the other hand, other formerly disadvantaged minorities, for example, Catholics, Jews, Southern Europeans, and Orientals, have advanced considerably in economic and social status. WASP (white Anglo-Saxon Protestant) cultural and economic dominance, although still significant, is diminishing.

After World War II, Anglo-America seemed ready for world political and economic leadership. The United States and Canada had the wealth, technological knowledge, and willingness to contribute to the reconstruction of the war-ravaged countries as well as to aid the underdeveloped countries. Much was accomplished in the postwar years, but the failure of the United Nations to prevent the buildup of military establishments, the struggle between Communist and anti-Communist blocs, and the inability of the Anglo-American countries to solve some of their internal and international problems have weakened their power and prestige.

A WEALTHY AREA

The apparent current slowdown in solving Anglo-American social and economic problems should not cause one to overlook the Anglo-American accomplishments of past centuries. Both the United States and Canada have advanced their frontiers of settlement to the Pacific, and are penetrating northward into the Subarctic and Arctic regions; they have changed from predominantly rural to urban economies, and have developed cultural, political, economic, and technological ideas which have pervaded and changed much of the world.

The rapid growth of material wealth in the United States and Canada has been attributed to their great natural resources: their extensive forests, offshore fisheries, fertile farmlands, countless freshwater lakes and rivers, and vast deposits of minerals. Undoubtedly these resources attracted early settlers and provided capital for economic growth. However, availability of resources alone provides an incomplete explanation of rapid development. Most Indian groups, although settled amid the same natural wealth for centuries, were not compelled to exploit it beyond satisfying their basic needs.

In Anglo-America, as elsewhere, the earth offers opportunities; it may present challenges, but it rarely dictates the human responses to these challenges. To what extent the resource potential of a place will be exploited at a particular time depends on a combination of human knowledge of the resource, technological capability, effective business organization, social incentives to think and work, and political setting favorable to development. To this lengthy list should be added historical accident, since many human activities have been located by whims, faulty perception, and other chance factors.

Thus, although some natural resources are essential, the real wealth of Anglo-America lies in its people—their knowledge, skills, and organization and their will to develop the raw materials of the earth they control. Human ingenuity converts a few cents' worth of Labrador iron ore into thousands of dollars' worth of steel tools, and changes a few bushels of Iowa corn into much more valuable pork chops, cornflakes, and margarine. The technology that makes these industrial miracles possible involves an accumulation and integration of techniques whose roots go back to Rome, Greece, Egypt, China, and even to our Stone Age ancestors. Nature, techniques, great leaders, and hard work combined to make Anglo-America the wealthy region it is today. Any unfavorable change in this combination of human factors is likely to decrease the production of wealth.

Measuring the Wealth

The wealth of any country consists of intangible items which cannot be measured in dollars but are of major importance to the nation. These include the skills, work habits, proportion of population of working age, and health of the people as well as the accumulations of technical and scientific knowledge available to the workers who need them in their work.

The figures ordinarily published on national wealth (for example, in *The Statistical Abstract of the United States,* 1973, p. 343) consist of tangible items which can be roughly evaluated in terms of dollars. These are:

1 Land resources (standing room, soil, minerals, flora and fauna)
2 Structures (buildings, fences, roads, railroads, etc.)
3 Tools and machinery
4 Goods in process of production
5 Inventories in warehouses and stores

The value of the measurable United States wealth (last estimated for 1968) was $3,079 billion dollars. Comparable Canadian data are not available, but the trends described below also occurred in Canada. The most important change in both countries was the decline in the proportion of wealth classified as land resources and a corresponding increase in the proportions attributable to structures, tools, and machinery. For example, in 1900 land resources represented 35 percent of the United States wealth and in 1968 only 23 percent; the value of farmland decreased from 17 percent of the total in 1900 to less than 5 percent in 1968. Similar analysis of other data shows the decreasing relative importance of agriculture (and other raw material production) in the national economy. This change was caused not by a decrease in farm and raw materials production but rather by an increase in manufacturing and especially service activities. These changes result largely from the huge investment of Anglo-American wealth in urban development. The outcome is discussed more fully in Chapter 3.

Such tremendous wealth is of little value without people. If the Anglo-American economies were to become so bankrupt that an attempt would be made to sell their wealth, only about one-tenth could be converted into a form of value detached from its labor force. Of what value would be structures in ghost towns or roads and railroads upon which no freight moved? Of what worth are farms without farmers or factories and shops without artisans, clerks, and customers? Anglo-America must be viewed as a going concern. Certainly it is a naturally wealthy land, but wealthy because well-integrated economies employing labor skilled in modern technologies have used the resources efficiently.

Wealth, Gross National Product, and Personal Income

National wealth is the accumulated capital of the nation. More important in following the growth of the national economy is the *gross national product* (GNP), the value of the total annual production of goods and services. But not all of the GNP can be spent by the consumers, for a considerable allowance must be made for the depletion of irreplaceable natural resources and depreciation of machinery and other capital equipment. In addition, most businesses reinvest portions of their earnings in the expansion and improvement of business. The amount left is paid out as wages, interest, and dividends to potential consumers, and this together with insurance payments and annuities represents *personal income.* Not all personal income is available for spending, as a considerable amount must be paid in taxes before the consumer determines his *disposable personal income,* part of which he may choose to save. For the United States in 1972 the GNP was $1,155 billion; personal income was $939 billion, of which $116 billion was absorbed by taxes and $63 billion was saved. This left the consumer $760 billion to spend on goods and services. The Canadian GNP (produced by about one-tenth the number of people) was estimated for 1972 at $103 billion; because of differences in accounting systems the detailed statistics of the two countries are not exactly comparable.

PROBLEMS
AND LIMITATIONS

Anglo-American leaders have generally thought of the future in terms of continued growth. Cities were expected to grow larger. Industrial output and consumer consumption would multiply together. The desert would be made to bloom, and new resources would be discovered in the sparsely settled West and North. Even after all the lands were occupied and all resources were tapped, scientists and engineers would tap nuclear power and synthesize resources. Many more people would be supported, and the present level of living of the wealthy would become the standard of living for the average Anglo-American.

This utopian picture has been at least obscured if not added to the "impossible dreams" of the 1970s. The pressure of events such as the energy crisis has impressed upon Anglo-Americans that they are one-sixteenth of the world's population but are consuming one-third of the earth's fuel, raw materials, manufactures, and services. No longer can Anglo-Americans rely on Arab oil or African copper. Even within Anglo-America, Canadians have

questioned whether exports of their oil, gas, water, forest products, and other natural resources should be continued in unlimited quantities to support the raw material-hungry economy of the United States. For both Americans and Canadians, questions, now more critical than ever, are being asked: Are there limits to growth? Will our culturally induced demands for more raw materials, more power, fancier and larger buildings be supportable in a finite world where many millions still lack the material requirements for a decent level of living?

If the authors' analysis is correct, there are four major problem areas:

1 Can the population growth of Anglo-America be restricted so as to match the desired standard of living for all its people?
2 Can the resources available to Anglo-America, both within the region and exchangeable through international trade, support the desired Anglo-American standard of living?
3 Can the pollution of air, water, and soil resulting from urban industrial developments in Anglo-America be sufficiently controlled so as to ensure a healthful environment for expanding concentrations of urban dwellers?
4 Finally, can Anglo-Americans learn to cooperate so as to provide a livable environment for themselves without pollution from industry, overcrowding in urbanized areas, and destructive conflicts between special-interest groups?

Geographers obviously cannot answer all these questions nor provide all the guidelines necessary for solving the problems inherent in these questions. Geographers do recognize Anglo-America as a physical and cultural area with unusual potential for a good life for hundreds of millions of Anglo-Americans. Furthermore, geographers hope that the complex problems now becoming apparent can be solved. The objective is not to provide for the largest number of people on the highest level of consumption, but rather to provide a homeland for a motivated, productive, and happy society. In so doing, we cannot neglect the present nature of Anglo-America nor the contribution of the past in shaping the present geographic patterns. The authors believe, however, that the problems resulting from the philosophy of unlimited growth imply dire consequences. Appropriate attention to these growth problems seems requisite to building the kind of civilization most Anglo-Americans desire.

Overpopulation

Compared with China, India, Japan, Belgium, and the Netherlands, each of which has more than 700 people per square mile, Anglo-America is not overpopulated. Canada has only 5 people per square mile, an unusually low figure, accounted for by the sparse population of the northern two-thirds of Canada. For Anglo-America as a whole (allowing for the almost uninhabitable areas), the United States density of 57 people per square mile (about 11 acres per person) is a fair estimate. But even with this huge per capita land resource, many rural areas are currently unable to support their populations and rural out-migration is common. If Anglo-Americans were willing to work as hard and consume as little as the average Chinese peasant, the Anglo-American land resource would be generous. But such a change in economic and social habits seems unlikely.

Within recent years Anglo-American birthrates have been declining steadily but not to the point of zero population growth. The annual rate of population increase in Canada for the last decade was 1.7 percent, in the United States 1.1 percent. These rates are lower than in earlier decades. But even if these low rates are maintained, the population of Canada would double by the year 2010 and that of the United States by the year 2030. It is noteworthy that the population growth rate for the United States in the first half of the 1970s fell below 1 percent.

The resulting population densities from continued increases at the above rates would not be intolerable if Anglo-Americans lived as frugally as most of the world's peoples. Unfortunately Anglo-Americans have spending and resource-consuming habits that evolved when land and natural resources seemed unlimited. Growth has become a way of life, and many Anglo-American industries and service businesses are dependent for their prosperity, or perhaps survival, on continued increases in the demand for goods.

Resources, Destructive Exploitation, and Illth

Geographers have long been aware of the need for the conservation of natural resources. Until recently most of our resources were believed adequate for centuries or at least several decades. Furthermore, new technologies and substitute materials were expected to solve any problem of shortages. Only within the last few years have the general public and the businessman become more aware of imminent crises. The shortage of low-sulfur oil and coal which do not pollute the air as much as high-sulfur fuels, the acceleration of our drain on local natural resources, the relative failure of recycling, the increasing dependence of our economies on overseas resources—all seem to have converged to advance the date for approaching crises. Nuclear power and nuclear-generated electricity, which were expected to replace fossil fuels, seem to many scientists, engineers, and laymen to pose greater environmental hazards than the fuels they were scheduled to replace.

Many resources such as the soil and forests may be exploited on a sustained-yield basis so that the resource is used no faster than nature can replace it. But certain activities such as mining necessarily use up the best ores first. If correct accounting procedures are followed, such depletion of resources is reflected in depreciation accounts. In many activities such as grazing and cropping, the quality of the pasture and soil may gradually

This slum has now been replaced by an urban renewal project. (Philadelphia City Planning Commission)

depreciate without any accounting entry being made to indicate the loss of capital. Such slow depreciation of resources may ultimately lead to the decline of the local resource-based economy. Use of a land resource so that economic value depreciates is called *destructive exploitation.* This practice, unavoidable in mining, should be discouraged in other enterprises.

The rarely used word *illth,* first used by John Ruskin, may be appropriately employed to describe a problem of which ecologically minded citizens are becoming increasingly aware. Illth is negative wealth.[1] Since wealth refers to anything which makes the earth useful to man, *illth may be anything which diminishes*

the usefulness of the earth to man. Thus smog, soil erosion, water pollution, the destruction of scenic places, and noise pollution might all be considered forms of illth. Such destruction of natural resources results from the focus of each individual on his own objectives with disregard of the consequences to others in the community. Certainly one of our pressing political problems is to prevent illth without unduly restricting individual liberty.

Pollution and Urbanization

Not many decades ago Anglo-American cities dumped raw sewage into rivers, and many industrial plants still dump chemical pollutants

[1] The word *wealth* originated from combining *weal* (well-being) and *th; illth* is *ill* plus *th.*

into lakes and rivers. Two decades ago pollution from internal combustion engines was looked upon as a nuisance and dirt producer rather than a health danger; today some urban air is "dangerous to health." The oceans, the ultimate garbage disposal, were also considered to be a reserve of seafood; today we know these two uses of the sea are inconsistent. Continued industrial growth seems more a threat than a promise to many.

The worst pollution threat is concentrated in and near large Anglo-American cities. There the massing of people and people-made pollutants increasingly surpasses the ability of air and water to dilute contaminants to safe levels. The natural ecological cycle consists of plants which absorb some pollutants and release oxygen to the air. But near large cities natural vegetation becomes scarce, and introduced trees, ornamental shrubs, and gardens are far from adequate in absorbing motor vehicle and industrial air pollution. Finally, some pollutants (most notably atomic waste) may continue to contaminate air, land, and water for thousands of years.

Can Anglo-Americans Solve These Problems?

Anglo-America is a wealthy region inhabited by many able and well-educated people. These people have originated life-styles which have been copied in part by many of the world's people—life-styles based on the prodigal use of material goods. The quarter billion of Anglo-Americans are using up many times their share of the earth's resources at a rate unparalleled in history. Are Anglo-Americans well enough informed, motivated, and organized to prevent overpopulation and resource exhaustion and eliminate pollution—problems which are basic to the solution of many unsolved economic, social, and political problems? Can Anglo-Americans overlook individual and group interests and cooperate in measures necessary to save Anglo-American society?

GEOGRAPHIC TOOLS IN REGIONAL ANALYSIS

Just as a doctor uses a stethoscope, x-rays, and blood tests to determine what is necessary to treat human ailments, the geographer must employ certain tools to analyze any part of the earth and its problems. Thereby he can determine how the space and resources are being utilized by men, whether a particular land use could be improved, and whether a plan for future use of land resources should be devised.

In short, the geographer's task is to explain the "where" and the "why" of a region's environmental and human resources—explaining the "where" is largely descriptive; examining the "why" is clearly analytical.

Differences among areas can be determined by personal observation, by systematic surveying and mapping, by remote sensing, by regional analysis, and by quantitative methods. When Anglo-America was first explored, the characteristics of places along certain routes, usually waterways or Indian trails, were noted. The features observed on such journeys may not have been representative of the areas traversed. In the mid-nineteenth century more accurate surveys were made as part of the planning for railroads; later land surveys were still more detailed, much more accurate, and very expensive.

Remote Sensing

Photographs or other images taken from a distance often survey the features of a part of the earth much more quickly and cheaply than these could be surveyed on the ground. Also, patterns never detected at the earth's surface often take on meaningful form only when viewed from a remote location, such as an orbiting satellite. This text includes sample images taken from the Earth Resources Technology Satellite (ERTS) which travels around the earth at an altitude of 560 miles and which by electronic sensors reproduces the features of square sections (115 miles^2) of the earth

The irregular pattern shown here in New Brunswick is typical of a glaciated area used primarily for forest industries. (New Brunswick Travel Bureau)

once every 18 days. Remote sensing of the Anglo-American environment has been carried on by a number of spacecrafts, including the Gemini, Apollo, Mariner, and Skylab satellites, as well as by ordinary aircraft. The images are produced on a variety of different films often employing a variety of filters so that fine distinctions may be made, such as between healthy crops and diseased crops or between different land uses. When remote sensing data are examined in the laboratory, the trained observer becomes aware of information which may have to be checked by geographers, geologists, or biologists on the ground.

The Map

The geographer's primary tool is the map, which is a portrait of a part of the earth on a relatively small scale showing certain features in a systematic way. Most of us are accustomed to using street maps of cities or road maps of states or regions. We use these primarily to guide us to some place we wish to visit. Accurate scientific maps tell much more: if the map were a large-scale street plan, it might show the exact width of the street, the sidewalks, the location and area occupied by each house, and perhaps even the extent and location of trees and gardens. The interpretation of maps can be a complicated undertaking, and the interested student may wish to examine books on cartography and map interpretation. At the same time, the student accustomed to reading maps realizes that a map can impart information in a single page or at a glance that might otherwise consume several pages of text. Thought of in this way, the maps in this book, which are both generous in number and easy to read, should serve the student to considerable advantage.

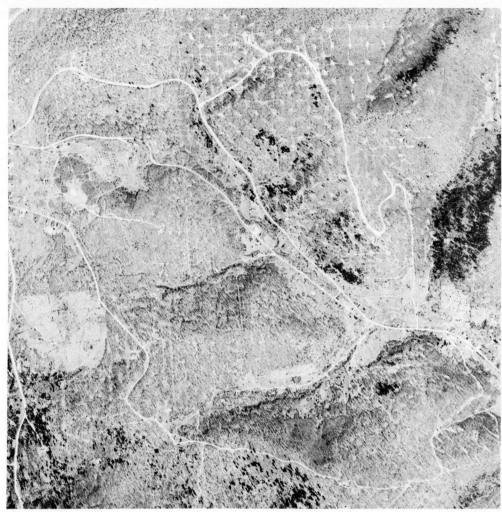

Regular patterns suggest the activities of man. On the Allegheny Plateau of northwestern Pennsylvania, an oil field in operation for a century shows that mining may last for considerable periods. The wells here are close together, and the pumps, connected by cables so that one engine powers several wells, create a distinctive pattern on the landscape. (USDA photograph)

Patterns   In flying over central Indiana, Illinois, and Iowa, even unskilled observers might notice that the majority of fields and country roads have a rectangular pattern. In the towns, most street patterns are likewise gridlike, and a map shows mostly rectangular county and township boundaries. This pattern is a result of the township-range survey (see Figure 5.2) upon which land titles have been based in most of the United States settled after 1790.

The recognition of geographic patterns may permit a trained observer to look for similar patterns to be repeated nearby or in other areas. Such repetitions raise the question of whether regions which have similar geographic patterns are similar in other ways. Unfortunately in most areas the individual patterns are not so uniform as in the rectangular patterns of the Midwest; the patterns for each type of data—for example, for climate, soils, vegetation, and roads—do not always match. These patterns may coincide in some regions but not in others. The landscape intertwines so many patterns that the resulting design may seem as complicated as in the most intricate Oriental rug. Yet the trained geographer can unravel these patterns and discover recurring regularities which give distinct descriptive characteristics to an area.

Regional Analysis

A major problem in making the various parts of Anglo-America a suitable home for man is the complexity of any large segment of the whole. Each area may seem to be a patchwork quilt of natural and man-made features. Add to these visible features the desires of the inhabitants for such objectives as increased economic security and opportunity, better housing and community life, and relief from the many major and minor annoyances, and the community seems to be a collection of chaotic features and unsolved problems. To compound the difficulties many of these features and problems seem to be the result of either historical inheritances or forces remote from local controls.

Regional planners and geographers find that it simplifies the comprehension of large and complex areas if they were subdivided into regions. *A region should have significant unifying characteristics which differentiate it from surrounding areas.* A region may be large or small. Thus Anglo-America is a very large cultural region characterized by a common language and traditions. The Everglades of Florida form a small region identified by its swampiness. The Tennessee Valley is a region bound together by its drainage into the Tennessee River.

Most regions used by geographers have arbitrary boundaries. Although regions may seem to have complex natural environmental

and man-made features, geographers believe that they can see order and patterns in these areas. Within the regions there are common phenomena, common problems, and human organizational features, including culture, routes, and governments. If the regions are natural (defined by landform features, climate, or vegetation), they may show few changes—at least in terms of a human life-span. But regions defined by cultural criteria may change as man changes; thus there was no Corn Belt until corn cultivation developed into a major land use and until American farmers evolved the technique of marketing corn by feeding it to livestock. Should some other crop (or industry) prove more profitable than corn or should Americans become vegetarians, the present activities within the Corn Belt would decline. That part of the United States would then have to be defined and characterized by some other activity.

Uniform regions and site Geographers find it convenient to distinguish two major categories of regions: *uniform* and *nodal* (Figure 1.1). Uniform regions are generally based on *site* characteristics, that is, on local features of or associated with the land included within the region, for example, soil, crops, landforms, type of farm, nature of the inhabitants, cultural characteristics, climate, and natural vegetation. Whatever characteristics are chosen as the bases for a uniform[2] region, they are prevalent throughout the region (although not always to the same degree). Thus, in most of its area Anglo-America has certain cultural characteristics that are lacking or rare in Latin America to the south or in Soviet Eurasia across the North Pole. Other examples of uniform regions are the *Colorado Plateau,* a Western area characterized by high plateaus dissected by deep canyons, and the *Mojave Desert,* an arid region in southeastern California, defined on the basis

[2] Some geographers use the terms *homogenous region* or *single-factor regions.*

of its low annual rainfall and subdued mountain and basin topography.

Nodal regions and situation The relationship of a central area to the surrounding countryside is characteristic of *nodal regions.* Such a relationship is commonly referred to as the *situation* of a place. For example, the *retail trading area of Indianapolis* is that region whose residents normally shop in Indianapolis stores; the *hinterland of Norfolk* is that inland area from which goods are normally shipped or to which goods are imported through the Port of Norfolk; the *log hinterland of Vancouver* is the coastal area from which logs are cut and transported to the sawmills in or near Vancouver, British Columbia.

Regional cores and boundaries The unique characteristics of nodal regions are often most pronounced in a central core within the region. This core is around the large city or other feature to which the surrounding area is related. The periphery of the region may be a transition zone between the adjacent regions and may have approximately equal qualities of each region. For example, if the criterion for determining the boundary between the trading areas of two cities is newspaper circulation, a transitional zone will have about the same number of subscribers to the papers from each of the competing cities.

Uniform regions may also have similar transition zones at the boundaries, but usually the core is not as sharply focused as in the nodal regions. The boundaries of either type of region may be sharp if some physical or cultural feature ends abruptly. For example, an international boundary may sharply limit the trading area of a city. A change in relief such as the steep edge of an escarpment or the edge of a marsh may prevent the extension of an agricultural region. In many cases regional boundaries are transitional rather than sharp, and the determination of a boundary involves consid-

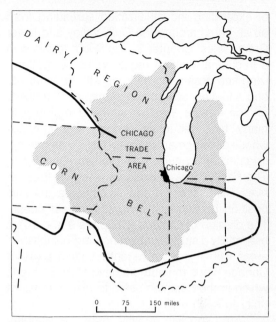

Figure 1.1 The Corn Belt is a uniform region in which most farming is centered on corn. Corn is also raised in the Dairy Region; but the farm focus is on dairy production, and corn serves mainly as fodder for dairy cattle. The Chicago Trade Area is a nodal region unified by its commercial focus on Chicago; a more refined classification might differentiate two nodal regions: the Chicago Retail Trade Area and the larger Chicago Wholesale Trade Area.

erable judgment by the geographer, as well as some exact measurement of the criteria being employed to define the region's main characteristics.

The variety of regional criteria In subdividing Anglo-America into regions related to human use, it becomes extremely difficult to follow consistent criteria. In this book, the authors use a variety of criteria in distinguishing their major regions: The regional analyses begin with Chapter 4, whose subject is the Atlantic Megalopolis, a highly urbanized seaboard area fringed by less settled lands. Chapter 5 examines the Central Lowland, a physiographic region which was rapidly settled initially to exploit its soil, forest, and mineral resources, but which now consists of an area of expanding industrialization spreading from urban cores around the Ohio Valley and lower Great Lakes. Chapter 6, *The South,* deals with a traditional cultural region which is modernizing and urbanizing in areas with unusual site and situation advantages. Chapter 7 focuses on the Interior West, a semiarid region with many high mountain ranges and plateaus whose development is based largely on mining, irrigated agriculture, and tourism. Chapter 8, *The Pacific States,* explores a region that derives climatic and trade advantages from its position bordering the world's largest ocean. The division of Canada (Chapters 9 and 10) is essentially a study contrasting long-established areas with the more recently settled parts of Canada. Thus the authors have several criteria which in their opinion serve to give a sense of unity to each region.

Any specific locality may be simultaneously in a variety of regions, each created by man to serve a particular purpose in his analysis or utilization of an area. Thus the Borough of Brooklyn, a major political subdivision of New York City, coincides with Kings County, a subdivision of New York State. Both of these units are political regions. Brooklyn is also part of the New York City Standard Metropolitan Statistical Area (SMSA), a creation of the U.S. Bureau of the Census. A banker might think of Brooklyn as part of the Second Federal Reserve District, the area served by the Federal Reserve Bank of New York. Brooklyn can also be considered a part of the northeastern United States, a part of the humid-continental climatic region, and a part of Long Island (which in turn is a part of the Atlantic Coastal Plain, a landform region). Obviously, regionalization can become exceedingly complex, but necessary if individual needs are to be satisfied.

Quantitative Tools

By its very nature geography lends itself to widespread use of quantitative techniques and computer technology. Many of the statistical methods used today are extremely complex, and the student so inclined should avail himself of the current wealth of literature in quantitative geography. This book employs graphs where appropriate, both arithmetic and semilog graphs (see Chapter 3). Two other devices utilized herein are *correlation* and the *location quotient.*

Correlation The development of computers has noticeably speeded up statistical accumulation and analysis of areas. Computers can be programmed to compare different kinds of data and even to draw maps to show the distribution of the data. By factor analysis, multiple correlation, and other techniques interrelationships can be measured in terms of statistical probability. For example, a recent study of the geography of poverty[3] lists these correlations (1.000 would be a perfect positive correlation):

1 Correlation of .458 between poverty in the United States and the distance to the nearest city of at least 250,000.
2 Correlation of .820 in the Dallas–Fort Worth SMSAs between poverty and proximity to either the Dallas or the Fort Worth Central Business District.

The location quotient In Anglo-America, most large cities (and all but a few states and provinces) have at least some of most types of business and social and political activities. Understanding of urban activities is not gained solely by noting that a certain metropolitan area has houses, apartments, supermarkets, garages, schools, banks, churches, each of the 19 major groups of industries, etc. It may, however, be significant that this metropolis has a relatively large number of textile mills and a disproportionately small number of schools. That is, what we want to know is how the city

[3]Richard L. Morrill and Ernest H. Wohlenberg, *The Geography of Poverty in the United States,* McGraw-Hill, New York, 1971, pp. 65–71.

is *different* from other cities, as well as in what ways it is similar. On another scale, the northeastern United States, compared with the United States as a whole, has more public transportation and a relatively small number of private automobiles per capita. This information permits one to characterize the Northeast in terms of these transport factors as being regionally different from other parts of the United States. A simple statistical device, the *location quotient*,[4] has been developed to show unusual regional concentrations of particular kinds of data. Consider Figure 1.2, a location quotient graph for all sources of income in the northeastern states of the United States.[5] If the bar for a particular category of income extends to the 1.0 line, this indicates that the region has the same per capita income from that economic activity as the United States. If the bar is only 0.5, income in that industry is only half of that in the United States; if 2.0, twice that in the United States per capita. Note that these location quotients are only a general estimate of the relative importance of industries: they assume, for example, that all labor is equally paid.

---

[4] The *location quotient* (LQ) is the ratio of the share of an industry in a region to the share of the same industry in the nation. It may be applied to other data, for example, employment, income, education, and health.

[5] Location quotients have been calculated in a number of ways using a great variety of data. The method used by the authors is as follows:

1 Calculate what *1 percent* (A) is of a selected United States or Canadian data category.
2 Multiply A (above) by the *percent of the national population* (B) in the region, SMSA, state, or province for which the location quotient is being determined ($A \times B = AB$)
3 To find the location quotient, divide the *data for the particular area* (C) by AB, or $LQ = C/AB$.

    Example: To find the California location quotient in transport equipment manufacturing.
    a The United States value added by manufacturing in transport equipment is $29,308 million; 1 percent = $293 million = A.
    b The population of California is 9.7 percent of that of the United States; $293 \times 9.7 = 2,842 = AB$.
    c California transport equipment is 3,213. This quantity (C) is divided by AB (2,842) to obtain the location quotient of 1.13. This method introduces into each calculation a per capita factor which is desirable because the problems considered in this book are mainly related to human use of earth resources.

INCOME   **THE ATLANTIC MEGALOPOLIS**

% Distribution   Location quotients: 1.0 = national average per capita

Employ-ment	Income	SIC source	0	1.0	2.0	3.0	4.0	5.0
1.4	0.1	Farms						
0.2	0.2	Mining						
4.7	3.9	Construction						
25.4	19.3	Manufacturing						
22.1	10.9	Trade						
6.0	4.3	Finance						
6.1	5.2	Transportation						
17.7	10.4	Services						
16.5	13.1	Government						
—	32.6	Other income*						
100.0	100.0	Total						

*Pensions, interest, dividends, annuities, insurance, etc.

Figure 1.2 The location quotient graphs show how any area compares in a given category with the country as a whole. Note that the huge agglomeration of cities extending from Boston to Virginia, described as the Atlantic Megalopolis (see Chapter 4), has a location quotient much below the United States average per capita income in the primary industries (farming and mining) but above average in finance, trade, and manufacturing. The two columns to the left show that income and employment are not necessarily distributed in any consistent relationship to the location quotient or to each other. Note, for example, *other income* which accounts for nearly one-third of the income of the Atlantic Megalopolis but which generates a negligible amount of employment. See Figure 1.3 below.

INCOME   **PACIFIC STATES**

% Distribution   Location quotients: 1.0 = national average per capita

Employ-ment	Income	SIC source	0	1.0	2.0	3.0	4.0	5.0
4.4	.9	Farms						
0.3	.3	Mining						
4.2	3.8	Construction						
19.9	15.3	Manufacturing						
21.4	11.4	Trade						
5.3	3.5	Finance						
6.2	5.2	Transportation						
17.2	9.8	Services						
20.7	16.3	Government						
—	33.5	Other income*						
100.0	100.0	Total						

Figure 1.3 The Pacific States include California, Oregon, Washington, Alaska, and Hawaii. Compare this chart item by item with Figure 1.2. How do you explain the differences?

Regional Systems and Synthesis

The preceding tools will produce analyses, descriptions, patterns, and other factual materials which if taken separately may or may not provide an understanding of the geography of a region. Increasingly, students of the social sciences have found it desirable to combine related forms of data into systems of interacting variables and then to correlate interactions among these systems. To some geographers the basic systems are those of:

A   Physical geography
1   The land as space for human activity, including spatial relations of one place to all other places on the earth
2   The landforms, climates, water bodies, vegetation, minerals, and soils which provide raw materials
3   The ecosystems (communities of organisms related to their physical environment)—for example, man as an organism as related to his biological and other environments

B   Cultural geography
Cultural systems among human groups, large or small, considered as:
1   Possessors of a wide variety of cultural traits and traditions
2   Part of political systems
3   Part of economic systems, as producers and consumers

4   Part of motivational or institutional systems (military, religious, etc.)

Obviously the above systems overlap, and for analysis each may need to be subdivided. Few persons know enough of the basic facts about the systems of which they are a part. Nevertheless they participate in decision making, and their decisions are based on their limited perception of the facts and issues of the problem at hand rather than on an understanding of the complete operation of the system.

A regional geographer, fully aware of the complex job being undertaken, must evaluate the major aspects of each area he is describing and present these as part of a larger region. The selection of the facts to be stressed will vary from region to region and with the intellectual background and interests of the geographer. Generally, however, two concepts should be expected in any regional treatment:

1   Considerable stress will be placed on interrelations among the major factors in each region.
2   Since each region is unique in its physical setting, economic and cultural history, and present development and problems, the organization used may differ from region to region. If the resulting product is a synthesis of the characteristics of each region rather than a catalog of facts, the text will achieve the spirit of regional geography.

SELECTED REFERENCES

Atlas of Canada, Queen's Printer, Ottawa, 1957. A new (1972) *Atlas of Canada,* available either in separate map sheets or in loose-leaf format, to be revised continuously, is published by the federal Department of Energy, Mines and Resources in Ottawa.

BLAIR, C. L., and B. V. GUTSELL, *The American Landscape, Map and Air Photo Interpretation,* McGraw-Hill, New York, 1974. Examples of geographic patterns illustrated by superb photos and topographic maps.

BOGUE, D. J.: *The Population of the U.S.A.,* Free Press, New York, 1959.

Canada Year Book (annual), Queen's Printer, Ottawa. Information Canada, Ottawa, will answer any request related to facts about Canada and will send lists of publications on requested topics.

CLAWSON, MARION: *America's Land and Its Use,* Johns Hopkins University Press, Baltimore, 1972.

GERLACH, ARCH C. (ed.): *The National Atlas of the United States of America,* U.S. Department of the Interior, Geological Survey, Washington, 1970.

Goode's World Atlas, 14th ed., Rand McNally, Chicago, 1974.

HAMELIN, L. E., and C. I. JACKSON, *Canada: A Geographic Perspective,* Wiley, Toronto, 1973.

HOLZ, ROBERT K. (ed.): *The Surveillant Science-Remote Sensing of the Environment,* Houghton Mifflin, Boston, 1973.

JONES, C. F., and P. E. JAMES (eds.): *American Geography: Inventory and Prospect,* Syracuse University Press, Syracuse, 1954. Includes a chapter on regions.

KALBACK, WARREN E., and W. W. McVEY: *The Demographic Bases of Canadian Society,* McGraw-Hill, Toronto, 1971.

LANEGRAN, DAVID A., and RISA PALM (eds.): *An Invitation to Geography,* McGraw-Hill, New York, 1973.

MANNERS, IAN R., and MARVIN MIKESELL (eds.): *Perspectives on Environment,* Association of American Geographers (AAG), Washington, D.C., 1974.

MORRILL, RICHARD, and ERNEST WOHLENBERG: *Geography of Poverty in the United States,* McGraw-Hill, New York, 1972.

MURPHEY, RHOADS: *The Scope of Geography,* Rand McNally, Chicago, 1973.

PUTNAM, D., and R. PUTNAM: *Canada: A Regional Analysis,* Dent, Don Mills, Ont., 1970.

The United States and Canada (Oxford Regional Economic Atlas), Clarendon Press, Oxford, 1967.

U.S. BUREAU OF THE CENSUS: *County and City Data Book: 1972,* Washington, 1972. New editions or supplements appear every few years.

———: *Statistical Abstract of the United States* (annual), Washington.

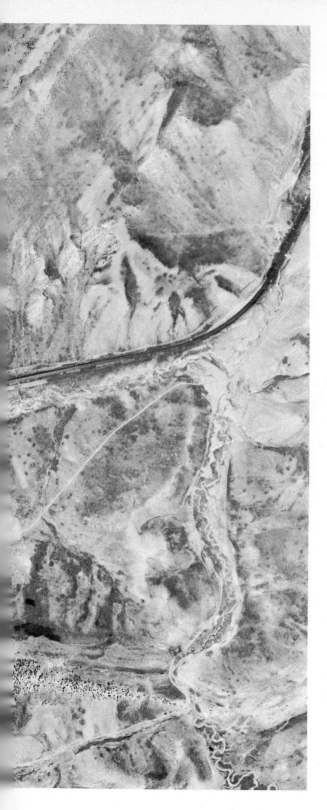

2
THE LANDS
AND THE SETTLERS

The settlement of a new land is no simple matter. It involves not only the physical nature of the settlement site but also the landscape and resources as the settlers perceive them—a perception biased by their culture and experience in a somewhat different environment. The lifestyle of the settlers was also influenced by local Indian cultures and by innovations diffused from their European or eastern American homelands. Within the new settlements the ideas and character of local (and later national) leaders altered the nature of the community and the customs of the settlers. Isolated from their homelands by slow transportation and communication, the pioneers were often forced to improvise new methods which proved valuable in problem solving in their new setting.

THE SETTLERS ENCOUNTER
ABORIGINAL AMERICA
The earliest settlers from Europe found that the land had already been used by aborigines and

This barren part of extreme southwestern Wyoming has been crossed by game trails, Indian trails, trapper routes, and by Mormons and other settlers. After having passed the highest point on its main route, the Union Pacific descends here along the headwaters of the Bear River, which drains into Great Salt Lake. The visible roads are of historic importance; the main highway (Interstate 80) is some miles to the north. (USDA photograph)

Figure 2.1 This is a useful but highly generalized map of the North American environment and sources of settlement.

was crisscrossed with a sparse network of trails, fields, huts, and villages whose location and arrangement had been determined by the customs and objectives of an earlier era. The aborigines lacked both the numbers and the technology to alter the land resources noticeably. Consequently the *organic* resources were rich with soils unleached, virgin forests and prairies stocked with game, pure air and water, and streams and offshore banks crowded with fish. To colonists from the well-settled, thoroughly tilled, not overfertile soils of Western

Europe, this almost free land, which could be bought (or conquered) cheaply from the Indians, was indeed a land of promise. The first generations of settlers thought in terms of a largely self-sufficient economy with the prospect of wealth from furs, fish, naval stores, and a few agricultural products in demand in Europe.

No scientific surveys preceded the first

settlements. The settlers perceived the New World piecemeal, and until the first decades of the nineteenth century much of the heart of North America was inaccurately described. Large areas were judged by what a few explorers found along river routes and by what Indians reported to white traders.

Vegetation was believed (in most cases correctly) to provide an indication of the fertility of the soil and of the climate in each area. Areas whose plant cover resembled that of areas known in Western Europe were assumed to have similar potentialities for agriculture. Spanish settlers entering the region from Mexico perceived potentialities in grasslands and semideserts. In contrast, English and French colonists were primarily interested in the extensive forests with their fur potential in the North and lumber and agricultural potential in the milder East.

Aboriginal Cultures

Ancestors of the aboriginal peoples probably first entered North America across the Bering Strait. Toward the end of the Ice Ages, Siberia and Alaska were linked together by a narrow land bridge which was attractive to primitive hunters following wild game herds. The exact dates of these migrations are still disputed but were probably at least 25,000 years ago. As the great glaciers of the late Pleistocene epoch melted, the sea level rose and the land bridge disappeared. Much later, perhaps 5,000 years ago, Eskimos crossed the Bering Strait to the American arctic tundras; they slowly and thinly settled a coastal zone 3,000 miles eastward to northern Labrador and Greenland where they encountered the Norse Vikings about the tenth century.

In contrast to the high densities in aboriginal central and southern Mexico, what is now Anglo-America was sparsely inhabited—at most there are believed to have been about 2 million Indians and 50,000 Eskimos north of the Rio Grande. These peoples were divided

into hundreds of tribal groups, possessing many distinctive languages and cultures. Most had a Stone Age culture less advanced than the indigenous cultures of southern Mexico from which agriculture and other cultural traits eventually spread into the Eastern Woodlands and some parts of the arid and semiarid Southwest.

The *material* features of most Indian cultures were closely related to the flora and fauna of their physical environment. To European settlers, the Indian provided trails, knowledge of the land and techniques for exploiting the land, and cheap labor in the fur trade. Eventually in most areas the settler found the Indian a nuisance to be pushed westward into unwanted lands, or exterminated. Lacking at first firearms, steel tools, and European scientific knowledge, the Indian, weakened by European-introduced diseases, liquor, and intertribal war, could delay but not stop European advance.

European Influences on Colonial Life-styles

The colonial civilizations that developed in America were influenced by religious, social, and economic traditions of Europe. In the seventeenth century, Western Europe politically and religiously was in turmoil; economically it was expanding and demanding raw materials from overseas. European society was highly stratified, and opportunities for the lower classes, no matter how skilled, were negligible. Land, and other means of rising into the favored classes, was not easily obtained.

America did not attract the timid. The Atlantic crossing required a hazardous voyage of two to three months. The *Mayflower,* only 90 feet long, carried 25 sailors and 102 passengers, crowded in with the domestic animals and stores needed during the voyage and to supply the new settlement. Such voyages attracted mainly the adventurous or the desperate who, discouraged by their prospects in Europe, be-

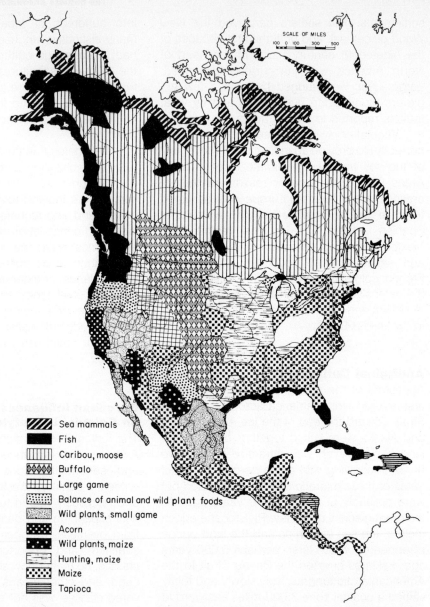

SCALE OF MILES
100 0 100   300   500

⫽⫽⫽	Sea mammals
▮	Fish
⦀⦀⦀	Caribou, moose
◇◇◇	Buffalo
▦	Large game
⠿	Balance of animal and wild plant foods
░	Wild plants, small game
⣿	Acorn
▬	Wild plants, maize
☰	Hunting, maize
⣏	Maize
≣	Tapioca

Figure 2.2 The food basis of American aboriginal life. Compare this map with Figure 2.4. (From Harold E. Driver and William C. Massey, "Comparative Studies of the North American Indians," TRANSACTIONS, The American Philosophical Society, vol. 47, part 2, pp. 177, 184.)

lieved their chances better in the New World. Many were willing to come as indentured servants. The trans-Atlantic voyage was usually much harder on political prisoners, convicts, and African slaves, all of whom contributed to the burgeoning colonial economies.

   The colonists had not been so much dissatisfied with life in Europe as with their place

in it. They came not to create a new type of society but to reproduce European settlements under conditions more favorable to themselves. Although temporarily subsistence farming was often necessary, the settlers did not intend to become peasants but rather to produce commodities for trade.

European trading companies and wealthy proprietors financed much of the early settlement. Their objective was to establish fortified trading posts at which furs, fish, timber, tobacco, and other crops could be collected and shipped to Europe. This system was modified by distance; when four to six months were required to send a message to London, Paris, or Amsterdam, control and support from overseas were tenuous. The colonists were forced to improvise, and by so doing they often established new institutions better suited to survival on the frontier.

The Frontiersman and the Moving Frontier

The new settlers had no desire to give up their European culture; in fact most of them started towns, churches, and schools soon after their arrival at their new homesites. Yet contact with the Indians, the problems of a new physical environment, and distance from the European homelands combined to modify their culture.

Not all settlers moved westward to the frontier; some found opportunities as clerks, artisans, or professional men in the established seaboard cities. Spatial links between the Western frontier and the Eastern cities were maintained; expansion of the frontier meant increasing trade in centers of earlier settlement.

The stereotype of the frontiersman was a pioneer farmer who built a log cabin and cleared land for crops and for pasture for his animals. The advance of settlement is often perceived as the advance of the agricultural frontier. The farmer was most influential in remaking a virgin land, but he did not advance alone. Other kinds of frontiers, each having distinctive characteristics, included the transient frontier of the fur trader and trapper, the boom frontier of the miner of precious metals, the fast-moving frontier of early cattlemen, and the carefully planned advance of the railroad

promoter and related real estate promotions. Each frontier advanced at a different pace—some of them overtook and pushed ahead of others.

The frontier did not always advance. Frontiersmen sometimes occupied an area, found it wanting in resources or unfriendly, and, after a struggle, retreated. Perhaps the land never was fertile enough or the climate humid enough for profitable farming. Elsewhere the resource—perhaps an ore vein or a forest—became exhausted, or changing market conditions converted a once suitable land use into an unprofitable venture. In some places people clung to a land use long after economic justification for such use had vanished.

ANGLO-AMERICAN COUNTERPARTS OF EUROPEAN HOMELANDS

The Northern Woodlands and Tundra

The first environment encountered by Indians from northeastern Asia as well as by European fishermen and fur traders was a land of long, dark, cold winters (Figures 2.3 and 2.4). Its snows lay unmelted on the ground almost until the advent of the short, warm summer. Spring arrived suddenly and the long, sunny days converted the frozen marshes into habitats for multiplying insects. The length of the summer days in part made up for the short growing season.

The forest (rear endpaper) is mainly coniferous—consisting especially of spruce, fir, and pine—although there are some birches and other deciduous trees. On its southern border, the forest is tall and useful for lumber. but on the northern border the trees are too stunted and too widely spaced to be commercially valuable; a 20-foot tree may represent a century of slow growth. The forest is rarely continuous because areas of bare rock, swamp, lake, and shallow soil inhibit its spread.

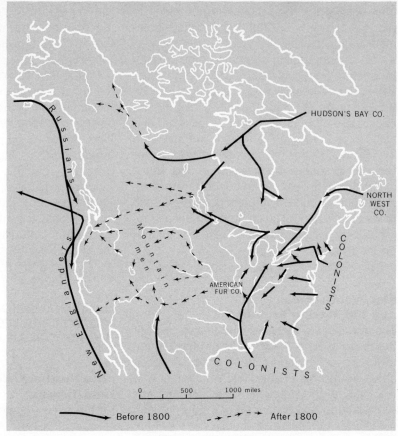

Figure 2.3 The fur traders whose routes are indicated on this map were responsible for much of the early exploration of the Anglo-American interior.

Soils[1] The common soil of the Northern Woodlands is an acid and sandy soil whose upper layer contains undecomposed needles and other raw humus. But much of the area, scraped clean by the former continental glacier or covered with glacial rock debris, lacks adequate soil for plant growth. Waterlogged soil, arising from glacially dammed streams, is another common handicap. Furthermore, in the northern part of this soil zone, *permafrost,* a condition in which the subsoil remains frozen

all year, blocks underdrainage. Such poor drainage develops *muskegs,* boggy areas partially filled with peat. There are a few isolated areas of moderately fertile soil, for example, the so-called Clay Belt of northern Ontario, but these make up a minute fraction of the whole Northern Woodlands.

Indians The Indians depended on hunting and fishing, and their main foods were woodland caribou and moose. The local groups of people were small and scattered because many square miles of hunting ground were needed to nourish a few Indian families. In summer, game was plentiful and was supplemented by

[1] Soil terminology is in a state of flux and technical jargon will be avoided. The National Cooperative Soil Survey has prepared a new soil classification (the *Seventh Approximation*) which is now being used by the U.S. Bureau of Soils; briefly the new system classifies each soil by describing, in a few syllables, the surface and subsurface layers. As most geographers are not completely familiar with the new terminology and most soil surveys now available use an older terminology, the authors will describe the soils where necessary in layman's terms.

berries, seeds, and roots; in winter, famine might result from poor hunting even though every kind of animal was considered potential food. Life was highly nomadic; the Indian followed the game on foot, on snowshoe, or by canoe. The conical tepees were easily moved; hides, fur, bark, wood, and stone were the major raw materials from which the simple household goods were constructed.

The fur trader and the route network
The depletion of wild animals and especially the competition from fur ranching have almost destroyed the trapping economy. But the contributions of past trappers and traders remain significant because they opened trails and routes across the country, established contacts with the Indians, and served as guides for later settlers. Some of their trading posts have grown into large cities, for example, Chicago, St. Louis, Detroit, and Winnipeg.

Viking visitors to the northeast coast traded in furs, as did a few European fishermen who visited Newfoundland and eastern Canada in about 1500, but such trading had little influence on the course of later settlement. About 1580 French fur traders sailed up the St. Lawrence estuary, and nearly 30 years later a permanent settlement was established at Quebec. Soon after, French traders, missionaries, and explorers pushed inland through the Great Lakes, reaching the Mississippi River in 1673 and gradually spreading their trade up the Mississippi tributaries. About the same time British colonists on the Atlantic seaboard were engaging in fur trading, although in many areas such trade soon became secondary to agriculture. In 1670 the Hudson's Bay Company was chartered by the British government, and soon its traders penetrated into Canada through Hudson Bay, competing vigorously with French traders based at Montreal (Figure 2.3).

After the Louisiana Purchase (1803) the traders and several American fur companies penetrated into a southward spur of the Northern Woodlands in the Rockies. The American Fur Company, organized by John Jacob Astor, even expanded its posts to Astoria at the mouth of the Columbia River. After the War of 1812, these posts came under the control of the Hudson's Bay Company. Fur trapping is still a leading industry in parts of northern Canada (although the total output is only about $1 million annually).

The pattern of resource use was frequently similar, whether the resource was fur, fish, soil, grassland, timber, or minerals. The westward advance of the frontier was motivated by the demand for some product which could be marketed in eastern Anglo-America or across the Atlantic. In each case, groups of people were dissatisfied enough in Europe or in eastern Anglo-America to take great risks and undergo considerable hardships to better their fortunes. Had beaver hats never become fashionable in Europe, Canada would have been more slowly explored and settled. Had fish and lumber been in surplus supply in Europe in the seventeenth century, New England might not have developed an economy centered on them.

The tundra and the Eskimo The Northern Woodlands grades northward into a treeless, lake-dotted tundra. The Eskimo inhabitants of the tundra are distinct in language and culture from the Northern Woodlands Indians. This vast polar and subarctic area has been only of minor significance in the settlement of Anglo-America, and more detailed discussion is deferred to Chapter 10.

The Eastern Woodlands
No sharp boundary separates the Northern and Eastern woodlands; indeed enclaves of Northern Woodlands occur on mountains within the Eastern Woodlands. Many of the same fur-bearing and game animals are found in both areas. The distinction between the two is that the Eastern Woodlands is suited for agricultural settlement. Even the Indians engaged in farming, although by no means as intensively as their European successors.

Early visitors to the Atlantic Coast noted

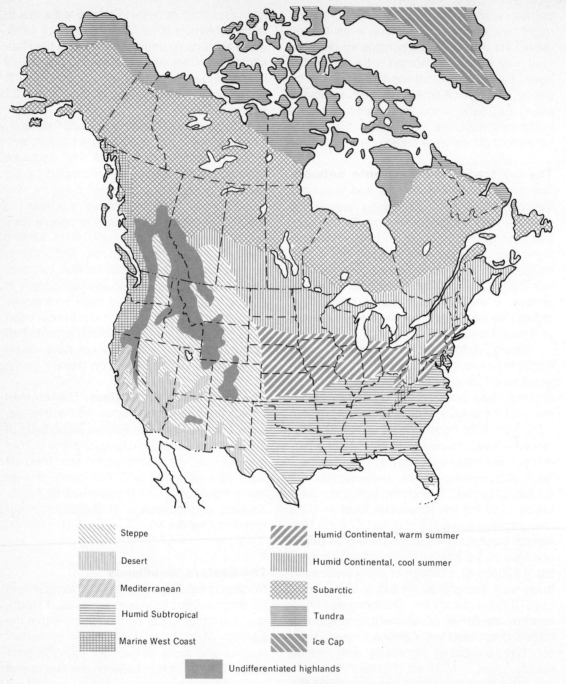

Steppe	Humid Continental, warm summer
Desert	Humid Continental, cool summer
Mediterranean	Subarctic
Humid Subtropical	Tundra
Marine West Coast	ice Cap
Undifferentiated highlands	

Figure 2.4 The climatic regions of Anglo-America. Note that since all climatic regions are based on averages, in exceptional years actual conditions may depart considerably from the conditions represented by each climatic type. (After Köppen, as modified by Trewartha.)

the tall timbers so in demand in a society based on wooden ships, wooden houses, and firewood for fuel. The Coastal Plain was the eastern edge of a million square miles of almost virgin forest, broken only by small clearings, marshes, lakes, and rocky barrens and, on its western margin, by areas of prairie (rear endpaper). In New England, white pine, birch, beech, maple, and hemlock were characteristic; southward, yellow pine, oak, chestnut, hickory, magnolia, and poplar predominated, and in the Southeast, yellow pines, rich in naval stores (turpentine and resin), were common along the coast. Cypress occupied the alluvial areas of the Southeast.

These tall Eastern forests were rarely impenetrable, for their thick, leafy canopy discouraged undergrowth. Trails suitable for pedestrian or horseman were easily blazed, if indeed they had not been already pounded out by bison and other animals and by Indians following game. The forests supplied food: in season berries, wild plums, crab apples, grapes, and nuts. Ducks, turkeys, pigeons, deer, rabbits, bear, raccoons, squirrels, and other animals provided meat from the land, and fish were plentiful in streams and lakes. Offshore the fishing banks, especially northeast of New York, had attracted European fishermen at least a century before the land was settled. For the small ships of the seventeenth century, the much indented Atlantic Coast provided innumerable harbors. Bays and river banks offered sites for fishing villages and small agricultural settlements.

Soils—productive if tilled carefully The Indians cleared parts of the forest when they needed new fields and would cultivate their hills of corn amid the stumps.[2] In the Eastern Woodlands soils often became exhausted after a decade. Then the Indians abandoned the old fields. The seventeenth-century pioneer had only slightly more agricultural knowledge than the Indian, but much better tools. After a few decades of settlement, he learned to use plant indicators as a guide to the soil potential.

The soils in the northern Eastern Woodlands are generally gray-brown or brownish in color, whereas to the south the soils are more likely to be red or yellow. Both soil groups include many soils which although initially fertile, become leached, acid, and eroded after continuous cultivation. If not eroded, most soils in both groups respond well to fertilization. The virgin gray-brown soils with a profile topped by leaf mold, beneath which lay a thick humus-rich topsoil and a heavier subsoil, were the more fertile. In the Great Lakes area these soils, formed from glacially deposited lime-rich material, are above average in structure and fertility. In the South soils were formed in regions of high average temperatures with heavy rainfall. Since Southern soils are rarely frozen in winter, when cleared they are subject to leaching and erosion throughout the year.

In the Eastern Woodlands (and other regions) many soil areas do not fit the preceding regional description. Within both soil regions described above, there are areas of alluvial and windblown (loess) soils which are above average in fertility. Underlying rocks and subsoil also influence the surface soil and add additional variety; thus limestone, glacial silts, and some crystalline rocks produced superior soils, whereas sandstone, former beaches, and glacial gravel influenced the soil adversely.[3]

---

[2] The barking or girdling of trees let the full sunlight onto the forest floor in a few months' time and thus made it ready for planting. The ground commonly was burned over before being planted, to free it of dead branches, dry leaves, and the light herbaceous vegetation that was present. The forest topsoil was dark with leafmold, rich in potash, and congenial to the heavily feeding Indian corn. In a few years wind completed the task of bringing down the dead timber. The deadened hardwood trunks and roots decayed rapidly in the moist, warm summers.

With one or two exceptions the plants cultivated by the Indians had originated far to the south of the United States under tropical or subtropical conditions. The list of native crops includes several kinds of corn, such as dent, flint, and sweet corn, various kidney or navy beans, squashes or pumpkins, the common sunflower, and the Jerusalem-artichoke. . . . Excepting the Jerusalem-artichoke, these are all annual plants which, in contrast to most of the crops of northern Europe, require warm weather for starting. Carl Sauer, "Climate and Man," in *Yearbook of Agriculture,* U.S. Department of Agriculture, Washington, 1941, p. 161.
[3] The Eastern Woodlands soils in the North were formerly classified as gray-brown podzolic soils; those in the South as red-yellow podzolic soils.

Indians contribute new crops The East-ern Woodlands Indians were of great value to the early settlers because they introduced Euro-peans to maize (corn), tomatoes, squash, lima and kidney beans, and many other plants, both wild and domesticated.[4] In general, these Indi-ans were dependent on agriculture carried on in clearings which were abandoned when the soil became exhausted. The Algonkian-speaking tribes in the north of the region were poorly organized groups who lived in small semipermanent villages of rectangular huts. More effectively organized and more warlike were the Six Nations of the Iroquois who con-trolled most of the Appalachian corridors. All these peoples traded among themselves, car-rying goods long distances on their backs or by canoes; all hunted, often following game trails (for example, the Buffalo Trace of south-ern Indiana) which later became pioneer roads.

South of the Algonkian area the Indian tribes were much more skilled in farming and lived in more permanent villages. In contrast to the Indians northward, workers specialized in crafts in the villages. Large clearings in the woods were planted in corn and beans (some-times two crops a year); tribes such as the Creeks of Alabama quickly adopted European crops, domestic animals, and tools when these were introduced by white settlers.

Farmers alter the woodlands As the ag-ricultural frontier advanced, the vegetation and the soil were soon greatly changed. The fences dividing the land into fields and pastures; the trails, roads and railroads; the farmsteads, hamlets, and towns visibly marked the advance of the frontier. Crops and domestic animals replaced wild indigenous plants and animals; even undesirable weeds and pests were intro-duced by the settlers.

Openings in the forests, natural meadows, and abandoned Indian fields provided some

[4]Tobacco is not listed because the variety planted in Virginia, Maryland, and elsewhere by Europeans was obtained from Indians in the West Indies. The potato from Peru was introduced to Anglo-America by way of Europe.

pasture for livestock, but grasses suitable for haymaking were rare. The introduction of Euro-pean grasses solved this problem, and in a few decades livestock industries developed along the coast, for example, on large estates around Narragansett Bay. Settlers moving inland often started farming by raising livestock which could be driven eastward to markets more economi-cally than crops could be shipped.

Northern settlement patterns and the small farm Climatologists divide this area climatically into two regions, *humid continental* to the north and *humid subtropical* to the south, the dividing line being the 32°F January isotherm (Figure 2.4). This isotherm is also approximately the boundary between the Northern and Southern settlement patterns: the former consisted of small farms, while the latter was characterized by large plantations and a planter aristocracy. There were many excep-tions to this generalization: for example, there were large estates in the Hudson Valley and southeastern Pennsylvania and small farms in the Southern plantation area. On the whole the small family farm of the North contrasted with the large plantation with black slave labor in the South.

As New England was settled at a time when Indians were a menace, the rural popu-lace were clustered, rather than spread out, around towns sited on such features as the fertile alluviums of the Connecticut Valley. Some of the hills were cleared for grazing, but many rugged or infertile lands remained un-improved—in fact, many areas once cultivated have since reverted to meadow or forest. The colonial New Englander raised crops, and es-pecially animals, to supply the towns, and oc-casionally had a surplus for export.

Eastern Canada developed agriculturally more slowly than New England; before the American Revolution its small population was interested mainly in fishing along the coast and in the fur trade inland. Several thousand French farmers occupied long, narrow farms along the St. Lawrence River, the land being apportioned under a feudal seignorial system like that of France. After the American Revolution, numerous loyalists migrated to the Maritime Provinces and eastern Ontario, settling in agricultural patterns similar to those in New England.

In the north the lowlands of the Hudson-Mohawk Valley might have appeared to offer a suitable land for pioneers, but until after the Revolution most of these lands were unavailable. The best lands in the Hudson Valley were owned in huge estates whose titles went back to Dutch colonial days. Westward the powerful Iroquois occupied the land, and to complicate matters, some of this land was claimed by both New York and Massachusetts. During the American Revolution the power of the Iroquois (allied with the British against American rebels) was destroyed; shortly the titles were assigned to a motley assortment of land companies. Two major groups moved westward then: first, loyalists who settled on lands in eastern Ontario which remained British, and, second, New Englanders. The latter, in contrast to the Southern pioneers, advanced in groups, clearing the woods and settling in towns, as had been the custom in New England. A major road (the Genesee Road) carved across New York State was used by New Englanders to settle the Western Reserve of northeastern Ohio, an area originally claimed by Connecticut. Several decades later the Erie Canal (completed in 1825) roughly paralleled the Genesee Road and increased the influx of settlers by the northern route.

Colonial eastern Pennsylvania was settled by the Quakers for whom the colony was chartered and by other groups who were attracted by the tolerant attitude of the Quaker proprietors. These included the Pennsylvania Germans (locally called Pennsylvania Dutch, *Dutch* being a corruption of the German *Deutsch*) and the Scotch-Irish. All three groups were hardworking settlers who tilled the soil well and in general got along with the Indians.

Across the Appalachians   (Figure 2.5) Most Appalachian ridges do not represent a formidable barrier. Rivers have cut through many of the ridges, and by following their winding valleys passes can be reached without difficult ascents. The Erie Canal crossed a broad divide at 578 feet altitude while the Cumberland Gap (where Tennessee, Kentucky, and Virginia meet) was at 1,650 feet. The landform barrier was probably less a problem than French and Indian opposition and the British Proclamation Line of 1763 in retarding trans-Appalachian settlement.

Meanwhile, Pennsylvanian and Southern migrants were pouring into the Ohio Valley by three main routes: (1) over Forbes Road from Philadelphia to Pittsburgh, (2) over the National Road (now U.S. 40) to the Ohio River at Wheeling, and (3) through the Cumberland Gap from the Great Valley. Thus by 1800 a great arc of pioneer lands was occupied from eastern Ontario down the Ohio Valley and into central Kentucky and Tennessee. A new landscape was being created in the Eastern Woodlands—patches of cultivated fields replaced the heavy forests, rough roads evolved out of Indian trails, and business and local industries arose in the small towns that grew at strategic sites. When negotiations with the relatively few Indians encouraged them to move westward, an area known as the Old Northwest was opened for settlement without much Indian warfare.

Southern settlement and the planter aristocracy   More sharply than in the North, society in the colonial South was divided into the planter aristocracy, the poor whites, and the Negro slaves. Cotton, which in the nineteenth century became "king" in the Southern economy, had little effect on initial settlement.

Along the South Atlantic Coast deep estuaries subdividing a broad coastal plain provided easy access to potential farmlands of the Tidewater Country. Planters laid out large plantations, cultivated at first by indentured servants, later by slaves. Crops not readily

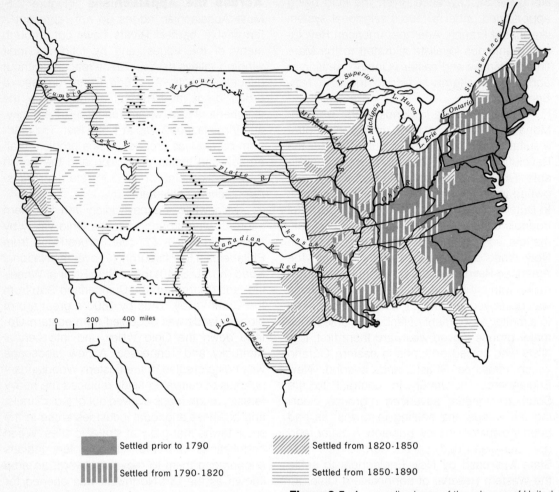

Settled prior to 1790

Settled from 1790-1820

Settled from 1820-1850

Settled from 1850-1890

Figure 2.5 A generalized map of the advance of United States settlement. The advance of the frontier shown here reflects mainly agricultural settlement.

grown in Europe, notably tobacco, indigo, rice, and, later, cotton, provided valuable exports. Timber and naval stores from the Coastal Plain forests supplied additional exports. Although the sandy soil soon lost its virgin fertility, there were extensive new lands awaiting to be cleared. In this physical setting the Southern planter aristocracy developed: farmers wealthy enough to own extensive lands and the slaves to work them.

Inland from the Tidewater was the more rugged, but initially more fertile, Piedmont, and westward, beyond the abrupt Blue Ridge, the even more fertile Great Valley. Much of the southern Piedmont was assigned in extensive

grants to Southern planters. Some of these grants were subdivided into large estates, others into small farms occupied by the less wealthy farmers migrating from the Tidewater. In contrast, the Great Valley and some of the narrower valleys in the southern Appalachians were settled by Germans and Scotch-Irish moving southwestward along the Great Valley. In such settings evolved the traditional pioneer farmer who built a log cabin, killed the forest trees by girdling, and then planted crops amid their stumps. The popular stereotype of the frontier farmer shown in movies and on TV had his origin in the valleys of the Appalachians as he conquered hardship and environment to create a farm and to supply food to his family. After the American Revolution, some land-poor peoples advanced rapidly into the southern half of the Wooded Midwest.

Southerners from the Carolinas and Georgia could avoid the Appalachians by following the Coastal Plain southwest and westward. From about 1820 to 1840, as soils in the Atlantic South became exhausted, "poor white" farmers and slaveholding planters alike moved into western Georgia and other parts of the Gulf Plain, seeking new lands to grow more cotton. Navigable rivers, flowing south to the Gulf of Mexico, provided an outlet for the cotton harvest for which increasing world demand provided a good market. After first settlement, the wealthier planters bought many of the better farmlands, building impressive homesteads while the "poor white" group raised corn, cattle, hogs, and some cotton on the poorer lands. Thus, some of the social patterns and classes of the Tidewater East moved west along with the agricultural frontier, maintaining a partial cultural unity throughout the whole South. The large plantations flourished, especially on the dark, limey soils of the Black Belt of Alabama and Mississippi and on alluvial strips adjoining the Mississippi and other rivers. The westward movement continued across the Mississippi, and before the Civil War a railroad was extended to the river at Vicksburg. In eastern Texas some settlers moved in overland from the Old South; others came by sea via the Gulf Coast. In this region westward migration of Americans encountered the northward migration of Spanish settlers from Mexico.

The Wooded Midwest Settlers from both the North and the South advanced into the Wooded Midwest, primarily an area between the Appalachian ridges and the Mississippi. Although the two streams of settlers intermingled, generally Kentucky, southern Indiana, and southern Illinois were settled from the South while Northerners were more common north of a line approximately connecting Cincinnati, Indianapolis, and St. Louis.

Especially on the flatter glaciated lands, the rectangular pattern of fields, roads, and town streets was characteristic. This almost geometric pattern in the regular spacing of modern settlements can be traced to the influence of the township and range (rectilinear) survey system (described in Chapter 5). Most of the area was settled after the Indians had been moved westward, and farmsteads were evenly spread over the land rather than clustered in or near towns for defense. In contrast to the irregular road pattern of the Appalachian Plateau and the Ohio Valley, this land of large rectangular fields was ideally suited for the mechanized agriculture that later developed. The soils and drainage offered some problems: for example, much of northern Indiana and adjacent Michigan and Ohio was swamp, a remnant from the Glacial Age, which had to be drained by ditch or tile before cultivation. Transportation to Eastern or Southern markets was another problem since the fertile loam soils areas commonly had boggy mud roads. Streams were used to float much farm produce southward to the Ohio and the Mississippi; later, canals were built to connect some of these rivers with the Great Lakes. By the mid-nineteenth century the railroad network connected the farmer to world markets; the cost of freight diminished, and prices received by the farmer rose accordingly. Although the farmer faced many problems from fluctuating farm prices and weather, his primitive pioneer existence had ended; soon his prosperous manner of living and extensive use of farm machinery dazzled the land-hungry peasants in Europe.

Within a decade after first settlement, the Midwestern farmer required manufactured goods. His economy was not based on crude handmade tools (although he used these until better ones became available). He preferred to buy tools and other manufactures and to specialize in his farming activities. He sold his

Contour farming and well-planned use of the terrain produce beautiful rural landscapes such as this area in southern Wisconsin. (USDA photograph)

produce to local merchants instead of rafting his goods to New Orleans, as the first settlers had done. City life developed quickly, and by 1820 Cincinnati, for example, was not only packing pork and milling flour but also manufacturing whiskey, furniture, clothing, pottery, cotton cloth, and steamboats. The urban landscapes which now dominate the Midwest were already apparent in the early settlement process.

Lumbering and Settlement

During the period of early settlement in the woodlands of eastern Anglo-America, trees were in surplus supply (Figure 2.6). Although settlers used them for housing, fencing, fuel, and even plank roads, the settlers' primary objective was the good soil beneath the forest. Timber which would bring premium prices today was burned in huge bonfires. Only in a few places, as in the pine forests of the coastal Carolinas, did much settlement result from the forests alone.

In contrast in the Pacific area the forest was first cut to supply lumber for California and East Asia, and later it found markets in eastern Anglo-America. The industry has continued for more than a century, and with the advent of tree farming, seems likely to continue indefinitely. North of Monterey Bay, California, to Anchorage, Alaska, a lush forest of tall conifers covered the coastal zone and extended inland 5 to 200 miles. In the south only a fraction of

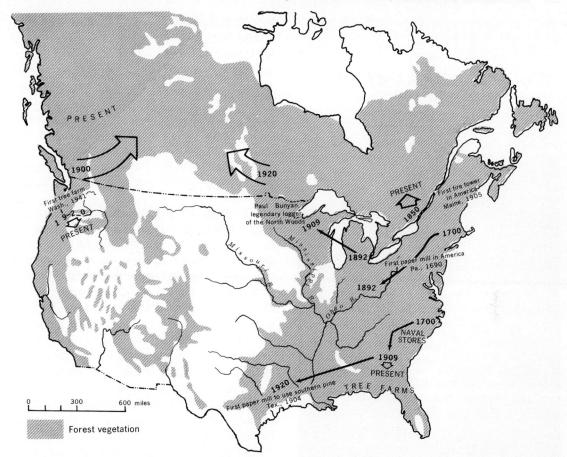

Figure 2.6 This map suggests the transient nature of Anglo-American lumbering. It is being stabilized by the widespread adoption of tree farms and by the selective harvesting of government-owned forests.

the original forests remains; the giant redwoods are dominant in the summer-drought, foggy area of northern California; Douglas fir, hemlock, and western cedar dominate in Oregon, Washington, and southwestern British Columbia; and Sitka spruce is the main species farther north. All may be used for excellent timber. These tall trees grow well in the humid climate with a lack of extreme daily seasonal weather changes.

One of the distinct regional characteristics of this North Pacific coastal region is the mildness of its climate, attributable in part to the prevailing air masses from the Pacific and in part to cool offshore currents. Summers range from cool to pleasantly warm depending on proximity to the ocean and latitude. Rainfall is moderate at lower elevations (30 to 50 inches

annually) but is higher in the mountains; much of it comes in the cool season when evaporation is slow. Lumbering in the slopes and farming in the limited valley areas encouraged the development of towns and permanent settlement.

The Indian tribes of the Pacific Coast (north of 40°) were culturally advanced people who made good use of their seafood and timber resources. Their homes were substantial rectangular wooden houses; in the northern section these were decorated with totem poles and other wood carvings. The land provided some game and berries, but their major source

The Pacific coniferous forest was used for woodworking long before European settlement, as this totem pole at Ketchikan, Alaska, indicates. (Travel Division, Alaskan Department of Economic Development)

though many small, portable sawmills did some of the cutting and milling, more permanent equipment was installed in certain river valleys and along railways, and lumbering towns arose at these places. Near the drier western areas within the mountains much forest land has been placed in reserve in national forests and parks, partly to provide recreation lands and partly to protect essential water supplies. In the Pacific Northwest the forest lands, too rugged or infertile for other uses, are being replanted with trees.

In eastern Canada, lumbermen were advancing north of the agricultural St. Lawrence Lowland in the second half of the nineteenth century. Forests have become a major Canadian asset. Pulp and paper manufacturing have continued to be the largest single manufacturing industry, and forest products provide several leading exports. Lumbering has opened up large areas which are unused for agriculture. Relatively few workers are needed, however, to harvest the timber, and most lumber towns (or camps) are small.

In the United States at the same time, lumbermen were harvesting trees on the Eastern lands too rugged or infertile for farming. In 1875 leading American lumbering centers included Williamsport (Pennsylvania), Indianapolis (Indiana), and Grand Rapids (Michigan). By the end of the century all these cities had become minor lumber handlers, as the lumbermen moved to the Great Lakes area into lands too cool and infertile for the corn-hog-beef-cattle type of farming prevalent in the Midwest.

Along the southeastern coast, forestry was a colonial industry, providing naval stores principally. Southern yellow pine was considered an inferior timber as long as northern white pine was available. Early in the twentieth century, the South became a leading lumber supplier—a permanent supplier because its forest matures more rapidly since the growing season is longer. Extensive lands of little value for other purposes became available to grow softwoods on the Coastal Plains and hardwoods in the Appalachians. But all these lumbering activities

of food was from the sea. Large dugout canoes, some equipped with sails, searched the estuaries, channels, and open sea for fish, which were eaten either fresh or dried. Farming was not practiced despite the availability of arable patches of lowland soils.

In the West, lumbering on the wooded mountains early supplied timber for local building, mine props, and fuel. Large-scale lumbering for Eastern markets began after the exhaustion of better-grade softwoods in the Great Lakes states, within the present century. Al-

(including related manufacturing) employ only a few hundred thousand persons, for as elsewhere, lumbering alone did little to establish permanent settlement.

Summary

By the middle of the nineteenth century settlers had occupied much of the Eastern Woodlands and in a few places, for example, southern Texas, central Illinois, and eastern Iowa, had penetrated the prairie. In Canada (with a few minor exceptions) settlement was restricted to the transition zone between the Eastern and Northern Woodlands, and much of the level land of Quebec and Ontario, south of the rocky Canadian Shield, had been occupied by this time. These were humid lands, and water was considered free and plentiful. Further advance would be into lands in which water was generally short in supply and where water surpluses had to be transferred from rugged areas to terrains more suitable for settlement.

SETTLEMENT PENETRATES THE WATER-DEFICIENT LANDS

The early explorers thought of Anglo-America as a land of boundless forests, punctuated by Indian trails and small Indian clearings. Within a century reports of extensive grasslands changed the European's perception of the interior, but the significance of this vegetation difference was not realized until later. Early travelers followed forest-bordered rivers into the grasslands, and the first settlers in the grassland areas sought well-wooded sites. Small grassy areas were welcomed as natural pastures, but extensive grasslands, requiring new tools and new techniques, were shunned.

The historian Daniel Boorstin[5] has pointed out "the vagueness of the land" in the minds of American settlers moving westward. Much of the character of the land, Boorstin asserts, was discovered and explored during the proc-

ess of settlement. Myths developed which exaggerated its resources, while other myths, such as that of the Great American Desert, stressed its handicaps and terrors. Certainly the Western lands were different from anything previously experienced by people brought up in the culture and environment of northwestern Europe. The Western grasslands and mountains were also a novel environment for second- and third-generation Americans raised in the forested East. Serviced by army units, land surveys, land offices, and government-financed railways, the settlers advanced into the West, and the half century 1840–1890 represents a migration rarely matched in human history in numbers, daring, and accomplishment. This movement into the prairies came about three decades later in Canada because the rocky, nonagricultural Canadian Shield was a barrier to be crossed between the farmlands of the East and the grasslands of the West. There was no such physical barrier in the United States.

The Prairies and Steppes

Adjoining the forest was the relatively humid prairie, originally a land of lush grasses, about a yard high in summer. Westward the tall grass changed to the short grass (steppe) as rainfall lessened, and the indigenous vegetation consisted of moderately high grasses mixed with dwarf grass, the latter becoming more dominant as soil moisture decreased. These grasses were probably much more luxuriant a century ago than they are now. Evidence has accumulated that this distribution of grasslands was in part a result of human interference. For example, the prairie areas of central Illinois are humid enough to support trees; indeed some steppe areas seem suited for prairie or even forest vegetation. Whatever the cause, the grasslands were interspersed by long fingers of woodlands in alluvial valleys and partly wooded areas in other settings.

In central Texas and in Oklahoma and along the eastern and northern edges of the

[5] *The Americans: The National Experience,* Random House, New York, 1965, pp. 221–274.

The sod house, shown here in Custer County, central Nebraska, about 1890, was the grassland settler's way of getting shelter with the minimum amount of wood. (USDA from Nebraska Historical Society)

prairie there are broad areas in which grassland and trees are intermixed. This transitional zone is called *parkland* across central Saskatchewan and Alberta, on the northern edge of the prairie. These parklands were of great value to early pioneers; for example, the Cross Timbers region of north Texas and central Oklahoma was a source of lumber for wagon trains about to cross the steppes to the west.

Animals The tall grasses of the prairie[6] and the mixed medium and short grasses to the

[6] The native prairie grasses were not the grasses common on the prairie today; Kentucky blue grass, timothy, white clover, sorghums, corn, alfalfa, and soybeans are among the introduced fodder crops which invaded the prairie. Westward the grasses are native (bluestem, wheatgrass, grama grass). The carrying capacity of the range is declining, 3 to 10 acres per animal unit per month now being required. In the southern Great Plains, grama and buffalo grass pastures offer equal grazing, provided the turf is reseeded. Sagebrush areas are of value for the grasses which grow between and under the sagebrush, and 9 to 15 acres may support an animal unit per month. In the desert areas the capacity of the range is less—in many places being nil. Open woodlands offer grazing equal to the short grass or even prairie areas.

west once supported numerous animals. Great herds of shaggy-headed bison (buffalo) ranged the entire area and even eastward into the forests as far as central Pennsylvania, following ancient trails which led to natural pastures, water holes, and salt licks. Other herbivorous animals were also plentiful: the pronghorn antelope, jackrabbits, squirrels, and prairie dogs. Feeding on these were the coyote and the wolf. Finally there were and are the pests, such as the Rocky Mountain locust, which at intervals invade the prairies.

Indians and the horse Most of the Indians who lived in the prairie-steppe region belonged to the Plains culture, which stressed hunting and war. The prairie tribes hunted bison, but also farmed and traded their tobacco and maize with the Indians of the steppe. These latter were warlike hunters who occupied the short grasslands, the Rockies, and parts of the arid intermountain plateaus and basins. They depended on bison flesh for food and bison skins to make clothing and covers for their portable tepees. Buffalo chips (dried bison manure) were a common fuel. In the seventeenth century, Plains Indian life was revolutionized by the acquisition of the horse, introduced by Spanish explorers and settlers. This gave the tribes greater mobility, increasing their ability both to hunt bison and to battle intruding settlers. The Indians and their lives now pictured—often inaccurately—in modern movies and TV are most likely to be the Plains Indians rather than the Indians of the Eastern forests.

New problems in the grasslands   The scattered prairies in the forested Midwest were welcomed by early settlers; these areas offered good, clear pasture, and when plowed, provided unusually fertile soil. In Illinois early pioneers sought farmsteads which included both woodland and prairie. Farther west the prairie dominated, and the settler needed new techniques and new tools. The small amount of available timber along the stream was inadequate for log cabins, fuel,[7] and rail fences. The virgin deep-rooted sod was not easily broken by a team and a cast-iron plow. Since stone to pave the roads or wood to surface plank roads was scarce, prairie roads alternated seasonally between deep mud and dust. Streams might be distant, and the machinery to dig deep wells was not available at first. Freight to market was so expensive that it took four bushels of Illinois grain to return cash to the farmer equal to that received for one bushel by eastern Pennsylvania farmers. The waves of settlers hesitated on the western margins of the forests as people sought new techniques and tools to move into this different physical environment. Moreover, people long accustomed to living in forested areas were at first suspect of a new land that supported few trees.

[7]Buffalo chips served as fuel. Sod houses reduced the need for lumber among early pioneers on the Western prairie.

The soils were fundamentally different than in the woodlands. Instead of being acid, they were neutral (or very slightly acid on the forest margins). Soils were increasingly alkaline as parklands gave way to tall grass and as tall grass was displaced by short grass. These soils had good structure, with humus derived from grassroots extending far below the surface. The chernozems, on the border between the prairie and the steppe, are blackish when freshly plowed, a color attributed to humus from decomposed grass roots. These fertile soils, with their ability to accumulate lime and their excellent structure, are first-rate farming soils, provided the rainfall is adequate for a good crop. Drought is a more serious problem than infertility. Westward on the short grassland, the soils are lighter in color because of lower organic content in rain-deficient areas. These also are good soils, provided enough moisture can be supplied by either irrigation or dry-farming techniques.

By about 1840 the prairie soils of Illinois, Iowa, and adjacent states became worth exploiting. Local prices of grain rose when the railroads arrived. New steel plows broke the sod with ease; the reaper and other tools facilitated harvesting, enabling the farmer to handle more acres with no additional hours of labor. Experience showed that after the sod had been broken, the rich grassland soils and the freedom from stones, sticks, and stumps encouraged the use of machinery. The trains which carried the grain and animals eastward returned with fuel, lumber, and manufactures from the East; later, cattle from the Western Plains were shipped east by rail for fattening. Within a few decades farmers transformed the grassland landscape into one in which the works of man—his fields, farms, and roads—were the dominant elements of the regional environment.

The cattlemen   Many pioneer settlers started as cattlemen. They drove or shipped surplus animals eastward while they were clearing their lands for large-scale tillage.

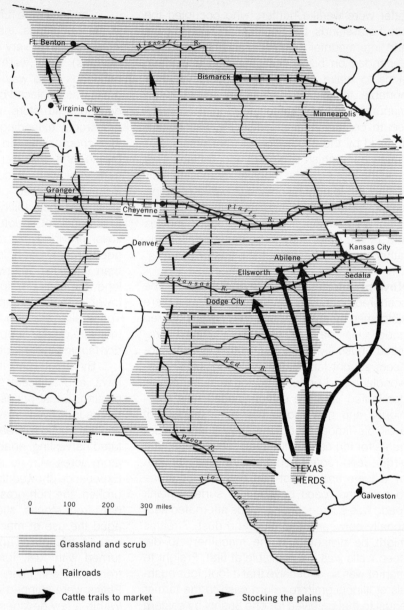

Ft. Benton

Missouri R.

Bismarck

Virginia City

Minneapolis

Granger

Cheyenne

Platte R.

Denver

Kansas City

Abilene

Ellsworth

Arkansas R.

Sedalia

Dodge City

Red R.

Pecos R.

TEXAS
HERDS

Rio Grande R.

Galveston

0   100   200   300 miles

░░░░░░ Grassland and scrub

┼┼┼┼┼ Railroads

━━▶ Cattle trails to market   ╌ ╌▶ Stocking the plains

Figure 2.7 The range cattle industry advanced northward and westward from 1850 to about 1880, as suggested by the arrows. The invention of barbed wire led to the end of the open range, so that today few Western ranches are unfenced.

About 1850 a new breed of cattlemen discovered the interior grasslands, especially those of Texas. Several decades of conflict started between these cattlemen and farmers after the Civil War, the struggle being most severe on the prairies and steppes along the advancing rail lines in Kansas. In 1865 mass cattle drives started northward because Texas herds had increased rapidly during the Civil War years when Eastern markets were inaccessible. The cattlemen aimed for the railroad, and the terminals of the cattle trails changed as the railroads advanced westward. A decade later the area of grazing lands was increased as cattlemen advanced northward east of the Rockies, occupying most of the Great Plains by 1880.

At first the rancher considered the range free, whereas the farmer occupied his quarter section more intensively and struggled to keep out intruding cattle. Wooden fencing was too expensive on the grasslands but the invention of the cheaper barbed wire (1874) soon ended the open range. After a decade or more of struggle, the Western grasslands were fenced. On the margins of cultivation, the fenced ranch (commonly including some cultivated land) replaced the open range. Later farming, by either irrigation or dry-farming techniques, provided some fodder for the livestock, and the two types of economy began to supplement one another.

The steppes The problems encountered on the prairies were accentuated on the steppes. There is no sharp landform or vegetation boundary along the eastern edge of the Great Plains. As the rolling lands of the Midwest rise gradually westward, annual precipitation decreases. Kansas, for example, with over 40 inches of precipitation in the southeast has less than 20 inches at the Colorado border. On the Plains most streams are intermittent, with sparse water (if any) spread over broad gravelly channels. The soils are alkaline, in places too alkaline. Although the little-leached, semiarid soils are fertile, their water supply may sometimes prove inadequate for profitable yields.

Several innovations in technology were needed to exploit the steppes; most were introduced in the Plains about 1880, during a period of above-average rainfall. Barbed wire enabled the rancher to regulate the grazing and breeding of his herds. Well-drilling machinery made deep wells economically feasible, and the variable-blade windmill harnessed the strong winds to pump water to the surface. Hard wheats, which not only yielded a superior bread flour but withstood shipment and storage

better than the soft wheats, flourished well in this semiarid environment. Hard wheats required a new type of flour mill—using rollers instead of grindstones—and such mills were introduced from Hungary. The huge wheat fields required larger machinery to plow the soil and to harvest, thresh, and bail the crop cheaply; factories in the Midwestern cities began producing machinery for these new needs. In the steppe areas, new water-saving techniques known as *dry farming,* used since the 1880s, were introduced.

These new techniques required access to the industrialized Northeast for supplies, machinery, and markets; such access was supplied by the railroads. The contrasting regional economics of the industrial East and the agricultural West began to integrate in this period. The first transcontinental railroad (the Union Pacific) reached the Pacific in 1869. Like many other Western lines, the Union Pacific was heavily subsidized by government loans and land grants (usually free rights-of-way and alternate sections of land in a broad zone, 10 or more miles wide parallel to the track). Thus the railroads had good reason to encourage settlement, both to get more freight and to sell land. Even today many Western railroads own lands of little agricultural value but which contain valuable minerals—especially petroleum and natural gas.

The Prairie Provinces The Canadian prairies were more favored by nature than the neighboring American Plains. The grasslands which occupy the southern third of the Prairie Provinces have equally fertile soils and, because of lower evaporation, more humid conditions than the American Plains. They have, however, a shorter frost-free season and were less accessible to pioneers and farther from adequate markets. The Canadian East provided a smaller market for flour than the American Northeast, and European markets were more distant. Most significant, a 500-mile rocky stretch of the Canadian Shield separated the Canadian prairies from well-settled eastern

This was a rich grassland in west Texas in 1903. Compare it with the same area (opposite page) forty years later. (USDA photograph)

Ontario, whereas the American prairies adjoined settled areas to the east and southeast.

The first few farmers in the Canadian area arrived via Hudson Bay; others came down the Red River from the United States. Finally in the 1880s the transcontinental Canadian Pacific Railroad provided direct connections to St. Lawrence River ports. The resulting settlement, more orderly than in the United States, was characterized by large farms, many devoted to mixed farming in the moister area, other raising mainly grain. In semiarid southern Saskatchewan and Alberta, cattle ranches were established; later, irrigation farming was added. The farmhouses, grain fields, and roads of the settled Canadian prairies looks much like these same features on the American Plains. But distant markets and transport costs remained a problem; it is twice as far from Peace River wheat fields to Winnipeg as from Denver to Kansas City; nearly twice as far from Edmonton to Montreal as from Minneapolis to New York.

The western edge of the Canadian spring wheat belt is further west than Los Angeles!

The Miner's Place in Western Settlement

Until 1848, the arid and semiarid West was an unfriendly wasteland to be crossed en route to Oregon or coastal California. With the exception of the Mormon settlement in Utah (1847), the scattered settlements of much of this shrubland can be attributed to the prospectors who in two decades scanned most of the West (Figure 2.8).

Elsewhere in Anglo-America mining had provided only minor and spasmodic impulses to settlement. In the East iron ore in quantities sufficing for small colonial furnaces was widely available. Because cheap wood was every-

Overgrazing converted the rich turf into an area of bunch grass and mesquite trees (almost valueless for grazing), which spread like an orchard over the land. (USDA photograph)

where available for fuel, coal had little attraction. Lead, widely used for bullets and brass, was in demand, and lead deposits provided a local attraction for settlement in the middle Mississippi Valley. The mining frontier did not advance steadily as did the farm frontier; rather it jumped from place to place.

The initial mining camps resulted from the discovery of gold in 1848 in central California, 40 miles east of Sacramento. In western Canada gold was discovered in 1858 in the Fraser River Valley. In both places metal was found in gravel beds from which it could be separated with inexpensive equipment and little technical skill. In the following decades prospectors explored the Western states and British Columbia in search of further mineral wealth.

For a decade or two, mining was carried on by small groups; thereafter it became an activity requiring capital, technology, and expensive machinery. To continue in operation, mines required sufficient deposits of ore to justify equipment, concentrating plants, a smelter, and the construction of rail connections. Such elaborate infrastructures created demands for other activities: the production of food for the miners, and the manufacture of mining tools and machinery. But mineral resources were soon exhausted, and the life of some mining towns was short; ghost towns became common throughout the West. However, some mining towns, for example, Denver, have remained even after nearby mines closed or became insignificant.

Desert Shrublands

The grasslands do not disappear suddenly at the Rockies; there are scattered grasslands west of the Rockies and large areas of desert shrub east of the Rockies, notably in central

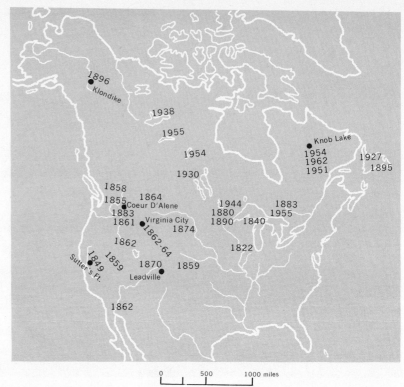

0   500   1000 miles

Figure 2.8 Selected dates of important ore discoveries in Anglo-America. In contrast to the advance of the agricultural frontier, mining development was more sporadic in both time and space. This map shows only a fraction of the mining strikes and a mere sampling of the names of important mining camps.

and southern Texas. However, the Rockies form a convenient boundary between extensive grassy turf to the east and areas westward of woody vegetation consisting of stunted bushes and trees adjusted to semiarid or arid climates. A drive along one of the interstate highways in the western mountains would give a cross-section view of a variety of vegetation forms in a patchy pattern; often sparsely wooded uplands, desert shrub lowlands, and almost barren areas appear at a glance. The plants are xerophytic (adjusted to drought) and able to take full advantage of rare rains.

North of about 37° (except in California), the growing season of the dry areas is generally less than 160 days, and winter is severe enough to have a snow cover for at least a month. In the Southwest, from Texas almost to the Pacific, mild winters are followed by scorching summers, with strong winds possible at all seasons. Variations in altitude, exposure

to the sun and wind, and distance inland from the Pacific create a great variety of local climates. Thus coolness and moisture characterize the mountaintops and high plateaus, scorching winds the open basins, coolness the shady canyons, and exceptionally mild weather the narrow strip along the Pacific Coast.

Water scarcity is the serious problem. Early travelers went from water hole to water hole. Much of the water originates outside this arid area, the surplus from the wooded mountains filling the Colorado, Gila, Rio Grande, and Pecos before these rivers flow into areas where evaporation greatly exceeds precipitation. The characteristic vegetation—whether mesquite, cactus, greasewood, creosote bush, sage-

The ghost town, symbol of a mining settlement whose ores became exhausted or unprofitable to exploit, is widespread in the West. This is Cabezon, New Mexico, about 65 miles west of Santa Fe. (New Mexico Department of Development)

brush, or evergreens—reflects the scarcity of moisture in the subsoil.

Indians   Two contrasting groups of Indians lived in the arid West. Most advanced culturally were the sedentary Pueblo Indians who built permanent villages of adobe, wood, and rock—usually on easily defended hilltops or mesas or in the mouths of caves, as in Mesa Verde. These peoples cultivated corn, beans, and other foods and, in the extreme southwest, cotton. They were skilled weavers, potters, and masons. In addition to the dog, the domestic animal common to all Indian tribes, these farmers had domesticated turkeys. They hunted for rabbits and antelope and collected wild nuts, but primarily they were peaceful farmers. They traded and sometimes fought with nomadic hunters (for example, the Navajos), whose tribes hunted in the same general areas.

In the northern part of the desert shrub-lands and in the forested Rockies, the Indians, culturally related to the Plains tribes, were resourceful hunters who often cooperated with the European beaver trappers. These "mountain men" followed the Rocky Mountains trails, and after the beaver were exhausted, some served as guides for agricultural settlers en route to Oregon or California.

Many of the other Indians of Nevada, Utah, and Southern California were primitive hunters and seed gatherers. In contrast to later white settlers, the Indians of southern California did little to improve the arid and semiarid lands which have since become among the most valuable real estate in the world. Indeed some of these Indians were economically among the

Indians developed impressive cultures on poor grasslands, as shown here in Pueblo Bonito, the largest of United States prehistoric ruins. When Europe was emerging from the Dark Ages, this 800-room town, now 100 miles northwest of Albuquerque, housed 1,200 people. (New Mexico Department of Development)

most primitive people in North America, depending mainly on acorns and seeds supplemented by whatever small game they could trap.

Soils, climate, and desert settlement

Soil acidity was not a problem for settlers in this region of alkali soils. Many of the soils are valueless for other reasons: they may become too coarse and shallow because the wind has blown away the fine sands and slit. Soils lack adequate humus because there is not enough plant debris to create it. This dry land proved to be unsuitable for the farm settler who could not adjust his moist-land tillage to new conditions; for decades after exploration, the area attracted mainly ranchers. The exceptions had religious motivations—namely the Spanish missionaries of the Southwest and Southern California and the Mormons who came to the flats east of the Great Salt Lake.

Has the Frontier Closed?

The historian Frederick Jackson Turner argued that the best free land had been occupied by 1890 and that with this closing of the agricultural frontier the course of American development changed. However, since 1890 much *more* land has been homesteaded than before that date. Much of the land occupied after 1890 was semiarid, usable because dry-farming, irrigation, and drought-resistant crops had been developed. Perhaps more significant than the actual occupying of the land has been the change in the nature of pioneering. As the frontier moved westward out of the Eastern

Woodlands, the agricultural pioneer equipped only with an axe, a rifle, some crude implements, a wagon, and some cattle had little chance of success. In the twentieth century more capital, better tools, and more agricultural technology have been available. Modern pioneering has become more an experimentation with new techniques than an advancement into unsettled areas. This new type of pioneering is still going on—in the deserts, on mountain slopes, and on lands which proved unprofitable when previously used. Thus those who have converted abandoned Southern croplands into managed forests, who have drained the tule marshes of the Central Valley of California, who have built artificial lakes in hill country and sold lakeshore sites for summer homes, are modern pioneers who are devising new uses for land resources.

Much of the land in the mountainous Interior West is still in the public domain and is little used; the shortage is not of land area but of usable land. There is even more unused land in central and northern Canada and Alaska. Many geographers believe that these subarctic and arctic areas of long, bitter winters, infertile soils, stunted trees, or swampy arctic tundra may remain unused except where richer-than-usual minerals are discovered. Perhaps new techniques, yet unforeseen, may advance the settlement frontier northward and also lead to new advances, for example, into Appalachian areas which are now in economic decline.

With the problems of pollution and overcrowding concentrated in urbanized areas and with looming resource shortages, Anglo-Americans need to explore the possibilities of spreading their settlements and searching for resources in thinly settled or unsettled lands. The new frontier may be in technologies which will make possible new potentials for good living in lands now considered submarginal.

SELECTED REFERENCES

BAKELESS, JOHN: *The Eyes of Discovery, The Pageant of North America as Seen by the First Explorers* (paperback), Dover, New York, 1961.

BILLINGTON, R. A.: *Westward Expansion,* Macmillan, New York, 1949, 1960, 1967. An interesting account of settlement by a historian who is well aware of the environmental background of American history. For another point of view, see THOMAS D. CLARK, *Frontiers in America,* Scribner, New York, 1959. Both volumes have detailed bibliographies.

BROWN, RALPH H.: *Historical Geography of the United States,* Harcourt, Brace, New York, 1948. A useful book, weakened by the author's discussing each area for only a limited period.

CHAMBERS, J. W. et al. (eds.): *Philips Historical Atlas of Canada,* Moyer Division, Vilas Industries, Toronto, 1966.

CLAIBORNE, ROBERT: *The First Americans,* Time-Life Books, New York, 1973.

DRIVER, HAROLD E.: *Indians of North America,* University of Chicago Press, Chicago, 1961. A good summary, by topics, with excellent maps. For a discussion of typical tribes in each region, see Robert F. Spencer, Jesse D. Jennings et al., *The Native Americans,* Harper & Row, New York, 1965.

HARRIS, R. COLE, and JOHN WARKENTIN: *Canada Before Confederation—A Study in Historical Geography,* Oxford University Press, Toronto, 1974.

HILLIARD, SAM B.: "Indian Land Cessions," Map Supplement No. 16, *Annals,* Association of American Geographers, 1972. The maps depict, at a somewhat generalized scale, how the nation grew at the expense of the American Indians.

HUNT, CHARLES B.: *Natural Regions of the United States and Canada,* Freeman, San Francisco, 1974. This is an expansion and revision of *Physiography of the United States* published in 1967.

KERR, D. G. G.; *An Historical Atlas of Canada,* Nelson, Toronto, 1960.

SAUER, CARL ORTWIN: *Land and Life,* University of California Press, Berkeley, 1967. A collection of articles, many relevant to this chapter, written by a leader in American geographic thought.

U.S. BUREAU OF THE CENSUS: *Historical Statistics of the United States: Colonial Times to 1957,* Washington, 1960. Updates are added at intervals. Sections A, C, J, K. L, M, and T are especially relevant to this chapter. Equivalent Canadian data are in M. C. Urquhart and K. A. H. Buckley (eds.), *Historical Statistics of Canada,* Macmillan, Toronto, 1965.

U.S. DEPARTMENT OF AGRICULTURE: *The Look of Our Land,* 5 volumes, Washington, 1970–1971. A descriptive stereo airphoto atlas of the rural United States.

ZELINSKY, WILBUR: *The Cultural Geography of the United States,* Prentice-Hall, Englewood Cliffs, N.J., 1973.

3

URBANIZATION AND URBAN CRISES, 1860–1970

In 1800 only 7 percent of all Anglo-Americans were city dwellers; by 1970 over 70 percent were living in cities. As the larger cities expanded in area, they absorbed many smaller towns and cities whose names are only remembered as belonging to neighborhoods. These enlarged cities were not planned for such growth nor were they planned for modern vehicles and industry. Eastern cities especially were laid out before the invention of the steamship, the railroad, the telephone, the automobile, and the airplane. To the citizen of the early nineteenth century, a shortage of fresh water and unpolluted air seemed inconceivable. Urban space was not at a premium then; and the congestion, crowding, and high noise level of modern cities were nonexistent because of so much almost unoccupied land to the west.

As the city became the symbol of modern enterprise, tall skyscrapers, templelike banks, and gigantic factories became testimonials to the achievements of civic leaders, business-

Port Alberni, British Columbia, on the west coast of Vancouver Island, is entirely dependent on the forest industry. Complete utilization of the trees is possible here where one company has sawmills, veneer plants, and a pulp and paper mill in the same site. Much of the forest on the background slopes has been cut over, but other nearby forest reserves remain untouched or are under forest management. (B.C. Government photo)

men, architects, and engineers. To many these planners of a more productive economy seemed prophets of an affluent era in which there would be enough for everyone and everything would be bigger and better. But as the cities grew a parallel set of problems developed: noise, air and water pollution; congestion, neighborhood decay, and urban slums; crime, political corruption, and grinding poverty within sight of extravagant opulence. While surplus labor from rural areas sought opportunities within the great cities and occupied once proud but decaying residential sections, urban leaders and middle-class workers migrated to the suburbs, thus unwittingly encouraging more decay in the older dwellings in the central city.

What happened was not only urbanization but an urban revolution which altered the life of Anglo-America. Along with the change of residence came an immigration of new workers, first from Europe and later from the rural areas. These peoples often spoke different languages or had a least different customs; they lived in separate neighborhoods, commonly on the "other side of the railroad tracks" where cheap housing clustered around the new factories was considered good enough for the new workers. Enough of these disadvantaged workers ascended the economic ladder so that it became the traditional American belief that hard work and at least moderate intelligence would enable any boy to rise toward the top. "Every boy has a chance to be president" said the school teacher, but for many the chance was infinitesimal.

This growing urbanization and its attendant social ills and exciting accomplishments resulted from a number of technological changes:

1   The growth of commerce led to the funneling of most business through large urban markets. With the growth of rapid communication (by telegraph, telephone, and radio) local markets reacted rapidly to changing world prices. Increasing regional specialization in certain products caused greater dependence on distant producers who could be contacted readily only through urban channels.

2   The growth of factories and the substitution of mechanical power for muscle broadened the market by making industrial products available at lower prices to a wider range of consumers. The needed raw materials, power, machinery, and labor could best be assembled at cities.

3   The adoption of powered agricultural, mining, and woodcutting machinery greatly reduced the demand for labor in the production of foods and other raw materials and thus reduced the demand for rural labor. This decline in rural employment led to wholesale migrations of workers to the growing cities.

All the above changes were superimposed on and integrated with a cultural and economic inheritance from an earlier age. During the first 250 years after Atlantic seaboard settlement, the Anglo-American economy was based on the production of food and raw materials; the prosperity of towns and cities was determined largely by their ability to serve nearby rural hinterlands. Our ancestors required food, clothing, shelter, government, amusement, professional services, and intellectual, artistic, and religious stimulation, as do modern Anglo-Americans. But the satisfaction of each of these needs required different proportions of their total time and income than today, and many of these needs were satisfied in different ways. In the colonial period, for example, many of the tasks now performed by city workers were performed by the farmer. The latter raised much of his own food and manufactured many of his implements. His wife spun thread from locally raised wool, wove cloth, and tailored it into clothing. The farmer hauled his produce to market and sold or bartered it in the marketplace. Services rendered today by physicians, lawyers, architects, entertainers, and other specialists were performed—perhaps rather amateurishly—by the farmer and his neighbors.

Later in the colonial period, rural inhabitants near the Eastern coast took advantage of specialized services available in the seaport towns, but on the frontier the almost self-sufficient economy continued into the nineteenth century. Manufacturing had already been started in many Eastern towns, large and small, but the products were mostly simple and turned out on a small scale. Large cities were few; in 1820 only seven American cities had populations exceeding 20,000. These were mainly commercial and transhipping cities, exporting the produce of their hinterlands and importing goods not locally produced.

THE GROWTH OF AMERICAN CITIES

Anglo-American settlement patterns were laid out when the production and processing of raw materials were the mainstays of the economy. Since then Anglo-Americans have been remaking their economy with more emphasis on service occupations, but usually building on settlement patterns established to meet the needs of the earlier economies. Some early settlements stagnated or declined, but the residents of each settlement have fought hard to maintain the value of their property and to find new activities to replace declining activities. Cities, which generate high land values per acre, have been expanding into and displacing productive orange groves in California, Corn Belt farms in the Midwest, cotton fields in Texas, and dairy farms in Ontario. The city, once the servant of the food and raw materials producer, has become the master.

In 1931, Mark Jefferson, a distinguished American geographer, noted: "Cities do not grow up of themselves. Countrysides set them up to do tasks that must be performed in central places." This is still true, but the "countrysides" stimulating the growth of most cities are no longer rural; today the great majority of city customers live within the same city, in its suburbs, or in other cities. The business of large metropolitan areas such as New York, Chicago, Toronto, or Los Angeles consists largely of performing services for residents of its own metropolitan area. This urban dominance is relatively new: in the United States the urban population first exceeded the rural population in 1920, in Canada in 1931.

The United States Economy in 1860

Just before the Civil War, about half the population of the United States lived west of the Appalachians. The frontier line extended approximately from San Antonio, Texas, to western Minnesota, with major outlying population centers in California and smaller settled areas near the north Pacific Coast, in eastern Utah, along the Rio Grande, and at the foot of the Colorado Rockies. Most large-scale industry was concentrated in the Northeast, and the major centers, including Boston, Buffalo, Cincinnati, Baltimore, Philadelphia, and New York, were distributed throughout an area which continues to be the major part of the *American Commercial-Manufacturing Northeast.* A sparse railroad net served this partly industrialized area, and connections westward reached only central Missouri and Iowa; southward connections were limited to a few through lines whose control became major military objectives in 1863–1864. Canals, the Great Lakes, and the Mississippi River system supplemented the railroads. Most of the roads were unpaved and unsuitable for long-distance transport.

In 1860 the feeling of regional consciousness was very apparent, and contributed to the Civil War. Already, regional differences in the economy were established. The Middle Atlantic states and New England emphasized industry, commerce, and the production of both perishable or bulky foodstuffs and raw materials for nearby markets. The Midwest was not lacking in industry, but its main function was the production of food for shipment east and south. The Southeast specialized in cotton and tobacco, while Texas was expanding as a cattle producer. Small towns were widespread throughout the settled East; most performed political and commercial functions but had

STRIVE TO EXCEL.

An American skirt factory about 1860. The operation is obviously mass production, but the sewing machines used are simple and the power is foot-generated. Clothing was fifth among American manufactures in 1860, exceeded by flour and meal, cotton goods, lumber, and boots and shoes in product value. In terms of labor employed, clothing was first, employing 42,749 male and 77,875 female workers. (This and the drawing on the next page are from U.S. Centennial Commission, *The United States on the Eve of the Civil War as Described in the 1860 Census,* Government Printing Office, 1963.)

some resource-based industries, for example, cotton ginning, grist milling, saw milling, tanning, and distilling. The West was relatively isolated, and only a few cities and widely scattered commercial towns served mining and range livestock industries.

For the whole country, more than three times as many people were employed on farms as in manufacturing. The Northeast accounted for 72 percent of industrial employment, the Midwest for only 12 percent, and the South for less than 10 percent. The most productive United States industries were cotton goods, lumber, shoes, men's clothing, and iron. The manufacture of tools and machinery was not unknown, but elaborate machines for industrial production were often imported. The system of subcontracting and subassemblies, so characteristic of modern industry, was almost unknown.

The United States: 1860–1920

The Civil War and the westward expansion of settlement produced great economic changes in the decades 1860–1880. The military needs of the Civil War and postwar reconstruction encouraged the growth of heavier industry; expansion of the rail net to the Pacific increased the demand for iron and steel. As the grasslands were occupied, agricultural machinery became heavier and more complicated. The expansion of gold mining supplied new capital, and the mining of other ores pro-

Wheeler's Patent Reaper at Work

duced more industrial raw materials. Immigration, after slackening during the Civil War, brought in over 5 million people in the next two decades, increasing both the industrial labor force and the market for its manufactures.

The 1880s were a pivotal period in American economic history. Indian wars were virtually ended, and the bison and untamed Western herds of semiwild cattle were gone; settlers had at least sampled most of the nation's lands. Three developments which were the culmination of post-Civil War growth are of note:

1   After 1880 the contribution of manufacturing to the national income every year exceeded that of agriculture (Figure 3.1). Actually both fields of activity were becoming much more productive, and each stimulated the other. Thus, the introduction of steam-powered farm machinery in the 1880s reduced farm costs and labor requirements and fostered industries which demanded more steel. More city workers demanded more food and raw materials: in turn this expanded market enabled the

Agricultural implements was twenty-third among American manufacturing industries in 1860. Its 14,814 workers supplied 2,423,895 farmers with simple machinery such as Wheeler's patent reaper shown here. By 1860, steel implements had largely replaced the wooden and iron-tipped implements common around 1800.

farmer to buy more manufactures. These employment changes are reflected in Figure 3.2.

2   After 1880 mineral fuels (coal, oil, and natural gas) surpassed wood as sources of power and fuel—in other words, fossil fuels were replacing forest fuels. This change resulted in part from the exhaustion of forests near the market, but perhaps even more from the rapidly increased demand for power and fuel and from the invention of internal combustion engines and dynamos to use fossil fuels.

3   In the 1880s (and later) the increase in the production of industrial raw materials continued rapidly, while agricultural production was increasing at a slower rate. Figures 3.3 and 3.4[1] show increased production of selected

[1] In contrast to many such graphs in which wheat is plotted in bushels, cotton in bales, and pig iron in tons, all the data here have been reduced to long tons. Thus we can note that the tonnage of pig iron nearly caught up with the tonnage of wheat in 1890 and 1900 and exceeded the wheat tonnage after 1900.

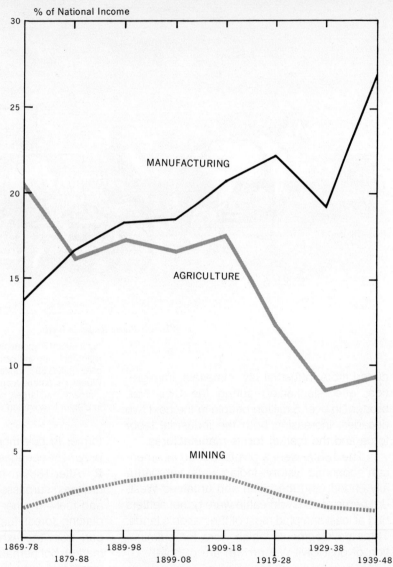

Figure 3.1 Changes in selected sources of national income: 1869 to 1948. Notice that these items never accounted for as much as one-half the national income; services (personal, professional, business, and governmental) have always been a major part of the national income. In recent decades, services have become relatively more important.

agricultural and nonagricultural commodities. A comparison of each agricultural commodity curve with each nonagricultural commodity curve shows that nonagricultural production was generally increasing more rapidly.

As a result of these changes urban population growth was stimulated more than rural growth, as indicated in Figure 3.5.

American Cities after 1920

The 1920 census reported that over half of the United States population lived in urban places. This census also defined a new type of resident, *rural nonfarm,* indicating that many rural

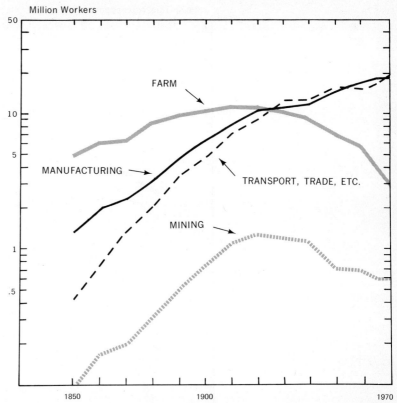

Million Workers

Figure 3.2 Employment in selected major activities: 1850 to 1970. The data in this graph and in Figures 3.3 to 3.5 have been plotted on a semilogarithmic scale so that, despite differences in magnitude, equal slopes on any curve represent equal rates of change.

people were not engaged in what were thought of then as rural activities. The urban population occupied surprisingly little land—only about ¹⁄₁₀ of 1 percent of the acreage in 1920. Population density in the United States as a whole averaged 35 persons per square mile but in cities ranged from 1,000 to 25,000 per square mile. Transportation facilities occupied twice as much land as cities, and rural lands used by city dwellers for recreation probably totaled more. In total, therefore, most of the *area* of the United States held very few people, and the landscapes remembered by persons now reaching retirement age are those of "unspoiled rural beauty."

As compared with cities in the 1970s, American cities of 1920 were much more compact; and their residents were more dependent on public transportation, especially the streetcar, and, in the larger cities, the subway, elevated railroad, and commuter railroad services.

The major shopping and business section was "downtown" (the Central Business District, or CBD), but for food and urgent purchases there were many neighborhood stores, mostly small. Factories were located close to the city center along the railroads or adjacent to waterways. People commonly walked as much as a mile or more to their jobs. In some very large cities executives and professional people sometimes lived in small nearby towns and commuted by train to work. Most Americans traveled more than 20 miles from home only on annual vacations, and automobiles had become fairly common only in farm areas and among the wealthier city people. Although the city was beginning to dominate America, its full suburban expan-

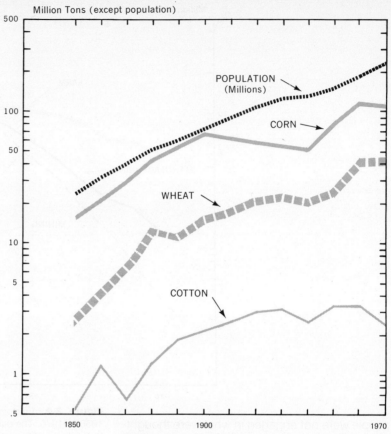

Million Tons (except population)

Figure 3.3 United States production of three major crops is compared with the growth of the American population. Data are plotted for census years only.

sion awaited the common ownership of the automobile.

Adjustments were also taking place in the rural areas. In 1920 for the first time, fewer farm workers had been counted than in the previous census. This resulted not from a decline in farm production but rather from increased output per worker, caused largely by mechanization and improved farm techniques. Consequently a considerable out-migration of younger workers was occurring in even the prosperous farm districts: some migrated to nearby cities; others moved to unoccupied parts of the country. The out-migration started in most of the Southeastern and Plains states in the decade 1910–1920. Many migrated to the more urbanized areas of the Midwest and Northeast, as well as to Florida, Texas, and the Pacific states. With higher per capita farm production, farm

living standards increased with the addition of such luxuries as running water, electricity, and telephones. Better roads and vehicles meant less rural isolation. The automobile made it possible for some members of farm families to work at least part of the time in nearby cities. Thus, former sharp lines between urban and rural living were beginning to blur.

Rapid urban growth in the 1920s brought about a host of problems. Most American cities had been laid out to serve modest populations with slow-moving vehicles. Urban water supplies and arrangements for the disposal of sewage and industrial wastes were inadequate for towns growing at rates of 25 to 50 percent per decade; in addition, increased per capita

Million Tons (except population)

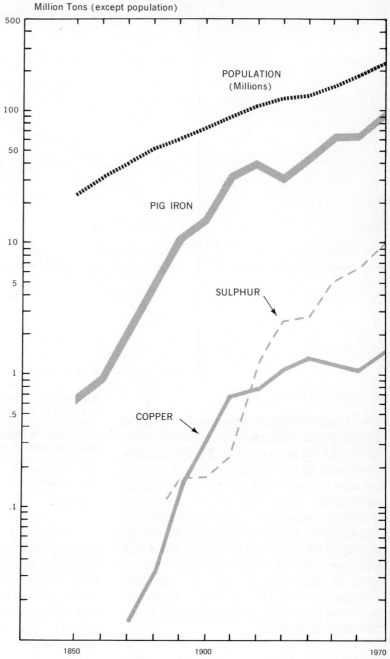

Figure 3.4 In contrast to the growth of agricultural production shown in Figure 3.3, the growth of industrial raw-material production rises much more rapidly than the population. The curves of raw-material production are, of course, affected by the competition of imports.

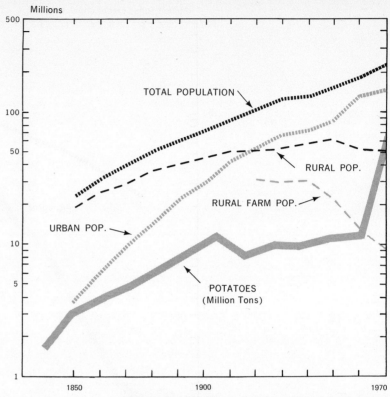

Figure 3.5 These curves show the relative increase in the urban and rural nonfarm population in recent decades. Potatoes are so widely used that it might be assumed that the potato curve would rise with the population since few potatoes are imported or exported. Perhaps the failure of potatoes to keep up with the population reflects the popularity of low-calorie diets, the lower-calorie requirements because of the smaller amount of muscular labor, or the use of substitutes such as sweet potatoes and rice.

use of water resulted from more and better plumbing and industrial use of water. Many cities were forced to tap distant water supplies. Traffic was by far the most universal problem because in many cities (except in the Eastern metropolitan areas) the private automobile gradually replaced public transportation. Trucks added to the congestion of streets designed for carriages and horsecars. We recognize that many of these urban problems are topics of discussion and lament in our daily newspapers; they are not recent problems— they were becoming apparent in large American cities 50 years ago!

THE ECONOMIC EVOLUTION OF CANADA: 1867–1970

Urbanization and related changes in Canadian settlement patterns paralleled those in the United States but usually occurred several decades later. For example, Canadian manufacturing did not equal farming as a source of income until World War I. Canadian tertiary activities (trade, transport, utilities, government, and services) grew rapidly along with manufacturing and construction (secondary activities). Primary industries (agriculture, lumbering, mining) remain and seem likely to remain more significant than in the United States.

Whereas in 1890 primary industries constituted about 36 per cent of the value added by goods-producing industries, this figure had declined to around 15 percent in the 1950s.

This relative decline in the primary industries was due mainly to increases in manufacturing. By 1970 Canadian manufacturing was valued at more than 20 billion dollars. During the 1960s this trend was reversed as the value of primary industry productions increased in Canada and by 1970 was about 22 percent of all goods-producing industries. Within the primary industries one of the significant changes by 1970 was that mining had replaced agriculture as the leader.

Federation

In 1867 the Dominion of Canada was established by the British Parliament with Ontario and Quebec as the core. These provinces had important lumber industries and livestock, dairy products, and wheat were major exports. New Brunswick, dependant mainly on lumber exports, and Nova Scotia, mainly a fishing province, agreed to federate on the promise that a railroad would be built to connect them with Montreal, thus making Halifax and Saint John ice-free ports for the St. Lawrence trade. Railways and canals soon developed interaction between the economies of Ontario and Quebec; but even though Prince Edward Island joined the federation six years later, close integration between the Maritime Provinces and central Canada was never really achieved.

British Columbia was a separate colony, isolated by the interior lands controlled by the Hudson's Bay Company. Title to most of the fur company's lands was transferred to the Dominion in 1869. In 1871 British Columbia joined Canada after being promised that a transcontinental railroad would connect it with eastern Canada; the province waited rather impatiently for 15 years before that promise was fulfilled—a contrast to the speed by which the American West was linked by railroads earlier. These rail connections did not lead to the immediate settlement of the Canadian West because world wheat prices were low from 1873 to 1893 and freight rates to world markets from the interior of Canada were prohibitive.

During the nineteenth century, the population of Canadian provinces grew slowly compared to the neighboring American states (Figure 3.6).

Prairie Settlement

In 1900–1910 settlement of the Prairie Provinces was stimulated by a number of human and technical changes. More efficient grain-handling methods were devised, reducing marketing costs. Demands for the good-quality hard wheat of these semiarid lands increased with the development of new types of bread flour. The introduction of early-ripening Marquis wheat reduced the risks of a killing frost before harvest. Immigrants flooded into the Prairie Provinces from Europe, and farmers' sons from Ontario moved to the new lands available in the west. The 1911 census showed a tripling of the Prairie Provinces' population. Some local manufacturing was established at a few cities, notably at Winnipeg, producing some consumer goods, but mainly processing agricultural products prior to export. Discoveries of coal, oil, and natural gas, chiefly in Alberta, supplied power and fuel for Prairie cities, but their faraway location in the interior of Canada made it uneconomic to export these products at that time.

Eastern Expansion

Prairie settlement increased the demand for Eastern manufactures, and United States' demands for Canadian raw materials further stimulated some Canadian industries. Railroad building required rail ties, steel rails, cars, and locomotives; greater wheat production required grain elevators, freight cars, lake freighters, and milling machinery; wood-pulp and newsprint exports required lumbering equipment, railroads, and paper-mill machinery.

Along the railroads across the Canadian Shield north of Lake Huron, nickel, copper, and iron ores were discovered around the turn of the century. The mineral, forest, and water-

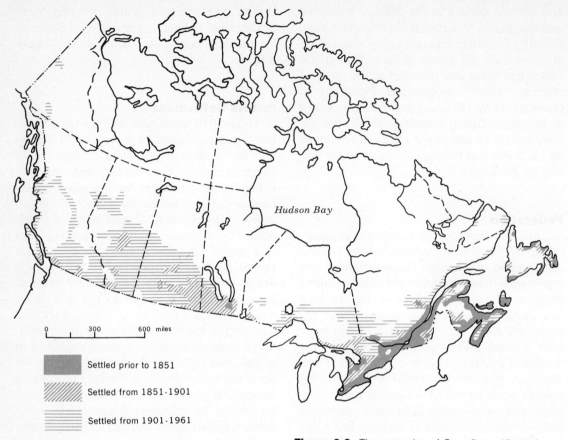

Hudson Bay

0   300   600   miles

▨ Settled prior to 1851

▧ Settled from 1851-1901

▤ Settled from 1901-1961

Figure 3.6   The expansion of Canadian settlement.

power resources of the Shield began to flow southward to the growing industrial cities of Ontario and Quebec. Thus, the raw materials of the Shield supplied the St. Lawrence Lowland cities (see Chapter 9). In both Quebec and Ontario, farm employment declined steadily after 1911, whereas manufacturing employment tripled between 1911 and 1951.

Population Growth

Although the Canadian population almost doubled from 1911 to 1951, the increase was not uniformly distributed. Ontario and Quebec were the two most populous provinces. In Quebec growth was mainly the result of natural increase of the French-Canadian people. The surplus farm population migrated to the trans-

portation hub of Montreal when the rural lowlands of southern Quebec were almost fully occupied. Montreal became Canada's largest city, reaching 1 million population in 1941. Ontario became the main industrial area, producing half of the value of Canadian manufacturing. These activities clustered into cities around the western end of Lake Ontario and westward across the peninsula jutting into the American Manufacturing Belt. In the west, British Columbia and Alberta showed a rapid percentage increase in population, but both started from small base figures; their increases were mainly the result of immigration from eastern Canada and from abroad. Although Canadian politicians and writers promoted the theme that "Canada's future lies in the North"—perhaps mimicking the popular appeal of United States "winning the West"—there was in fact very little northern settlement. Most population clustered into urban centers across the southern part of the country, and these cities had the same general physical appearance—their commercial strips and types of housing—as American cities to the south.

Thus Canada somewhat later underwent an economic and demographic transformation essentially similar to that in the United States. Although rural activities occupy the bulk of the productive acreage, the cities produce the bulk of the income.

EVOLVING PATTERNS AND URBAN CRISES

Combined industrialization and urbanization have erased many differences among the well-settled parts of Anglo-America. From southeastern Canada to Florida to California to British Columbia, the supermarket, the gas station, the freeway, the motel, and many other man-made features are remarkably ubiquitous. Ideas that originate in one part of Anglo-America are soon diffused by mail, telephone, television, and travel to all but the most isolated places. The regional differences, so sharp in Indian societies and conspicuous even earlier in this century, have been smoothed and in places overlaid by the sameness of an industrial and urban society. The freeways and the smog of Los Angeles are being duplicated in other metropolitan areas. Climatic differences remain, but even these have less differentiating effect on a predominantly urban society housed increasingly in air-conditioned homes. There is more variety in rural landscapes—the orange groves of humid Florida present a different appearance from the irrigated cotton fields of California and the dairy farms of Wisconsin.

The increasing urban concentration has at the same time created new patterns on the land. Anglo-Americans, blessed with an overwhelming supply of motor vehicles, have become remarkably mobile; intricate transportation networks have spread over the land. These routes have made possible cheap and rapid shipment of a wide range of goods, and many specialized activities have developed to serve regional and even continental markets.

Central *nodes* have evolved where routes come together. On these crossroad sites commercial and industrial cities have been able to compete in specialized services that depend on access to a wide market. These cities developed into size and spatial hierarchies,[2] a cluster of small cities being served by more specialized functions of a medium-sized city, and a cluster of medium-sized cities being supplied by a large city whose citizens offer a greater variety of specialized services.

Urban Agglomerations and Dispersion

Transportation provides cities not only with the goods and services their citizens require but also with a market for the goods and services they have to sell. With the increasing urbanization of the Anglo-American economy and its linking together by transport networks, it seems likely that more giant metropolitan areas (megalopolises) will develop similar to the Atlantic Megalopolis consisting of a string of cities from Boston to Washington, D.C. Among other similar agglomerations of growing size and complexity are Detroit-Chicago-Milwaukee, Buffalo-Cleveland, Dallas–Fort Worth, San Diego–Los Angeles, San Francisco–Sacramento, and Oshawa-Toronto-Hamilton.

Because of the congestion in these large urban complexes, certain industries are moving to small cities or suburbs. In many cases the economic advantages of proximity are being weighed against the social desirability of dispersion and low-density surroundings.

[2] The concept of urban hierarchies will be more fully developed in Chapter 5.

Fontana was originally an agricultural settlement near San Bernardino in Southern California, laid out in rectangular farms irrigated by the melting snows of the San Gabriel Mountains to the north. During World War II, the Kaiser steel mill was constructed to service Pacific Coast shipyards and other war industries. Since the war, it has supplied steel for new industries developing in the Los Angeles area. (Kaiser Steel Company)

The Detroit Area—Crises and Planning

While the changes described above were taking place, most Anglo-Americans assumed that enlightened business and political leaders would be able to make the needed alterations in the growing cities. Riots and other signs of urban unrest in the 1960s indicated that piecemeal planning had been inadequate to solve the burgeoning problems. Overall plans seemed necessary, and cities that did not already have some sort of planning agency established one. One of the cities that suffered most from central city riots was Detroit, a city which has been well studied by geographers and urban planners alike. Although Detroit was no worse than many other metropolitan areas, it is used as an example because the three-volume study by Doxiadis Associates has been published by the Detroit Edison Company. Action has been taken by the city and its businessmen to redesign the inner city, and much

has been accomplished along the riverfront and around the cultural center. The Doxiadis Plan covers a much wider area and would be much more expensive; there are many common concepts in the two plans.

The Urban Detroit Area—Doxiadis style

The Doxiadis study indicates that there is a gap between the speed of urban growth and human ability to cope with the problems resulting from this growth. The difficulty arises in part from the tendency to consider the political city apart from the international, national, regional, metropolitan, and local settings to which most urban problems are related. A further difficulty results from the attempt to solve

Kennedy Square is an example of open space created in downtown Detroit. (City of Detroit)

urban problems on the basis of short-term costs and benefits, whereas the consequences of the solutions adopted may last a century or more.

Detroit's rapid population growth, stimulated largely but not entirely by the automobile industry, brought in immigrants from a variety of ethnic groups. Canadians represent the largest foreign group, many of them having moved across the Detroit River from Windsor, Ontario. There are also distinct Polish, Italian, German, and Slavic sections. More recently large numbers of Southern blacks and "hillbillies" from Appalachia have added to the cosmopolitan aspect of the city as well as to its social and economic problems.

Detroit SMSA,[3] in common with most American metropolises, consists of a *central city* area which is surrounded by suburbs; a part of this central city is described as a *critical area*—in this section the unattractive living conditions widespread in a central city are most common. In general the central city is occupied by people who because of old age, poverty, or racial discrimination live in an area of older, poorly maintained housing amid a section devoted to industry, transportation, and

[3] The Standard Metropolitan Statistical Area consists of a county with a central city of at least 50,000 inhabitants and contiguous counties if they meet certain census standards of urbanization and employment.

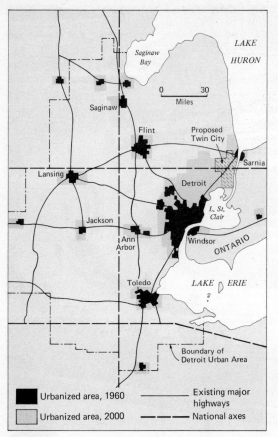

Figure 3.7 The Urban Detroit Area, as used in the plans of Doxiadis Associates, includes parts of three states and two nations.

other activities which create noise and air pollution.

As in the majority of metropolitan areas, Detroit's central city population decreased by 9.5 percent in the 1960s, while the population of the metropolitan area increased by 11.6 percent. Generally this reflects an out-migration to the suburbs, especially of the higher-paid workers. This is shown by the 1972 per capita income estimates which were nearly $3,000 higher for the Detroit SMSA than for the central city. Thus the city of Detroit, with a higher per capita need for municipal services, has a lower tax base to finance such services. The out-migration of residents is also being accompanied by a corresponding suburban

development of shopping centers, business headquarters, and industrial plants. The consequence seems to be that the heart of the city will continue to decay as wealth and productivity move to the suburbs. To arrest this trend, urban renewal must make the central city attractive to the skilled and higher-paid workers. But this is difficult because of the present low levels of education and income in the ghetto. Employment in the dominant automotive industries involves a high proportion of blue-collar workers and a low proportion of people in the service industries. Poor as much of the area is, its working economy still provides considerable income to thousands of landlords and hundreds of thousands of workers. Complete redevelopment of an established area often involves destruction of still useful buildings, displacement of hundreds of thousands of residents, and other changes which are expensive in terms of both money and disruption of human life-styles.

The Doxiadis concept-plan for the Urban Detroit Area   Only a very general statement[4] of the Doxiadis plan can be given:

1   A city cannot be planned without reference to its surrounding region. Thus, the Urban Detroit Area (UDA), the basis for planning, includes all southeastern Michigan counties (see map, Figure 3.7), nine counties in northwestern Ohio, and three counties in Ontario.

2   Major proposals in the plan include:
a   Revitalizing and remodeling central Detroit by eliminating congestion, creating more green spaces, and providing improved housing and public transportation.
b   Creating a twin city to Detroit north of Lake St. Clair to relieve congestion in downtown Detroit, to construct an additional lakeport, and to provide room for industries not now in the Detroit industrial area.

[4] Based on volume III of the Doxiadis study, which has 399 elaborately illustrated pages.

Parts of older downtown Philadelphia have been renovated to create the atmosphere of colonial Philadelphia. (Philadelphia City Planning Commission)

c Creating new axes for transportation and development to supplement the existing expressways extending westward from Detroit and Toledo and southward from Bay City and Flint to Toledo. One of new axial routes would extend westward from the new St. Clair metropolis to north of Lansing, the other southward from Saginaw. Both new axes pass through largely rural areas suitable for the development of new industrial and commercial centers.

d Developing an integrated transportation system that features express routes along major axes, high-speed transportation within the large cities, and community transit in the smaller cities. The objective would be to provide public transportation from home to job with a maximum travel time of 35 minutes and an average journey of less than half that time.

e Creating a network of recreational areas so that every home would be within walking distance of at least a small facility, within 20 minutes by transport from larger parks, and within 90 minutes of rural recreational belts.

f Providing a network of residential communities filled into a rectangular plan developed from the rectilinear township-range survey. To keep interpersonal relations on a human scale, the smallest unit would have a local school, a shopping center, and

In the Society Hill section of old Philadelphia, the renovated houses, modern buildings, and the docks along the Delaware River have been integrated into a pleasant urban landscape. (Philadelphia City Planning Commission)

community services. For certain more complicated services, these communities might be combined into groups of six or more.

Implementing a regional plan   The Doxiadis plan, outlined above, required five years of work by a large staff. The difficulties of carrying out such a plan are almost insuperable; yet the problems with which Anglo-American cities are faced are so great that some sort of orderly plan seems a necessity. Here are a few of the major problems involved:

1   The assumptions on which the plan is based may prove to be partly erroneous. In light of current ideas favoring zero population growth and reduced resource consumption (with reduced urban pollution), an urban area population of, say, 10 to 15 million seems undesirable.

2   Without the prospect of rapid growth, the huge funds required to implement the plan will not be obtainable.

3   The plan will almost certainly damage certain existing businesses and be opposed to the wishes of large numbers of property owners.

4   Many of the improvements expected to result from the plan may not become apparent for years after the funds have been expended.

Columbia, Maryland, is a completely planned new town combining urban and rural landscapes. This photo shows the downtown service and shopping center and one of the villages into which the residential areas are divided. (The Rouse Company)

Many of the details in the Doxiadis plan have been successfully tried in other Anglo-American cities; for example, the scheme of separating pedestrian streets from roadways has been used in Minneapolis, Sacramento, and Montreal. Green belts have been developed in many new suburban communities and in central city urban renewal. Chicago has introduced high-speed public transit along some of its freeways, and Los Angeles is building a bus lane along one of the more congested freeways. These novel ideas are most easily introduced where new communities are built on rural land, as in Irvine, California, and Columbia, Maryland.

Is the Large City Needed?

The growth of large cities started in an era when communication and transportation were slow. Life in a large city had many advantages: access to capital, leadership, skills, government, and markets. But in the past half century technology has made it possible to have most of the above advantages without physically living in the central place. Telephone and television enable the transaction of as much business and the rapid diffusion of information in the suburbs as in the central city. Where direct personal contact is required, jet planes make it possible to reach any major city overnight. The migration to the suburbs suggests that most people might be happier living in small or medium-size cities in which contact with the open countryside is within reach. Already a number of planned communities have been started on this concept.

Even if suburban settlement seems ideal to some, it is unlikely that the large cities will be abandoned. Many still prefer to live in large metropolitan areas. These cities represent huge accumulations of wealth—housing, stores, offices, roads, and factories which would be of little value without inhabitants.

Various plans for urban renewal have been tried in most large cities. The most obvious areas for urban renewal are the slums. In some cases the alternate housing created there has proved too expensive for the residents, and they have simply moved to other ghettos. In some cities, for example, St. Louis, large new apartment projects have been vandalized and abandoned. Somewhat greater success has been attained in building model suburban cities, but these have often proved too expensive for those most in need of better housing. Better and more comprehensive planning seems needed, but the cost of reconstruction of an entire city is staggering and far beyond the budgets (and credit) of the cities that need it most. The consequence is that most urban renewal is being handled piecemeal with inadequate budgets. Such "bandaid" planning cannot solve major social and economic problems in the cities.

In 1870 Anglo-America had less than three dozen cities of over 50,000 in population. As urbanization and industrialization advanced, a utopian reformer, Edward Bellamy, wrote *Looking Backward, 2000–1887,* which portrayed a future America characterized by cooperation, brotherhood, and an industrial machine which would meet all human needs. As the year 2000 approaches, our crystal ball does not produce Bellamy's rosy image. While our cities have grown to mammoth size, ugliness, strife, insecurity, and air, water, and noise pollution have offset many of the advantages of urban living. Increasingly the central cities seem to be the abode of the disadvantaged, and the ghetto seems to be the most rapidly growing type of central city community. The financially more successful citizens take refuge in surrounding suburbs or in luxury apartments near the central city.

Anglo-American society, organized into increasingly larger and more complex units, seems to have overwhelmed the individual. Its institutions are so large and severe and control so many people that the individual seems helpless in their grasp. Perhaps communities should be organized on a smaller scale with open country between each community, but it is not clear what the economic base of such cities would be. If man cannot live with the mammoth city, he will have to develop a new form of central place to perform the urban-type functions now so dominant in Anglo-American society.

SELECTED REFERENCES

BOGUE, DONALD J., and CALVIN L. BEALE: *Economic Areas of the United States,* Free Press, New York, 1961. Rather encyclopedic, but a convenient, quick reference and regional analysis.

BORCHERT, JOHN R.: "American Metropolitan Evolution," *Geographical Review,* vol. 57 (1967), pp. 301–332.

————: "America's Changing Metropolitan Regions," *Annals* AAG, vol. 62 (1972), pp. 352–373.

CITY PLANNING COMMISSION OF NEW YORK: *Plan for New York City,* Six volumes, M.I.T., Cambridge, Mass., 1969.

DEGLER, CARL N.: *Out of Our Past,* Harper & Row, New York, 1959, especially chaps. 9, 11, and 13.

DOXIADIS, C. and ASSOCIATES: *Emergence and Growth of an Urban Region: The Developing Urban Detroit Area,* Detroit Edison Company, Detroit, 1966, and later. A study that includes most of the Great Lakes region, although the focus is on Detroit.

DUNCAN, OTIS D., et al.: *Metropolis and Region,* published for Resources for the Future, Inc., Johns Hopkins, Baltimore, 1960, chaps. 1–4, 7–11.

EASTERBROOK, W. T., and H. G. J. AITKEN: *Canadian Economic History,* Macmillan, Toronto, 1956.

EDITOR AND PUBLISHER: *Market Guide* (annual), 850 Third Avenue, New York 10022. Gives data on all counties and SMSAs, and especially detailed industrial data on cities that have daily newspapers.

FEDERAL RESERVE BANKS: Each bank publishes a journal or review as well as special studies. The reports issued by the Boston, Philadelphia, Richmond, Cleveland, St. Louis, Kansas City, Atlanta, Dallas, Minneapolis, and San Francisco banks are especially valuable to geographers.

HOOVER, EDGAR M.: *The Location of Economic Activity,* McGraw-Hill, New York, 1948. A clear theoretical analysis of the economic forces that influence the location of production.

INNIS, H. A.: *Settlement and the Mining Frontier,* University of Toronto Press, Toronto, 1936.

JACKSON, J. N.: *The Canadian City,* McGraw-Hill, Toronto, 1973.

JACOBS, JANE: *The Death and Life of Great American Cities,* (Vintage Books) Random House, New York, 1963.

JENSEN, MERRILL (ed.): *Regionalism in America,* paperback edition, University of Wisconsin Press, Madison, 1965.

LEWIS, PEIRCE F., DAVID LOWENTHAL, and YI-FU TUAN: *Visual Blight in America,* Resource Paper No. 23, AAG, 1973.

LITHWICK, N. H.: *Urban Canada: Problems and Prospects,* Central Mortgage and Housing Corp., Ottawa, 1970.

PERLOFF, H. S., E. S. DUNN, JR., E. E. LAMPARD, and R. F. MUTH: *Regions, Resources, and Economic Growth,* published for Resources for the Future, Inc., Johns Hopkins, Baltimore, 1960. A statistical analysis of the changing economic geography of the United States, 1870–1954.

PRED, ALLAN R.: *The Spatial Dynamics of U.S. Urban-Industrial Growth: 1800–1914,* M.I.T., Cambridge, Mass., 1966.

RAND MCNALLY: *Commercial Atlas and Marketing Guide* (annual). Available only by subscription. See libraries.

RENGERT, GEORGE F.: "Coping with Urban Stress: The Case of School Dropouts in Philadelphia," *Proceedings,* AAG, vol. 6 (1974), pp. 120–124.

ROSE, HAROLD M.: *The Black Ghetto: A Spatial Behavioral Perspective,* McGraw-Hill, New York, 1972.

SALES MANAGEMENT: *Survey of Buying Power* (annual), 630 Third Avenue, New York 10017. Population, income, and sales data by states, provinces, counties, and cities, both in dollars and in percentages of national totals.

U.S. BUREAU OF MINES: *Minerals Yearbook* (annual), vol. 3. *Area Reports* is especially pertinent.

U.S. CIVIL WAR CENTENNIAL COMMISSION: *The United States on the Eve of the Civil War as Described in the 1860 Census,* Washington, 1963.

U.S. DEPARTMENT OF AGRICULTURE: *Yearbook of Agriculture* and *Agricultural Statistics* (both annual) are generally of interest to geographers. For the innumerable special studies and pamphlets published by this department, see current price lists.

U.S. DEPARTMENT OF THE INTERIOR: Popular reports are being issued on various states—for example, *The Natural Resources of Wyoming.* A variety of special reports are also issued on land utilization problems.

U.S. GOVERNMENT: Yearbooks or handbooks obtainable from U.S. Government Printing Office, Washington, D.C. 20402. (Free price lists are available on such subjects as maps, commerce, soils, agriculture, and weather.)

U.S. OFFICE OF BUSINESS ECONOMICS: *Growth Patterns in Employment by County: 1940–1950 and 1950–1960,* 8 vols., Washington, 1965 (one volume on each O.B.E. region); *Survey of Current Business* (monthly).

4

THE ATLANTIC MEGALOPOLIS AND THE ADJACENT NORTHEAST

Nearly 50 million people are concentrated in the highly urbanized area extending from Maine to eastern Virginia. The region consists of an urban core of almost continuous cities adjoined by a less settled area which functions as a recreational area, a source of certain raw materials, and a provider of perishable food-stuffs such as milk. On the Atlantic margin deep indentations and harbors connect with natural routes inland so that the region is essentially a series of gateways connecting coastwide and overseas trade with the Central Lowland (Chapter 5).

This is the cultural hearth of the United States where events ranging from Pilgrim settlement and the Declaration of Independence to the innovation of the assembly line and large-scale industrial production occurred. Between Massachusetts and Virginia were forged many institutions, including American democracy, the immigrant melting pot, Yankee ingenuity, big business, trade unions, and political machines.

Geographers subdivide the American cul-

The economic capital of the Atlantic Megalopolis is New York City. Many business decisions controlling the American economy are made on Wall Street, near the southern tip of Manhattan Island. Artistic and fashion decisions are made in the Midtown District, upper right. (The Port of New York Authority)

tural hearth into three centers from which varied culture traits, including housing, land tenure, dialects, and manners, diffused inland and southward: (1) New England, from which peoples and their way of life went westward; (2) New York City, New Jersey, and eastern Pennsylvania (the Midland), whose people influenced areas westward and southwestward; and (3) the plantation area around Chesapeake Bay, which helped mold the traditional South. Regional cultural distinctions are believed to have been stratified by the 1820s. But the boundaries of these three cultural areas have never been defined and have been further blurred by southern migrations northward and vice versa. Later, groups of immigrants entering the country mostly through the Port of New York had their first contact with American culture in the Midland Hearth; many carried European cultural traits westward and formed distinctive localized groups, such as the Scandinavians in the rural northern Midwest and the Germans in the cities of Buffalo, Cincinnati, Milwaukee, and St. Louis.

The longest settled, most economically mature, and most intensively developed part of the United States has been variously called *Megalopolis,* the *Atlantic Megalopolis,*[1] the *Atlantic Metropolitan Belt,* or *Bos-Wash* (Figure 4.1). This agglomeration of cities, villages, and suburbs, with its incongruous assortment of street plans, is gradually being merged into a complex economic unit, incorporating such historic centers as Boston, New York, Philadelphia, Baltimore, Washington, Richmond, and the Hampton Roads ports. Each year the open spaces between these cities become smaller; along the transport axes of the region the open space consists mainly of cemeteries, parks, and airfields, The Atlantic Megalopolis houses nearly one-fifth of the nation's people who produce about one-quarter of its value added

by manufacturing and handle nearly one-third of its wholesale trade.

The Atlantic Megalopolis has other characteristics besides statistical leadership:

1 Although it produces all kinds of manufactured goods, the Atlantic Megalopolis is relatively lacking in raw materials, and these make up a large proportion of the tonnage of goods shipped into the region.

2 The region is highly dependent on a network of ocean, inland waterway, rail, highway, pipeline, and air routes to bring in the huge amounts of raw materials, fuels, and foods the region requires. Indeed it is the major focal point of Anglo-American and overseas routes.

3 Despite the huge local demand for fuel and power, much of the region is almost lacking in local fuel resources.

4 Although nearby farms have been made highly productive, they supply only a fraction of the huge food demands of nearly 50 million people,

5 New York and many smaller cities within the region have been centers of national and even world leadership in specific activities. There is a great concentration of professional workers in almost every specialty and subspecialty.

6 The Atlantic Megalopolis includes a tremendous diversity of local specialization: thus Boston is a leader in education and electronics; Hartford in insurance and aircraft engines; the Delaware Valley in heavy industry; the Chesapeake area in seafood, vegetables, and some heavy industries; and Washington in government. The region has the advantages of both division of labor and large-scale operations within a compact area easily accessible to leading American markets.

7 Although the Atlantic Megalopolis is congested, its unrivaled opportunities for jobs, business deals, entertainment, social activities, political intrigue, and even crime attract people from throughout the United States and many foreign countries.

[1] The term *Megalopolis* was used by Jean Gottmann to apply to the Boston-Washington area. Other megalopolises are now developing in Anglo-America; hence the term *Atlantic Megalopolis* is used to identify the "first" megalopolis.

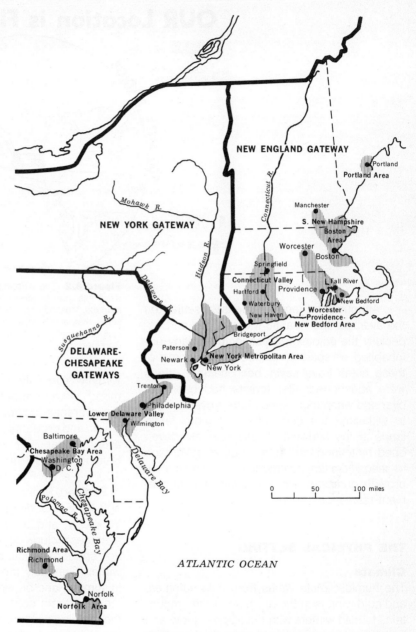

Figure 4.1 The Atlantic Megalopolis, as discussed in Chapter 4, includes a highly urbanized core and adjacent less built-up areas which largely service the urban core. The megalopolitan areas developing along the lower Great Lakes, with extensions southward toward the Ohio and Upper Mississippi valleys, may eventually challenge the supremacy of the Atlantic decision-making areas.

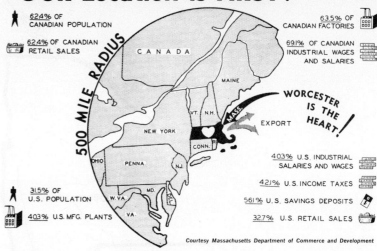

OUR Location is FIRST!

62.4% OF CANADIAN POPULATION

62.4% OF CANADIAN RETAIL SALES

63.5% OF CANADIAN FACTORIES

69.1% OF CANADIAN INDUSTRIAL WAGES AND SALARIES

500 MILE RADIUS

CANADA

MAINE

VT. N.H.

MASS.

WORCESTER IS THE HEART!

EXPORT

NEW YORK

CONN.

OHIO

PENNA.

N.J.

40.3% U.S. INDUSTRIAL SALARIES AND WAGES

4.21% U.S. INCOME TAXES

5.61% U.S. SAVINGS DEPOSITS

32.7% U.S. RETAIL SALES

31.5% OF U.S. POPULATION

40.3% U.S. MFG. PLANTS

MD.

W. VA.

VA.

Courtesy Massachusetts Department of Commerce and Development

Figure 4.2 The Worcester Chamber of Commerce has used this map to stress its central place relationship to markets. Most other cities in the Atlantic Megalopolis could show that a 500-mile radius around their cities would include equally large markets. (Worcester Chamber of Commerce)

Although the region is densely settled *on the average,* the Atlantic Megalopolis and especially the adjoining areas include many uninhabited or sparsely settled areas. Some of these areas have never been settled; others were abandoned after forests had been cut over and when local agriculture proved unable to withstand the competition of more fertile lands in the Midwest. These sparsely developed hinterlands are now of great advantage to megalopolitan communities to which they provide domestic water supplies and convenient recreational areas.

THE PHYSICAL SETTING

Climate

The humid climate varies from mild summers and cold winters in the north and in the mountains to mild winters with occasional snow and hot sticky summers around the nation's capital. It is difficult for modern megalopolitans to imagine what life was like without air conditioning and central heating; yet their ancestors survived under these conditions in the past and contemporary residents get a sample when there is a power blackout. The climatic averages are not extreme. The precipitation data

for New York City, Portland, Maine, and Richmond average about 40 inches annually, but the averages include downpours of rain, blizzards, and droughty periods. July temperatures average near 78°F in Richmond, Washington, Baltimore, and Philadelphia (with maxima of 100°F+); 74°F in New York City; and 68°F in Portland, Maine. January temperatures average 19°F in Burlington, Vermont; 32°F in New York City; and 39°F in Richmond, but these averages include occasional severe cold waves and spells of almost springlike weather in midwinter. Generally the rural landscape is green in summer and brown or snow-covered in winter. In autumn cold waves from the north end the growing season. To the visitor from Southern California both the seasonal contrasts and varied weather from day to day are striking.

Landform Regions and Associated Activities

Four landform regions, each roughly parallel to the Atlantic Coast, are found from New Eng-

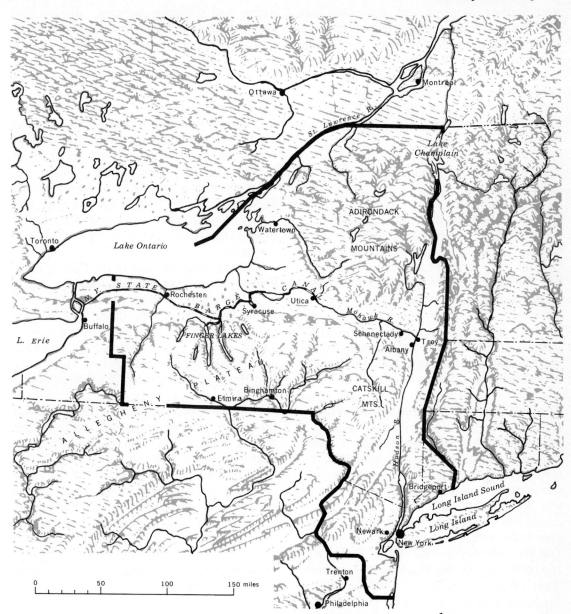

Figure 4.3 Landforms of the New York Gateway. (Base map copyright by A. K. Lobeck. Reprinted with permission of The Geographical Press, Hammond, Inc.)

land to Alabama, but they occur in different proportions in each part of the Atlantic area. The following description applies particularly to the Atlantic Megalopolis and the adjacent Northeast.

The Coastal Plain This low-lying flattish sandy region is found mainly on Cape Cod in

New England, includes Long Island and eastern and southern New Jersey, and broadens to 90 miles in the Chesapeake Bay area. Many of the deep bays are blocked by barrier beaches formed by coastal currents; behind the beaches lagoons and extensive tidal marshes are common and, unless sprayed, provide ideal breeding places for mosquitoes. The numerous small harbors are suited only for fishing vessels and small yachts; ports for larger vessels are concentrated around New York Bay, upper Delaware Bay, Chesapeake Bay, and Hampton Roads. Contact with the sea has always been easy.

The virgin soils of the Coastal Plain, although not rich, were good enough in colonial days for five or more crops of tobacco, after which the planters cleared new land. In Virginia, the bulk of tobacco cultivation has shifted to the Piedmont, but southern Maryland farmers, by applying mammoth quantities of fertilizer, still continue tobacco production.

The soils of the Inner Coastal Plain are mainly sandy loams which warm up rapidly in the spring. These easily worked soils, although not very fertile, respond well to fertilization, yielding a great variety of farm produce including potatoes, garden vegetables, and berries for nearby urban markets

The fall line and the Piedmont The inland boundary of the Coastal Plain is known as the fall line—a name derived from the falls on streams which dropped abruptly from the hard rocks of the Piedmont to the softer sediments of the Coastal Plain. Because in places this physical boundary both offered waterpower and formed the head of ocean navigation, it was an excellent site for cities—indeed Trenton, Wilmington, Baltimore, Richmond, and others may be described as fall-line cities. Other cities such as Philadelphia and Washington are astride the fall line but did not derive the benefits ordinarily attributed to the fall line.

Partly because of tradition and partly because of nearness to metropolitan markets, agriculture is the major occupation on the Piedmont. The well-kept brick houses and barns, the manicured fields, the diversity of crops seem almost a combination of the best in American and Western European agriculture. The crystalline rocks have provided heavy

loams, well suited for orchards, dairying, and poultry farming when fertilized. In Pennsylvania a small limestone area, the Lancaster Plain, produces cigar tobacco, grain, and fine livestock. The fields fitted to the contours on the farms and the well-cared-for appearance of many towns have been attributed to the thrifty immigrants from the Rhineland who settled here in the early eighteenth century. Scotch-Irish farmers made a similar impact on the land in many localities. Pennsylvania farmers devised a system of farming now common in the Midwestern Corn Belt: They bought lean mountain-bred cattle and hogs and fattened them on local grain before selling them in Eastern cities.

On the western edge of the Pennsylvania Piedmont rises a discontinuous crystalline ridge of sparsely settled, wooded hills, commonly called South Mountain. This modest barrier, separating the Piedmont from the Great Valley, can be easily traversed by highways such as the Pennsylvania Turnpike. Historically the "mountain" funneled transverse traffic through its gaps and thus influenced the location of cities such as Reading, Lebanon, and Harrisburg. Its mineral resources are minor, but its iron ores are still used by the Bethlehem steel industry.

The New England equivalent of the Piedmont is less fertile with much more land in woodland and pasture. Ridges rising above the rolling to hilly New England Upland surface form the well-wooded Berkshire Hills, the rounded Green Mountains, and the higher, more rugged White Mountains, all used mainly for vacation areas today.

The Ridge and Valley Province (folded Appalachians) West of the Piedmont–New England Upland, worn-down remnants of folded sedimentary rocks occupy a belt 20 to 90 miles wide. In cross section these ridges and valleys seem almost like huge pieces of corrugated paper. The wooded narrow ridges rise to an even skyline; in the intermediate valleys dairying and poultry farming occupy the small fraction of the land suitable for farming. The folding of the rocks has converted some limestone layers into marble, sandstones into quartzite, and soft bituminous coals into hard anthracite coal, all historically important minerals which are no longer of major importance to the economy.

Just as the Coastal Plain encouraged movement between the industrial Northeast and the more agricultural South, the widest and most continuous Appalachian valley (commonly called the Great Valley) performed the same transport function inland. This wide lowland, with fertile soils from the underlying limestone and shale, extends from the Hudson River to Alabama. Prosperous Pennsylvania Dutch and Scotch-Irish farmers occupy the flatter lands. The minerals of the valley include cement rock,[2] slate, and iron ore; each has contributed to the location of industries in Great Valley cities: for example, the steel industries of Bethlehem and Easton and the cement industries around Allentown.

The narrower valleys west of the Great Valley have considerable dairy and poultry farming, but only a small fraction of the land is tillable. The mining of anthracite coal, once a major source of employment, now provides only a modest number of jobs, and deserted tipples and huge piles of waste rock separated from the coal are memorials to a declining industry. Anthracite coal cannot at present compete with bituminous coke in the steel industry, or with fuel oil and natural gas in domestic heating. The forests which made this area a major lumber center a century ago have since been cut over. The major anthracite cities—Scranton, Wilkes-Barre, Hazleton, and others—are stagnant, kept alive mainly by a modest success with textiles, clothing, and other industries whose main requirements are cheap labor and/or nearness to the megalopolitan market.

---

[2] A kind of clayey limestone which can be converted into cement with very little, if any, other materials added.

The Allegheny Front and Plateau The Allegheny Front rises abruptly 1,000 feet or more west of the Ridge and Valley Province. Although dissected by the canyonlike valleys of the Susquehanna tributaries, the front represented a considerable barrier to early travelers. Now crossed by two interstate highways and with adequate railway connections, the population of the rural Allegheny Plateau nevertheless remains small. About one-third of the land is in farms. Dairying for metropolitan markets is the major rural activity.

The Megalopolitan Model

To the contemporary social scientist, *a model is a simplification of reality which portrays the essential patterns of complex situations without confusing them with minute details.* In the Atlantic Megalopolis such a model can be easily devised. The landform regions are parallel to the coast, and although they are modest barriers to modern civil engineers, they were significant barriers to early settlers and therefore influenced the settlement patterns still dominant in this region. Estuaries attracted early settlers, and the estuary with the most spacious natural harbor and with the best natural corridor into the Central Lowland enabled New York City to become the megalopolitan capital and the leading American city. Human as well as physical features must be included in a full explanation: for example, if Governor De Witt Clinton had not initiated the Erie Canal in the 1820s or if people in Baltimore, Norfolk, Philadelphia, or Boston had been willing to spend the sums necessary to lay out an easy trans-Appalachian route, New York City might not be the dominant metropolis today.

The present model displays three basic geographic features:

1 The old gateway ports were located generally on estuaries which lead to the interior. Most of these cities have taken on functions only indirectly connected with the original gateway function.

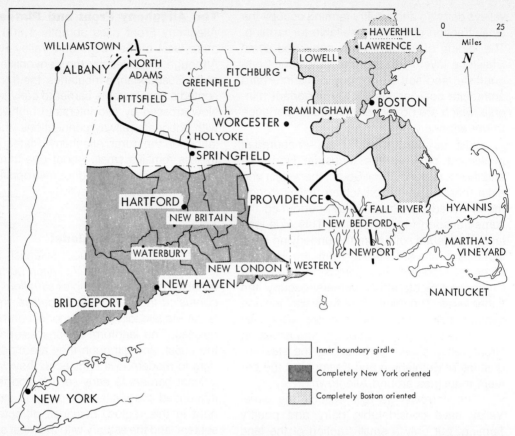

Figure 4.4   How New York has taken away much of the hinterland claimed by Boston is shown by this map based on a median boundary line derived from seven hinterland criteria. (From Raymond E. Murphy, *The American City*, McGraw-Hill, 1966, after Howard L. Green, "Hinterland Boundaries of New York City and Boston in Southern New England," *Economic Geography*, vol. 31 (1955), fig. 9. Used with permission of McGraw-Hill Book Company.)

2   A well-settled elliptical zone connects these gateway cities and makes up the heart of the Atlantic Megalopolis. Within it are suburbs, industrial towns, and educational and recreational centers. Its boundaries are uneven and slowly pushing westward. Within this megalopolitan zone, much of the economic activity consists of serving neighboring cities.

3   The remainder of the Northeast consists of rugged areas with scattered industrial cities, mostly small except along corridors to the interior, such as the Mohawk Valley. The bulk of the nonmegalopolitan Northeast is used for resorts, dairying, lumbering, scattered mining, and fishing along the coast. There is still much unused or little-used land.

Gateways to the interior require special mention since they are foci of critical decision making. Shall the goods handled at the port be simply transshipped, or should they be stored, processed, financed, bought or sold before being forwarded? To which destinations should they be shipped? Shall the port city maintain showrooms, commodity exchanges, stock exchanges, insurance companies, and banks to handle the trade and perhaps control and stimulate it? Should the commercial center be close to the sea or nearer the head of navigation: At New York or Albany? At Wilmington, Philadelphia, or Trenton? At Norfolk or Baltimore? Decision making includes many functions not connected with the gateway functions, and these are likely to be concentrated in the larger cities, for example, political decisions in Washington and financial decisions in New York.

THE NEW YORK GATEWAY

In the early seventeenth century the Dutch established fur-trading posts on southern Manhattan Island and upstream at the site of Albany. By the outbreak of the American Revolution most of the land draining into the Hudson had been at least sparsely settled. Although New York was a major colonial port, it was neither as populous as Philadelphia nor as influential as Boston. But after the Revolution, the aggressiveness of its merchants, the regularity of its shipping services, and the rise of a transshipment service to smaller Atlantic ports aided its growth. The foreign trade of New York quadrupled from 1800 to 1830 when New York became the most populous American city. About the same time the settlement of western New York and Ohio and the opening of the Erie Canal stimulated further traffic through New York. Railways, canals, and turnpikes rivaled one another for traffic to and from the interior. Whichever vehicle was used, the best natural route led to New York; by 1860 five-eighths of all American foreign trade was channeled through that city.

New York was also the major port through which immigrants entered the country. They clustered together in neighborhoods where they could seek employment or socialize within their own language groups. Although many immigrants moved inland, others replenished their meager funds by working in such industries as clothing, packing, and construction. Low-cost immigrant labor was a major factor in New York City industrial development.

New York City is the most convenient place to collect the data, ideas, and advice necessary to make decisions.[3] No one pretends to know everything about business, but with telephones, libraries, experts, national offices, and representatives of foreign governments close at hand, relevant data on almost any problem can be assembled rapidly. Thus New York has become a testing laboratory for new ideas, styles, books, art, businesses, and security issues. On the highest level, New York is an international capital, the scene of the debates and behind-the-scenes maneuvers in the United Nations. Above all, New York is a focus of controls: financial, technical, commercial, political, and artistic. Decisions are made there which may alter the ways of life throughout the world.

With the slowing of European immigration in the 1920s, migration from other parts of the country took on a growing importance. Many of the new residents were from the Midwest; they sought greater employment opportunities in the nation's business capital. Lack of opportunity in the South and Puerto Rico sent multitudes of blacks and Puerto Ricans into the Harlem section around 125th Street. In 1960 New York City's population was 14 percent black; in 1970 21 percent of the population was black. After World War II European refugees flocked into the city; as a result the residents of European birth exceeded the black population in 1960 and 1970. Thus, New York retained its cosmopolitan image; foreign-language newspapers were commonly seen on the street, and public notices were often posted

---

[3] The importance of New York City in decision making does not mean that New Yorkers dictate national trends. In most cases the decision makers examine the situation throughout the nation and decide what policies will appeal to the largest part of the national market. For example, buyers from department stores and specialty shops visit New York to see showings of the new women's clothing styles offered by New York manufacturers, who may be influenced by styles exhibited earlier in Paris and Rome. The buyers order the dresses. suits, etc., which they believe their customers will purchase. The manufacturers receive and prepare the orders, which constitute the styles available to American women. Usually the new styles are promoted by fashion magazines and by women who may have purchased the models designed earlier in Paris and Rome. The decision as to which styles will become available is made in New York but not necessarily by New Yorkers.

in English, Spanish, and Italian. The newcomers usually settled in the central city, but as they achieved financial success they often joined the trek to the suburbs.

The Metropolis and Its Hinterland

Much of the growth of New York is based on its ability to serve its hinterland. It is difficult to determine exactly the extent of this hinterland; for some services it includes most of the world. Probably every part of the United States is served by New York in at least several important respects. The area mapped (Figure 4.3) as the New York Gateway is based largely on the boundaries of the New York Federal Reserve District, an area within which New York business connections are of outstanding importance.

The Hudson-Mohawk route   The most developed sector of the New York hinterland is along the Hudson-Mohawk route. North from New York City the wide, brackish Hudson estuary is adjoined by well-settled suburbs which soon give way to the wooded recreational lands of the Hudson Highlands. Clearly visible to the west of the Hudson are the so-called Catskill ''Mountains,'' actually the eastern edge of the Allegheny Plateau. This resort area is also a major source of the New York City water supply.

A few miles north of Albany the New York State Barge Canal (formerly the Erie Canal) and major rail-highway routes turn westward up the Mohawk Valley, finally connecting with the Great Lakes at Buffalo. Most of this transport route is adjoined by pastoral rolling countryside, largely used for dairy farming but with some specialized orchard and vineyard areas.

Specific industries in each city along the Erie Canal route are attributable to local resources or to the founding of a factory by a local businessman. For example, one urbanized area consists of the three cities of Albany, Troy, and Schenectady. Albany, first a fur-

trading post, was selected as state capital in 1790. Besides functioning as a political center and transport junction, the city has developed diversified industries such as paper and machine tools. Neighboring Troy is best known for shirt manufactures which were initiated by the local invention of detachable shirt collars and cuffs. Schenectady, now noted for the sprawling General Electric factories, owes its specialty to the decision of Thomas Edison to buy factory buildings to house his electric machine works there.

Syracuse arose on the site of an Indian village. Like many other large cities Syracuse has the advantage of being located at the junction of two landforms, the Lake Ontario plains and the Appalachians, and uses the resources of both. In addition it had a crossroads position, being at the head of a north-south route following one of the Finger Lakes into central New York State. After the Civil War the city turned to the manufacture of metal products. Today durable goods, for example, electrical equipment and pottery, are the leading industries.

Rochester has a geographic setting in many ways similar to that of Syracuse; yet differences in both environment and leadership have given it a distinctive character. The settlement was founded about 1790 to use the waterpower of the Genesee River for sawmilling and flour milling. As grain production shifted westward, the economic base changed to seeds and orchards, and to the use of immigrant labor to manufacture ready-made clothing. Industrial emphasis changed again because of the leadership of a handful of science-oriented men. Outstanding was George Eastman, who in 1880 turned his hobby into a business after inventing the dry photographic plate. Consequently photographic equipment and instruments now dominate in industrial Rochester.

Each of these cities serves as a central place for the nearby agriculture and industries in the small towns along the route, and each is well connected with the other large cities

Much activity in New York City is concentrated on the "sidewalks of New York." On New Year's Eve, crowds concentrate in Times Square (at Broadway and Forty-second Street) to await the arrival of the New Year. (Wide World Photos)

along the interior line. In turn, these cities look to New York for business decisions, advertising, and markets.

Other routes   The other major routes focusing on New York parallel the coast and connect the megalopolitan capital with the New England, Delaware, and Chesapeake cities. The traffic over these routes, both freight and passenger, is very heavy and is handled by rail, expressway, and air. Much less important routes tap the trade of interior New England and southern New York State. The most important of these was based on the anthracite railroads, designed to bring eastern Pennsylvania coal to urban markets. Several of these railroads extend to Lake Erie through moderate-size industrial cities such as Scranton and Binghamton.

The Local Geography of the New York Metropolis

Physical setting   The local geography of New York City was far from ideal for early settlement. The land around New York harbor is poorly suited for farming. Ice Age glaciers scraped the surface soil off New England and deposited a mass of sand and boulders on Long Island. North of Staten Island a long ridge

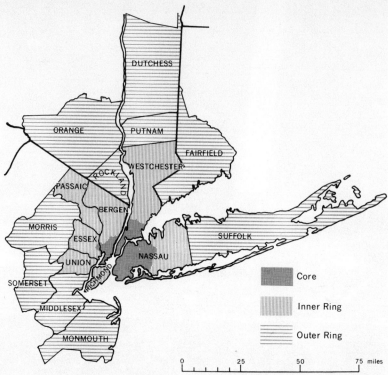

Figure 4.5 Three zones used in planning for the extended New York Metropolitan Region. (After Hoover and Vernon)

of igneous rock rises gradually to form the Palisades, a columnar wall of basalt along the western shore of the lower Hudson. West of this upland, a low-lying marshy area was an ideal home for mosquitoes for which New Jersey was once famous. East of the Hudson River a prong of the rocky, ice-scoured New England Upland extends south to form the hard base of the boroughs of Bronx and Manhattan. Twenty miles north of New York City a spur of this rock prong extends southwestward and is cut by the Hudson River, forming the scenic Hudson Highlands.

The main site advantage of New York City has been its broad channels formed by the submergence of ancient river valleys. The depth and width of the Hudson estuary made it suitable for ocean liners as well as for humbler craft. East of Manhattan the so-called East "River" provides a sheltered route via Long Island Sound to southern New England and via the Cape Cod Canal to Boston. New York Har-

bor requires no tidal basins; its 20- to over 40-foot-deep channels handle large tonnages with very little congestion; less favorable reports can be given about its land-based traffic where in wharves and truck terminals transshipment is often slowed to a snail's pace.

The Core and the CBDs The major subdivisions (Figure 4.5) used below follow the scheme used for planning the extended New York Metropolitan Area. The *core* includes four of the five boroughs (counties) of New York City as well as Hudson County, New Jersey. This central area includes a number of Central Business Districts identifiable by their tall buildings and high commercial, financial, and other service employment. Of these CBDs, that of the southern part of Manhattan Island is of outstanding national and international importance (Figure 4.6).

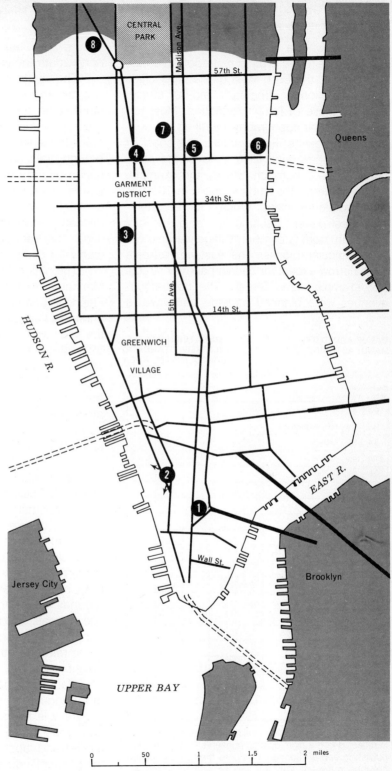

Figure 4.6 The Manhattan CBD. The older part of the city includes City Hall (1) and the produce markets (2). The midtown business district developed between Pennsylvania Station (3) and Grand Central Terminal (5). Times Square (4) is commonly thought of as the center of the theatrical district although most of the theaters are to the north of it. Recent developments are Rockefeller Center (7), the United Nations (6), and Lincoln Center (8).

Many of the urban patterns described below will be found in other metropolitan areas, especially in the East. Most of the older cities have a section of irregularly laid-out streets such as those of lower Manhattan. Most too have had their topography modified by construction projects. For example, the coast of Manhattan has been filled in to create additional land: Greenwich Street, for example, which bordered the Hudson shore in 1830, is now two blocks inland. When a more systematic street pattern became desirable, the city northward from Greenwich Village was laid out in rectangular blocks. The east-west streets were narrow except for certain parkway streets (for example, 42nd Street). The north-south avenues were planned as wide parkways, a feature which has proved a great advantage to north-south traffic.

The center of the downtown core in 1871 was marked by the railroad terminal at East 42nd Street and Fourth Avenue, the site of the present Grand Central Terminal. Other railroads terminated on the New Jersey shore and brought their passengers and freight to Manhattan by ferry until 1909–1910 when railway tunnels under the Hudson and East rivers were completed. With the decline of long-distance railroad passenger service, Grand Central Terminal and Pennsylvania Station are used primarily for commuting services.

The national and international business of Manhattan is divided between the Wall Street Financial District (where the Stock Exchange and most financial institutions are located) and the Midtown Office District (between 34th and 59th streets). The midtown section also includes the theatrical and the main shopping districts. Residences for the office workers in the downtown and midtown business sections are supplied by many apartments and rooming houses, especially in Greenwich Village and along the narrower east-west streets.

Near the central city of most large cities are usually the areas of social and economic problems. The western edge and eastern bulge of the Manhattan CBD, somewhat away from the main course of business, consist of poor tenements which became ghettos. Many of these slums are gradually being replaced by modern apartments. Noisy narrow streets and rows of old houses with few parks and playgrounds are found in the many densely populated areas. Undoubtedly this unattractive, congested environment contributes to the high crime rate and other social problems in these neighborhoods.

Manufacturing in the CBD consists largely of loft industries, that is, industries which occupy single floors (or less) of large buildings and whose main requirement is nearness to market and labor. The largest loft industry is the garment industry (located about in the center of the CBD) whose many subcontractors

VALUE ADDED BY MANUFACTURING

GREATER N.Y.C.–N.E. NEW JERSEY STANDARD CONSOLIDATED AREA

% Distribution   Location quotients: 1.0 = national average per capita

Employ-ment	Value added	SIC source	0	1.0	2.0	3.0	4.0	5.0
5.4	8.3	Food products						
NA	NA	Tobacco products	NA					
3.4	3.0	Textiles						
17.2	12.9	Apparel						
0.6	0.4	Lumber						
1.6	1.3	Furniture						
3.2	2.9	Paper products						
10.4	15.3	Printing						
6.5	14.8	Chemicals						
0.3	0.8	Petro-coal products						
2.2	2.0	Rubber–plastic						
1.9	1.2	Leather						
1.6	1.9	Stone–clay–glass						
2.3	2.4	Primary metals						
5.4	5.4	Fabricated metals						
5.3	5.6	Machinery						
9.1	8.5	Electrical machinery						
4.0	6.7	Transport equipment						
2.6	2.7	Instruments						
100.0	100.0	All categories						

Figure 4.7 The decision-making function of New York is reflected in the high location quotients for printing and publishing and for apparel. Compare the two distribution columns to the left: Why are they so different in the apparel, food products, printing, and chemicals categories?

This once middle-class Harlem apartment section is now the center of the Manhattan black community. Some streets at times are reserved for playgrounds. (Photograph by Charles Harbutt, Magnum Photos)

must keep in close touch with one another; with the wholesalers of yardage, dresses, suits, and trimmings; and with the creators of changing styles.

The population of Manhattan averages 68,000 per square mile, not counting the million or more tourists and business visitors who spend most of their daytime hours in the Manhattan CBD. Each morning converging subways, railways, ferries, and buses bring over a million workers into the CBD and take them home at night. At least half come from the core, but about 600,000 commute from the inner and outer rings. In strong contrast to other American metropolitan areas, few workers travel to the CBD by private automobile since parking space is expensive and rush-hour expressway driving is much slower than the frequent rail and bus services.

Because space in the Manhattan CBD is so costly and crowded, many businesses di-vide their work between the inner and outer sections of the city. For example, most publishers have their offices in the Midtown Office District, but their books and magazines are printed in and shipped from suburban towns or even distant cities. Insurance companies have their main offices in the CBD, but much of their clerical work is performed in suburbs. Most of the city's wholesalers have their showrooms in Manhattan, but their warehouses may be in the suburbs. More than half of all value added by manufacturing in New York City is still produced in Manhattan, being concentrated in industries where style or design are more important than bulk, for example, apparel and jewelry. The concentration in the CBD is even more apparent in the service industries.

Some of the boroughs[4] around Manhattan seem to be merely dormitories for workers commuting to Manhattan. This description might fit the Bronx, which is largely a lower- and middle-class residential area with more than half its workers employed elsewhere. On Long Island, sprawling Queens, originally consisting of many small towns each with a considerable community consciousness and distinctive street patterns, is somewhat similar to the Bronx. Brooklyn is different. Before it merged with New York City, it was a separate city, and it is now the most populous borough in the metropolis. Like Queens, its early settlements were a number of separate towns, many founded by early Dutch settlers. Although two-fifths of its workers are employed elsewhere, Brooklyn has an active business center of its own, including a CBD across the East River from lower Manhattan. Brooklyn leads Manhattan in industries involving weight or bulk: for example, food products, chemicals, and fabricated metal products. Although some factories are scattered along the railroads, most are located on or near docks of the East River or Upper New York Bay. Although most passenger liners dock in Manhattan, freighters are likely to unload either in Brooklyn or in Hudson County, New Jersey.

The use of Hudson County illustrates how physical difficulties may be overcome if a site is strategically located. The Jersey shore is overlooked by a mile-wide upland of volcanic rock, 400 feet high in the north and less than 100 feet high in the south. The well-settled summit of the upland is flat or rolling in places; the narrow lowland to the east has been filled in a mile or more to make land for terminals and docks. Six railroads now cross Hudson County and terminate at its docks. Much of their freight is handled financially in Manhattan but physically never enters that overcrowded

island. The bulkier Hudson County industries (petrochemicals, fabricated metals), concentrated to the south in Bayonne, contribute to air pollution which in much of the New York core now surpasses that of Los Angeles.

The inner ring (Figure 4.5)   The inner ring includes towns and cities which had (and in many cases still have) independent economies of their own before they were integrated into the Metropolitan area. Cities such as Newark have sizable CBDs as well as specialized industries. The inner ring is especially suitable for industries requiring space.

Each part of the inner ring has distinctive characteristics; for example, Newark has durable goods manufacturing as the principal source of employment in contrast to the core where nondurable goods are far ahead. With a deep-water port, uncongested connections by four railroads, and numerous highways, Newark is well suited to produce fabricated metal goods and machinery.

Westchester County, just north of New York City, is well known as a residential county for upper-class commuters. Gracious homes with ample lawns and gardens contrast with the tenements of Manhattan. With a seaport at Yonkers and inland connections via the Hudson-Mohawk route, this uncongested area with a well-educated labor force is attractive for many industries such as automobile assembly and printing. Nassau County, east of Queens on Long Island, in many respects duplicates Westchester County as a commuting, residential, and light industrial county. Its indented bays on Long Island Sound and its beaches and lagoons on the Atlantic shore offer intensively used recreational possibilities.

Most of the inner ring has many of the advantages of the core without its congestion and high land prices. In fact, some of the typical Manhattan CBD industries (apparel and printing and publishing) have begun to move to the inner ring. Available land in the inner ring is being rapidly occupied; thus the once

---

[4] The boroughs coincide with counties but have local governments which are a part of the New York City government. The Borough of Brooklyn is also Kings County; the Borough of Manhattan (New York County) comprises Manhattan Island.

The John F. Kennedy International Airport, about 10 miles east of Upper New York Bay, was constructed on marshy land adjoining Jamaica Bay. (The Port of New York Authority)

marshy areas such as the Hackensack Meadows between Newark and Jersey City are becoming industrial areas.

The outer ring The outer ring includes much land yet unused for urban purposes: farmland, wooded hills, sandspits, and tidal marshes. It provides water supplies for New Jersey cities and parts of New York City. The outer ring also provides a small but significant part of the food of the metropolis: both Suffolk County on eastern Long Island and rural northern New Jersey have intensive farming, producing perishable foods, for example, Long Island ducklings.

Bridgeport, Connecticut, is an example of an outer ring city. Its local industries manufacture such diverse goods as machinery, sewing machines, and firearms. The original location of its industries depended on its once-important port and the traditional skill of Con-

necticut metal workers; today, however, location near the New York market is its major advantage.

New York City: Still a Leader
Given contemporary speed of communication and transportation, many functions once performed in New York are being shared with other cities in the Atlantic Megalopolis as well as with cities to the west such as Detroit, Chicago, Atlanta, Dallas, Los Angeles, and San Francisco. Nevertheless the New York Gateway, with one-eighth of the nation's people, still retains leadership in many fields. The decision-making activities, the functions as a gateway between the Atlantic nations and the United States, and many services provided for the

Minuteman National Park, barely 20 miles west of downtown Boston, scenically typifies rural New England. The Park houses the "original" minuteman statue, North Bridge and Battle Road where the initial battle of the Revolutionary War raged, and a migratory bird refuge. (Crane Miller)

Atlantic Megalopolis are concentrated in the Greater New York Area. Closely connected with this urban giant are the suburbs, the Atlantic beaches, the hills and mountains inland which give the city worker some relief from the noise, pollution, and congestion of the central city. The parts of the city the visitor sees often seem depressing and confusing, with slums and other signs of urban decay adjoining spectacular skyscrapers and striking vistas. The tourist comes as a visitor to see the sights—theater, concerts, arts, the United Nations, the Fifth Avenue shops, and Rockefeller Center. The working New Yorker is less confused—he is a cog in a complex but functioning cultural, economic, and social machine. He feels he is in the center of things, events, and opportunities and that he can do his job well. The New Yorker is quite aware of the many unsolved problems of the New York community; yet life

there can be exciting, and many New Yorkers would not want to live anywhere else.

THE NEW ENGLAND GATEWAY[5]
During the first two centuries of Anglo-American history, New England surpassed or equaled other areas in several measures of leadership, for example, shipping, manufacturing, education, and literature. Today its income totals less than half that of the New York Metropolitan region, but New England capital,

[5]Historically and conventionally, New England comprises six states, but Fairfield County, Connecticut, has been excluded because it has become economically merged with the New York Metropolitan Area.

skill, and intellectual leadership still exert major influences on national development. Its importance as a gateway has diminished, much of its foreign trade now being handled through the Port of New York.

New England is no longer noted for its great natural resources. Early settlers found six resources of which they took full advantage: (1) fish from adjacent banks; (2) natural harbors; (3) oak and white pine suitable for shipbuilding and other construction; (4) small areas of fertile soil; (5) waterpower easily harnessed; (6) small deposits of lead, copper, and bog-iron ores. Although natural resources were a major factor in the past New England economy, compared with other Anglo-American regions local resources were scanty. The soils are generally stony and infertile, and the rough terrain is rarely suitable for modern mechanized farming. The forests have been cut over, and pasture or inferior stands of timber occupy the former areas of tall virgin forest. The climate is cold and raw in winter and is too cool in summer for the profitable growth of many crops. Minerals today are of minor importance. Most New England development in the last two centuries has resulted from the skill and energy with which the settlers used the little bounty that the land offered.

Land and Settlement

Rough topography characterizes the landforms of New England. Except for small coastal plains and a few alluvial or glacial lowlands, New England is a much dissected upland of hard crystalline rocks: largely granite, gneiss, and marble. The upland, commonly 300 to 1,000 feet high except for steep north-south ranges rising a few thousand feet above the general level, has been scoured by continental glaciers which planed off the hilltops and filled in the valleys. Boulders, clay, and sand deposited over the surface blocked stream channels to form innumerable lakes, ponds, and swamps. Projecting into the upland are fertile basins covered with glacial soil such as that in the Boston and Narragansett basins. Use of the environment influenced settlement patterns. Village settlements and farms came to the areas of fertile soil. Where streams descended from the upland, early industry and millsites were located.

Agriculture   With adequate rainfall and a fairly long growing season in sheltered valleys, colonial farmers thrived. Until about 1830, wheat, wool, and beef were produced for urban markets and even for export. With the growing exploitation of better soils in the Midwest, most New England farms could not compete. As a consequence, about half of the cropland went out of production. Today New England obtains nearly all its flour, beef, pork, butter, and cheese and much of its fresh, canned, and frozen fruits and vegetables from outside its borders. Many of the descendants of early New England farmers moved westward; others moved into the cities to work in the factories; some still live on the farm but work at least part-time in the city.

The remaining New England farms are generally small (about 200 acres) and specialize in a few crops. Farmers near the megalopolitan markets benefit by high prices for their dairy products, poultry, and vegetables. For this reason the limited productive lands are tilled so intensively that Massachusetts and Rhode Island are among the leading states in value of crops per cultivated acre. In a few areas there are local specialties: potatoes from Aroostook County, Maine; blueberries from coastal Maine; cranberries from Cape Cod; and wrapper tobacco from the central Connecticut Valley. Nevertheless the traveler in New England may note that farming occupies a minute proportion of the area. Wooded hills and mountains, lakes and marshes, and extensive pastures are more characteristic than cultivated fields.

Extractive industries   The visitor to New England may be so impressed by the extensive forests and the numerous fishing ports that it

Figure 4.8 Landforms of New England. Very little of New England is plain, the uplands in most areas sloping down gradually to a rockbound coast. (Base map copyright by A. K. Lobeck. Reprinted with permission of The Geographical Press, Hammond, Inc.)

seems incredible that natural resources contribute so modestly to the present regional economy. Fishing, for example, yields a catch of about $50 million annually. Although this is one-eighth of the annual fishing catch of the United States, it is only equal to the personal income of a New England city of 30,000 people. Mining (mostly quarrying) yields about the same annual value, much of which consists of

sand and gravel used for concrete. New England forests now produce less than 2 percent of American lumber. In a similar environment, but with a much smaller population, these natural resources are much more significant, in relative terms, in the adjoining Maritime Provinces of Canada.

Manufacturing   Manufacturing still accounts for about one-third of New England's earned income. The region must import most of its industrial raw materials; its waterpower must be supplemented by large imports of coal and petroleum. Many of its factories are old and often not easily accessible to modern trucks because the streets and roads were designed for the horse-and-buggy days. Yet with all these handicaps New England continues to produce industrial goods—especially those goods that benefit from skilled labor, advanced engineering techniques, and emphasis on quality. Smaller New England industries process local raw materials such as Maine lumber, Vermont marble and maple syrup, and Atlantic fish.

In this century industries based on semiskilled labor and automatic machinery have moved to other regions where labor and power were cheaper and markets somewhat nearer. The cotton textile industry has been the prime example of this migration: until the 1920s New England was an undisputed leader in textile production, but this preeminence has long since shifted to the South. On the other hand, eastern New England is one of five dominant national centers for research and development; Massachusetts, for example, has more than twice its per capita share of the nation's research and development projects.

The infrastructure and service functions   The New England economy is based primarily on services rather than on the production of tangible goods. Two-thirds of the income is derived from services and from payments unrelated to current civilian production. Services, such as insurance, underwriting, advertising, publishing, scientific research, designing, and machinery repair, are especially important in New England. Many of the services rendered contribute to the efficiency of its man-

ufacturers; other service activities are themselves basic ("export") industries serving major markets both in and outside New England.

Urban Patterns and Income Patterns

Settlement and occupational patterns are reflected in the geographic distribution of income. The three northern, largely rural, states account for over 18 percent of the population but only 15 percent of the New England income; in southern New England four SMSAs account for over half of the regional income. New England income is concentrated in three urbanized areas: the Boston Basin, which now extends economically to the lower Merrimack Valley, the Narragansett Basin including Providence and the Blackstone Valley, and the Connecticut Lowland and several adjacent valleys. Aside from these basins, most of New England is rural, with a sprinkling of small to medium-size cities each with a few industrial specialties. The three major industrial areas are connected by interstate highways, and suburban developments are gradually welding the major cities into a continuous megalopolis.

The Boston area   About 3.4 million people reside in nearly 100 towns and cities which focus on the central city of Boston (population 641,000). In the days of New England maritime supremacy, Boston was the leading American port, sharing its trade with nearby Gloucester, Marblehead, Salem, Lynn, and Quincy. Today visitors flying into Boston's international airport can see the urbanized area spreading across the low-lying Boston Basin, onto the low rimming hills, and northward into the Merrimack Valley. The intricate network of street and road patterns cannot be understood unless it be realized that this urban crazy quilt started as a multitude of towns[6] and villages whose design fitted local topographic conditions.

[6] Political organization in New England differs from that in other states. Although each state is divided into counties, the subdivisions of the county, the towns, are the major local governments. These, like townships elsewhere, may include both rural and urban areas. See Raymond E. Murphy, *The American City*, McGraw-Hill, New York, 1966, pp. 20–21, 434–466.

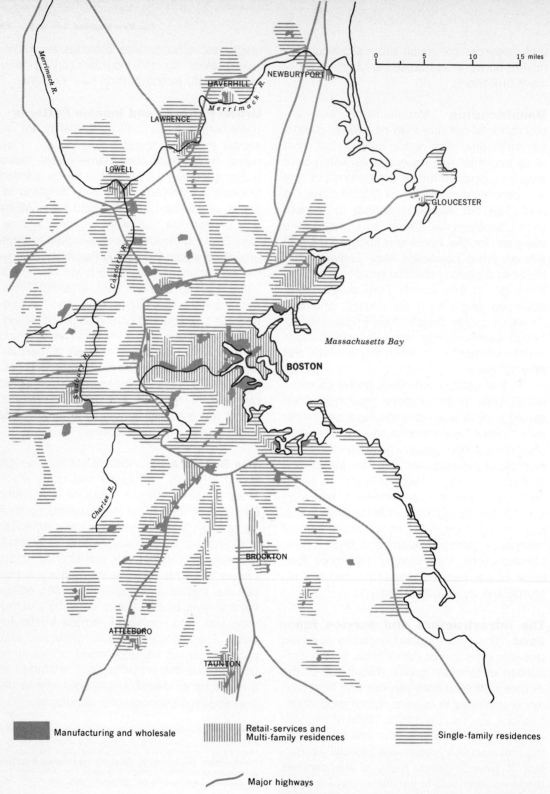

Figure 4.9 The Boston metropolis has sprawled out, industrially, commercially, and residentially, beyond the limits of the Boston Basin but the focus on Boston Harbor is still evident.

Manufacturing and wholesale

Retail-services and Multi-family residences

Single-family residences

Major highways

Boston eastward from Prudential Center. Just south of the CBD, the "last mile" of the Massachusetts Turnpike from New York emerges from beneath the Center. In the background, Logan International Airport and Boston Inner Harbor provide a focus of transportation at the mouth of the Charles River; but from here inland the river is neither deep nor long enough to accommodate commercial shipping in the way the Hudson River has for New York City. (Crane Miller)

The Boston Basin was first altered by glaciation and later by man. When first settled in 1630, it consisted of plains interrupted by numerous swamps and ponds, above which rose low glacier-deposited hills. The city of Boston occupied the bulging end of a narrow peninsula on which rose Beacon, Copps, and Fort hills. The well-sheltered shores of the city provided adequate spaces for wharves only 6 miles from the open sea. With Massachusetts Bay and the Charles River permitting local waterborne traffic, Boston became an ideal political and commercial center for Massachusets. Soon the city became so crowded that other towns were established on nearby well-drained lands: Cambridge, Roxbury, Charlestown, Somerville, Newton, and Quincy. Later marshy areas were drained or filled, extending the present shoreline well beyond the original coast; for example, the Back Bay project, commenced in 1856, filled in the flats adjacent to the neck of the Boston peninsula, and on it a rectangular street pattern was added to the meandering streets of old Boston.

The original commercial nucleus (CBD) was on a cove east of Beacon Hill. When railroads entered the city between 1835 and 1855, lines from the north crossed the Charles and stations were built on reclaimed land north of the CBD. The expanding CBD gradually filled most of the area between the railroad terminals and between Beacon Hill and the docks to the east. Boston thus developed a business center focused on about a square mile; in the present century this became so crowded that many business activities moved to suburban locations.

The outward movement has been aided by new transport lines. A freeway cuts through the older part of downtown Boston; inner belt and outer expressways intersect the innumerable roads fanning out from the harbor. While sky-scrapers are rising in old Boston, new science-oriented industries line the encircling express-way now nicknamed "Electronics Row." Like many Eastern cities, Boston is both an old and a new city: remnants of the buildings and land-scapes of the colonial period have been pre-served; narrow streets and monotonous brick factories are reminders of an early industrial age. Elsewhere the curving streets of ranch-type houses, the broad parking lots of subur-ban shopping plazas, and beautifully land-scaped suburban industrial parks make Boston as new as any other American city. Although Boston is primarily a commercial and service center, manufacturing accounts for one-third of all employment. Boston claims to have the largest group of engineers and scientists in the world; hence it is not surprising that the elec-tronics industry is the leading branch of indus-trial employment and that transportation equip-ment and machinery are in second and third place.

Industries are found throughout the Bos-ton SMSA, but the newer industries are con-centrated in some 43 industrial parks. The city of Boston has a wide variety of manufactures, whereas suburban satellites are likely to have only a few each; thus Gloucester specializes in fish packing, Beverly in shoes and shoe machinery, and Lynn in electrical goods and shoes. The industries are generally those in which resources play a small part compared with skilled labor and technology.

The other types of employment in Boston are similar to those found in many other Ameri-can cities. A third of all Bostonians perform commercial and financial work; in addition large numbers are employed in government and services. The remainder work on con-struction, transportation, public utilities, and a great variety of miscellaneous projects. Essen-tially these workers are not producing goods but services. Some of these activities, for ex-ample, university education, scientific re-search, insurance, publishing, and investment banking, serve the entire country; others, such as wholesaling, newspaper publishing, govern-ment, transportation, and banking, serve New England primarily; the remainder, including retail trade, nonspecialized medical services, and entertainment, serve mainly the Boston area. As we study other cities, these types of regional and local activities need not be noted, but one should not forget that they are charac-teristic of most large cities.

At one time Boston was a junction of ocean and inland waterway routes; later it be-came a railroad center and a great ocean port. More recently it has become a focal point for freeways and airlines, although its rail and ocean routes are still important. Boston is no longer a major East Coast port. Its annual ton-nage is about one-fifth that of New York and

VALUE ADDED BY MANUFACTURING **BOSTON SMSA**

% Distribution

Location quotients: 1.0 = national average per capita

Employ-ment	Value added	SIC source	0	1.0	2.0	3.0	4.0	5.0
7.5	9.2	Food products						
NA	NA	Tobacco products	NA					
1.6	1.4	Textiles						
5.0	4.1	Apparel						
0.6	0.5	Lumber						
1.1	0.9	Furniture						
3.7	3.8	Paper products						
9.6	11.2	Printing						
2.2	3.7	Chemicals						
0.2	0.3	Petro–coal products						
4.1	3.9	Rubber–plastic						
4.7	3.0	Leather						
0.9	1.0	Stone–clay–glass						
1.2	1.5	Primary metals						
5.7	2.5	Fabricated metals						
9.8	13.3	Machinery						
15.0	16.3	Electrical machinery						
7.1	6.0	Transport equipment						
7.2	12.9	Instruments						
100.0	100.0	All categories						

Figure 4.10 Compare this chart with Figure 4.7. Why the differences in location quotients and employment dis-tribution?

is less than that handled by Philadelphia, Baltimore, or Norfolk.

Boston satellites The history of three satellite areas of Boston will serve to illustrate the changing adjustments of New England cities to the competition of other areas and to their environmental setting.

In 1823 a cotton textile company moved from Waltham to Lowell, establishing a mill to use the greater waterpower there. By the middle of the century steam power was introduced to supplement waterpower, and woolen textiles became important. Industry expanded, and immigrants (Polish, Greek, and French-Canadian) came in to supplement a labor force originally recruited from New England farms. After World War I many mills (especially cotton textiles) moved south, and Lowell obtained new industries including electronics, printing, and clothing.

Manchester, New Hampshire, on the Merrimack River with its many falls, recapitulates the history of many older New England cities. Founded in 1722, it remained a minor rural village on the muddy "Mast Road" over which tall timbers were hauled to coastal shipbuilding yards. A canal built around Amoskeag Falls in 1807 permitted produce to be shipped out from central New Hampshire; the new and much used river route connected with the Lowell-Boston Canal. Several small industries were started in Manchester (so renamed in 1810 after the leading English textile city). Little industrial development occurred until in 1831 the Amoskeag Manufacturing Company bought up land and water rights to use the potential power from the 85-foot drop in the river level. Gradually a huge textile mill was built which during the next 75 years attracted labor from the declining New Hampshire farms. At one time this huge mill employed two-thirds of the city's workers; in 1935 it became bankrupt.

In the next few years the city suffered from a flood and hurricane. These catastrophes forced local businessmen to reorganize the urban economy. The Manchester SMSA with 113,000 people, long the commercial center for southern New Hampshire, now has added technological industry attracted by locally trained skilled labor. Textiles and clothing are still important, but electronics is now the principal single source of employment.

South of Boston a sandy area consisting of islands (Nantucket, Martha's Vineyard), Cape Cod, and the shores of Buzzard's Bay was until a century ago the headquarters of a prosperous whaling industry. Today most of the area is a vacationland for urban New Englanders and New Yorkers. Its principal whaling port,[7] New Bedford, although its fishermen still specialize in the scallop catch, earns much more by manufacturing, for example, clothing and metal tools.

The Narragansett Basin Somewhat larger than the Boston Basin in area but with only one-fourth the population, the Narragansett Basin seems better endowed by nature. Its bay, subdivided by islands and peninsulas, provides marvelous harbors and local water transportation. Its soils are more fertile and its climate milder than in the Boston area; its streams provide excellent waterpower sites, one of which powered the first textile mill in America. But Boston, founded a few years earlier, remains the regional hub, while Providence serves as capital and commercial center of only tiny Rhode Island. Its excellent natural harbor attracts mainly oil tankers, private yachts, and fishing vessels. Its slower development as compared with Boston is a reminder that *people* are the important component in successful man-land relationships.

[7] *Nowhere in all America will you find more patricianlike houses; parks and gardens more opulent than in New Bedford. Whence came they?—All these brave houses and flowery gardens came from the Atlantic, Pacific, and Indian Oceans. One and all they were harpooned and dragged up hither from the bottom of the sea.*

In New Bedford, fathers, they say, give whales for dowers to their daughters, and portion off their nieces with a few porpoises apiece. . . .

Herman Melville's *Moby Dick*

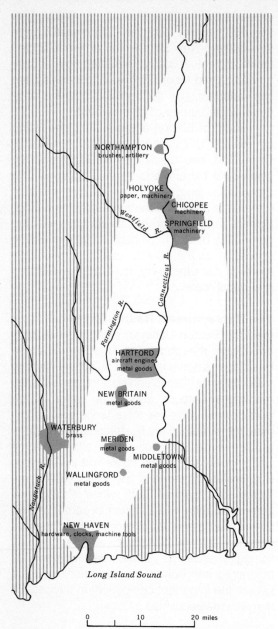

NORTHAMPTON
brushes, artillery

HOLYOKE
paper, machinery

CHICOPEE
machinery

Westfield R.

SPRINGFIELD
machinery

Connecticut R.

Farmington R.

HARTFORD
aircraft engines
metal goods

NEW BRITAIN
metal goods

WATERBURY
brass

MERIDEN
metal goods

MIDDLETOWN
metal goods

WALLINGFORD
metal goods

Naugatuck R.

NEW HAVEN
hardware, clocks, machine tools

Long Island Sound

0   10   20 miles

Figure 4.11 Because of adjacent farming areas, navigable waterways, and local waterpower, most of these cities are located in or near the Connecticut Valley; but their continued prosperity depends on the skills of their workers, their relations to allied industries, and their access to markets in Megalopolis, the nation, and overseas.

Industrially the Narragansett Basin repeats the Merrimack Valley story with a few variations. Cotton textiles powered by the Blackstone River and later by the Fall River (which dropped 130 feet in a quarter mile) were the major industry. When waterpower proved inadequate in the 1850s, Fall River pulled ahead of Lowell as a cotton textile producer as a result of its tidewater location being better suited for coal imports. In the 1920s Fall River was the leading cotton textile city in the country, and it now specializes in garment manufacture. Fortunately the area attracted other industries. For example, Providence and nearby Attleboro produce half the costume jewelry in the nation. Silverware is a closely related industry, and over 700 firms work in precious metals.

The economy of the Narragansett Basin illustrates how the people of once-Puritan New England have changed. Newport and other waterfront resorts attract vacationists, high society, and at times a jazz festival. Woonsocket, a diversified manufacturing center north of Providence, is known as *La Ville du Nord* because of its large French-Canadian population. Five-sixths of all Rhode Island church members are Roman Catholics, but remnants of Puritan New England can still be found in museums and in old houses carefully preserved.

The Connecticut Lowland and New Haven   West of the Blackstone Valley pleasant country roads wind through a sparsely settled upland, containing much woodland and the large Quabbin Reservoir which supplies water to Boston. Less than one hour by Massachusetts Turnpike west of industrial Worcester lies the fertile trough of the central Connecticut Valley, first settled 15 years after the Pilgrims landed at Plymouth. On alluvial soil (above average in fertility for New England), frontier farmers raised crops and fattened cattle to be driven to the Boston market. An early industry critical to a pioneer community was the manufacture of muskets; from this developed the

Springfield Armory. Later other mechanical industries were established; for example, the first successful automobile in the United States was constructed in Springfield in 1892–1893. Today, machinery, electrical goods, and toys are representative Springfield products.

Three years after settlement in central Massachusetts, other settlers approached the Connecticut Lowland from the south, founding New Haven in 1638. The rocky Connecticut coast is the edge of a low, glacier-scoured upland trenched by numerous streams which have eroded almost parallel valleys. These valleys provided millsites and waterpower for early industry.

Hartford is the major metropolitan center of Connecticut. Once reached by ocean shipping, it is now only a minor river port unloading coal and fuel oil. In addition to its aircraft engine industry and political importance as a state capital, Hartford is a leading insurance center, having the home offices of some 40 insurance companies. The reasons for this are largely historical: New England has long had a surplus of capital, and financial businesses including insurance are outstanding in many large New England cities.

The industrial emphasis in Connecticut is largely on metal manufactures designed by artists or engineers and produced by master craftsmen. This industry, at least as old as the Republic, is characterized by two methods originated there and now widely used in all modern industry. Chauncey Jerome devised a technique of stamping out brass parts from sheets instead of laboriously cutting each part by hand; this made possible the cheap production of clocks and watches. Also about the end of the eighteenth century, Eli Whitney (also known for his invention of the cotton gin) began making muskets with interchangeable parts and machine-bored barrels. These techniques and the development of machine tools by Elisha Root and others made possible assembly-line methods of production.

Rural New England

North of the industrial urban areas is a charming land of winding tree-lined roads and changing landscapes of woodlands, pastures, fields, old farmhouses, and huge barns. In the valleys the roads pass through a string of small towns and occasionally a city not submerged in the grime of an industrial society. The town center is usually a parklike common, shaded by tall elms and faced by a tall-spired white church and a variety of ancient shops and buildings, all in good repair. In the more scenic areas a cluster of old resort hotels with broad porches along with modern motels serve the tourist trade. The townspeople are proud of their town and give the visitor directions to handicraft shops, maple sugar factories, town museums, and other sights. Prongs of this less urbanized New England extend south between the thickly settled valleys so that anyone can sample the area by leaving the truck-laden freeways.

Above the town and farm-strewn valleys rise the rounded Berkshire Hills and their northward extension, the somewhat higher Green Mountains of Vermont. To the east are the rugged White Mountains of northern New Hampshire and northwestern Maine. All have beautiful resort areas with lakes, fishing streams, and hiking trails in summer and ski slopes in winter.

The northern three-quarters of Maine contains much empty land. However, forests that were once cut over are now yielding a modest second harvest of lumber and wood pulp. Its half million people are concentrated in a few places: in the Penobscot Valley, along the coast, and in the potato area of Aroostook County. The major commercial center is Bangor, a river port serving a vast region of woods and lakes and providing an outlet for its newsprint, pulp, and lumber. Along the coast are fishing towns which have developed a considerable resort business. The adjacent countryside, where used at all, produces poultry, dairy products, blueberries, and Christmas trees.

Portland, the most populous SMSA in rural New England, is the leading commercial and financial center for about half of the million people living in Maine, plus the thousands of summer residents. Its well-sheltered harbor is a major fishing port; like other New England ports there are more imports than exports. Exports are mainly local products such as wood pulp and fish, but some wheat is received from Montreal for export when the St. Lawrence River is closed by ice. Portland and other urban areas along the southern edge of rural New England may be annexed by northward megalopolitan expansion in coming decades.

THE DELAWARE-CHESAPEAKE GATEWAYS

In contrast to New England, the deeply indented Delaware and Chesapeake gateways lead to extensive areas of soil, mineral, and forest resources. Their coastal lowlands extended much farther inland and the soils were initially more fertile. Agricultural exports assumed early importance, especially near Chesapeake Bay where in the Tidewater country both plantations and slavery became the basis of the colonial economy. In Pennsylvania, settled somewhat later, agriculture was not neglected, but because many colonists had industrial skills, small-scale manufacturing started a few years after the founding of Philadelphia (1682). Historically the broad settlement pattern evolved in relation to the distribution of local resources which in turn were related to the landform regions described earlier.

Throughout the last two centuries this region has been characterized by balanced agricultural, commercial, and industrial activities. In recent decades governmental activity in the Washington–Hampton Roads area has stimulated the southern ports of the Atlantic Megalopolis.

Today the Delaware-Chesapeake gateways constitute essentially an urban area; resource-based activities, although they now occupy much of the land, yield only about 2 percent of the regional income. The resources, quite adequate for modest needs of a century or more ago, are now subordinate to imported fuels, raw materials, and foodstuffs in the regional economy.

The immigrants were varied in both national origin and way of life, and their heritages still add diversity to the regional culture. South of the Mason-Dixon line (named for the surveyors of the southern boundary of Pennsylvania), the original settlers were Catholic and Protestant landlords, indentured servants, and black slaves. To the north, attracted by the liberal Quaker government of William Penn, Mennonite and Amish Germans, Scotch-Irish, and other groups occupied the land. In recent decades blacks from the South Atlantic states have flooded into the larger cities. There migrants are able to afford only ill-maintained, old row houses which form extensive ghettos.

The Mason-Dixon line traditionally separated the planter aristocracy of the South from the small-farmer and skilled artisan-merchant society of the North. While this division has never been as sharp as tradition has implied, the planter heritage is generally centered around the Chesapeake Gateway and the farm-artisan heritage around the Delaware Gateway. The Maryland-Virginia area still is largely a part of the traditional South with its emphasis on family connections, traditional etiquette, and class-conscious patterns of racial relations. The characteristic economy is best illustrated on Chesapeake Bay, especially along the Eastern Shore which attracts yachtsmen and amateur fishermen. Here many of the wealthier citizens of Baltimore have built luxurious homes overlooking the bay.

Chesapeake Bay is known for seafood: crustaceans, mollusks, and fish. Megalopolitan seafood restaurants claim "the fish upon your plate today, slept last night in Chesapeake Bay." The low-lying peninsulas between the many estuaries branching off the bay support vegetable industries and associated foodpack-

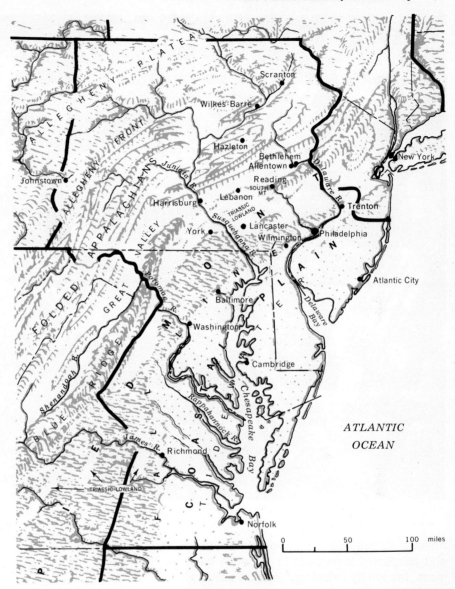

Figure 4.12 Landforms in the Delaware-Chesapeake Gateways. Conspicuous features are the topographic features which parallel the coast and the major streams which cut across the grain of the relief features. (Base map copyright by A. K. Lobeck. Reprinted with permission of The Geographical Press, Hammond, Inc.)

ing plants. Local areas specialize in hogs, poultry, dairy products, and tobacco. Because groundwater conditions vary, some fields must be drained by tile while others are watered by overhead pipes to offset brief droughts at critical growth periods. Many farmers contract in advance for the sale of their crops to canners or to shippers who get them to Northern markets before local Northern crops are ready.

Inland from the fall line the rolling terrain is more likely to be devoted to wheat, dairying, beef cattle—all integrated into a highly diversified agricultural system. In both areas rural

Since before the American Revolution, Lancaster County, Pennsylvania, an especially fertile part of the Piedmont, has been well tilled by Pennsylvania Dutch farmers. The use of contour strip farming to reduce erosion is a modern innovation. Agriculture is highly diversified with a scientific system of crop rotation, including livestock. (USDA)

housing ranges from small clapboard homes and substantial farmsteads to luxurious mansions, the variety reflecting the stratification of the planter society.

Social customs are less aristocratic north of the Mason-Dixon line where Quakers, Germans, and Scotch-Irish were alike in being thrifty and industrious. The cities and most towns have a cluster of mansions and middle-class sections—both located in or near the suburbs. Working-class homes and ghettos and some exclusive as well as more modest apartments are sited near the CBDs in the central cities.

Philadelphia, Center of the Delaware Gateway

In 1682 William Penn selected the site for Philadelphia on high, dry land 4 miles above the marshy land at the confluence of the Delaware and Schuylkill rivers. Where the winding rivers were only 2 miles apart, a wide street (Market Street) was laid out. In contrast to colonial New York and Boston, a rectangular grid was designed with space for parks and spacious lots.

By 1776, Philadelphia had become the largest city in Anglo-America. Industrially the city rivaled New England but specialized more in goods depending on raw materials; for example, in 1785 a completely mechanized flour mill was perfected and Philadelphia remained the leading United States milling center until after the Civil War.

North of Philadelphia a number of towns including Germantown and Frankford were founded soon after the central city. In these the main streets were oriented to the through roads and not to the rectangular street grid of Philadelphia. Camden and West Philadelphia were ferry towns, located across from each end of Market Street.

When the railroads were built, their tracks were laid as much as possible in unsettled areas such as the rocky or marshy lands on each side of the Schuylkill. These lines provided convenient sites for nineteenth-century factories. Canals, together with the railroads along the Schuylkill, brought coal from the anthracite coal fields to the north and the northwest.

A route westward The need to tap its hinterland soon became apparent to Philadelphia merchants. After 1800, they became aware of the rising competition of New York City, but they had no easy natural corridor inland comparable to the Hudson-Mohawk route. A dirt road to Lancaster, an area settled early in the eighteenth century, was traversed at first by pack trains, later by Conestoga wagons.[8] As this route proved too slow and overcrowded, in 1796 the state government completed the wide Lancaster Turnpike, with a paved center of crushed stone. In 1834 the turnpike was supplemented by a railroad from Philadelphia to Columbia on the Susquehanna River. The transport line was extended by canal and barges up the Susquehanna and its tributary, the Juniata, to the Allegheny Front. Barges were mounted on wheels and pulled by

[8] Named for the Conestoga, a tributary of the Susquehanna River, these wagons later played a major role in Western settlement.

stationary engines over the summit to be refloated on a tributary of the Ohio. This winding route later became the main line of the Pennsylvania Railroad. Although in recent years this railroad has competed successfully with New York's water-level route, in the nineteenth century it was so slow that Philadelphia lost much Midwestern trade.

Modern Philadelphia William Penn's careful planning proved far from ideal for twentieth-century Philadelphia. The spacious lots and open blocks disappeared. Demands for central city housing led to the construction of thousands of blocks of brick houses, with marble sills and steps, each attached to its neighbor; because of the high price of the land these houses were erected on probably the narrowest lots in the United States. Streetcars on the narrow streets started the congestion, and the automobile age brought traffic almost to a standstill. Fortunately, however, subway lines had been built under Broad and Market streets, and these have increased the flow of people.

Philadelphia is an example of the kind of urban renewal that is going on in other large cities. Government and private renewal activities have partially opened the crowded city. A parkway was cut diagonally from the Schuylkill across the blocks of brick houses to City Hall Square. Later the Pennsylvania Railroad moved its main terminal to 30th Street, west of the Schuylkill, and placed its downtown tracks underground, thus providing new building sites in the CBD. Finally a large mall has been opened around Independence Hall, and urban renewal projects have renovated many older portions of the city. The most spectacular renewal has occurred along the waterfront where efficient port terminals handle about half the tonnage of the Delaware Valley ports.

Although the central city decreased slightly in population from 1950 to 1970, it still accounts for much of manufacturing employment in the SMSA, leading in most industrial categories. The heavier industries, petroleum refining and chemicals, are located on the

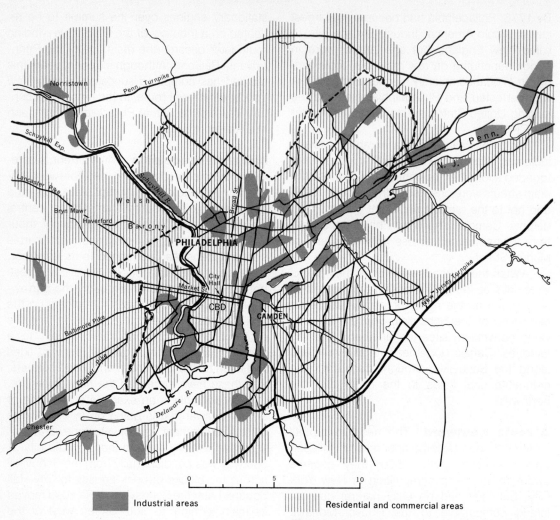

Industrial areas   Residential and commercial areas

Figure 4.13 Unlike most colonial cities, colonial Philadelphia had a street plan essentially oriented to the cardinal points of the compass; the plan of the outlying areas was greatly influenced by the converging roads and by street plans established in once-independent towns.

lower Schuylkill; other industries are generally along the railroads. More widely distributed are the clothing, food products, printing and publishing, and textile industries which together account for nearly half the city's industrial employment.

West of the city is the so-called "Welsh Barony" with Welsh town names such as Merion, Bryn Mawr, Bala Cynwyd, and St. Davids, now all upper-class commuting towns along the main line of the Pennsylvania Railroad. Nearby are famous liberal arts colleges; huge estates carved out of the rolling Piedmont; and historic Valley Forge, King of Prussia, and Hopewell Furnace. Contemporary factories house electrical and computer industries so elegantly that some have been mistaken for college campuses.

Two satellite cities Trenton, 20 miles upstream from Philadelphia, and Wilmington, the same distance downstream, are independent metropolitan areas which seem destined to be absorbed into the Philadelphia metropolis. Both cities are located on navigable water on the Coastal Plain; both have expanded westward onto the Piedmont. The Trenton SMSA includes the New Jersey capital and the educational and scientific activities around Princeton University, but much of its employment is in the manufacture of consumer goods. Development across the river from Trenton has been stimulated by the opening of an integrated steel plant, using imported ores and Appalachian bituminous coal.

The Wilmington SMSA straddles upper Delaware Bay, the two segments being connected by a bridge carrying a New York–Washington expressway. The central city was founded by Swedes in 1638 on the Christina River. After a modest growth as a flour-milling town, its industrial emphasis was changed by the Du Pont family in 1802. Starting as a producer of black powder, the Du Pont industrial empire has expanded, producing in the Wilmington area such varied products as explosives, dyes, cellophane, nylon, paints, and synthetic rubber.

The Delaware River Port Authority The port facilities from Wilmington to Trenton are coordinated under an interstate port authority similar to the Port of New York Authority. By weight the Delaware Gateway traffic is nine-tenths that of New York. However, New York handles much more general cargo with a high value per ton. Delaware Gateway imports such bulky commodities as petroleum, iron ore, gypsum, and coal. A few heavy manufactures are shipped out, but the high-value-per-ton exports tend to be shipped via New York which offers more frequent service. It is somewhat ironic that this valley whose industries once developed on a base of plentiful raw materials is now growing in part because of its ability to import raw materials.

VALUE ADDED BY MANUFACTURING   **PHILADELPHIA SMSA**

% Distribution   Location quotients: 1.0 = national average per capita

Employ-ment	Value added	SIC source	0	1.0	2.0	3.0	4.0	5.0
7.5	10.3	Food products						
0.4	0.3	Tobacco products						
3.7	3.0	Textiles						
8.1	5.0	Apparel						
0.5	0.3	Lumber						
1.1	1.1	Furniture						
3.9	4.7	Paper products						
5.9	6.5	Printing						
5.8	14.1	Chemicals						
1.9	5.0	Petro-coal products						
2.5	3.3	Rubber–plastic						
0.6	0.3	Leather						
2.3	2.5	Stone–clay–glass						
5.4	7.1	Primary metals						
7.9	8.9	Fabricated metals						
8.4	8.7	Machinery						
10.6	10.8	Electrical machinery						
4.7	5.8	Transport equipment						
2.1	2.3	Instruments						
100.0	100.0	All categories						

Figure 4.14 Is Philadelphia a highly diversified, industrialized SMSA? Account for each industrial category which has an unusually low location quotient.

The Chesapeake Gateways

There were difficulties in establishing the interior gateway functions for the southern third of the Atlantic Megalopolis. Although settled early in American history, the Appalachian barrier to the west delayed interior penetration for many decades. One result, however, was a consolidation of agricultural and manufacturing activities in the coastal section, along with the early growth of important urban centers. But the hinterland did have resources, and the landform barrier eventually was penetrated, and the influence of the cities of the Chesapeake region gradually extended inland. The regional ties, however, are still stronger in a north-south alignment than toward the interior, and the cities and economy are very much a functioning part of the Atlantic Megalopolis.

Much of the industrial and governmental income arises from port functions. Chesapeake Bay and the tributary Hampton Roads and Potomac estuary make up the world's most spacious harbor, large enough to anchor most of the world's ships. Tides are negligible, fog and storms are rare, and channels are easily maintained. The ports are not as near Europe as the ports to the northeast, but this makes little practical difference since trans-Atlantic freight rates are about the same from all ports from Hampton Roads to Portland, Maine.

The principal handicaps of these ports had been: *first,* the routes inland over the mountains were high and winding, and, *second,* the immediate hinterland was relatively undeveloped. The first handicap was overcome by the completion of three coal-shipping railroads across the mountains, providing slow interior freight connections by rail; later improved highways carried adequate truck services. As to the second handicap, heavy industries developing near Baltimore have increased trade of all kinds, and the growth of federal activity has increased industrialization and military needs. Especially important to port development, the Interstate Commerce Commission has recognized that the shorter distances from Chesapeake ports to interior points should be reflected in lower through rates on general cargo than via more northerly ports.

In the Chesapeake Gateway there are four distinctive urban areas. Baltimore is a smaller version of Philadelphia with its seaport handling bulk goods and with a variety of industrial and commercial activities. Washington is primarily a national capital and its other functions are of minor rank. The Hampton Roads SMSAs somewhat resemble Baltimore in their port trade but are dominated by the federal defense establishments. Richmond is one of the major Southern cultural and financial centers with its industries dominated by tobacco products. The specific character of each place represents the combined result of geographic and historic forces.

Baltimore   The city was founded in 1729 to take advantage of the waterpower from the fall line and the natural harbor of the Patapsco estuary. Waterpower was used to grind wheat from the adjacent Piedmont into flour which was shipped to the West Indies. In 1797 when Washington was being constructed as the nation's Capital, Baltimore dredged the Patapsco, filled in adjacent marshlands, and built wharves so as to be able to serve as a port for Washington.

The success of Baltimore merchants caused the city to grow much faster than nearby Annapolis, a longer established town with attractive old buildings. Baltimore became a wholesale center not only for the Chesapeake Gateway but for Virginia and the Carolinas. Culturally it rivaled Richmond as a center for planter society, and its wealthy citizens promoted cotillions, horse racing, and gourmet dining. While British forces were being repulsed at Fort McHenry (which commanded the entrance to Baltimore harbor), Francis Scott Key wrote the "Star Spangled Banner," which later was set to the tune of a popular drinking song. Baltimore attempted to develop its interior hinterland by the Cumberland Road (now U.S. 40) and by the Baltimore and Ohio Railroad, one of the first railroads built in the United States.

The urban functions of Baltimore complement those of Washington. Early Baltimore industry consisted of processing perishable seafood and farm produce along with the manufacture of consumer goods for its wholesale trading area. Since the federal government discouraged the building of factories in Washington, Baltimore performed many industrial functions for the Capital city. Recent growth has been in the durable goods industries for which proximity to West Virginia coal, a fine harbor, and access to distant raw material were significant. An example of heavy industry is the integrated steel plant built by Bethlehem Steel Company at the mouth of the Patapsco. Improved coastwise transportation increased in-

The inner harbor of Baltimore is close to the downtown business section. (Baltimore Promotion Council)

teraction within the region. For example, the deepening of the Chesapeake and Delaware Canal enabled coastwise vessels sailing east to avoid the 150-mile trip down Chesapeake Bay; similarly the Atlantic Intracoastal Waterway enabled barges and small boats to reach Southern ports without using the open sea.

A variety of suburbs have developed in the Baltimore-Washington area—some compactly planned while others are examples of urban sprawl. One of the better examples of urban planning is Columbia, whose 14,000 acres are 10 miles west of downtown Baltimore. The city with a population in 1972 of about 20,000 may house 110,000 when completed in 1981. Employment for residents is available in nearby Baltimore and Washington or in 60 factories near the city. To avoid congestion the city is divided into a downtown center and seven villages, separated from each other by green-belts. Each village is divided into neighborhoods, each having its own recreational facilities, elementary school, and convenience store. Each village center has more elaborate recreational facilities, a secondary school, churches, a supermarket, a bank, and other commercial services. The downtown area includes a community college, theaters, restaurants and night clubs, and other facilities usually found in a city of 100,000. All the factories are in rural settings, away from but easily reached from the residential villages.

The Washington SMSA   The federal Capital had an independent and somewhat artificial origin, being established because of its central location. In 1790 the most populous state was Virginia with half again as many people as second-place Pennsylvania. Because the American people were concentrated east of the Appalachians then, Washington was suited more for the federal Capital than it is today. Originally the District of Columbia was to have been square, but in 1846 Congress, not foreseeing the future growth of federal business, returned the Virginia portion (now Arlington County) to that state. The Coastal Plain portion of the city, low-lying and marshy, was occupied by many major government buildings, and the area near the State Department Building is locally known as Foggy Bottom. The high humidity from the Potomac and Anacostia rivers and adjacent marshes is responsible for the hot sticky weather for which Washington is noted.

Generally Washington was well planned. The center of the city is a hillock upon which the Capitol was built. The northwest quadrant includes the major buildings and the CBD, and on the higher Piedmont, the embassies and several fashionable residential sections. The land-use patterns of Washington are different from other East Coast cities because of the lack of extensive industrial zones.

The District of Columbia has a peculiar combination of monumental buildings; old residential sections with brick row houses, many of which have deteriorated into ghettos; and some modern residential and apartment house sections. Elaborate plans have been drawn up for renovating the central city, but only small parts of these plans have been carried out. One-third of the labor force works for the government, and many of the others serve government employees and tourists. The migration of blacks into the East Coast cities became apparent in the census of 1960 which reported that Washington became the first large American city with more than half nonwhite residents. The suburbs of Washington are largely white.

Just as commercial and industrial activities are moving outward in other cities, many governmental services and buildings are being moved to suburban sites near Washington; for example, the National Institutes of Health and the Naval Medical Center are in Bethesda, Maryland. Private research centers, shopping centers, and factories working on government contracts or benefiting from government research are also located in suburban satellites.

Hampton Roads   The first permanent English colonists in Anglo-America settled near the entrance to Chesapeake Bay. Tobacco farming, the former economic base of colonial Tidewater Virginia, is now unusual there. Much of the farmland north of the James River has reverted to forest or been converted to urban use, including fishing villages, military installations, and retirement residences. Toward Richmond the better-drained, slightly higher land is devoted to general farming, including some dairying, poultry raising, and truck farming. South of the James, a section that grew cotton until the incursion of the boll weevil now specializes in peanuts and peanut-fed hogs (Smithfield hams).

Physically, Hampton Roads (Figure 4.15) is somewhat like New York Harbor, but in economic development the Virginia area, although growing, is far behind New York. The immediate hinterland of New York is much richer in industry and purchasing power, and its interior hinterland is more easily reached and more productive. Hampton Roads growth is mainly based on a superb harbor strategically located to guard and to service militarily and commercially the central Atlantic Coast.

The Hampton Roads area has no outstanding CBD such as Manhattan to draw both local and more distant business. Indeed many urban banking, insurance, government, and tourism activities are more centered in Richmond. The many towns and cities include samples of the architectural style of other Chesapeake cities: There are colonial towns such as Williamsburg and Yorktown, ports with business sections with narrow streets, beach resorts, army and navy installations, modern residential suburbs, and innumerable monuments and markers commemorating historic events.

Physically, the Norfolk-Portsmouth SMSA

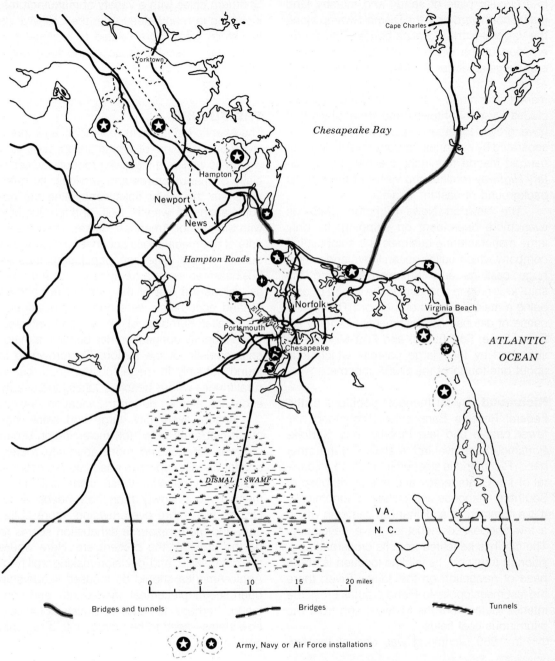

Cape Charles

Chesapeake Bay

Yorktown

Hampton

Newport

News

Hampton Roads

Norfolk

Virginia Beach

Ellizabeth

Portsmouth

Chesapeake

ATLANTIC
OCEAN

DISMAL · SWAMP

V A.

N. C.

| 0 | 5 | 10 | 15 | 20 miles |

Bridges and tunnels   Bridges   Tunnels

Army, Navy or Air Force installations

Figure 4.15 The Hampton Roads area consists of scattered military, naval, and commercial harbor installations backed by urban service areas.

is a circular plain of sandy and marshy land jutting northward from the Dismal Swamp along the Virginia–North Carolina border. The southern part of the circle is still rural, producing early vegetables for Northern markets as well as dairy and other produce for the Norfolk market. The much indented northern circle includes a variety of towns and street plans that have grown together except where they are separated by estuaries, military reservations, or railroad marine terminals: the peripheral *Military Highway* reminds the visitor of the historic background of eastern Virginia.

The Newport News–Hampton SMSA is even more dependent on shipping. Its only large manufacturing business is a shipbuilding company which builds ocean liners and makes huge castings and turbines. Adjoining the shipyards are the coal docks, the export of coal being a major function of the port. The significance of defense establishments—Langley Air Force Base, Fort Eustis, and Fort Monroe—is illustrated by their large payrolls which total about one-fourth of the SMSA income.

Richmond   By far the least populous of the Federal Reserve Bank cities, Richmond has fewer people and less income than Norfolk-Portsmouth, its rival in the state. On the other hand, Richmond is steeped in tradition as capital of the Confederacy and is a storehouse of Southern memories and culture. Economically it is a commercial and financial center in which a few specialized industries have developed. The city has benefited from its crossroads position in transport. Its fall-line location is at the head of navigation on the James River; there the fast megalopolis-to-Florida routes cross the interior routes from the Midwest and from the bituminous coal fields.

In 1860 Richmond was one of the few Southern cities with a variety of manufactures, including iron and steel. After the Civil War its industries were more related to regional raw materials, especially tobacco and food products.

THE FUTURE

The Atlantic Megalopolis represents an impressive concentration of accumulated skills and wealth as well as a massive productivity, especially of manufactures and services. Its gateways are the major links connecting the accumulations of wealth, skill, and productivity with the interior American market. The inhabitants of the megalopolis account for nearly one quarter of the American population; thus its businessmen serve a tremendous local market as well as the rest of the world. The patterns of land occupance were originally developed for smaller numbers of people and vehicles. Consequently congestion has become a major characteristic of the region. Overcrowding is found not only in megalopolitan areas but in rural fringes whose beaches, lakes, and beauty spots are jammed during the vacation season.

Almost every city, large and small, has made elaborate plans for implementing urban renewal, for building more adequate routes, and for opening up more adequate recreational facilities. In general, these plans are implemented more slowly than new needs arise. Growth with more overcrowding, more pollution, and more resource exhaustion seems to be the order of the present era. Here where the data, skills, and decision-making ability of Anglo-America should be focused, leadership often seems piecemeal, inadequate, and confused. Perhaps the former British colonies—now states—need to be merged into a regional government.

SELECTED REFERENCES

ALEXANDER, LEWIS M.: *The Northeastern United States,* Van Nostrand, New York, 1967. One of a series of regional paperbacks.

DANSEREAU, PIERRE (ed.): *Challenge for Survival: Land,*

Air and Water for Man in Megalopolis, Columbia University Press, New York, 1970.

ESTALL, R. C.: *New England: A Study in Industrial Adjustment,* Praeger, New York, 1966.

FEDERAL RESERVE BANK OF BOSTON: *New England Business Review* (monthly). At least half the issues of the *Review* have material of value to the geographer.

GOTTMAN, JEAN: *Megalopolis: The Urbanized Northeastern Seaboard of the United States,* Twentieth Century Fund, New York, 1961.

————: *Virginia in Our Century,* University of Virginia Press, Charlottesville, 1969.

GREEN, CONSTANCE M.: *American Cities in the Growth of the Nation,* Harper & Row, New York, 1965.

HIGBEE, EDWARD: *The American Oasis,* Knopf, New York, 1957, especially chaps. 8 and 9.

HOOVER, E. M., and RAYMOND VERNON: *Anatomy of a Metropolis,* Doubleday, Garden City, N.Y., 1962.

KLIMM, L. E.: "The Empty Areas of Northeastern United States," *Geographical Review,* vol. 44 (1954), pp. 315–345.

LEMON, JAMES T.: *The Best Poor Man's Country; A Geographical Study of Southeastern Pennsylvania,* Johns Hopkins Press, Baltimore, 1972.

LEWIS, GEORGE K.: "Population Change in Northern New England," *Annals,* AAG, vol. 62 (1972), pp. 307–322.

LEWIS, PEIRCE F.: "Small Town in Pennsylvania," *Annals,* AAG, vol. 62 (1972), pp. 323–351.

MARYLAND DEPARTMENT OF ECONOMIC DEVELOPMENT: *Maryland Economic Atlas,* Annapolis, 1967.

MILLER, E. WILLARD: *An Economic Atlas of Pennsylvania,* State Planning Board, Harrisburg, 1964.

MURPHY, RAYMOND E.: *The American City: An Urban Geography,* 2d ed., McGraw-Hill, New York, 1974.

NATIONAL CAPITAL PLANNING COMMISSION: *The Proposed Comprehensive Plan for the National Capital,* Washington, 1967.

NATIONAL CAPITAL REGIONAL PLANNING COMMISSION: *The Regional Development Guide 1966–2000,* Washington, 1966.

PATTON, D. J.: "General Cargo Hinterlands of New York, Philadelphia, Baltimore, and New Orleans," *Annals,* AAG, vol. 48 (1958), pp. 436–55.

PRICE, EDWARD T.: "The Central Courthouse Square in the American County Seat," *Geographical Review,* vol. 58 (1968), pp. 29–60.

SEWELL, R. W. DERRICK: "The New York Water Crisis," *Journal of Geography,* vol. 65 (1966), pp. 384–389.

THOMPSON, JOHN H. (ed.): *Geography of New York State,* Syracuse University Press, Syracuse, 1966.

U.S. DEPARTMENT OF AGRICULTURE: *The Changing Fertility of New England Soils,* Agricultural Bulletin no. 133, Washington, 1954.

VERNON, RAYMOND: *Metropolis: 1985,* Doubleday, Garden City, N.Y., 1961.

VICERO, RALPH D.: "French-Canadian Settlement in Vermont Prior to the Civil War," *Professional Geographer,* vol, 23 (1971), pp. 290–294.

WARD, DAVID: "The Industrial Revolution and the Emergence of Boston's Central Business District," *Economic Geography,* vol. 42 (1966), pp. 152–171.

WILSON, H. F.: *The Hill Country of New England: 1790–1930,* Columbia University Press, New York, 1936. An interesting study of changing occupations in Vermont and New Hampshire.

WRIGHT, JOHN K. (ed.): *New England's Prospect,* American Geographical Society, New York, 1933. Old but excellent background material.

5

THE CENTRAL LOWLAND

After the American Revolution, the agricultural frontier advanced quickly across the Appalachians. Most pioneers did not settle in these mountains but crossed into the Central Lowland, first occupying the low plateaus of the Ohio Basin. The soils of this plateau area, mostly not considered fertile today, were in a virgin state equal to those on the Atlantic seaboard. But the Ohio Basin was the gateway to more fertile plains, drained by the upper Mississippi and its major tributaries, the Ohio and the Missouri, and now the home of one-third of the United States population. Rich in soil, forest, fuel, and mineral resources, moderate in relief, and connected by an excellent system of natural waterways, the interior was indeed a land of promise. Yet even its riches were not limitless. The bulk of its forests have been stripped away; some fuels and minerals must now be shipped in; and in the eastern part of the lowland a food deficit exists. Soil leaching and erosion along with stream pollution and local overcrowding have played considerable havoc with the land. Except for its western and

Commercially, Chicago is the outstanding SMSA of the Central Lowland. Note the skyscrapers marking the Loop, the diverging railroads, the artificial harbor, and the park area on filled land along the Lake Michigan shore. (Chicago Aerial Survey)

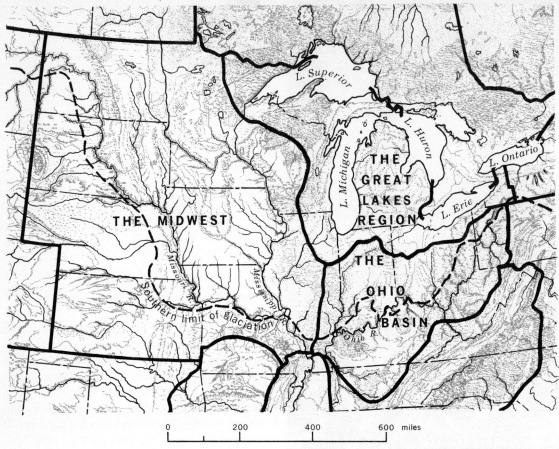

0   200   400   600 miles

Figure 5.1 The subdivisions of the Central Lowland are neither topographically nor economically sharply delimited; each is bounded by a transition zone. (Base map copyright by A. K. Lobeck. Reprinted with permission of The Geographical Press, Hammond, Inc.)

northern margins, the Central Lowland depends on manufacturing and urban services for its principal source of income. Its settlement patterns, however, still contain many relicts of its earlier farm history; in the Midwest especially, it is apparent that the towns and routes were planned initially to serve the farmer.

THE PHYSICAL SETTING

Most of the Central Lowland consists of sedimentary rocks—sandstones, shales, limestones, and coal—deposited in a great marine gulf which once occupied the central United States. In the extreme north, especially near Lake Superior, older crystalline ore-bearing rocks occur close to the surface. Although the

resources of these rocks provided important industrial raw materials, they had little effect on the major settlement patterns. More important to the settlers was the Glacial Age which ended about 11,000 years ago in the Great Lakes region and which modified soil and drainage patterns. The thick layers of ice scraped soil and stone from Canada and the upper Great Lakes region and deposited them irregularly as far south as the Ohio and Missouri valleys. This gigantic movement of the earth's surface materials exposed ancient ore-bearing rocks around the upper lakes and covered rough sections in the lower lakes region with deposits of lime-rich soil-forming minerals; blocked waterways to form swamps, marshes, and lakes; and in places radically changed the direction of drainage. Most spectacular, huge tongues of ice dug out the basins of the Great Lakes, the largest group of freshwater bodies on earth.

The Central Lowland was largely smoothed by glaciation north of and between the Ohio and Missouri rivers. In many areas the land was made so level that tiling and ditching were required to make the wet soil tillable; in other sections low moraines added variety to the landscape. In the unglaciated south the land was rough but rarely rugged. Compared to the small valleys of the Appalachians, this lowland appeared to be good farm country to the settlers.

The climate was varied and was indicated to newcomers by the flora. The tall hardwood forests were associated with hot summers and cold winters—a regular seasonal rhythm that was humid in most years but often erratic during the growing seasons. The changeable weather had spells of heavy rain and periods of drought: cool or cold waves were followed by warm or hot waves. To the north coniferous trees indicated shorter and cooler summers, longer winters, and usually less fertile soils. Westward, prairie grasses with a fringe of trees along the streams indicated a subhumid climate. The soils were almost neutral, dark, and rich in humus. Further west the shorter grasses indicated greater danger of drought.

THE SURVEY AND SETTLEMENT PATTERNS

The settlement of the Central Lowland began after the American Revolution; a little more than a century later the land was comfortably filled although migrants continued to stream into the cities. In the first decades two streams of settlers could be identified; first, those who entered from the Southeast via the Great Valley and Cumberland Gap; second, groups from the Northeastern states came either via the Hudson-Mohawk route or across the mountains to Pittsburgh. The earlier settlements had little geographic regularity—being scattered on the eastern edge of the lowland.

In 1785 Congress provided for a new system of surveying which had a great influence on field and road patterns and even on most city plans. Starting from a parallel of latitude as a baseline and from a principal meridian, federal surveyors divided the land into square townships, 6 miles on each side. Each township was subdivided into 36 sections 1 mile square (640 acres); Figure 5.2 illustrates the system. The rectangular system of land surveying encouraged an even spacing of farmsteads, roads, and towns. Departures from the general plan were necessitated by water bodies; swamps were avoided, whereas stream and lake sites were sought for domestic water supply, navigation, and control of crossings. In the less settled northern parts, the rectangular road and farm system is less conspicuous, but the survey is marked by the grid of county and township boundaries. As the region was settled, towns which were sited either on lake harbors or where major roads and railroads crossed rivers grew more rapidly into commercial centers than other towns.

In the well-settled areas, the urban centers developed a hierarchy of commercial functions. The smaller towns (second-order places in Figure 5.9) with local retail functions are served by a smaller number of third-order places which also offer wholesaling and other specialized services. Even more specialized services and a greater number of services are offered by the still smaller number of fourth-order places which are commercial capitals for subregions, for example, Grand Rapids, center of western Michigan. Even larger places are regional business capitals for extensive hinterlands: Detroit for the area with automotive industries; Cleveland for north and central Ohio; Buffalo for the eastern end of Lake Erie. Chicago, serving as a subnational business capital for the entire Central Lowland, also performs many national functions.

RECTANGULAR COORDINATED LAND DIVISION SYSTEM

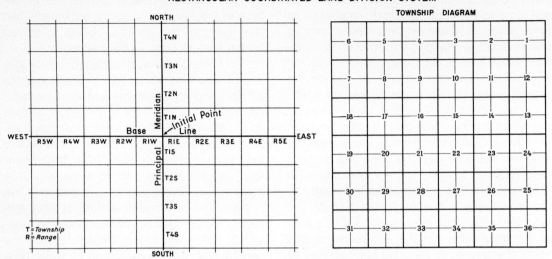

Figure 5.2 The rectangular patterns so characteristic in most of the trans-Appalachian United States can be traced to the rectangular survey which divides each state into 36-square-mile townships measured from selected initial points. Each can be identified (as shown on the diagram to the left) by an abbreviation, for example: T2S, R4W. Within each township, sections of 1 square mile are identified by numbers (diagram to the right). (USDA)

Changing urban patterns Following the initial development of the rail lines and town patterns, immigrants from Europe entered the Central Lowland beginning in the 1840s and 1850s. At first settlers were primarily from Northwestern Europe. Commonly, they settled in groups, for example, rural clusters of Germans, Swiss, and Scandinavians in Wisconsin and German urban clusters in Buffalo, Cincinnati, St. Louis, and Milwaukee. As urbanization and industry developed, immigrants from Eastern and Southern Europe provided labor during the early 1900s.

Settlement patterns were altered after World War I: with the mechanization of farming, the demand for farm labor decreased and in most years after 1921 migration from farms exceeded migration to farms. Three groups migrated to the cities:

1 The well-educated children of Midwestern farmers, who usually had little difficulty in finding jobs and adjusting to urban life.
2 White migrants from Appalachia (and other areas where educational standards were low), who had much more difficulty than the children of Midwestern farmers and moved into neighborhoods with deteriorating old housing.

3 The most disadvantaged groups, rural blacks from the South Central states, who generally moved into poor housing in the central city where ghettos evolved.

The inflow into the Central Lowland declined after 1924 when overseas immigration was severely cut by the Immigration Act; consequently the less skilled migrants from rural areas were employed in low-skilled jobs formerly filled by new arrivals from Europe. With the common ownership of the automobile, many middle- and upper-class whites moved to suburban homes, thus making central city neighborhoods available for disadvantaged immigrants who needed housing near work or near public transportation.

The changing settlement and occupational patterns in the Central Lowland have created a host of problems. To simplify the analysis, this huge region has been subdivided into three regions, each with somewhat distinctive prob-

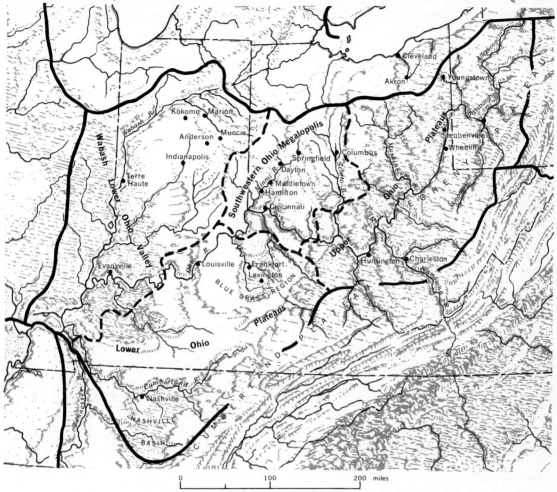

0   100   200 miles

Figure 5.3 Landforms and subregions of the Ohio Basin. The relief of the Ohio plateaus is not great but includes many abrupt escarpments and bluffs. (Base map copyright by A. K. Lobeck. Reprinted with permission of The Geographical Press, Hammond, Inc.)

lems: the Ohio Basin, the Great Lakes region, and the Midwest. No sharp boundaries separate these regions, and the problems discussed under each region are to some degree found in the other two. For the Ohio Basin, the economic decline of farm and mining areas and increasing water scarcity and pollution are stressed. For the Great Lakes region, the themes are the focusing of water and overland routes at lakeshore points and urban planning problems including pollution. For the Midwest the transition from a farm-based economy to an urban-based region is considered with emphasis on Midwest examples.

THE OHIO BASIN (FIGURE 5.3)

This region, mainly draining into the Ohio River (excluding the Tennessee Valley), consists of two landform zones, each elongated approximately southwest-northeast. The northern section is a glaciated plain of undulating fertile land which has been converted into productive farmland. To the south is a broader, less fertile plateau zone, low in the west and higher to the east and southeast, into which are incised the Ohio and its tributaries.

Water Problems

The two parts of the Ohio Basin are tied together by their similar problems and complementary resources: the floods and pollution of the Ohio Valley cannot be controlled without regulation in both zones. People on the glacial plain depend on the plateau for coal, recreation, and some special products such as tobacco, hardwoods, glass, steel, and chemicals. The plateau economy depends on the lowland for governmental assistance and a wide variety of manufactures and services.

The critical question is how much should be spent to control the Ohio and its tributaries. A river basin is an example of a multiple-use region. The water may be used for consumption in homes or industry, for production of power, or for navigation. Very little of the water is actually consumed; rather it is polluted chemically, biologically, and thermally. Most of this pollution can be cleaned up at a cost. A further problem is the irregularity of the flow of the streams because of fluctuations in precipitation. The effects of this irregularity can be controlled by building adequate dams—again at a cost. The problem is especially complicated because the river cannot be controlled for a single purpose; each improvement for one purpose creates advantages and handicaps for other uses, making it awkward to allocate costs to the beneficiaries.

Floods The drainage area of a river system forms a physical region. What happens in one part of such a region affects the residents in most other parts. For example, severe floods caused in part by upstream deforestation and in part by heavy spring rains and rapid melting of snow in some years, have caused severe damage along the industrial and commercial waterfronts in all river cities, including Pittsburgh, Cincinnati, and Louisville. The defense against floods has been twofold: levees to protect the shore against encroaching water, and dams and forests to impound the floodwaters upstream. Flood-control reservoirs are gradually being built with funds provided jointly by federal and state authorities. Many of these provide by-product uses in the form of lakes for recreation and domestic water supply. The most thorough attempt to control floods has been the Tennessee Valley Authority (see Chapter 6), whose watershed affects only a 40-mile section of the lower Ohio Valley.

Navigation In the spatial system of interacting Ohio Basin economies, the river is a major mover of commodities. The Ohio and several major tributaries are controlled by a series of dams and locks on which a minimum 9-foot channel is maintained. Maintenance of navigation involves some dredging because the Ohio carries a heavy burden of mud, the result of upstream erosion. River cargo consists of a few relatively bulky commodities: coal from the plateau, petroleum and other raw materials shipped upriver from the Gulf Coast, and some heavy manufactures. Some distant shipments of raw materials are included; for example, the coking coal of the eastern plateau is needed for metallurgy in areas where inferior local coal is used to generate power. The Ohio River tonnage is huge, exceeding that of either the Panama or Soo canals. This traffic is expected to increase further both because of greater demand and because of improvements that are now being undertaken in channels and locks.

Power The Ohio system aids power generation in two ways: its tributaries supply waterpower, and its waters are used in the process of generating carboelectric and nuclear power. Most of the hydroelectric power that can be developed economically has been harnessed; in each state within this basin the capacity of carboelectric power plants greatly exceeds the hydroelectric capacity. The further generation of thermal power is partly limited by the cooling ability of the Ohio's waters.

Water supply   Water is one of those multiple-use resources which is used in diverse ways by different people. Many towns use the rivers for domestic water supply; others dump their sewage into the rivers. Industrial and coal mine wastes add considerably to the river's load, so that much of the Ohio resembles an open sewer. Much water is drawn from the river for industrial use; most is used for cooling and then returned hot, in a few places hot enough to injure fish which may have survived other forms of contamination.

Recreation   Although much has been done to reduce pollution, in the industrialized sections the Ohio is no longer satisfactory for fishing or swimming. Today the best recreational facilities are upstream on the tributaries.

Employment and Income

The Ohio Basin is a major industrial area of the nation. It exceeds the national average in manufacturing and mining; these two occupations provide, respectively, about 30 and 3 percent of total employment of people in the basin. Nearly two-thirds of all manufacturing employment is in durable goods; mining employment is largely in coal mining. Metals and fuel were the foundations upon which regional industry has been built.

Population and Migration

One-tenth of the American people live in the basin, and together they are a cross section of the social and ethnic peoples of the nation. They include the descendants of Scotch-Irish settlers in the Appalachian Plateau, Germans settled around Cincinnati, Eastern and Southern Europeans and Southern Negroes attracted by industrial employment, and Southern aristocrats in the Bluegrass and Nashville Basin. The Ohio Basin, except in a few cities, has been a region of slow economic growth with net out-migration reflecting the lack of adequate

local opportunities. The poor soils of the plateaus have given cause for much farm abandonment and consequent migration to local and distant cities. In many counties this decrease in farm population began in the last century. The reduced employment in coal mining has caused additional out-migration from smaller cities and towns and has increased unemployment among those who remained. The number of man-hours worked in coal mining (now less than one-third of the 1940 figure) has declined much more than the tonnage mined because of the introduction of strip mining and of machinery. It remains to be seen whether coal mining will revive in the 1970s as a result of shortages of other forms of fuel and power.

The Upper Ohio Plateaus

The Allegheny Plateau consists of almost horizontal sedimentary rocks, including numerous beds of high-quality bituminous coal, limestone, clay, glass sand, salt, and some iron ore. Toward the east especially, the rocks have been slightly folded, and this folding has helped to concentrate oil and natural gas. The streams are incised 500 to 1,000 feet in the uplands; gentle slopes are limited to uplands and narrow flats along the streams. The landforms of the plateau are not particularly suitable for agriculture.

The Pittsburgh SMSA   Pittsburgh is often thought of as a city founded to use local coal. But coking coal was not used in Pittsburgh furnaces until 1859. A brief historical account gives a more adequate explanation. In 1754, the French established Fort Duquesne on what is now known as Pittsburgh's *Golden Triangle.* Following British victories over the French, Fort Pitt was established on the site of Fort Duquesne and British settlers entered the area. After the American Revolution, settlement was accelerated, and Pittsburgh, at the junction of Forbes Road from Harrisburg, the Cumberland

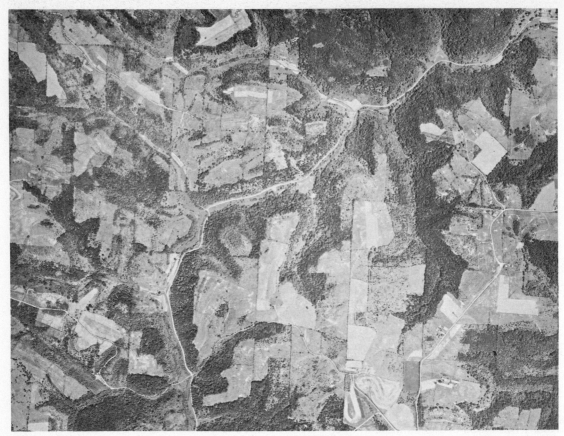

The upper Ohio plateaus include much intricately dissected land, which was mostly farmed in the last century but is gradually reverting to woodland and pasture. Other areas have been urbanized or at least temporarily made useless by strip coal mining. The area shown in Athens County, southeastern Ohio, is used for dairying and other livestock activities. (USDA)

Road from Baltimore, and the navigable Allegheny and Monongahela rivers, proved an ideal spot to start boats and rafts down the Ohio to Kentucky or even New Orleans. In Pittsburgh, an iron foundry using local iron ore, limestone, and charcoal supplied cannon to Perry's fleet on Lake Erie in 1813 and to Jackson's army at New Orleans. Further stimulation to the steel industry came from the demands of the Civil War; the expanding railroad network; and the industrial genius of Carnegie, Frick, and others. Also in the 1860s the oil industry developed 100 miles northward up the Allegheny Valley, providing another important fuel and raw material for western Pennsylvania industry.

For many decades, the Pittsburgh area led the country in steel production. The so-called "Pittsburgh Plus" pricing policy (by billing all steel, no matter where produced, as if shipped from Pittsburgh) helped maintain the local industry although Great Lakes centers were nearer to both Lake Superior iron ore and Midwestern markets. Because of the steel industry Pittsburgh received (and in part deserved) a reputation of being a dirty, smoky city crowded into congested valleys.

The Pittsburgh SMSA occupies a low plateau, much broken by steepsided valleys whose streams are as much as 500 feet below the rolling upland. Generally, heavy industry

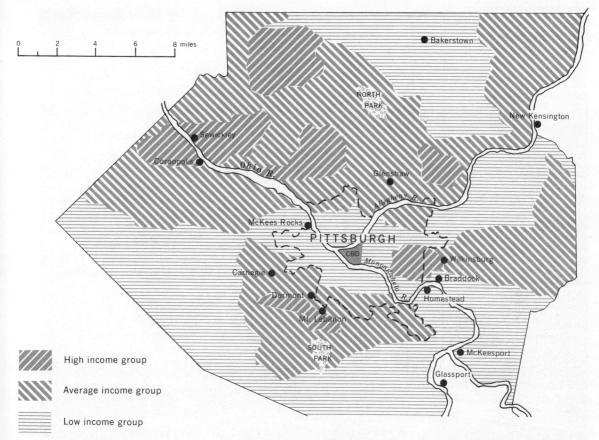

0   2   4   6   8 miles

High income group

Average income group

Low income group

Figure 5.4 This map of Allegheny County, the heart of the Pittsburgh SMSA, shows that the high-income areas are on the uplands away from the rivers, railroad tracks, and heavy industries. (Data from Greater Pittsburgh Chamber of Commerce)

occupies the narrow lowland strips, while better-appearing urban and suburban settlements are on the heights (see Figure 5.4). The irregular topography resulted in the development of variously oriented street grids; these, in turn, increased the difficulties to traffic already funneled into bottlenecks by bridges, tunnels, and steep slopes.

After World War II, Pittsburgh leaders decided to tackle four major problems: smoke control, flood control, sewage disposal, and urban renewal. Improvements in the urban environment have gradually taken place. The city adopted strict smoke control regulations which were later extended to all Allegheny County. The 71 local governments in Allegheny County put into operation a sewage control program which removed most of the offensive charac-

teristics of county streams. A federal dam-building program has controlled all but the most severe floods. More obvious to the visitor has been the creation of a park where the Monongahela and the Allegheny join to form the Ohio. East of this point, the CBD (in the Golden Triangle) has been largely renovated with the Gateway Center (a cluster of skyscrapers). Handsome highway bridges at Point State Park funnel traffic into expressways along both river waterfronts. On the slopes east of the Golden Triangle, slums have been replaced by modern apartments and a civic arena with a retractable roof. An attractive cultural center

An oblique aerial photograph of the renovated Golden Triangle of Pittsburgh. In the background, The Cathedral of Learning, an educational skyscraper, stands out on the University of Pittsburgh campus. (Photograph by Dick Brehl, Associated Photographers, Inc.)

is located a mile farther east on the upland. Although urban renewal consisted largely of office buildings, public buildings, and expressways, about 100 acres of apartment houses were built in the central city. But Pittsburgh remains essentially a city of single homes; some luxurious, some middle class in monotonous rows, and some workers' homes precariously perched on steep slopes.

Heavy industries still account for about half the Pittsburgh SMSA manufacturing employment. Industrial expansion continues but with no appreciable increase in industrial employment. Employment increases have been rather in white-collar jobs with corresponding decreases in farming, mining, and automated industry. The population growth for the SMSA has stopped, but environmental improvements in recent decades in Pittsburgh suggest that growth in human quality and opportunities may be more indicative of human progress than mere population growth.

Outlying areas The plateau north of Pittsburgh produces high-grade oil; the southern part has bituminous coal well suited for coking. Cities such as Youngstown, Steubenville-Weirton, and Wheeling are little Pittsburghs with somewhat fewer commercial and financial functions. In addition to steel, manufactures include pottery, glass, and chemicals—heavy industries originally based on local raw materials. Only slow growth is predicted for these cities and the surrounding countryside, because the good industrial sites are crowded, water for industrial expansion is scarce, and adjacent uplands are much dissected.

Population decrease in West Virginia

West Virginia has suffered from population decline since 1950 and from net out-migration since 1920. The mechanization of coal mining, and hilly to mountainous terrain which resulted in marginal or submarginal farming, caused a steady drop in employment. Can industrial development solve some of the problems of this scenic mountain state?

Charleston is capital of the state which has had more severe problems from unemployment and out-migration than any other American state. Local brines, combined with nearby coal and limestone, led to the foundation of the Charleston chemical industry. Scientific and engineering skills undoubtedly had much to do with the growth of such complicated chemical industries as the production of nylon, rayon, synthetic rubber, and plastics. These industries are aided by ample coal-generated electricity, an industry which in itself requires few workers. The significance of Charleston's industries to the state is indicated by the fact that the city produces one-third of West Virginia's value added by manufacturing but employs only one-fifth of the state's industrial workers. Not all industrial growth produces corresponding industrial opportunity in this automated age.

The Potential Southwestern Ohio Megalopolis

The Ohio Valley has been well linked to the Lake Erie cities. Early settlers to the middle Ohio descended the river from Pittsburgh or Wheeling. Others came via Lake Erie, crossing the low divide either to the upper Ohio or to its Muskingum, Scioto, or Miami tributaries and thence to the middle Ohio. About 1830 to 1850

VALUE ADDED BY MANUFACTURING PITTSBURGH SMSA

% Distribution — Location quotients: 1.0 = national average per capita

Employment	Value added	SIC source	0	1.0	2.0	3.0	4.0	5.0
5.4	6.4	Food products						
NA	NA	Tobacco products (NA)						
NA	NA	Textiles						
1.2	0.5	Apparel						
NA	NA	Lumber						
0.5	0.4	Furniture						
1.2	1.3	Paper products						
2.7	2.7	Printing						
2.1	5.0	Chemicals						
0.2	0.2	Petro-coal products						
1.1	1.0	Rubber-plastic						
NA	NA	Leather (NA)						
5.3	5.5	Stone-clay-glass						7.7
33.2	40.4	Primary metals						
7.9	9.1	Fabricated metals						
10.4	12.6	Machinery						
6.6	9.1	Electrical machinery						
1.9	1.8	Transport equipment						
2.4	2.2	Instruments						
100.0	100.0	All categories						

Figure 5.5 What proportion of all value added by manufacturing in Pittsburgh is accounted for by heavy industry? What is the proportion of all industrial employment in the heavy industries? Note: NA means "not available"; this indicates that so few businesses are in that category that the Bureau of the Census cannot disclose the data without giving confidential information.

canals traversed parts of these valleys to carry trade from Cleveland to Pittsburgh, Columbus, and Portsmouth, and from Toledo to Dayton and Cincinnati.

The Cincinnati-Dayton SMSAs Cincinnati illustrates the good fortune a city has in being well situated in relation to business-generating areas in each period of its economic history. Founded about 1790 as part of a plan to settle the rolling lands in the Miami and Little Miami valleys, Cincinnati soon became a major Ohio port where three natural routes crossed. Some 15 miles westward the Ohio River turned sharply south, making Cincinnati a logical transfer site for pioneers bound for central Indiana to change to overland transport. Manufacturing developed to pack the meats and grind the grain from the agricultural areas to the north and west; other industries were established to supply tools and consumer goods for farm markets. In the 1830s a canal connected the city with Toledo, and in the next decades railroads converged on the city.

The older part of Cincinnati spread along bottomlands and river terraces. The wholesale district was established near the river, and behind it arose the CBD. The industrial area was originally along the river, but industrial ribbons later stretched inland along the valleys descending from the encircling upland and along the route to Dayton. The river is still important for importing fuels and raw materials, but most industrial goods are shipped out by rail, truck, or plane.

Modern Cincinnati specializes in several types of industries: manufactures which convert raw or partly processed materials into finished products, for example, soap and chemicals; metal products of high value per ton, such as truck trailers and machine tools.

Nearby Dayton started as an agricultural service center for the upper Miami Valley. Although it would be an oversimplification to attribute Dayton's later growth to a number of inventions, these certainly were turning points in its history. Shortly after the Civil War cash

registers from Dayton introduced a new era in merchandising records. Motor generators, invented in Dayton, provided farms with electricity before rural power lines became commonplace. The Wright Brothers built the first successful airplane there and flew regularly at a field now part of the huge Wright-Patterson Air Force Base. Charles F. Kettering developed the electric starter for automobiles and improved ignition systems, antiknock gasoline, and other automotive products which led to General Motors' expansion in Dayton. This city's industrial growth is a reminder that people and ideas are as important as transport and raw materials in modern industrial location and growth.

Columbus The advantages of the Miami River valleys also are found in the Scioto-Muskingum watershed, whose commercial capital is Columbus. Although initial growth was as a state capital and farm marketing center, other activities now provide more employment. Industry employs more people than trade, which employs the next largest number of people. In third place is government employment (including education), which has been increasing more rapidly than total employment. At present, Columbus, with no water connections and few local raw materials, competes successfully on the basis of central location; excellent road, rail, and air connections; and political leadership.

Smaller cities The rectangular system of rural land settlement, as elsewhere in the lowlands, developed a multitude of rather evenly spaced county seats, each performing commercial and service functions for the surrounding farmlands. With the displacement of much farm labor by machinery, these cities sought and found industries that could use former farmhands and cheap, uncongested factory sites. Some of these cities originated their own industries to serve the surrounding area; for example, the steam shovel was developed in Marion, Ohio. Many of the industries

THE EVOLVING REGIONAL PATTERN

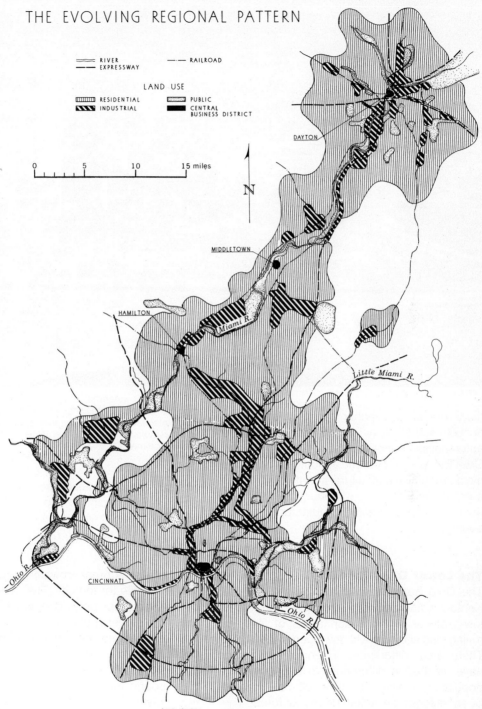

Figure 5.6 The open area between Cincinnati and Dayton is filling up so rapidly that planners have already laid out future land use. (Cincinnati Planning Commission from Cincinnati Chamber of Commerce)

The Louisville waterfront has been redesigned so as to replace the rundown buildings which formerly adjoined the CBD. Interstate 75, extending inland, connects Louisville with Nashville, Birmingham, and Mobile. (Louisville Chamber of Commerce)

made use of the mechanical skills of workers accustomed to repairing farm machinery and automobiles. Although this Ohio part of the Corn Belt is a prosperous agricultural area, the most productive agricultural county, Darke, has a *gross value* of all farm products slightly less than the *value added* by manufacturing in that county.

perous. Their business is centered on four sizable cities: Cincinnati, Louisville, Lexington, and Nashville; all four are well connected with each other by freeway, rail, and air.

The Lower Ohio Plateaus

The Ohio Basin in southern Indiana, central Kentucky, and adjacent Tennessee consists of low plateaus within which areas of level or rolling land alternate with low but rugged lands. There areal differences in underlying rocks have resulted in differences in economy and population density. The hilly sections, formed by sandstones, are suited mostly for forest. The more fertile, less rugged lands are underlain by limestone and other relatively soft rocks; they are generally more populated and more pros-

Louisville A break in water transport established the site for the city. The river at the falls of the Ohio drops only 26 feet in 2 miles. While these rapids were not impassable at high water, they encouraged the transshipment of goods overland from Louisville to Portland or Shippingport below the falls. Although a canal was built around the falls in 1830, it did not stop the growth of Louisville. The city became a distributing center for growing southern Indiana and part of the Bluegrass Region and central Kentucky.

The traditional industries of Louisville were dependent on either the produce or needs of its immediate hinterland, such as whiskey and tobacco products. Recently, introduction of new industries such as household appliances have given heavier industries predominance.

The Bluegrass and Nashville Basin The Kentucky Bluegrass Region with its gently undulating surface, originally covered with grass 2 to 3 feet tall with scattered groves of trees, proved ideal for raising beef cattle, horses, tobacco, corn, and wheat. Accessible both from the Ohio and via the Cumberland Gap, its lands were settled by farmers before 1800. On its phosphate-rich limestone soils they developed a horse-racing aristocracy with "gracious homes, fences of white board or stone, and lovely green pastures and hay-fields."[1]

Lexington, first settled in 1779, recorded its first horse race a decade later. Nearby is Bourbon County after which the distinctive beverage distilled from corn is named. Burley tobacco, for which Lexington is the world's largest market, is another Bluegrass product. Industrial diversification has come in the past decade, as illustrated by the establishment of a business machine industry there.

Nashville Basin is the Tennessee equivalent of the Kentucky Bluegrass Region. A typical estate there contrasts with poorer farmsteads in most of the sandstone-shale areas: its 355 acres are mainly pasture in bluegrass, clover, and other hay crops. The soil is shallow but fertile, rich in lime and phosphate; none of the land is in corn, wheat, or other row crops conducive to erosion. The farm produces mainly livestock—100 beef cattle, 140 lambs, some wool, and perhaps a few pedigreed horses.

Nashville, capital of Tennessee, brings together the trade of diverse areas: the cotton and hardwoods of the Mississippi Plain, the

poor farms of the Tennessee Highland rim located both east and west of the Nashville Basin, and the developing industries of the Tennessee Valley. Although considered by some people to be a Southern city, Nashville business ties are more to the north. Its industries include synthetic fibers and a great variety of consumer goods. Some of its nationally known service industries include religious publishing and the recording of country and Western music.

The Wabash–Lower Ohio Valleys

This subregion illustrates how a farm economy changed to become an urban-industrialized economy. The northern two-thirds of this area is rich glaciated Corn Belt, in most respects a continuation of the characteristics of west central Ohio. Blessed with local resources such as hardwoods, proximity to coal, local gas fields, and plentiful farm produce and farm markets, its towns turned early to manufacturing. Its industries, long established to process farm products and supply farm needs, expanded, using labor migrating from the southern hills or displaced by machinery on the nearby farms. Indianapolis, the state capital, still has large stockyards, food-packing plants, and fertilizer plants, but some of its present specialties—engines, machinery, and pharmaceuticals—result from its convenient location in relation to major manufacturing regions rather than from local resources. North and east of Indianapolis, a cluster of county seats (Muncie, Marion, Anderson, Kokomo) boomed in the 1880s when natural gas discoveries encouraged the manufacture of glass. These cities are now outposts of Detroit, producing automotive parts. These industrial developments explain why in Indiana, a state noted for its corn, beefsteaks, and pork chops, the 1971 civilian income obtained from farms was $671 million but from manufacturing it was $7,140 million; from other urban activities nearly another $8,000 million can be added.

The lower Wabash Valley has experienced

---

[1] *Soil,* Yearbook of Agriculture, U.S. Department of Agriculture, Washington, 1957, p. 368.

fluctuations in economic development. Evansville, for example, had a net out-migration of more than 21,000 in the 1950s. Unemployment was high until new industries were obtained, mostly of the durable goods type, such as refrigerators. A huge aluminum plant, which takes advantage of cheap coal, Ohio water, and Ohio barge transportation, improved the regional economy.

The Future of the Ohio Basin

This region consists of a relatively prosperous northern glacial plain and an economically declining low plateau area amid which certain cities such as Cincinnati, Pittsburgh, Louisville, Lexington, and Nashville are prosperous. The plateau countryside is scenic and centrally located between the well-populated Great Lakes states and the growth regions to the south, especially in the Piedmont and Florida. Many of the more energetic and better-educated people from the plateau have migrated to cities outside the plateau or to the local urban centers where leadership has been outstanding. All forecasts for the plateau area are for only slow growth, with many areas of stagnation or decline. If good land becomes scarce in the world, this plateau with its many advantages for a home for man represents a challenge to American economic planning: the underdeveloped lands are not all in foreign countries!

THE GREAT LAKES REGION

The Great Lakes are politically divided between the United States and Canada, but this division does not prevent cooperation; the two countries are pressured into joint action by problems of resource use, pollution, and trade. This section of the chapter will consider the resources and problems of the lakes from the American side and examine also the parts of adjacent states most dependent on the lakes.

The water area of the Great Lakes is over 95,000 square miles, or approximately the size of Oregon. The lakes and their outlet, the St.

Lawrence River, provide a navigable waterway (with the help of canals) of 2,340 miles from Duluth to the Atlantic Ocean. The lakes drain an area of nearly 300,000 square miles, and the huge amount of water is stored in basins which range in depth from a maximum of 1,333 feet in Lake Superior to a shallow 210 feet in Lake Erie. The major impediments to navigation are the St. Mary's rapids which drop 20 feet between lakes Superior and Huron, the Niagara Escarpment (which drops about 200 feet), and the former rapids of the St. Lawrence River between Lake Ontario and Montreal.

The economy of the Great Lakes region demonstrates the changing relationships to natural resources. Until the end of the eighteenth century, this area was of interest mainly to the fur trader and trapper. A half century later its southern half had been occupied by farmers, and its northern half was being opened to obtain forest and mineral raw materials. The latter, in turn, were manufactured into farm implements and wagons, railroads, and boats to haul farm produce eastward. Before the end of the nineteenth century, the lakes linked Upper Lakes ores, lumber, and limestone with Appalachian coal, and brought Midwestern grain and meat to Eastern markets. The waters of the lakes have become a natural resource and not simply a means of transport.

Business activity around the Great Lakes is enormous, second only to that of the Atlantic Megalopolis. Its population, two-thirds the numbers of the Atlantic Megalopolis, is concentrated near the lower lakes. Despite the historic importance of raw materials of the hinterland, production is mainly in urban places—indeed two-thirds of its personal income is concentrated in four metropolitan areas: Chicago, Detroit, Cleveland, and Buffalo. The region is the leading industrial part of the country. Its rank in all other activities—farming, mining, trade, and services—is also high. For a long time its trade was carried by combinations of lake, canal, rail, and highway routes to Atlantic ports, but since 1958 the region is connected by the Great Lakes–St.

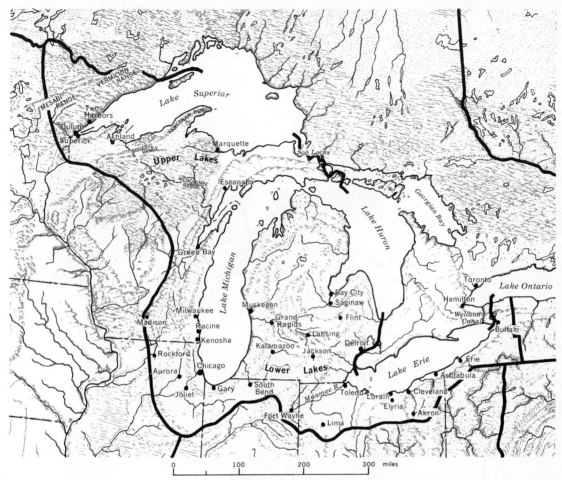

Figure 5.7 Landforms of the Great Lakes region. (Base map by A. K. Lobeck. Reprinted with permission of The Geographical Press, Hammond, Inc.)

Lawrence Seaway directly with Atlantic ports two-thirds of the year. This latter slow route generally handles bulk cargo, while general cargo is shipped by the more southerly rail and highway routes.

The Great Lakes region obtains over two-fifths of its civilian income from manufacturing and contract construction. Trade is the second largest source of income; trade and service together account for half of the total regional income. Farming produces less than one-thirtieth of the income provided by industry. Mining income is still smaller, many ores and oil and gas now being shipped in. Finance, transportation, utilities, and, especially, services and government—each yields much

more income than the crops, livestock, lumber, and minerals which first attracted settlers to the region. Much more important today to the regional economy are central location in relation to Anglo-American population and the well-developed transportation, communication, utility, and other services used by industry.

The Lake Erie Ports

Transshipment points have provided sites for the growth of great cities, and the Lake Erie shore—especially those places which offered

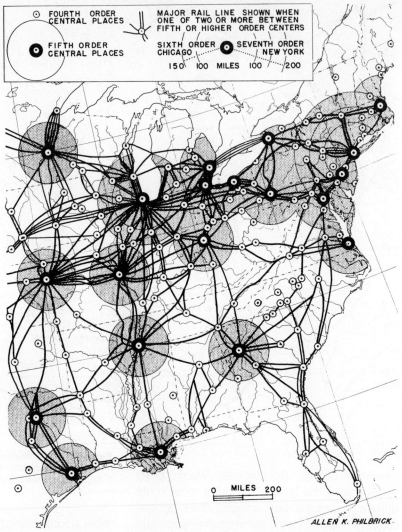

AREAL FUNCTIONAL ORGANIZATION IN THE EASTERN UNITED STATES

⊙ FOURTH ORDER CENTRAL PLACES

◉ FIFTH ORDER CENTRAL PLACES

MAJOR RAIL LINE SHOWN WHEN ONE OF TWO OR MORE BETWEEN FIFTH OR HIGHER ORDER CENTERS

SIXTH ORDER CHICAGO ⊙⋯⋯◉ SEVENTH ORDER NEW YORK

150   100 MILES 100   200

0   MILES 200

ALLEN K. PHILBRICK

Figure 5.8 Philbrick has divided the urban centers into orders of cities, all fitting into a hierarchy. The seventh-order center, New York, is an international capital as well as the primate city in the United States. Chicago is the primate city of the interior United States. Fifth-order cities are major focal points for clusters of large cities; they are usually regional economic capitals with central banking functions. Fourth-order cities are transshipment points with commercial controls over only part of a state or over parts of several adjacent states. (This figure and Figure 5.9 are from Allen K. Philbrick, "Principles of Areal Functional Organization in Regional Human Geography," *Economic Geography,* vol. 33 (1957), pp. 306–336.)

sheltered harbors—provided suitable places for city development. The Erie ports received grain, lumber, and ores from the upper lakes and shipped bituminous coal to industrial Ontario and other lake ports. The Erie ports soon became major wholesale, retailing, industrial, and financial centers, connected by major east-west railroads and highways paralleling the lakeshore. As the lakeside economies grew, the heavy industries benefiting by cheaper fuel and raw materials spawned other

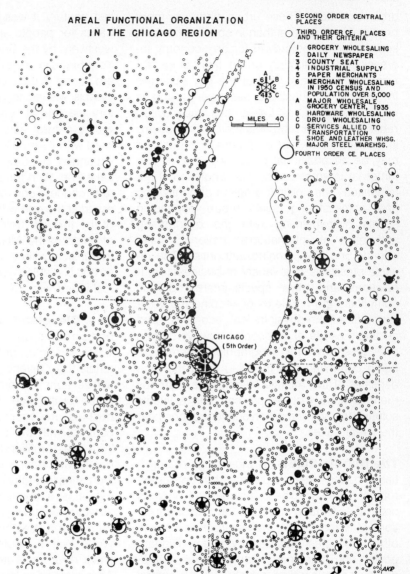

AREAL FUNCTIONAL ORGANIZATION
IN THE CHICAGO REGION

○ SECOND ORDER CENTRAL
PLACES

◯ THIRD ORDER C.E. PLACES
AND THEIR CRITERIA

1 GROCERY WHOLESALING
2 DAILY NEWSPAPER
3 COUNTY SEAT
4 INDUSTRIAL SUPPLY
5 PAPER MERCHANTS
6 MERCHANT WHOLESALING
  IN 1950 CENSUS AND
  POPULATION OVER 5,000
A MAJOR WHOLESALE
  GROCERY CENTER, 1935
B HARDWARE WHOLESALING
C DRUG WHOLESALING
D SERVICES ALLIED TO
  TRANSPORTATION
E SHOE AND LEATHER WHSG.
F MAJOR STEEL WAREHSG.

◯ FOURTH ORDER C.E. PLACES

0 MILES 40

CHICAGO
(5th Order)

Figure 5.9 The regular distribution of small cities (second-order) is partly the result of the rectangular survey. This map also shows that these cities are lined up along railroad routes. Second-order cities have mainly local functions; third-order cities also have wholesaling and other specialized functions. The classification of these cities is somewhat arbitrary; for example, Gary, Indiana, is classed as third-order, but it is fourth-order in some respects.

manufactures—especially those producing machinery and consumer durables. Light industries also were established, especially food packing and processing, partly using nearby farm products and partly using grain shipped in by lake.

Potential megalopolises A Great Lakes Megalopolis may develop. As suggested in the example of Detroit in Chapter 3, such urban

growth might be in the form of urban networks over the countryside with adequate rural agricultural and recreational areas between the urban corridors. These urban patterns, more predictable in general than in specific location, seem a logical outgrowth for an economy increasingly substituting urban technology for rural raw materials. One of the raw materials for which no substitute has been found is water; since the Great Lakes have ample water, rapid urban expansion near their shores seems likely *if pollution can be controlled*. Fresh air may be an additional casualty if smoke and fumes of internal combustion engines cannot be limited. The political problem of controlling and administering such urban expansion seems overwhelming with the overlapping authorities of international, national, state, county, and city planning authorities. The diverse pressures of a variety of business organizations and other special-interest groups complicate the problems of keeping the landscape fit for the physiological, economic, and aesthetic needs of its people. However, when one sees how the geographic patterns are being controlled and modified amid the high densities of the Atlantic Megalopolis, perhaps there is hope that people can find a livable solution for evolving urban concentrations near the Great Lakes.

The Buffalo SMSA A wide range of activities and land uses are dispersed through metropolitan Buffalo. These include fruit growing near lakes Ontario and Erie; the tourist attractions of Niagara Falls; the electrochemical and other industries attracted by cheap Niagara power; the machinery, transportation equipment, and flour-milling industries of the central city; the commercial and financial services of the CBD and its adjacent well-sheltered harbor; and the steel mills of Lackawanna. Despite this variety of activities Buffalo is primarily an industrial city producing durable goods and bulky nondurables. Its growth is partly due to a remarkable ability to combine skillfully raw materials, water, and power.

The industrial activities could be (and are) located elsewhere along the lakes, but Buffalo has had unusual locational advantages. In the last century it was the gateway to the Great Lakes for people and products which moved westward by the Erie Canal across upper New York State. In this century it has been the eastern end of Great Lakes water transport (unless vessels wished to go through Canadian territory via the St. Lawrence Seaway). Starting with a natural harbor on Buffalo Creek (now lined with flour mills), its port has been greatly expanded by breakwaters and docks along Lake Erie. With the advent of railroads, special rate concessions allowed grain to be processed at the port without losing the advantages of the through freight rate from inland points of origin to the Atlantic Coast. To this *milling-in-transit* privilege was added *milling-in-bond* so that Canadian grain could be processed and reshipped without paying United States duty.

The Cleveland area Cleveland, another port similar to Buffalo, takes advantage of both water and land transport to assemble raw materials. The Cuyahoga River divides the city into two sections and provides a harbor for lake ore boats for the steel industries. These heavy industries are supplied also by railroads that connect with the coalfields to the southeast. With over 2 million local customers, Cleveland needs, and has, a variety of consumer goods industries including clothing and food processing. It is a cosmopolitan city: its industries attracted skilled immigrants from Northwestern Europe and later from Eastern Europe; during World War II Southern migrants came from black rural areas and from white Appalachia. As in most cities, many of the middle and upper classes moved to the suburbs, and ghetto conditions developed in the central city.

Cleveland, like Pittsburgh, is an example of how older industrial cities are attempting to renovate their commercial cores to balance the outward flow of business. Cleveland first developed an urban plan in 1902. In downtown Cleveland the Union Terminal Building was constructed on Public Square, and later a stadium, an airport, and docks were constructed nearby on filled land along the lakefront. An

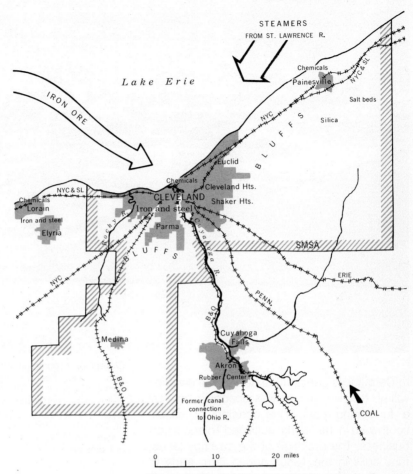

Figure 5.10 Some factors which account for the economic development of the Cleveland SMSA.

expressway through the downtown area and frequent suburban rapid transit service from Union Terminal to outlying parking lots were later efforts to open up the congested city. More recently, capital from the steel industry financed the modernization of 163 acres east of downtown Cleveland; this Erieview project has 80 acres of parklike plaza, a 40-story office building, a federal building, an auditorium, and high-rise apartments. At the same time Cleveland is expanding outwardly, and its planners are talking about a megalopolis to include Ashtabula, Akron, Elyria, and Lorain.

One of the outlying cities is Akron, in which more than half the industrial workers manufacture rubber products. Although B. F.

Goodrich moved there in 1870, Akron was still mainly a farm-marketing center with diversified small industries in 1910. The growth of the automobile industry attracted other tire companies because Akron already had experience with this industry.

The Toledo SMSA Similar to Buffalo, Toledo's rise was based in part on the junction of river and canal routes with the lake. There were, however, distinctive differences between the two ports in local resources which are reflected in the present industrial mix. The Maumee Valley is an example of how regional functions can change. Until 1827 when a road

to Detroit was constructed across the swampy valley, the river mouth was occupied only by a fur-trading post. The opening of canals southward in the 1840s multiplied Toledo's port business. The drainage of the swampy lacustrine soils in the 1850s added farm trade to other Toledo business. In 1888 a glass company was attracted by the discovery of nearby oil, gas, and glass sand deposits, and today four major glass companies justify Toledo's claim to be "Glass Center of the World." Petroleum refining developed about the same time. These industries still remain although the local resources have been exhausted; fuels and raw materials are now brought from Texas, Illinois, and West Virginia.

As local resources declined in relative importance, Toledo's industries depended more and more on excellent transportation. Having 11 railroads, the city claims third rank among United States rail centers; the port is the largest handler of soft coal in the world, shipping Appalachian coal to Canada and upper lake ports. Toledo, also an importer of

Cleveland, in common with many cities fronting on the Great Lakes, has constructed an artificial harbor with docks on filled land. The Cuyahoga River, the localizing factor in the establishment of Cleveland, contributes its water and its refuse to polluted Lake Erie. The location of the railroad terminal can be identified by Terminal Tower, the skyscraper to the right. (Cleveland Chamber of Commerce)

general cargo, possesses the only United States free-trade zone on the Great Lakes.

Michigan and the Automobile
There was no impelling reason why the Detroit area should have become the American automobile region; in fact, early automobile manufacturing did well at such widespread places as Bridgeport (Connecticut), Cleveland (Ohio), South Bend and Indianapolis (Indiana), and Kenosha (Wisconsin). Detroit, however, had such men as Ford, Olds, Buick, and Leland who were willing to risk their money and invest their time in the new industry. Previously established vehicle and engine industries provided a trained labor supply. The major market

Ford Motor Company's River Rouge manufacturing complex in Dearborn is the largest concentration of closely knit factories in the United States. The Rouge is the only Anglo-American plant at which iron ore, limestone, and coal are unloaded on the docks; smelted into iron; converted into steel; and transformed into engines, frames, bodies, and parts which are assembled into automobiles. (Ford Motor Company)

was in the Midwest, and Detroit businessmen turned out products which captured that market.

Although steel is the principal material in modern automobiles, the early automobile had a wooden body made of materials then plentiful in Michigan forests. Fortunately for the area, the iron ores of the Lake Superior area supplied new raw materials when steel bodies were introduced. Today, a multitude of towns and cities within a 200-mile radius of Detroit supply parts and subassemblies for the industry that accounts tor one-fifteenth of all United States industrial production. Although automobiles are now assembled in many large metropolitan areas, the decision-making functions of the industry are concentrated in and near Detroit.

Detroit SMSA Detroit, beginning as a French fur-trading post, became a port about 1830 for pioneers settling the well-drained area north of the Maumee Valley. From Detroit the

first railroad to reach Chicago from the east was completed in 1852, and international railroad connections across southern Ontario provided a fast route to New York. Farm trade; the exploitation of Michigan lumber; and farm machinery, wagon, and bicycle industries gave Detroit industrial importance long before the automobile entered the scene.

Detroit has often been discussed as a one-industry city because so much of its industry—steel, glass, machine tools, metal stampings, etc.—delivers much of its products to the automobile industry. South of the skyscrapers of the Detroit CBD, industries line the Detroit River for several miles, spewing their wastes into the river which flows into and pollutes Lake Erie—perhaps beyond recovery. Four-fifths of its industrial workers are in the durable goods industries; nevertheless, it has over 10,000 workers each in its food, clothing, textile, printing, pharmaceutical, and chemical industries.

In Chapter 3 the basic features of the Doxiadis proposal for the Urban Detroit Area were outlined. Since then the city of Detroit has drawn up elaborate plans for revamping the inner city. Goals specified are:

1 To intensify the sense of structure and coherence by building character into neighborhoods, pathways, and open spaces in an attempt to differentiate the parts of the city.
2 To increase the diversity within the inner city in order to increase the choice of what people can do, what they see and experience, and the ways in which they move throughout the area.
3 To provide more opportunity for leisure activity.
4 To make the parts of the city more accessible to more people.

The plan, in common with plans of many metropolitan areas, attempts to revivify the inner city as a commercial, educational, artistic, and residential center, combining past and present values in a city for the future:

While currency has replaced furs and trading posts with towering banks, the Inner City is still tied to the land patterns of days when Messieurs Beaubien and Rivard tilled the soil. Much of the local street system is based on the subdivision patterns of the narrow French farms extending from the riverbank north, divided, and redivided through the years with the resulting matrix of small blocks, as unsuited to the 20th Century as an economy based on furs. Houses on narrow lots crowd the tiny islands in a torrent of cars. Store fronts line the French roads, catching at passing cars with flashing signs. But the historical order has pre-

vailed: the radial axes, the major institutions along the city's spine, Woodward Avenue, the containment of Grand Boulevard, the Bridge, the Island, and the River. The structure remains, the context has evolved.[2]

Other Michigan cities It is difficult to find a Michigan city that does not make an important contribution to automobile manufacture. Some are almost dominated by the motor companies. Pontiac has most of its industrial labor working for one automobile company. Flint, once a lumber center and later a wagon manufacturer, is more diversified. Although about 70,000 industrial workers are in the leading transportation equipment category, its other industries supply materials used in automobile manufacture, for example, automotive enamels and oil filters.

Grand Rapids, the only large Michigan city not dominated by Detroit, is the major business center for western Michigan. Located on a minor fall line, 30 miles up the navigable Grand River from Lake Michigan, Grand Rapids used local waterpower and water supply to become a lumber-mill town. Later it became known throughout eastern Anglo-America for furniture manufacturing—still an important industry employing one-seventh of the industrial labor force. Its durable goods industries also produce such items as refrigerators and automatic merchandising machines. Whereas local resources were once important factors, the city now pumps part of its water from Lake Michigan and gets gas and fuel oil by pipeline from the Southwest.

Rural Michigan Agriculture is still a major activity between the many cities of southern Michigan. Along the eastern shore of Lake Michigan winter weather is moderated by the lake, thus permitting fruit growing. Beginning about 50 miles north of Grand Rapids, the cutover land has much infertile soil. The remainder of northern Michigan is a wooded,

[2] Quoted portions from *Detroit 1990: An Urban Design Concept for the Inner City,* City of Detroit, no date.

lake-studded land which attracts the vacation trade in the summer and hunters in the autumn and winter. But as population increases in southern Michigan, the lakes to the north become more crowded in summer, the camping places are filled, and game is becoming scarce. Urban population of the Great Lakes cities affects even the once-empty parts of the region.

The Upper Lakes

Except for its extensive ores and somewhat poorer soils the Lake Superior area resembles the northern part of lower Michigan. It has had difficulty in maintaining its economy. Its extensive forests (about which the Paul Bunyan legends grew) were cut over early in this century; their slow regrowth provides wood suitable mainly for pulping. The lumber companies made little attempt to replant the trees, abandoning title if the land lacked mineral resources. Fire destroyed huge areas. Today state governments are encouraging tree farming with some success. The metamorphic and igneous rocks underlying the forest were rich in ores, but the best of these are almost exhausted. The soil, mostly rocky or sandy, is farmed only where pockets of good soil permit dairying and potato farming. The numerous lakes and streams and the cool summers provide attractions for hunters, fishermen, and campers, but this business is highly seasonal. Past development has been based on natural resources, shipped elsewhere for manufacture.

Copper and iron Mining has been a major primary activity in the upper lakes. The earliest commercial copper mining was in 1844 in the Keweenaw Peninsula of Michigan; iron ore mining began in 1846 in the Marquette Range. The mining prospects were sufficiently good in 1855 to justify the opening of the Sault Ste. Marie Canal, commonly called the Soo. Later, ores were (and still are) shipped from the Menominee and the Gogebic ranges, using the ports of Marquette, Escanaba, and Ashland.

Minnesota ores were not tapped until near the end of the century from the Vermilion Range, and the first Mesabi ore was moved to Duluth in 1893. The 50 to 70 percent iron-content hematites, largely recoverable by open-pit mining, are now approaching exhaustion. The future of Minnesota iron mining depends on taconites with 20 to 30 percent iron content. These need to be upgraded to be competitive with higher-grade ores: 2 tons of taconite rock are condensed into 1 ton of pellets.

The Duluth-Superior SMSA One-third of the subregional population is concentrated around the sheltered harbor at the head of Lake Superior. Originally a fur-trading post, Duluth became a significant port when the railroad from St. Paul reached it in 1870. Its huge grain elevators and ore- and coal-loading docks indicate the kind of raw materials that flow through the port. Unlike most cities of its size, Duluth-Superior SMSA has little industry, being primarily a commercial and transshipment center.

The Chicago Megalopolis

The regional economy of the western Great Lakes region focuses on Chicago, core of an urbanized lakeshore extending 125 miles from Milwaukee to Gary. This urban agglomeration slightly exceeds New York City (not the New York SMSA) in income and population. Like that city, it developed because its leaders took advantage of converging land and water routes. The southern Lake Michigan region had the additional advantage of being adjacent to the world's richest agricultural area; it had the handicap of being, before the opening of the Welland Canal and the St. Lawrence Seaway, almost 700 miles from ocean ports.

The population of the Chicago Megalopolis was estimated in 1973 at 10 million people, occupying an area slightly smaller than New Jersey. The 1960–1970 population growth rate approximated that for the United States as a whole, and as in most SMSAs,

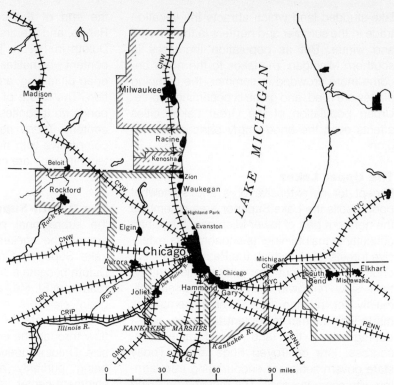

Figure 5.11 From Milwaukee to Michigan City, SMSAs are continuous. The gap between the Calumet District and South Bend is now being developed as a result of a new port near Michigan City.

growth included a decreasing population in the central cities balanced by rapid peripheral growth.

The physical site of Chicago An examination of Chicago's site and position makes it seem an almost inevitable location for a large city. A short portage across a low divide of unconsolidated sediments indicated several places where canals could be built to connect streams tributary to Lake Michigan with tributaries of the Illinois River. The portage at Chicago, used in turn by the Indians and fur traders, later was dominated by Fort Dearborn. The shore itself is flattish and fairly well drained in places, and consists either of lacustrine deposits formed when glacial Lake Michigan had a higher level or of sand dunes and morainal ridges which paralleled the shore. Lake Michigan provides an unlimited municipal water supply, and since it is slightly higher than the Illinois River tributaries, lake waters could be used to fill canals connecting with the Missis-

sippi system. To the west and southwest is a rich farmland, a source of business for Chicago shippers and of food for growing urban populations. Finally, between Lake Michigan to the north and the Kankakee Marshes to the south was a natural corridor for east-west routes.

The growth of Chicago into a great city reflected the settlement (1830–1850) of the Illinois prairies, southern Wisconsin, and, later, around the upper lakes (for the lumber). Chicago was the gateway to the West before it was connected to the East by rail in 1852. By 1860 Chicago had 112,000 people, and its grain elevators, stockyards, and sawmills—dependent on regional natural resources—were supplemented by factories processing raw materials and supplying farm implements and consumer goods. Heavier industry was established toward the end of the century. Railroads fanning out westward gave Chicago merchants control of a vast wholesale market; mail-order merchandizing extended its Midwestern retail market. The Chicago Board of Trade, the leading Anglo-American exchange for farm products, became as influential in these commodities as Wall Street was in stocks and bonds.

Although the natural advantages of Chicago now seem so obvious, its growth was related to human decisions there and elsewhere. If Eastern railroads had continued to build westward, thus avoiding the necessity of changing trains at Chicago, its railway business might have been considerably less. If businessmen in St. Louis had exploited their Mississippi and western railway trade more effectively, that city might have remained, as it was until 1870, the business capital of the Central Lowland. Greater leadership might have come from people in Milwaukee or even Duluth in exploiting Wisconsin and Minnesota trade. Chicago's growth, not inevitable, depended on business leaders who utilized its natural advantages and overcame its handicaps.

The Loop and the railroads The Chicago CBD grew up on a rectangular peninsula, about a mile square, enclosed on the east by Lake Michigan and on the west and north by the Chicago River. Because the Loop was initially a quagmire in wet weather, streets and buildings were elevated several feet above the original level to ensure dry pavements. The major railway passenger terminals are on the fringe of this area, and rapid transit lines went around the Loop on elevated tracks.

The areal patterns of land use can be seen from the top of a Loop skyscraper: railroad tracks converging toward the CBD, the fashionable apartments along Lake Shore Drive, the smoke of heavy industries along the southwestern curve of Lake Michigan, and solid strips of industries along the rail lines and main highways. Along the northern and western edges of the Loop, boats and barges carry cargo along the Sanitary and Ship Canal.

There are many similarities between the Chicago and New York CBDs. The Loop and adjacent parts of the CBD have loft industries and other types of activity also found in the Manhattan CBD. The hotel-restaurant-theater area is clustered within the Loop but offers less variety than its New York counterpart. Libraries, museums, and educational institutions are found on the fringes of the Loop as well as in several outlying locations, for example, Evanston and Jackson Park. As in New York, the land area was extended by filling up the adjacent shores; over 1,000 feet of downtown Chicago (including Grant Park) projects into what was once Lake Michigan. Port business, although large and growing by Great Lakes standards, is less conspicuous than in Manhattan, much of the bulky cargo being relegated to outlying waterway sites.

Chicago industry Chicago has almost every kind of industry (Figure 5.12) and is not lacking in any main category. Many of the bulkier industries, for example, meat packing, have left the city. In terms of number employed, the production of durable goods accounts for three-fifths of the manufacturing employment. Employment in manufacturing is slightly more than one-third of the total and is almost equaled by commercial employment (trade, transportation, finance). As in any large metropolis, employment in professional, educational, and other services is also high.

Chicago suburbs Like most metropolitan cities, Chicago includes many satellite communities; some of the older of these have been incorporated into the city. Except for major highways which converge toward the CBD, both in Chicago and in satellite cities the street pattern is rectangular, thanks to the original land survey. Semicircular belt expressways and commuter railways connect the satellites, thus bypassing central city congestion. The suburbs vary in quality and local community spirit, some being dormitory towns for commuting workers, some being clustered around factories, a few being exclusive residential centers which have also educational institutions and "scientific" industries. Cities such as Elgin, Aurora, and Joliet were distinct urban centers before they were absorbed into the Chicago SMSA. These cities are similar in function and areal patterns to the cities in the Outer Ring around New York.

The Calumet area East Chicago, Hammond, Gary, and smaller Indiana industrial suburbs form an industrial district along the Calumet River, adjacent to the similar heavy industrial district in southeast Chicago. Seventy-five years ago the Calumet sand dunes and marshes were little used except by railroads converging on Chicago. About 1890, an oil refinery was built at Whiting and a steel plant at East Chicago; in 1905, after a careful survey, the United States Steel Corporation selected a sand dune site on which to build an integrated steel works to supply the Chicago market. The attractions of Gary were obvious: excellent lake and railroad connections; unconsolidated materials which could be easily bulldozed into level land; port sites and unlimited fresh water; cheap access to Minnesota hematite, Michigan limestone, and Appalachian coal; central location amid growing automobile, farm machinery, and construction-steel markets; and a huge potential labor supply. All these advantages proved ideal for industries producing heavy or bulky goods. Employment is concentrated in a few cyclical industries; for example, over half the industrial workers are in the steel industry.

VALUE ADDED BY MANUFACTURING   **CHICAGO-N.W. INDIANA STANDARD CONSOLIDATED AREA**

% Distribution   Location quotients: 1.0 = national average per capita

Employment	Value added	SIC source	0	1.0	2.0	3.0	4.0	5.0
8.0	11.5	Food products						
NA	NA	Tobacco products	NA					
0.3	0.2	Textiles						
2.4	1.6	Apparel						
0.8	0.5	Lumber						
2.0	1.5	Furniture						
3.2	3.0	Paper products						
8.7	9.3	Printing						
4.5	9.6	Chemicals						
1.2	2.5	Petro-coal products						
2.7	2.3	Rubber-plastic						
0.4	0.3	Leather						
2.0	2.1	Stone-clay-glass						
12.9	12.6	Primary metals						
10.8	10.2	Fabricated metals						
11.0	10.9	Machinery						
13.8	12.4	Electrical machinery						
2.8	3.4	Transport equipment						
3.2	3.5	Instruments						
100.0	100.0	All categories						

Figure 5.12 Compare this chart with Figure 4.7. Why are textiles so unimportant in the Chicago area? In what ways does the New York area differ industrially from the Chicago area?

The Milwaukee SMSA The lakeshore urban strip almost connects Chicago with Milwaukee. Urban centers, notably Kenosha and Racine, were sited initially by small river-mouth harbors. A larger harbor, formed by the junction of three streams close to the lakeshore and enlarged by dredging and breakwater construction, provided the site for Milwaukee. Railroads now follow these converging valleys, along which cluster most of the long-established industries.

Milwaukee was another port that depended on its natural resource hinterland. Here German and Polish immigrants during the middle of the last century processed and shipped the lumber, grain, and animal products produced in southern Wisconsin. Many of the immigrants were political refugees who, being more skilled and better educated than other immigrants, founded the mechanical industries for which Milwaukee is noted. To supply the local market they established breweries whose products are now sold throughout the United States.

Milwaukee is now the commercial center for most of Wisconsin; half of the state's trade is in its 11 southeastern counties. Milwaukee and other Wisconsin ports are preparing termi-

This modern dairy farm, with acres of corn and huge silos and barns, is located in Walworth County, southeastern Wisconsin. Although the total sale of farm products gives the county the highest per farm rate in Wisconsin, the value added by manufacturing in the small cities of the county is about twice the farm sales. The manufacturing labor force is about twice the size of the farm labor force. Most farms are highly mechanized and require few full-time workers. (USDA)

nal facilities to make expanded use of the Great Lakes–St. Lawrence Seaway. Compared with Chicago, these ports have the advantage of less congestion and newer equipment, and they have access to a high-quality labor force drawn in part from nearby Wisconsin farms.

Eastern Wisconsin cities and farmlands On the northern fringe of the Chicago Megalopolis, eastern Wisconsin supplies many farm products directed primarily toward Chicago. This is a green land of neat white farmsteads with tall silos, of scattered lakes and wooded ridges and hillocks, amid which a sprinkling of neat towns and small cities specializes in serving the adjacent countryside and manufacturing a few specialties. The largest towns are on the southeastern margin, and the country roads that lead into them are paved to support the heavy milk tank trucks which concentrate Wisconsin's well-known product at butter, powdered-milk, and cheese factories. In

the center and north, industry is largely based on local raw materials; further south, more diversified industry based on skilled workmanship is characteristic.

Are the Great Lakes a Permanent Resource?

The growth of industries in the Great Lakes region resulted from a high degree of human technology being applied along the world's greatest inland seas. Excellent land and water transport brings raw materials from both nearby and distant sources. The cities, once service centers for the nearby food and raw material areas, are now major markets as well as suppliers of goods and services to broader world markets.

The prosperity of this region is based in part on the domestic water supply, navigation, fish, and climatic modification contributed by the Great Lakes. Will these advantages last? In the 1930s the sea lamprey eel entered the Great Lakes and greatly reduced the catch of lake trout, white fish, and other commercially valuable fish. Soon after, the alewife (a kind of herring) entered the lakes and by the 1960s had so multiplied that their dead bodies polluted the beaches and waters of Lake Michigan. In much of the lower lakes commercial fishing disappeared. Pollution from sewage and industrial waste almost annihilated the fish in Lake Erie and southern Lake Michigan, and most beaches in these lakes became too contaminated for swimming. The introduction of coho salmon may conquer the alewives and add a new food resource to the lakes.

The line of big industrial cities around the west and south sides of Lake Erie found it convenient to dump their domestic and industrial wastes into the lake, ignoring that the lake had other purposes for other people. Human activities have speeded up the aging of the lake, a process involving an increase of nutrients in the lake which depletes the oxygen available for fish. The excess of chemical and biological wastes is making it increasingly difficult to purify the water supply for domestic use. These processes, most advanced in Lake Erie and in parts of lakes Michigan and Ontario, are likely to spread to all the lakes. Can controls be instituted to preserve the lake resources upon which the lives and livelihoods of millions of Anglo-Americans depend?

The problem is further complicated because the international border runs through the Great Lakes and international cooperation and agreement are necessary for most control measures. Because most of the industry and population pressure is on the American side of the lakes, Canada expects the United States to pay the larger share of the clean-up costs.

Studies have examined this problem in considerable detail; the controls involve the cooperation not only of two nations but of thousands of state, provincial, county, and municipal governments as well as of many powerful corporations. The human and political problems may be greater than the environmental problems.

THE MIDWEST

The Midwest, as considered here,[3] consists of most of the West North Central states to which have been added the western parts of Wisconsin and Illinois which have much in common with their western neighbors. Agriculture still dominates the landscape in most of this region. Although only one-seventh of the income is directly attributable to farming and ranching, many of the factories either process farm products or produce goods for use on the farm. Likewise, many of the commercial and governmental services are related to agricultural needs.

The agricultural regions (and their problems) discussed below extend eastward into the Great Lakes region and the Ohio Basin. To the west there is no sharp change agriculturally at the western borders of the Dakotas, Nebraska, and Kansas; to the south the wheat farming of Kansas continues across northwestern Oklahoma into the panhandle of Texas. On the western margin, land use varies from decade to decade, sometimes from year to year. As the jet-age traveler flying across these regions can see, the ranches and the dry-farming and irrigated areas send innumerable fingers across these boundaries so sharply depicted on generalized agricultural maps.

The following characteristics apply to the Midwest as a whole but to different degrees in the various parts of the region:

1   Agricultural areas, while increasing in pro-

[3] The term *Midwest* is used in a variety of ways by Americans. It is used here as a convenient term for the western part of the Central Lowland which once largely agricultural is now urbanizing around large cities.

Figure 5.13 Landforms of the Midwest. All the landform features are minor, consisting mostly of low hills, bluffs, water bodies, and marshes. Can you find a city not located on a stream? Instead of including an agricultural regions map, we have labeled the approximate location of the agricultural regional cores. These regional boundaries are rarely sharp and change with market conditions and agricultural innovations. (Base map by A. K. Lobeck. Reprinted with permission of The Geographical Press, Hammond, Inc.)

ductivity, are providing less farm employment because of changes in technology and changes to a larger scale of the profitable farm unit.

2 The surplus rural population has resulted in a net out-migration from most of the rural area for several decades. Housing, towns, and local government in predominately farm areas exceed the need for them. Net out-migration occurred in every decade since the 1920s in every Plains state (except in Minnesota in the 1930s); in the 1950s 800,000 more people moved away from these states than moved into them; in the 1960s the net out-migration was 619,000. In both of the Dakotas there have

For beef cattle, this modern, mechanized, paved feedlot operation in Iowa has a capacity of 200 to 300 head. The actual feeding time is 20 to 30 minutes, depending on the amount of grain with the silage. (USDA)

been actual population declines in every decade since 1930.

3 Rapid growth in the larger cities has provided increased employment in the eastern half of the region.

4 Most of the Midwest is relatively free from pollution and offers uncongested space for cities provided an economic base for such new cities can be found.

The Midwest, except for small areas around the larger cities, remains a land of farmers who with a maximum of machinery and a minimum of hired labor in favorable seasons produce record-breaking yields for national and world markets. The use of city-made machinery, fertilizer, seed selection, and antibiotics has made it possible for an outstandingly

successful farmer to become a wealthy man. Along with generous soil resources, the region has benefited from terrain level enough to encourage a development of a close network of roads and railroads and to facilitate the wide use of machinery.

The agricultural units originally laid out in 80- to 320-acre homesteads have, in recent decades, become too small for efficient farm management. While the larger farms have yielded huge crop surpluses, many small farms are on the verge of bankruptcy and survive only because of part-time employment off the farm. Nearly one-third of the farms in the Plains states have sales of under $5,000 annually;

many are occupied by retired farmers, part-time farmers, and others taking advantage of cheap rural housing. Many of the out-migrants are of prime working age; this accounts for the fact that the Plains states have 20 percent below the national average in the 18 to 44 age group and 10 percent above the national average in the over-65 age group.

Humid Farm Regions and Representative SMSAs

About one-ninth of the land of the United States (excluding Alaska) and about one-third of its cropland are included in this humid area of highly diversified farming. The region is characterized by crop rotation, chemical weed control, fertilization, and the marketing of the bulk of its crops as livestock products. The outstanding crop is corn, which occupies one-fifth of the cropland: somewhat more in the south (commonly called the "Corn Belt"), and somewhat less in the north (the "Dairy Belt"). The soils, generally derived from lime-rich glacial deposits or from windblown silts, were initially fertile, but when carelessly tilled they may become leached and eroded. Local soil variations based on slope, nature of soil materials, and drainage conditions are common; fortunately most farmers are skilled in adjusting their tillage, fertilizers, and crops to the varied soils in their fields. The rotation of cleanly cultivated corn and soybeans with such ground-covering crops as hay and small grains, and the common inclusion of nitrogen-depositing clover, alfalfa, or soybeans, help to maintain soil fertility.

The Corn Belt   This region was described by Smith and Phillips in 1940 as

a seemingly endless expanse of black or dark-brown flat or gently rolling land upon which is a seemingly endless succession of farms with rich crops of corn, oats, hay or wheat and herds of big, cubical cattle or fat, cylindrical hogs. The homes, some good and some not

so good, and the big barns are usually sheltered behind a windbreak of trees and surrounded by yard, garden, orchard, and perhaps feed lots, the whole comprising 2 to 4 acres. There is commonly a hog pasture of 1 to 10 acres; a cattle and horse pasture of 10 to 30 acres; a hayfield of uncertain size; the rest of the farm is given over to growing grain. . . . This is not a land to thrill one who loves hills, wild landscape, mountain panorama, waterfalls, babbling brooks, and nature undisturbed. In this flat land of food crops and murky streams, rich with silt and the odor of pigs, man must find thrills in other things, perhaps in travel, print, radio or movie.[4]

This *was* the land of the small independent farmer who by dint of hard work and by keeping up with new techniques through farm journals, agricultural experiment station bulletins, and the advice of county agricultural agents earned a good living on his 80 or more acres. When land prices rose, many such farmers sold out and retired in town or perhaps in the milder climates of Florida or California. But the Corn Belt is no longer the place for the young farmer with little capital; farms, machinery, and livestock may require a $100,000 investment, perhaps much more in coming decades. It was estimated in 1969 that for optimal production a two-man hog farm required a capital investment of $360,000 including 770 acres of land; a two-man cash-grain farm required $900,000 and 1,641 acres. Farms valued at $1,000,000 are ceasing to become a rarity.

In Iowa, the typical Corn Belt state, the average farm was 150 acres in 1900, 240 acres in 1969. In 1900 the farmer required almost 150 man-hours to produce 100 bushels of corn, and in 1970 only 7 man-hours sufficed; machinery, fertilizer, and pest killers had largely replaced muscle and sweat. The conversion of small-scale farming to big business (now called agribusiness) is far from complete. In western Iowa, for example, of almost 1,000

[4] J. Russell Smith and M. Ogden Phillips, *North America*, Harcourt, Brace, New York, 1940, p. 369.

Modern machinery on an eastern Nebraska farm. (USDA)

farms averaging 275 acres, 40 of them were less than 10 acres in size. Many of the larger farm businesses till additional acreages by renting nearby land from retired farmers or absentee owners. The type of modern Corn Belt farming varies with farm size and location: the smaller farm sells little of its crops and specializes in feeding a variety of livestock: beef cattle, hogs, and possibly poultry; the larger farms specialize in grain sold in the market.

The feed-grain livestock farm may be illustrated from two somewhat different farm areas. In Iowa the basic fodder is obtained from an annual rotation of corn, soybeans or oats, and meadow with an extra year in meadow on the sloping land and an extra year in corn on especially flat land. Permanent pasture occupies the slopes along a small stream. Although many calves are raised on the farm, money is needed to buy additional livestock from western ranches for "finishing." Fertilizer use may be

high, especially on the mediocre soils where manure and crop rotation do not make up the huge soil-nutrient requirements of high-yielding hybrid corn. The farmer's business is no longer simple tillage and livestock feedings. In order to compete, his techniques must be scientific and his market judgment must be sound. If the farmer has been especially successful, a new ranch-type house typical of middle- or upper-class suburbia may be added to the farm equipment.

Iowa cities Much of Iowa's industry is based on the processing of food or the production of farm equipment. Des Moines, founded in 1843 as a military post, is at the junction of the Des Moines and Raccoon rivers, a fact considered significant when water transport was important. Many of its modern activities are service industries including regional federal offices, universities, insurance offices, and the publication of farm journals. These and other commercial activities far surpass industrial employment, which is only one-fifth of the total.

Except for fewer governmental functions, similar characteristics are found in other Iowa cities such as Davenport, Cedar Rapids, and Waterloo. Most Iowa cities are commercially tributary to Chicago to which they are connected by a variety of rail and highway routes. Some of these cities are outliers of the Commercial-Manufacturing Core, and Iowa is sufficiently close to its western edge to be absorbed into that belt in coming decades.

Eastern feed-grain livestock farming

East of the arbitrary boundary of the Midwest, Corn Belt farming is also common. In central and northern Indiana and Ohio, glaciation has produced a great variety of soils within a small area: sandy ridges, rolling areas of silt, and low-lying muck soils. Much of the land has been drained by tile; in fact, the amount of drained land there exceeds that in the Mississippi flood-plain. The basic crop remains corn, which with soybeans makes up about half the crop acreage. On this once-wooded land, soils are more acid and less fertile than in the prairie; consequently larger applications of lime and fertilizer are needed to produce high yields. The combination of products varies from section to section and even from farm to farm; hogs are the principal product in the south, with more emphasis on dairy products northward.

Cash-grain farming

In some areas where the land is especially level or where markets are nearby, cash-grain farming replaces the more traditional livestock economy. The yields per acre obtained by some cash-grain farmers are very high. The *Farm Journal* (November 1965) reported 125-bushel-per-acre wheat, 8-ton alfalfa, and whole counties averaging 120 bushels of corn. The same magazine gave an example of an Illinois farm averaging 200 bushels of corn per acre on 550 acres. How was it possible to obtain yields more than twice the state average? The farmer spaced his rows only 20 inches apart, and applied 2 tons of limestone per acre every other year and 200 pounds of potash and 225 pounds of anhydrous ammonia per acre every year.

Peoria exemplifies a medium-size city in the Illinois cash-grain area. It gained commercial importance because at its port Mississippi steamers transshipped their cargo to barges. Grain provided the raw material for its numerous breweries and distilleries; many of its other manufactures are farm-related, for example, food packing, farm machinery, and wire fencing.

The general farming region and St. Louis

From northern Missouri southward the vegetation of the undulating prairie gradually changes to forest cover. The terrain becomes rougher, changing to open hills, outliers of the low but dissected Ozark Plateau. The rural population, both human and animal, thins out, and a type of general farming, including corn, wheat, dairying, and root crops, replaces the more intensive Corn Belt farming. The character of this region is the trans-Mississippi counterpart of the low plateaus adjoining the Ohio Valley. On the northeastern edge of this area is St. Louis, a city which arose more because of trade routes than the surrounding farm economy.

The monumental arch at the St. Louis waterfront memorializes its historic position as the "Gateway to the West." There in 1764 a French trading post was established where a bluff overlooked the Mississippi. Its position was well served by water transport. A few miles upstream, the Missouri provided a river route northwest to the Northern Rockies; a few miles farther north on the east bank the Illinois River provided access to the Great Lakes; and 140 miles downstream the Ohio joined the Mississippi.

These St. Louis locational advantages have been used in diverse ways during the past two centuries. Until 1817 St. Louis was primarily a fur-trading center. Then, with the beginning of steamboat traffic, it became a major river port where freight was transshipped from the smaller upstream boats to the larger river steamers going southward. In the middle-nineteenth century shallow draft vessels penetrated 2,000 miles up the Missouri. In 1857 the first railroad connected East St. Louis with the Atlantic Coast via Cincinnati, a line of great importance in moving Union troops from Virginia to the Mississippi Valley. During the Civil War, St. Louis was a Union military base and a supplier of goods and munitions for Union armies down the valley.

After the war the city resumed its position as a major trading center for the Mississippi Valley. The first bridge across the Mississippi was completed there in 1874. In the 1870s, St. Louis became the main wholesale and industrial center for the area to the south and southwest.

The St. Louis SMSA has many nearby natural resources. Adjacent Illinois has coal and oil; larger supplies of oil and natural gas are available in Oklahoma and southern Kansas. The Ozark Plateau of southern Missouri provides lead, zinc, iron ore, timber, and hides. The better farmlands to the north and east and down the Mississippi provide a great variety of crops: cotton, corn, wheat, soybeans, and fruits—all used in St. Louis industries.

The warehouses and older factories are clustered in St. Louis, especially along the waterfront and the railroads; the newer factories are more likely to be sprinkled in the suburbs. The lighter types of industry are commonly manufactured in St. Louis, Missouri, whereas the Illinois side generally has the heavier industries. St. Louis resembles Chicago (and most large metropolises) in that it is encircled by industrial and residential satellites. The central city has a population of only 600,000, but the SMSA total is nearly 2,500,000.

The St. Louis SMSA is one of the most diversified metropolitan areas in the United States. For example, its distribution of employment by occupations includes most groups and is about the average for urban United States. Its largest industrial groups—food packing, transportation equipment, and machinery—are well diversified; for example, transportation equipment includes aircraft, motor vehicles, and railroad shops.

Missouri River cities   A number of cities along the Missouri are within the western Corn Belt, but their business is based on their function in connecting diverse regions. Before the railways penetrated beyond the Mississippi, fur traders, military units, and prospective settlers sailed by river steamer to convenient points, where they outfitted themselves for the journey across the Great Plains (Figure 5.14).

The location of Kansas City was significant because there the Missouri turns northward and the Kansas (Kaw) Valley provided a route westward. This was the eastern end of the Santa Fe and Oregon trails and, after the Civil War, the collecting point for the grain of the adjacent Corn Belt, the hard winter wheat of Kansas, and the cattle of the central Plains. Its port is still of importance, and its rail, highway, air, and financial connections have made it a growing commercial center. Its Federal Reserve Bank, for example, serves an area to the west extending beyond the Rockies and southward into Oklahoma and northern New Mexico (Figure 5.15).

The elevators, flour mills, stockyards, and packing houses of Kansas City are still important, but the city also caters to the more complicated needs of farmers and ranchers by manufacturing feeds, farm implements, and portable storage bins, and by serving as a headquarters for numerous farm organizations.

The growth of Council Bluffs and Omaha dates from 1863 when railway construction of the first transcontinental line began westward. Soon other railroads converged on Council Bluffs to make connections with the Union Pacific. Although Council Bluffs developed railroad shops and grain elevators, it has now become subordinate to Omaha to which two-fifths of its workers commute. In addition to its

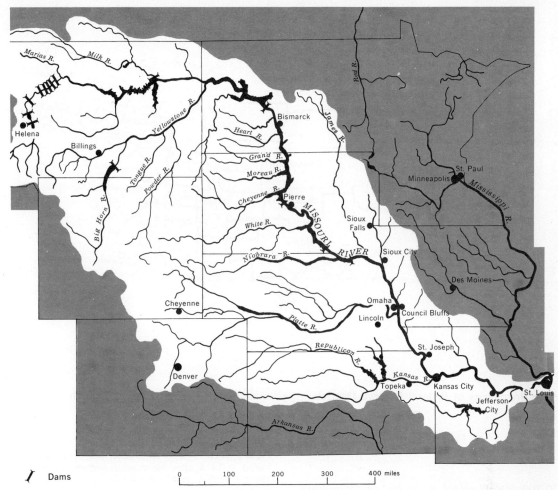

Dams

| 0 | 100 | 200 | 300 | 400 miles |

Figure 5.14 The location of cities on the Missouri River was originally due to river transportation, which is today of minor importance. The western tributaries of the Missouri were not navigable, but did provide water for early travelers across the plains.

railroad and meat-packing industries, Omaha has about 40 insurance companies as a major secondary industry. Nationally, it is significant as the headquarters of the Strategic Air Command.

The Dairy Belt In most of Michigan and Wisconsin and along the Mississippi Valley north of Burlington, Iowa, the land is better suited for hay and pasture than for grain. Dairy farms require a much smaller investment than the larger Corn Belt farms, and the farmer makes a living by intensive year-round work. Corn and other grains are grown mainly for fodder. This wooded area of low but rolling-to-

rough relief is the domain of the dairy cow; although beef cattle, hogs, and poultry are common, the Holstein and other dairy breeds are most conspicuous. Generally the soils are acid and require considerable liming and fertilizer. Because the winters are long, huge barns and tall silos which maintain the herds through the winter are dominant landscape features.

The dairy farmer's product varies with local custom and equipment and with distance

Drawn by R.W. Galvin, Cart

—— Boundaries of Federal Reserve Districts —— Boundaries of Federal Reserve Branch Territories

✪ Board of Governors of the Federal Reserve System

◉ Federal Reserve Bank Cities   • Federal Reserve Branch Cities

Figure 5.15 The Federal Reserve Districts were delimited in 1914 after the presentation of testimony by interested cities. Within a year after the districts were established, minor revisions proved necessary. Thus northern New Jersey was transferred from the Philadelphia to the New York district, and central Wisconsin was shifted from Minneapolis to Chicago. Why do most of the districts extend westward from the Federal Reserve Bank cities? (Note that Alaska and Hawaii are in the Twelfth District.) (Board of Governors, Federal Reserve System)

to the market. Near large metropolitan areas milk is generally shipped fresh although seasonal surpluses may be converted into cheese and dried milk. Cream is shipped to fairly distant markets, for example, from Wisconsin to New York City. More isolated farmers are likely to market most of their product as Class 2 milk, that is, milk to be processed into butter, cheese, or powdered or evaporated milk. Trade in milk and milk products illustrates the general rule for most staple commodities that prices are determined at major urban markets and prices elsewhere are set by these prices less freight.

Minneapolis–St. Paul The northern counterpart of Kansas City is the Twin Cities SMSA, strategically situated as the commercial center of the Ninth Federal Reserve District, often

called the Upper Midwest. The first European settlement (1819) was at Fort Snelling on a bluff overlooking the junction of the Minnesota and Mississippi rivers and guarding the routes leading to easy portages to Lake Superior. The well-wooded countryside, studded with attractive lakes, provided valuable hardwoods; southward and westward the bison-stocked prairies offered potential pastures and fertile farmlands. In 1841, St. Paul was established at the head of navigation on the Mississippi.

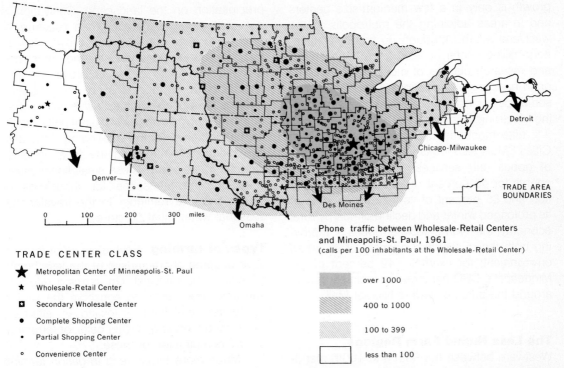

TRADE CENTER CLASS

★ Metropolitan Center of Minneapolis-St. Paul

★ Wholesale-Retail Center

▣ Secondary Wholesale Center

● Complete Shopping Center

• Partial Shopping Center

○ Convenience Center

Phone traffic between Wholesale-Retail Centers and Mineapolis-St. Paul, 1961
(calls per 100 inhabitants at the Wholesale-Retail Center)

over 1000

400 to 1000

100 to 399

less than 100

Figure 5.16 The Minneapolis Federal Reserve District has a hierarchy of cities and towns focused on the Twin Cities. The commercial influence of the Twin Cities may be measured by the volume of telephone calls from outlying areas. Would you expect this urban hierarchy to function differently than in the Chicago area (Figure 5.9)? Note that the two hierarchies are plotted on slightly different criteria. (Data from maps from The Upper Midwest Research and Development Council)

Just before the Civil War, annual steamboat arrivals there averaged nearly a thousand, mostly from downriver. St. Paul became the political capital and its port the focus from which roads and railroads radiated into the new state (1858). Minnesota's subsequent settlement was jointly stimulated by the Homestead Act of 1862 and by the efforts of railroads to settle lands acquired by congressional land grants. Early settlers had been mainly from the older Eastern states, but for decades after the Civil War, Scandinavians poured into the hinterland of the Twin Cities.

Minneapolis started as a manufacturing village (1848) first utilizing the power of the Falls of St. Anthony to saw lumber, later to grind wheat from the prairies. Minneapolis was at a convenient river crossing since the Mississippi Gorge impeded crossings for 10 miles downstream. Today Minneapolis and St. Paul cooperate, sharing, for example, an airport, a baseball team, and a metropolitan planning commission; in 1890 their rivalry was so bitter

that both cities falsified census returns in an attempt to outdo each other.

St. Paul possesses a large stockyard and such industries as paper products, Scotch tape, household appliances, and farm machinery. Commercially its business hinterland is mainly eastward, including northwestern Minnesota and western Michigan. Generally these are dairying, lumbering, and mining areas with stagnant populations except near St. Paul itself.

Minneapolis, now somewhat larger in population and in business, is the major financial and commercial center for a huge area extending north to Canada and west to central Montana. Much of its commercial hinterland has a declining rural and small city population;

growth is only in a few medium-size centers and in areas adjoining the metropolis to the west and south. Although no longer a major flour-milling center, it retains the head offices and research centers of most of the nation's grain-handling organizations. Minneapolis has some special industries such as those producing electronic controls.

Like most metropolitan areas, the Twin Cities SMSA also looks inward for many sales of goods and services. The metropolis accounts for 45 percent of Minnesota's population and 55 percent of its income. In spite of its prolonged winter and decline of nearby rural economy, the Twin Cities metropolis is improving both the quality and quantity of its urban environment; for example, 40 percent of the Minneapolis CBD has been completely rebuilt around the automobile-free Nicolet Mall.

The Less Humid Farm Regions

Westward between the 96th and 100th meridians, water becomes a scarce commodity away from streams fed by the melting snows of the Rocky Mountains; farming changes from a business to a gamble. Indeed it must, if the farmer depends on rain which, for example, in one county in central South Dakota, ranged in 28 years from 9 to 26 inches annually; during the same period wheat yields varied from 3 to 16 bushels and in 3 years the wheat crop failed completely. With high risks from drought, plant disease, locusts, hail, and wind erosion, not to mention fluctuating wheat prices, it is not surprising that the farmer wants crop insurance, soil banks, price supports, and other forms of governmental aid. The farmer spreads his risk by using drought-resistant sorghum and rye grass, dry-farming techniques, cattle, and, where possible, some irrigation. Farms must be large since per acre yields are low except on irrigated land. The average farm occupies about 1 square mile, but toward the western margin of the region the average size in some counties is 6 to 10 square miles.

The person flying over the rural lands west of the Missouri River can see the effects of low

precipitation on the landscape. Cultivation is not continuous; strips of green (pasture or grain) alternate with strips of brown (fallow) near the scattered farmhouses and are islands of cultivation amid a sea of brown or gray grassland in spring. Most of the tributary streams have been dammed with small earthen dams, looking from the air like giant pollywogs— the blunt "head" (of the lake) being at the dam and the reservoir forming the tapering body stretching upstream. These small linear reservoirs dot the landscape for thousands of square miles, a reminder to the traveler that seasonal water must be stored.

Types of farming Several types of farming have become characteristic of the less humid regions in the Midwest. *Dry farming* refers to any techniques used to conserve the limited soil water: mulching, fallowing in alternate years, strip cropping, shelter belts, or terracing, or any combination of these.

Much more intensive is *irrigation farming* in which water which fell as rain or snow on the Rockies is used to supplement the modest local precipitation. Most of this water is obtained from and used near transverse surface streams; less common but locally significant is irrigation water either obtained from artesian wells or pumped from underlying aquifers.

Stock farms (*ranches*) provide another way of reducing risks. Such farms must be large and must have a dependable stream or underground water which can be pumped to the surface. Some land is devoted to crops including hay; grain crops which fail to mature may be used for fodder. Most farms in this region today have some cattle; whether a farmer is classified as a stock farmer depends on whether his stress is primarily on beef rather than grain.

Several types of farming are based on the relation of the farm worker's residence to the fields. *Sidewalk farming* is done by farmers who live in town and drive out to their fields when work needs to be done; another version of this type of migratory farmer has moved into town so that his family may have the benefits of better schooling, hospitals, and town social life. *Suitcase farming* is done by the farmer who works on a number of farms, commonly in different latitudes, so that the periods of heavy work come at different times of the year on each farm. A week is sufficient for the harvest on the average wheat farm. The suitcase farmer's equipment is transported by truck, and his family may move with him in mobile homes. By combining one or more winter wheat farms with a spring wheat farm, his labor is better distributed and his risk from local drought reduced. In many cases farm work is performed by migratory work groups who work on contract for absentee landlords.

The Spring Wheat Belt One of the great wheat surplus areas of the world is the Red River Valley, an area of rich black lacustrine soils. The farm products may be spring wheat, dairy cattle, potatoes, flax, sugar beets, soybeans, or clover, or more likely a combination of several of these. Drought is rare; in fact, the soils are often difficult to till in spring because of excessive moisture. However, the growing season is short; the farmer must work fast to get the maximum crop from his extensive acreage (average about 500 acres) before winter comes. Large machinery and mass production methods are conspicuous on the huge flat fields.

West of the Red River Valley, the land is rolling and is less humid; the tall grain elevators loom on the horizon long before the market towns become visible. In eastern North Dakota, the land is largely in spring wheat. To the west, cattle and sheep gradually become the predominant sources of income. Work there is highly concentrated in the summer season, resulting in under-utilization of manpower during the winter. In North Dakota, industries are almost entirely related to agriculture or mining.

An agricultural state South Dakota, including parts of three farming regions, can be used as an example of the distribution of income in an agricultural economy. In 1971 its 663,000 people had a total personal income

of $2,320 million, of which $435 million was classified as farm income. Another major source of income ($300 million) was trade, most of which was in farm products or in goods sold to farmers. South Dakota's industrial income ($135 million) is also related to farming because 71 percent of all industrial employment is in meat-packing and other food products industries. Thus, although in 1970 44 percent of the South Dakota population was urban and 30 percent was rural nonfarm, most of the former group earned their living by performing services for farmers.

The western edge of South Dakota is ranch country bisected by the wooded Black Hills whose lumbering and gold-mining activities add some diversity to people's income. Three railroad lines and six through highways handle west-east traffic including tourist and other through traffic. Except around the Black Hills the towns are small, and there are many sparsely populated counties. Even the capital, Pierre, has less than 10,000 people and no sizable industries. Eastward, population density increases, crops become more important, but livestock still exceed crops in value; the railroad and road net thickens, counties are smaller in size, and county seats are larger in population. The only SMSA, Sioux Falls (95,000), is on the eastern border of the state.

South Dakota family incomes are fairly high in the counties with cities, but extremely low (50 to 70 percent of the United States average) in the numerous counties containing Indian reservations. With cold winters and drought-ridden summers, and being somewhat isolated from Anglo-American population centers, South Dakota seems likely to continue to provide agricultural produce, a few minerals, and some tourist services; but its outlook for major urban growth seems poor.

The Winter Wheat Belt Although the products of the two wheat belts are similar, the seasonal work schedules are different. In most of the Dakotas winter is too severe for crops, whereas in Kansas wheat is planted in the fall and harvested in early summer. Corn, sorghum, and other summer crops may enter into the crop rotation. Generally, hard winter wheat and beef cattle bring in cash income; other crops are used for fodder. As in the Dakotas, the farms become larger to the west; large machinery owned by traveling teams of farm workers is characteristic, and cattle graze on lands too rough or infertile for cultivation.

Cities in the Winter Wheat Belt   The largest city is Wichita, whose leading source of employment is durable goods manufacturing. The outstanding industry is aircraft assembly, attracted by the high percentage of clear days suitable for testing planes. The city also has industries to serve its agricultural hinterland, for example, food packing.

The growth of Wichita suggests that urban industry may be able to counterbalance the decline in farm employment. In the Corn Belt and the Winter Wheat Belt the majority of cities between 10,000 and 50,000 population showed substantial increases in both population and employment. Many of these cities had small manufacturing plants in addition to food processing. Small towns away from metropolitan areas were less successful in holding their populations. Nevertheless, although Kansas experienced a 3.2 percent population increase from 1960 to 1970, it had a net out-migration of 140,000. It appears that many activities can be expanded in the Plains states, such as employment related to oil production, but so far such expansion has not sufficed to make up for the decline in farm employment.

Two ranching subregions   In the Flint Hills of eastern Kansas the country appears drier than it is, and the westward traveler seems to pass directly from the Corn Belt into a range-land of nearly 5 million acres. In part the stony soil is too thin for crops, but the rain suffices for a lush growth of bluestem grass. Some of the grassland is the result of human decisions about the use of the environment rather than the physical limitations of the environment. Much tillable land is kept for grazing because

it is owned by ranchers with business connections to the southwest. Cattle, locally bred or fattened after arrival from Texas ranches, produce luscious steaks and contribute, along with the Corn Belt, to Kansas City stockyards and slaughterhouses. "K.C." steaks are often featured in restaurants from Texas to the Rockies.

Much of western Nebraska consists of sand dunes which support an ample prairie grass cover. The valleys have local water supplies and meadow sufficiently damp to yield good crops of hay. This is beef cattle country, somewhat richer than most of the semiarid grazing lands.

From the air the many ranch regions show a surprising number of small bodies of water. Ponds dot the landscape, some created by damming streams, others fed by windmills. Large reservoirs store the floodwaters of rivers once noted for their undependable water supply. Along the Platte and other streams, ribbons of irrigated land appear dark green in summer, yielding fodder crops such as alfalfa. As farms and ranches are merged into larger units, most of the newer units contain some irrigated land.

THE AMERICAN HEARTLAND

The vast Central Lowland, containing one-third of the nation's population and producing one-third of its income, is probably the largest single piece of good land in the world. It has been exploited by an energetic people using new industrial and agricultural techniques to turn out a huge per capita material output which has lifted most levels of Anglo-American society to a standard of affluence unmatched in most of the world. Along with this material advance, a relatively democratic society has fused together diverse peoples. Although much leadership remains in the Atlantic Megalopolis, the Central Lowland has made equal contributions to the American economic and social fabric.

Unfortunately all these marvels have taken place within such a short time that many side effects from this rapidly changing economy have not been anticipated. The deification of technology and industrial growth has brought about resource shortages and air, water, and noise pollution. The growth has been most concentrated in the lower Great Lakes region where pollution has gotten most out of hand. At the same time technology has created machines which have created unemployment in the farm, mining, and forest industries. In turn the displaced workers have flocked into the metropolitan areas, creating social, economic, and political problems with which the cities were not prepared to cope. These problems are not unique to the Central Lowland or even to the United States, but in the Central Lowland there seems to be the space and other resources to solve these problems.

SELECTED REFERENCES

BAUGHMAN, ROBERT W.: *Kansas in Maps,* Kansas State Historical Society, Topeka, 1961.

BOWMAN, MARY J., and W. WARREN HAYNES: *Resources and People in East Kentucky,* published for Resources for the Future, Inc., Johns Hopkins, Baltimore, 1963.

BROWN, ROBERT H., and PHILIP C. TIDEMAN: *Atlas of Minnesota Occupancy,* Minnesota Atlas Company, St. Cloud, 1961.

CUTLER, IRVING: *Chicago Metropolis of the Mid-continent,* The Geographic Society of Chicago, 1973.

Detroit 1990, An Urban Design Concept for the Inner City, City of Detroit, no date.

HART, JOHN FRASER: "The Middle West," *Annals* AAG, vol. 62 (1972), pp. 258–282.

—— and RUSSELL B. ADAMS: "Twin Cities," *Focus,* vol. 20 (February 1970), pp. 1–11.

HIDORE, JOHN J.: "Supplemental Irrigation in the Upper Mississippi Valley," *Professional Geographer,* vol. 19 (1967), pp. 184–188.

KINGSBURY, ROBERT C.: *An Atlas of Indiana,* Indiana University, Department of Geography, Bloomington, Occasional Publication No. 5, 1970.

KNUDTSON, ARVID C., and REX W. COX: *Upper Midwest Agriculture: Structure and Problems,* Upper Midwest Research and Development Council and University of Minnesota, Minneapolis, 1962. There are also other studies in this series.

KOLLMORGEN, W. M., and G. F. JENKS: "Suitcase Farming in Sully County, South Dakota," *Annals,* AAG, vol. 48 (1958), pp. 27–40.

——, and D. S. SIMONETT: "Grazing Operations in the Flint Hills–Bluestem Pastures of Chase County, Kansas," Annals, AAG, vol. 5 (1965), pp. 260–90.

LEOPOLD, ALDO: *A Sand County Almanac,* Oxford, (paperback), New York, 1968. A naturalist's view of a small part of rural Wisconsin and the broader issue of conservation.

MALIN, J. C.: *The Grassland of North America,* privately printed, Lawrence, Kansas, 1948.

MATHER, E. COTTON: "The American Great Plains," *Annals,* AAG, vol. 62 (1972), pp. 237–257.

MAYER, HAROLD M., and RICHARD C. WADE: *Chicago: Growth of a Metropolis,* University of Chicago Press, Chicago, 1969. Excellent illustrations and text on the historical geography of a regional capital.

MILLER, E. W.: "The Industrial Development of the Allegheny Valley," *Economic Geography,* vol. 29 (1953), pp. 388–404.

Numerous publications of the state agricultural experiment stations are of value, e.g., *Soils of the North Central Region of the United States,* University of Wisconsin Agricultural Experiment Station Bulletin 544, Madison. 1960.

OTTOSON, H. W. (ed.): *Land and People in the Northern Plains Transition Area,* University of Nebraska Press, Lincoln, 1966.

PHILBRICK, A. K.: "Principles of Areal Functional Organization in Regional Human Geography," *Economic Geography,* vol. 33 (1957), pp. 306–336.

——: "The Nodal Water Region of North America," *The Canadian Geographer,* vol. 8 (1956), pp. 182–187.

REINEMANN, M. W.: "The Pattern and Distribution of Manufacturing in the Chicago Area," *Economic Geography,* vol. 36 (1960), pp. 139–144.

SMITH, J. RUSSELL, and M. OGDEN PHILIPS: *North America,* Harcourt, Brace, New York, 1940.

THROWER, NORMAN J. W.: *Original Survey and Land Survey,* published for Association of American Geographers by Rand McNally, Chicago, 1966.

U.S. DEPARTMENT OF AGRICULTURE: *Soil,* Yearbook of Agriculture, Washington, 1957. This and other agricultural yearbooks provide excellent source materials. See also, *Power to Produce,* Yearbook of Agriculture, 1960, and for statistical details, *Agricultural Statistics* (annual), Washington.

WEAVER, JOHN C.: "Crop Combination Regions in the Middle West," *Geographical Review,* vol. 44 (1954), pp. 175–200.

6

THE SOUTH

What is commonly called the "South" includes an extensive area having long, hot, humid summers and short, mild winters, with a social culture influenced by the heritage of the plantation system, black slavery, and the Civil War. In this area "cotton was king," although tobacco, peanuts, corn, sweet potatoes, and hogs added some diversity to farming; manufacturing was not dominant, but a few areas produced textiles, tobacco products, furniture, and other simple manufactures. This was the traditional South, and the current South is still influenced by many of these former conditions and characteristics. But cotton is no longer king, and it is possible to travel over much of the South without seeing any cotton.

It is difficult to define the boundaries of the South. The U.S. Census includes 16 states in its South, spreading from Delaware to Texas. The regionalization of the Office of Business Economics (O.B.E) includes in the Southeast all the states south of the Potomac and the Ohio plus Arkansas and Louisiana. This book uses the O.B.E. Southeast as a starting point for its South, but excludes the northerly edges already discussed under the Atlantic Mega-

This satellite image taken 560 miles from the earth shows a cross section of the southern quarter of the Florida Peninsula from the Miami-Palm Beach Megalopolis westward across the Everglades to south of Naples on the Gulf of Mexico. (NASA)

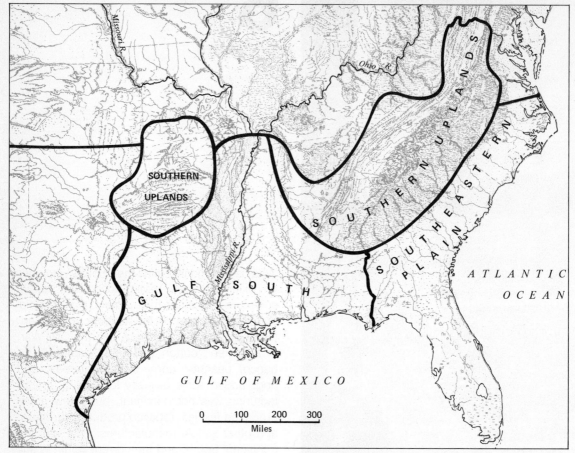

Figure 6.1 The subdivisions of the South reflect relief in the Southern Uplands and commercial orientation elsewhere. (Base map by A. K. Lobeck. Reprinted with permission of The Geographical Press, Hammond, Inc.)

lopolis and the Ohio Basin and adds the petrochemical area of the Texas Gulf Coast.

The South (as considered here) occupies about one-seventh of the nation's land and houses one-fifth of its people. As a whole, the region is well below the national average in per capita income, but it contains progressive areas, especially in Florida and the larger cities. Improvements have been made in raising living and educational levels, lessening racial discrimination, and modernizing cities, but much remains to be done. Considering the recent tendency of Americans to move toward milder climates, the South seems likely to increase in relative importance in the national economy.

Although the South is a unit in the minds of many Southerners, for geographic analysis it is desirable to divide it into three broad regions (Figure 6.1).

THREE SOUTHERN REGIONS

1 *The Southern Uplands,* sometimes called the Upper or Upland South, forms a borderland between the South and the Central Lowland. This region was less influenced by slavery and the plantation system than the other two regions. Its problems arise from declining employment in farming and mining and consequent out-migration; much of the region is characterized by poverty. Its advantages are its central location close to well-settled areas and its natural beauty.

2 *The Southeastern Plain,* a climatically mild coastal lowland, suffers from a variety of soil and drainage problems. Tree farming and specialized agriculture provide good incomes for a minute proportion of the labor force; in southern Florida the resort and retirement community booms have developed a dynamic economy.

3 *The Gulf South* has much physical resemblance to the Southeastern Plain, but it has additional resources: petroleum, natural gas, salt, sulfur, and the alluvial soil of the Mississippi floodplain. The exploitation of these resources employs a small fraction of the population; poverty is a serious problem for those unable to find a place in mechanized agriculture, mining, and industry.

All three regions are in transition from an agricultural raw material economy to an industrial economy. No sharp boundaries separate these regions, and the region in total has many common distinctive features, potentialities, and problems. Life in the South still has a regional accent; but television and the southward infiltration of Yankee industry and tourists have broken down its former regional semi-isolation. Today many Southern cities look much like Northern cities except in carefully preserved older sections such as downtown Charleston, South Carolina. Nor are the Southern problems unique: the North and West also have race riots, rural and urban slums, traffic congestion, and urban renewal. The South has its prosperous industrial centers as well as a rural unemployment problem more serious than that in the Midwest.

Each Southern region has certain problems whose solutions contain economic and social potentialities. The Southern Uplands, blessed with attractive settings, a mild climate, and adequate water resources, offers many homesites, industrial sites, and recreational possibilities. There, close to the worst Appalachia problem areas, amazing progress has been made in the present century with private industry, community leaders, and the TVA providing leadership. On the Southeastern Plain the proper management of soil and water and mild climate have attracted subtropical farming, lumber industries, and an influx of settlers desiring to avoid cold winters. The Gulf South's wealth of alluvial soil, although still productive, yields only a fraction of the income from industrial and commercial development stimulated by petroleum, natural gas, sulfur, salt, and lumber. Although the South has both an aggregate and a per capita income below that of its Northern neighbors, the region remains a huge market; when (and if) the levels of living of its large population can be raised to national levels, it may become the largest Anglo-American regional market. This internal market will develop demands for goods and services such as are already perceptible in progressive centers such as Atlanta, Charlotte, and Houston. These three metropolitan areas already have an average per household income close to that of Los Angeles and St. Louis.

Climate and Vegetation

The Southern life-style is considerably influenced by the humid subtropical climate and related vegetation patterns. High humidity, a seasonal rhythm with more rainfall during the warmer half of the year, and considerable variation from day to day within each season are characteristic. The length of the frost-free period distinguishes the North from the South. In the South the growing season lasts at least half of the year (thus permitting the cultivation of subtropical crops such as cotton and peanuts). Along the Gulf Coast and in the Florida peninsula the growing season is at least nine months. Winters are generally short and mild; summers are long and often oppressive, but outdoor activities are possible all or most of the year. The gardening period is almost continuous, and deciduous trees are green most of the year.

Certain cultural features may be attributed

to the subtropical climate. Architects in the South are more concerned with keeping cool than with keeping warm; consequently such features as high ceilings, porches, cross ventilation, and shade trees have high priority. Contemporary upper- and middle-class houses as well as stores and office buildings have air conditioning, but many retain the previously noted architectural features which preceded air conditioning.

The Southern climate is far from uniform. In the Appalachian valleys, the 40° January average at Knoxville, for example, is only slightly warmer than in St. Louis where the January mean is 32°. On the coastal lowlands, for comparison, a 50° January average means pleasantly warm weather on sunny days. The midwinter traveler approaching the Gulf Coast will find a yellow-brown landscape a dozen miles inland; he may also find the leaves of deciduous trees being raked off the lawn in December. The Southern tourist season reaches a peak in late winter after springlike weather arrives in February. In summer the vegetation is lush, thunderstorms are heavy and frequent, and the humid heat slows the pace of human activity. In the more humid areas, Spanish moss drapes the trees, insects are plentiful, and any shade is welcomed. In central Georgia twice as much power is used for annual air conditioning as in Chicago; in winter only one-third as much fuel will be needed for heating as in Chicago, But when record-breaking cold waves bring 10° temperatures to New Orleans and zero weather to Atlanta, local heating systems prove inadequate and car radiators may burst.

The characteristic vegetation results from the combined influences of latitude, altitude, soil, moisture, and man. The oak-hickory forest common in the Southern Appalachians resembles the forest once common in Connecticut. The Piedmont and some parts of the Coastal Plain still have considerable remnants of the original oak-hickory-pine forest. Today the more southerly Coastal Plain is largely planted

in longleaf (slash) pine, the more northerly plain and much of the Piedmont in shortleaf (loblolly) pine. Within the Coastal Plain the floodplains have oak, gum, and bald cypress; areas along the Texas-Louisiana coast and in interior southern Florida are dotted with various kinds of lush prairie. Although cleared areas in fields and pastures are apparent in this vegetative blanket, the South generally is a land of trees without the broad vistas of cultivation so common in the Corn Belt.

Relief and the Problem of Water

The landform regions are essentially a continuation of those noted in the Atlantic Megalopolis: Coastal Plain, Piedmont, ridge and valley, and plateau. The Coastal Plains and the Piedmont sections are wider in the South, and the mountains are somewhat higher and broader. In both the South and the North the mountains are rainy and the streams tend to produce floods; generally in the South the flood problem is more severe, especially in the broad Mississippi floodplain and along the streams flowing from the rainy Appalachians to the Ohio Valley.

Climatologists classify the South as humid. Water surpluses are more a problem than water shortages. The Tennessee Valley dams and reservoirs, the levees along the Mississippi and its tributaries, and the drainage projects in coastal regions are all parts of the major problem—to keep or put water where men want it and to store water when it is not wanted.

Soils, drainage problems, and land use are closely related. In the mountainous and hilly areas and the Piedmont, soil erosion is a serious problem which has been lessened by the damming of streams, the terracing of hillsides, and the conversion of steeply sloping areas into pastures and orchards. On the Coastal Plain and on the alluvial plains of the Mississippi and smaller rivers, the nature of the soil and land use is controlled by hydrological conditions. The coastal fringes are unsettled except where sandy offshore islands and coasts provide resort sites or where, as in Louisiana and Texas, oil, gas, salt, or sulfur are exploited. With the exception of New Orleans the ports are sited on well-drained land or bluffs; most of the ports are on deep bays or up navigable streams.

The plain is partly swampy amid the dominant forest. Still further inland the Coastal Plain is occupied by sandy soils which are productive if well fertilized. Former lagoon areas with limy soils, such as the Black Belt of Alabama and Mississippi and the coastal prairies of the Gulf Coast west of the Mississippi, provide excellent pasture for cattle. The most productive agriculture is on the alluvial lands. For example, of the 42,000 square miles of Mississippi alluvium about half remains in swampy forest; and on the rest soybeans, cotton, rice, or sugarcane is cultivated, the exact crop depending on local soil and climatic conditions.

Soils and Rural Patterns

Most Southern soils are leached and especially lacking in phosphorus, nitrogen, lime, and humus. The soil remains unfrozen and unprotected throughout the winter; hence leaching and erosion continue all year. Many farmers, poor in both working capital and techniques, can harvest crops only at the expense of reducing their soil capital. One-quarter of all United States fertilizer is used in this region; more could profitably be applied. Although the long growing season and the generally humid weather aid crop growth, they also facilitate the multiplication of pests and plant diseases. Thus, for successful farming, this region requires careful soil management, including possible drainage and supplementary irrigation, pest controls, and heavy fertilization.

Soil drainage and climatic differences obviously do not entirely account for the local agricultural geography. Demands for cotton, tobacco, peanuts, early vegetables, citrus fruit, phosphates, naval stores, timber, resort and retirement facilities, as well as the position of each area in relation to the movements of peoples, have determined the timing of particular developments. Nevertheless, the localization of many of these activities on the Coastal Plain can today be largely explained in terms of climate, soil, and drainage, even though the accidents of history and the decisions of local leaders must be considered in explaining the details of development.

THE SOUTHERN UPLANDS

The hills, mountains, and plateaus which separate much of the South from the Central Lowland provide a paradox. This scenic region, located amid the most populated areas in the country, is characterized by economic and social backwardness, and large parts are almost rural slums. An imaginative federal project, the Tennessee Valley Authority (TVA), has greatly aided one part of this region, but much remains to be done. Many of the more ambitious people in these regions have migrated; local industries are largely slow-growth ones which offer modest employment at low wages.

The uplands are varied both in relief and in settlement patterns. In the wooded, moderately rugged Cumberland Plateau the hills rise to an even skyline and croplands and pasture occupy limited areas in the valleys. Because the land system was not based on a rectangular survey, in the uplands especially farm and county boundaries are very irregular. The older towns are along the trans-Appalachian routes; these and more isolated towns on the branch valleys engage in lumbering or coal mining.

Southeast of the sharp high edge of the Cumberland Plateau (the equivalent of the Allegheny Front in Pennsylvania) are the wooded, almost parallel Appalachian ridges and intervening valleys. Of these, the broadest and most significant is the well-settled limestone valley of the Tennessee, a part of the Great Valley corridor used by pioneers migrating southwestward. To the southeast rise the rounded crystalline Great Smokies, their well-

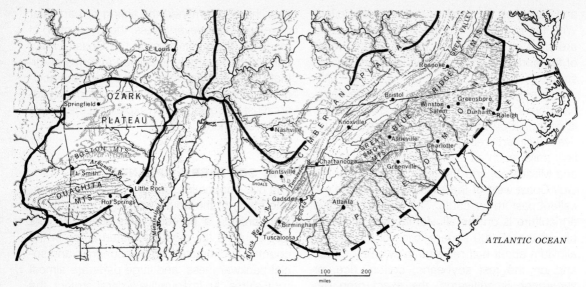

Figure 6.2 Landforms of the Southern Uplands. The boundaries of the subdivisions discussed can be identified from the physiographic symbols. Note that a small part of the northeastern corner of the region has been omitted because of the awkward shape of the region. (Base map copyright by A. K. Lobeck. Reprinted with permission of The Geographical Press, Hammond, Inc.)

forested slopes used today mainly for recreation; beyond, the steep Blue Ridge overlooks the hilly to gently rolling Piedmont, with its woodland and pasture and its rundown homesteads amid prosperous poultry and cattle farms.

Appalachian History and Culture

Toward the end of the eighteenth century, the lowlands in the coastal states were largely occupied by large estates. The earliest settlers who moved inland to the Appalachians selected the areas with limestone soils, but others were not dissatisfied with their poorer holdings. Although markets were distant, their corn could be concentrated into whiskey before shipment, and their livestock could be driven to market for ready cash. A farm in the Appalachians with 10 or 20 acres of tillable land, plus the forest's game, nuts, berries, and timber resources, provided them a standard of living well above that of the European peasant. A conservative society with many folk arts developed among people who had infrequent contact with lands and peoples beyond their valleys and coves (mountain hollows).

A transportation network evolved slowly.

Through routes traversed the Great Valley and crossed major gaps to the Piedmont and the Bluegrass, but there was no network of paved roads to serve the backcountry before 1930. Railroads extended the length of the Great Valley before the Civil War, and a few north-south lines developed soon after, but some local lines into the coalfields were not completed until World War II. Railroads speeded up the exploitation of the forests and the coalfields. These developments attracted immigrants who added nationality diversity to the Scotch-Irish and English strains. The settlement of the Ouachita and Ozark highlands occurred decades later but followed the same general pattern.

Appalachian Valleys and the TVA

Tremendous economic progress has occurred in the Great Valley from eastern West Virginia to Alabama. Between the Blue Ridge and the high edge of the Cumberland Plateau the val-

The highest TVA dam, Fontana Dam in North Carolina, rises 480 feet and can produce 202,000 kilowatts of electricity. The Great Smokies are rounded, wooded mountains, soaked annually by heavy rains and well suited to store water for downstream use. There are many pleasant acres for recreational use. (TVA)

leys provide easy routeways southwestward. These fertile valleys are formed on less-resistant rock, and many are drained by several streams. The many river gaps and some notches in the ridge tops provide narrow passes across the mountains on each side. Cities such as Knoxville and Chattanooga developed near each gap and at junctions between valley routes and gap routes.

Although not isolated from the adjacent South, the Appalachian valleys, at least as far south as Knoxville, were settled from the north. The wheat, corn, tobacco, hay, dairy products, and apples suggest a type of farming characteristic of southeastern Pennsylvania. Rich soils formed on limestone, and mediocre soils on shale characterize the land resource. Small farmers rather than planters till the land; both rural and city populations are overwhelmingly white. These facts caused the people in many southern Appalachian valleys to be neutral or pro-Union during the Civil War.

The TVA Industrial development in the Great Valley preceded the Tennessee Valley Authority by many decades; however, TVA did stimulate further growth. Why was this valley chosen for a new experiment in federal activity? The Tennessee River, rising in the rainiest part of the Appalachians, was a major source of flood-waters to the Ohio-Mississippi system. The river had been navigated during high water, but its water levels had proved uncertain. Various local improvements, attempted over a period of a century, failed to solve the problems of shoals, floods, and low water. During World War I, a dam at Muscle Shoals, northern Alabama, produced power for nitrate production, but a more comprehensive program was needed for flood control, navigation, and more power.

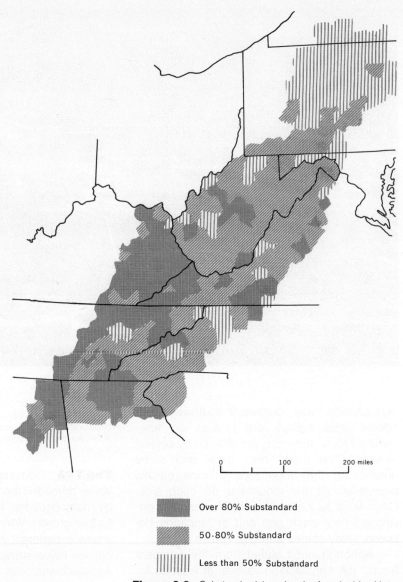

0   100   200 miles

■■■■ Over 80% Substandard

//// 50-80% Substandard

|||| Less than 50% Substandard

Figure 6.3 Substandard housing in Appalachia. Note that the Appalachia area includes some areas that are not part of the Southern Uplands. (After Maryland Department of Economic Development)

Revamping the river was no simple task: its headwaters, shared by four states, converged on the Great Valley of southeastern Tennessee. Obviously a number of dams were needed to control the river, but these dams would flood the best farmlands, require locks for navigation, and generate cheap power as a by-product. Such a comprehensive project was beyond the capacity of any state government or corporation.

The Tennessee Valley Authority, authorized by Congress in 1933, constructed 25 dams which converted the main stream and some tributaries into a chain of lakes (Figure 6.4); this created a 9-foot channel from Knoxville to the Ohio River. The cheap power generated at the dams attracted so much activity to

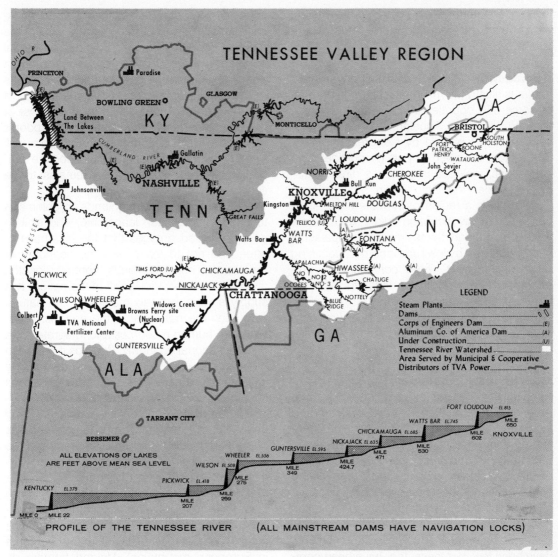

Figure 6.4 The Tennessee River rises in the rainier parts of the Appalachians and for this reason is a major contributor to Mississippi floods. The dams have converted much of the river into a series of lakes. Although the dams on the Mississippi and its tributaries hold back much potential flood water, the spring flood of 1973 demonstrated that the Mississippi system is far from being completely controlled. (TVA)

the valley that supplemental carboelectric plants became necessary to meet local power demands, and a huge nuclear power plant is now under construction. TVA moved many farmers from the flooded lands, teaching them to use modern farm methods to conserve the soil on their new lands and to plant forests on land unfit for tillage. All in all, TVA was the best example of regional planning the world had seen. It has controlled floods, provided a needed waterway, and raised the regional level

of living. Older centers have been stimulated into new economic growth, and even the small cities have felt the favorable impact of regional development. The Tennessee River now provides a connecting link between the Ohio Valley and the Interior South. Petroleum and grain move upstream; coal and stone come downstream.

Appalachia   A later example of government action is illustrated in Appalachia. It is an area of some 360 counties in 11 states being developed under the Appalachian Regional Development Act passed by Congress in 1965. The region, bounded in part by political considerations, includes large areas already discussed under the Ohio Basin. In landforms Appalachia is a region of intricately dissected plateaus, narrow mountain ridges, and narrow valleys. In human terms, most of Appalachia is characterized by low rural incomes, declining rural employment, and considerable outmigration. However, it also includes prosperous counties, especially in the Great Valley. Most of the population is urban and rural nonfarm; only 350,000 are classified as farm residents.

Appalachian problems   The problems of Appalachia have not been unique in Anglo-America. Farm populations have declined and farmlands have gone out of cultivation there just as they have in the hills of New England and southern Indiana. Coal production has declined because of competing fuels. Mining employment has declined even more because of strip mining and mechanization, but this has also occurred in southern Illinois. Schooling has been backward, and public improvements have been few, but these, too, have been common elsewhere where the tax base has been small. Inadequate roads have been especially serious in the rugged Appalachians where costs are high. Perhaps the most serious handicap has been the out-migration of the better educated and more energetic. Businesses such as coal mining, lumbering, and manufacturing in the larger towns and cities are controlled by corporations whose ownership and administration are outside Appalachia.

However, the situation is not entirely gloomy. Certain urban activities and services such as good communications and repair facilities that are part of the growth sector of the national economy have improved the regional economy. Although rugged relief brought about isolation in the past, the populated parts of the area now have greater accessibility. On the main roads it is possible to cross most of the highlands in an afternoon; on the poorer roads in a day. Whether improved roads will further aid local development or speed the emigration of the better workers remains to be seen.

A solution of the highlands' problems is to obtain the capital, leadership, and skill to develop the advantages that the hills have to offer, and not to try to rival the economy of the plains. These highlands, centrally located amid the more populous half of the nation, can supply a variety of raw materials. The natural resources are not lacking; the need is to develop the human resources and integrate them into the national economy. Perhaps it has been a mistake to consider Appalachia as a single unified region; instead the Cumberland Plateau should be considered in relation to such adjoining growth centers as Cincinnati and Louisville; to the south the economic success of the Great Valley, the Smokies, and the Blue Ridge must be looked for in relation to Birmingham, Atlanta, and Charlotte.

Appalachia is not free from physical handicaps (although travelers in Austria and Switzerland may consider Appalachian handicaps modest compared with those already overcome in European mountains). Upland farmers do suffer from the small and disconnected areas of level land and from the length of roads necessary to connect modest straight-line distances. In the more isolated areas the economy suffers from the lack of experience with resort business. Help, however, has not been lacking: it has come from the TVA, area redevelopment programs, such state projects as the Kentucky Mountain Parkway, and numerous privately endowed educational projects. Even with all this help, though, the reversal of a regional downtrend has not been easy, especially where

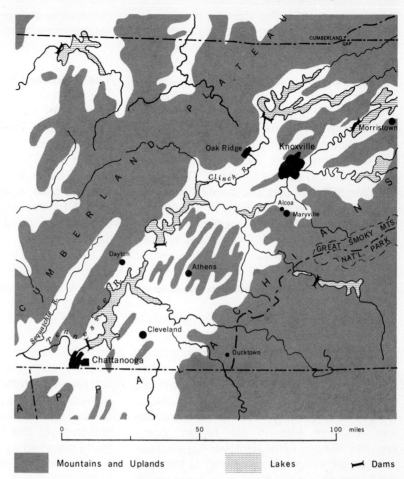

Figure 6.5 This map shows the most developed area in the TVA project. Note that the valley is subdivided by ridges and is by no means as flat as it appears on more generalized maps.

the residual population is above average in age, below average in education, and lacking in capital.

Urban populations Roanoke provides an example of the growth of Appalachia cities. Located strategically where the Roanoke River cuts a gap in the Blue Ridge, the town was unimportant until 1882 when the Norfolk and Western Railway established its western headquarters there, thence pushing its lines west into the Appalachian coalfields. Its transport functions were increased as a result of connections to the Great Valley rail route. Later, being in an area of declining rural population, Roanoke's modest wage level and labor surplus attracted industrialists producing such

goods as textiles, furniture, and electric machinery. These same advantages of labor surplus, cheap power, and low costs have also attracted a variety of industries to a cluster of small cities (Bristol, Johnson City, Kingsport, etc.) on the Virginia-Tennessee border, each producing relatively simple manufactures such as rayon, paper, furniture, and clothing. These advantages are widely available in the region, but are exploited only where alert businessmen have integrated them.

The two large cities in Appalachia, Knoxville (400,000) and Chattanooga (305,000), are located about 100 miles apart on the Tennessee River. Both have grown slowly in population as a result of a net out-migration in the last decade. Knoxville was a railroad junction and commercial center; later it attracted manufactures such as furniture and mine equipment. The availability of power has attracted special industries to the nearby area, such as aluminum at Alcoa and atomic energy at Oak Ridge.

Chattanooga has more industrial than commercial and service functions. During the Civil War this river port was the most strategic rail junction in the South. Early in this century the city developed industries which were common elsewhere in the region such as textiles, woodworking, and iron fabrication. Its excellent rail network permitted raw materials to be assembled easily and manufactured goods to be sent out to Eastern markets.

The largest city, Birmingham (739,000), is another slow-growing SMSA with a net out-migration. Birmingham is a steel producer, aided by coking coal, iron ore, and limestone all being mined locally. Other raw materials such as cement, concrete, gypsum, and plaster are all available locally. The city has one of the less attractive sites in the region, being crowded into one of the narrower Appalachian valleys. Just as rural incomes are low throughout Appalachia, in the three cities noted above personal incomes are not as high as the national average. Poverty and low incomes become more apparent in these Appalachian cities, whereas rural poverty is dispersed and less obvious throughout the scenic countryside.

The Blue Ridge and the Great Smokies
This tadpole-shaped area of rounded, wooded mountains, rising to over 6,000 feet, is largely recreational. Marginal farmlands occupy the valley and the lower slopes; towns and small cities are dispersed and few. Its resources are scenery, a mild but rainy climate, waterpower, lumber, and a few peripheral mineral deposits such as copper ore at Ducktown, Tennessee. The only metropolitan center is Asheville, the

commercial and recreational metropolis for the southwestern North Carolina Piedmont.

The Southern Piedmont
The Piedmont is a transitional subregion between the Appalachian Uplands and the Coastal Plain. The Piedmont stands out conspicuously on a map showing soil erosion (Figure 6.6). The region is not particularly high or hilly; rather it has the characteristics of an elevated plain which has been intricately dissected by streams. Its reddish sandy soils, derived from quartz-rich crystalline rock, are badly eroded.

Agricultural land use is changing. Cotton, corn, forage crops, and oats were once leading crops in the Piedmont, but their acreage has declined and cotton, for example, has almost disappeared. Forest, pasture, and orchards are occupying an increasing share of the land. Because many of the farmers entered the area from the North, the characteristic farm is small and owner-operated in contrast to the Southern plantation. The rural population is moderately dense, but full-time farming occupies only one-tenth of the population, most residents being classified as urban or rural nonfarm.

The larger cities are supported by a cluster of tributary industrial towns. On the population map these cities and towns form an irregular crescent from Raleigh, North Carolina, to Anderson, South Carolina, called the "Piedmont Crescent of Industry." An area of much sparser population southeast of this crescent separates the interior Piedmont towns from the fall-line cities.

Industrial growth The increased industrialization of the Piedmont during the present century has been attributed to such local raw materials as wood, cotton, and tobacco, and to nearby coal and hydroelectric power. No doubt these have been advantageous, but generally the raw materials could have been shipped to Northern factories and markets as cheaply or more cheaply than their products.

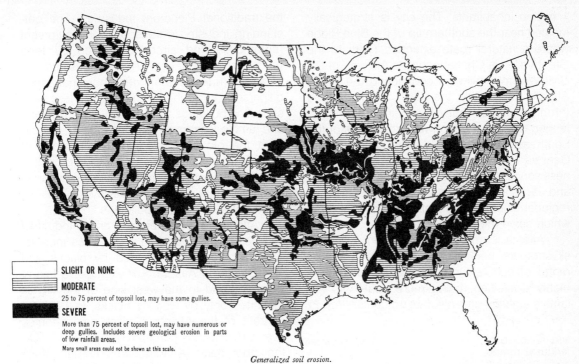

SLIGHT OR NONE

MODERATE

25 to 75 percent of topsoil lost, may have some gullies.

SEVERE

More than 75 percent of topsoil lost, may have numerous or deep gullies. Includes severe geological erosion in parts of low rainfall areas.

Many small areas could not be shown at this scale.

Generalized soil erosion.

Figure 6.6 Severe soil erosion is not limited to the Southeast; but with heavy, often torrential, rainfall and soil commonly unfrozen throughout the winter, it is not surprising that it is concentrated there. (USDA)

Cheap, cooperative labor has been more important; in 1971 Piedmont industrial wages averaged 20 percent below those in the Northeastern States. Other attractions—less restrictive labor laws, moderate taxes, low land prices, a mild climate, newer and more modern factories and machinery—have assisted the southward migration of Northern industry. At first the new industries were relatively simple: textiles, tobacco products, and furniture; in recent decades Piedmont industry has become increasingly diversified although textiles still account for nearly half the industrial employment.

The commercial functions for the industrial area are focused on Greensboro, Charlotte, and Greenville. Although the Piedmont contains seven metropolitan areas, much of the industry is found in smaller cities and towns, and much of the industrial labor is rural nonfarm. Interaction within the industrial crescent is facilitated by a good rail network and by Interstate 85, locally called the "Textile Highway."

Several cities illustrate the variety and increasing maturity of industry. The Greensboro–High Point–Winston-Salem SMSA has the greatest industrial employment; to the traditional tobacco product, textile, and furniture industries have been added chemical, paper, fabricated metal, and electrical industries. Charlotte, second in population in the Carolinas, ranks third in industrial employment, being more noted as a wholesaling and transportation center. Greenville, South Carolina, has highly diversified textile, clothing, and textile machinery industries.

The Atlanta SMSA Atlanta is a latecomer among Southern cities. It was founded as a railroad town in 1836, destroyed by Sherman in 1864, and then rebuilt to become the commercial hub of the Southeast. Atlanta is now one of only three Southern SMSAs with over

1 million inhabitants. The city is strategically located near the southern tip of the Blue Ridge where a natural route extended north to the Great Valley at Chattanooga. At the time of the Civil War four railways connecting the South Atlantic area with the Gulf South passed through Atlanta. Today it remains the unchallenged rail, air, and highway crossroads of the Southeast. Its wholesale area includes the Georgia Piedmont, and its financial and business services extend to Birmingham, Nashville, and Jacksonville. Atlanta is the head office, or regional office, for a number of national firms which serve the South.

Atlanta is an extremely modern city with skyscrapers, freeways, tall hotels, and a wide range of cultural activities. Its industries are highly diversified, being more related to Atlanta's function as a distributing center than to the traditional Piedmont industries. The outstanding industry is transportation equipment (automobile and aircraft) followed by food products and printing. These industries are located in numerous, modern industrial parks, dispersed throughout the city; these low sprawling buildings, with attractive landscaping and ample employee parking, are a far call from the old congested industrial zones of some Northeastern cities. Because of crowding in the central city, company offices have been dispersed near suburban freeways in clusters of attractive low office buildings.

Atlanta's commercial and industrial services have brought in a generous income. This high income is shared by blacks and whites alike in Atlanta. For example, a luxury neighborhood in the west side of the city is inhabited only by wealthy blacks. In 1969 65 percent of the Atlanta families had incomes over $10,000 (26 percent over $15,000). On the other hand, Atlanta had one-sixth of its families with incomes below $5,000; most of these live in the central city, which is 52 percent black. In the 1960s, the net in-migration of blacks into Atlanta was 32,000, while the net out-migration of whites was 82,000. The net in-migration of whites into suburban Atlanta was 170,000. Comparable population movements are occurring in Northern cities.

VALUE ADDED BY MANUFACTURING   ATLANTA SMSA

% Distribution   Location quotients: 1.0 = national average per capita

Employment	Value added	SIC source	0	1.0	2.0	3.0	4.0	5.0
9.1	15.9	Food products						
NA	NA	Tobacco products	NA					
4.0	2.1	Textiles						
5.9	5.5	Apparel						
0.9	0.7	Lumber						
3.7	2.9	Furniture						
5.7	6.4	Paper products						
7.3	9.5	Printing						
3.9	8.0	Chemicals						
NA	NA	Petro-coal products	NA					
.8	0.7	Rubber–plastic						
1.6	1.0	Leather						
3.3	4.5	Stone–clay–glass						
2.4	2.4	Primary metals						
4.3	4.5	Fabricated metals						
3.5	3.5	Machinery						
2.7	4.0	Electrical machinery						
32.9	26.7	Transport equipment						
NA	NA	Instruments	NA					
100.0	100.0	All categories						

Figure 6.7 How does this chart reflect the industrial history of Atlanta? Why is transport equipment so important?

The Ozark-Ouachita Uplands

Two hundred miles of Gulf Coastal Plain separate this subregion from the Appalachian area; yet the two have much in common. The subregion has several environmental handicaps. The Ozark Plateau, the topographic counterpart of the Allegheny-Cumberland Plateau, is less rugged and lacks the latter's coal. The soils in the western area, formed from sandstone rather than limestone, are fertile only on the narrow floodplains. South of the Arkansas Valley, the Ouachita Highlands rise less than 3,000 feet but contain areas almost as rugged as the Blue Ridge.

Like the Appalachian Uplands, the Ozark-

From the beginning Atlanta has been a transportation hub, and it is hardly surprising that expressways, tracks, skyscrapers, and parking lots are conspicuous in this view of a progressive Southern city. (Atlanta Chamber of Commerce)

Ouachita Upland is one of decreasing population, having many isolated areas with submarginal land and peoples. Above-average incomes are found only in the cities in the Arkansas Valley, traversed by several major highways and railroads. Like most of Appalachia, most of the subregion seems likely to support only a sparse population by forestry, cattle raising, and some resort business.

Little Rock In contrast to the rural Ozarks, Little Rock (with a population of 340,000) has a more prosperous economy. Located astride a regional boundary, where routes from the Gulf Plain converge on the Arkansas Valley, it has benefited from its central position to become a leading commercial center. Manufacturing, until recently concentrated in industries related to local farming and lumbering, is now predominantly in durable goods, especially metal products.

THE SOUTHEASTERN PLAIN

Both in the Southeastern Plain and the neighboring Gulf South, soil and drainage conditions are major factors in determining land-use patterns. Both regions are subtropical in latitude, and this plus proximity to the sea ensures a mild, humid climate, often oppressive in summer and punctuated by occasional cold spells in winter. The two regions have much in common: extensive forests, swamps, and marshes; herds of cattle; and remnants of the plantation economy. The Southeastern Plain has more citrus fruit, tobacco, commercial vegetables, and resort activities. The Gulf South has more major mineral resources—petroleum, natural gas, salt, and sulfur—more fertile soils (alluvial and loessial); and more land in cotton, rice, and sugarcane. The rural patterns of the

Figure 6.8 The Southeastern Plain has traditionally been an area of water surplus with many swampy or marshy areas. Urbanization in SMSAs, especially in Florida, has locally changed the problem to one of water shortage. (Base map copyright by A. K. Lobeck. Reprinted with permission of The Geographical Press, Hammond, Inc.)

Southeastern Plain are conveniently described by belts which almost parallel the Atlantic Coast.

The fall line Before roads and railroads were constructed, streams now considered too shallow for navigation were used to bring in immigrants and their supplies and to ship out the crops. The head of navigation was the edge of the Piedmont where falls or rapids blocked the streams. This fall line, where freight was transshipped, provided logical sites for waterpower and aided the growth of inland commercial and political cities, including Raleigh, Co-

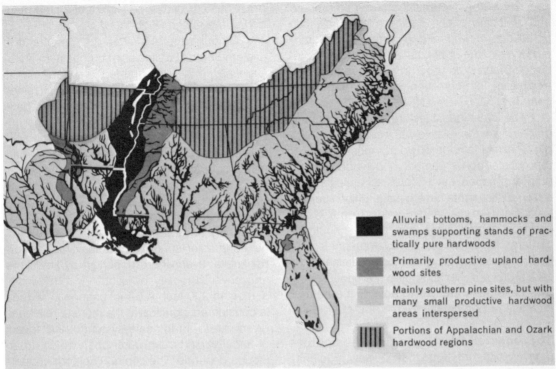

Alluvial bottoms, hammocks and swamps supporting stands of practically pure hardwoods

Primarily productive upland hardwood sites

Mainly southern pine sites, but with many small productive hardwood areas interspersed

Portions of Appalachian and Ozark hardwood regions

Figure 6.9 This map of the lumber resources of the South also shows the location of the alluvial areas and the Southern Uplands. Can you locate the fall line? (American Forest Products Industries, Inc.)

lumbia, Augusta, Macon, Columbus, and Montgomery.

Adjacent to the Piedmont is a belt of once pine-clothed sand hills (in places rising higher than the adjacent Piedmont) which suffer from excessive soil drainage. In both areas the farms, irregular in size and shape, are being converted from cotton farming to diversified farming, supplying vegetables, fruit, dairy, and poultry products for fall-line cities. About three-fifths of the land is covered by commercial forests. The irregular field patterns contrast with the rectangular patterns of the Midwest; the Piedmont and Coastal Plains are more scenic but give a sense of disorder in the landscape.

The Middle Coastal Plain The environment here is favorable to agriculture. The surface soils, light-colored and sandy, are underlain by reddish and yellowish layers of sands and clays. Cotton is still grown but less than

in the past; corn, sweet potatoes, and other subsistence crops are grown everywhere, at least for the local market. Areas with local specialties (which commonly extend into adjacent soil regions) include tobacco in North Carolina and southern Georgia; peaches, peanuts, and pecans in Georgia; and truck crops in South Carolina.

The lumber industry (Figure 6.9) dominates the Middle Coastal Plain. Small commercial forests are common, and the well-labeled miles of forests owned by paper companies are conspicuous. The natural vegetation is largely loblolly or longleaf (slash) pine; about half the land is in commercial forest. The long growing season matures pulpwood in a decade, whereas saw timber takes two or three times as long. Used first for its naval stores (turpentine, pitch, and tar), then for cheap timber and as a raw material for making corrugated board and wrapping paper, southern pine now can be used for newsprint and other paper. Southern forests are now the major producer of United States pulpwood. In many areas forests also serve for recreation, grazing, and water control.

The forest industries are the basis of manufacturing in the relatively few cities in the Middle Coastal Plain; other wood industries are at the coastal ports. Lumber and woodworking, pulp and paper, naval stores, chemicals, and a few textile plants have caused cities such as Valdosta, Georgia, and Sumter, South Carolina, to become more than local agricultural centers. These industrial developments have been modest; the growth of these cities has not offset rural out-migration, and not enough new jobs have been created to absorb the natural increase of population.

The coastal fringe   The coastal environment is different from that in New England; in the South too much water is a common problem. The Southeast Coast is almost everywhere bordered by fringing bars and spits, backed by broad sounds, lagoons, tidal marshes and swamps. The offshore bars have formed islands wide enough to be the sites of resort cities, for example, Miami Beach. These sandy strips, formed by alongshore currents, may be 100 miles long, as in eastern Florida. Elsewhere, such as the Sea Islands of Georgia and South Carolina, roughly oval islands make up the offshore barrier. Almost every part of the coast has inlets adequate for small boats; the larger river mouths and indentations have become the location of the major ports. Inland the almost continuous line of lagoons and marshes made it relatively easy to construct the protected Atlantic Intracoastal Waterway which extends the length of the Atlantic Coast.

The inner edge of the coastal fringe is known as the "Flatwoods." Pines occupy the better-drained soils, and cypress the swampy soils, and there are scattered areas of marsh grass, almost barren coastal dunes, and mangrove in southern Florida.

Although there is much good cropland in eastern South Carolina and southeastern North Carolina, only one-quarter of the land is cropped. The old plantations which once raised rice and indigo on diked alluvial soils have gone out of cultivation, leaving the lumber industry to dominate the countryside. Paper mills, rayon mills, and woodworking establishments support the town populations.

The Rural Florida Peninsula

Both the land and people gradually take on a new character south of Jacksonville. The low peninsula, everywhere underlain by limestone and covered locally by sands or muck, rises at most to 200 feet. A 5-foot change in altitude is considered significant; the modest relief has given rise to an intricate system of two layers of underground fresh water upon which urban Florida depends. The central "upland," underlain by slightly uparched limestone, collects much of the subsoil water which feeds the St. Johns River, Lake Okeechobee, and the Florida Everglades. So much water for domestic use has been pumped from these freshwater reservoirs that in some coastal areas salt water has invaded the aquifers.

The long growing season, indicated by palm trees along the coast, justifies the clearing, cultivation, and intensive fertilization of infertile sands to produce berries, potatoes, and early vegetables. Nevertheless much of the land remains in pine forest. The exposed limestone in the slightly higher central upland forms a sandy, easily worked soil which is used for tobacco and general farming in northern Florida and for citrus fruits in the central peninsula.

In southern and central Florida, there are many sandy and limey areas, commonly rather marshy, whose lush grasses growing all year support huge herds of beef and dairy cattle. With proper drainage, these generally warm lands can be used and, in extreme southeast-

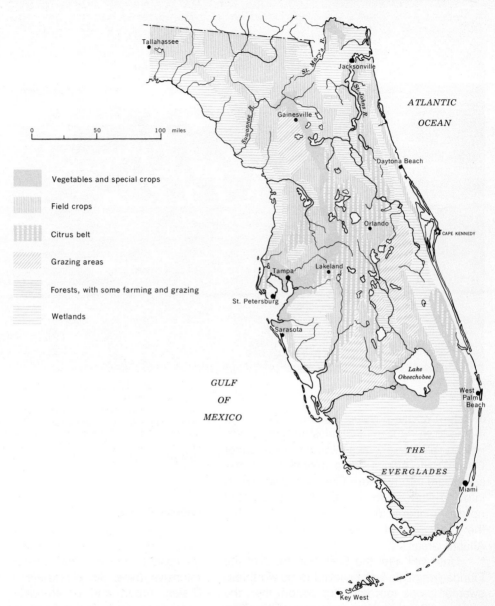

Figure 6.10 Although the Florida peninsula is flattish, it has considerable variety in land use because of small differences in drainage and temperature conditions.

ern Florida, are used for limes, sugarcane, and winter vegetables.

Settlement Except for Florida most of the Southeastern Plain was well settled by 1820. The demand for naval stores, tobacco, rice, and indigo, and later the increasing demand for cotton spurred the extension of the planta-

tions. Since it was believed that white labor was not suited for field work in the hot, humid growing season, Negro slavery became so widespread that Negroes predominated in many counties. A white aristocracy developed

On the drained muck soils of southern Florida, winter vegetables are a valuable crop, harvested with the latest machinery. This celery harvester travels 5 to 6 feet a minute, permitting the harvesting of 24 rows of celery. The machine and its crew cut, trim, wash, sort, and pack the celery in crates before it leaves the harvesting area. (USDA)

a culture whose physical evidences still stand in fine town houses in Charleston and Savannah and planters' homes throughout the former Cotton Belt. After 1820 a migration set in— southward into northern Florida and westward into the Gulf South. In part this represented normal frontier expansion; in part it reflected the abandonment of exhausted fields in the Atlantic areas.

Until well after the Civil War, most of the Florida peninsula was believed to be worthless swamp; it was too damp for cotton, then the dominant Southeastern cash crop. The citrus boom started in central Florida in the 1880s, and a railroad reached Tampa in 1884, Miami in 1896. The Florida peninsula had little inheritance from Negro slavery, and today blacks make up only 10 to 20 percent of the population. Many of the recent settlers in the peninsula are yankees or Cuban refugees, so that the social atmosphere is clearly different than elsewhere on the Coastal Plain.

Urban Florida

A general principle in land economics is: when land is equally suited for several uses, the most intensive use of the land pushes out the less intensive uses. As elsewhere in the United States, urban and urban-related uses take precedence over farming, ranching, and forestry; furthermore when urban development creates demands for rural products and services, specific rural occupance is distributed in relation to urban markets for dairy products and other perishable foodstuffs.

The pattern of urban distribution in this subregion differs from north to south. North of the Florida peninsula the cities and towns were originally seaports or local political or commer-

The Lake District of central Florida, pictured here southeast of Winter Haven, is a leading orange and grapefruit area. The climate is characterized by adequate rainfall and is almost frost-free; as a rule the occasional winter night frosts are not severe enough to damage the groves. Temperatures are moderated by the many lakes formed by solution of the limestone rock underlying the sandy soil. (USDA)

cial centers. In recent decades many of these have added industrial and other functions. In the Florida peninsula many of the early towns were at first military posts, then resort and retirement centers; their development as industrial and metropolitan centers came later. In the following analysis note how each metropolitan area has somewhat distinctive functions from the others; note also how these functions have changed with the passage of time.

The Miami–Palm Beach Megalopolis

Developed largely in the last half century, three SMSAs with a 1970 population of 2¼ million form an almost continuous urbanized strip about 5 miles wide extending 90 miles from north to south. The offshore bar has been settled mainly for resort and residential use. Behind the bar, a navigable lagoon separates the resort area from the business and industrial portions of the megalopolis. Recreational and tourist activities are not lacking west of the lagoon but tend to be concentrated along the waterways and along the north-south highways. The sandy section extending about 5 to 10 miles west of the urbanized area is devoted to dairying and other farm activities supplying the coastal cities. Westward the marshy or swampy Everglades are almost uninhabited except around Lake Okeechobee.

The oldest city in the area is Fort Lauderdale, founded in 1837. Its seaport, Port Everglades, capable of handling most ocean shipping and by far the busiest port in southeastern Florida, receives petroleum, cement, and other raw materials not produced on the peninsula. To the north is stylish Palm Beach (on the offshore bar) and, across the lagoon, West Palm Beach. Visitors to Palm Beach remember its palatial hotels, mansions, and large waterfront estates.

The most populous SMSA is Miami with its satellite cities, Miami Beach on the bar, and to the south, Coral Gables, fronting on Biscayne Bay. Until the arrival of the railroad in 1896, Miami was a small Indian trading post. Rapid development began in the 1920s, and Miami soon became known as a resort center with accommodations to fit modest as well as deluxe budgets. At the same time Miami became the wholesale and banking center for southern Florida.

The coming of the Air Age changed Miami from a peripheral to a central location. Miami International Airport became the focal point where air routes from Anglo-America connected with air routes from all over Latin America. Because of dislike of political conditions in Cuba, Miami became the destination of thousands of Cuban refugees; downtown Miami became almost as Latin as it had been Anglo-Saxon.

Meanwhile Northerners had discovered Florida as a place to retire or even to seek employment. The population of southern Florida became more "Northern" than typically "Southern"; blacks make up less than one-fifth of the populace. On Lincoln Road, the main shopping street of Miami Beach, New York accents predominate in the tourist season; indeed Miami Beach resembles Atlantic City (plus palms). To serve more permanent residents, real estate promoters first laid out the sandy areas and then ditched the swampy areas, piling up the dredgings from the channels to provide each house with a dry site adjacent to its own boat landing. All this construction and the needs of consumers required a multitude of goods and services—especially goods designed for warm weather living.

Tampa Bay and the west central peninsula Well-sheltered Tampa Bay adjoined by much well-drained land would seem to have been an ideal place for settlement; yet Tampa had only 720 people in 1880. The coming of the railroad in 1884, combined with the orange orchard boom and transfer of the cigar industry from Key West to Tampa, converted that village into a city. Tampa became primarily a commercial and industrial city: its major industry is food packing, cigar making, and agricultural chemicals, the latter based on huge phosphate deposits east of the bay. Its port, the busiest in Florida, imports a variety of raw materials, especially petroleum and fertilizer materials for the chemical industries.

The retirement function of Florida is illustrated by St. Petersburg, noted for its large proportion of old people who can enjoy an inexpensive retirement there. More luxurious are many of the homes around Sarasota, 30 miles south of Tampa. Lakeland, the same distance east of Tampa, is the gateway to a cluster of conservative residential towns in the lake and citrus area of central Florida.

The Orlando trading area The first railroad to Tampa reached Orlando several years earlier, resulting in a citrus development in Orange County. Orlando, much less populous than Tampa and Miami, is nevertheless the largest city between Jacksonville and Fort Lauderdale. Attractively located amid several dozen lakes, large and small, the city is an important junction for expressways and railroads. Until recently people in its trading area depended largely on citrus growing, retirement residences, and resorts, but the rise of the Cape Kennedy Space Center to the east added electronic, missile, and instrument industries. The elaborate Disney World amusement park has multiplied the tourist business of the area.

The Jacksonville trading area Jacksonville is the southernmost of a number of ports which serve the unevenly settled Coastal Plain characterized by few large cities. These inland areas, producing lumber, tobacco, peanuts, and cattle, once depended on water traffic on streams now little used for this purpose. Jacksonville and other river-mouth ports were the major points of contact from the interior settlements to the outside world. Later, road and railroad nets focused on the established ports, and Jacksonville became the major commercial and banking center for the Florida peninsula and adjacent Georgia. For a century and a half Jacksonville has shipped lumber and other naval stores as well as regional crops. Manufacturing is largely concerned with the processing of local food and wood raw materials and the processing of imports for regional markets such as agricultural chemicals. Savannah and Charleston are in many ways counterparts of Jacksonville. All three cities are located on estuaries; all handle exports and imports of raw materials; all serve a hinterland with small towns and cities, forest and farm activities, and much sparsely settled land.

Georgia-Carolina Ports

The Georgia and South Carolina ports are more ''Southern'' in atmosphere. Savannah is built around long-established squares, each with a character of its own, while the Savannah River is lined with docks, many with associated factories processing lumber, wood pulp, cotton, chemicals, and fertilizer. In few American cities is the visitor so aware of the past as in downtown Charleston; on a tongue of land between the Ashley and Cooper estuaries, facing on a spacious bay guarded by the ruins of Fort Sumter, the pastel-colored houses of the antebellum and colonial periods have been charmingly maintained; even the gas stations are designed to fit the colonial setting. Inland the Savannah trading area extends to the edge of the Piedmont, including three growing fall-line cities, Augusta, Macon, and Columbus, all of which also have major commercial bonds with Atlanta. The rural portions of the area generally have decreasing populations; farms are becoming larger and more mechanized.

In Georgia, where nearly one-fourth of all personal income originated from government sources (three-fourths of this from the federal government), government activity is becoming more important than agriculture in accounting for the distribution of people and business. Cities such as Augusta, Macon, and Columbus all receive sizable portions of their income from nearby federal government camps.

Upstream the modern industries of Charleston almost duplicate those of Savannah. Elevated expressways bring traffic to the busy modern port, industrial center, and naval and air bases. The agriculture of the adjoining Coastal Plain, specializing in tree farming, cotton, tobacco, and vegetables, has only modest importance to Charleston. Inland on the fall line, Columbia, the state capital, although populous and productive as Charleston is primarily a political and commercial center.

North Carolina ports, and their inland agricultural hinterlands, are transitional in location between the South and the Atlantic Megalopolis. When ships were smaller, these ports were of considerable significance, but their business has been modest compared with nearby Hampton Roads. Northeastern North Carolina is separated from the sea by bars, shallow sounds, and extensive swamps; thus the ports of North Carolina are awkward to approach; much of the tonnage handled through Wilmington and Morehead City is coastwise or local. Over five-sixths of North Carolina exports by value are shipped through out-of-state ports, especially Norfolk.

The agriculture of the North Carolina Coastal Plain continues to be productive with major emphasis on flue-cured tobacco. Increased income, but not population growth, has resulted from the industrialization of a dozen or more small cities, for example, Fayetteville (textiles, furniture). The only metropolitan area, Raleigh, is tied more closely with the Piedmont Industrial Crescent than with the Coastal Plain.

The Future of the Southeastern Plain

A basic Southeastern problem has been the low level of living. South Carolina in 1973 had a median family income $1,969 below the national average. The highest family incomes are in the Florida peninsula and in the urban centers throughout the region. Incomes are lowest in the Middle Coastal Plain where urbanization is least advanced. Everywhere the income for nonwhite males is sharply below that for white males, for nonwhite females lower than for all other groups. In 1969 12.7 percent of the families were classified as below low-income level in Florida; in South Carolina, 19.0 percent. Poverty is human hardship, not merely an unfortunate statistic.

In settlement history, the Coastal Plain (except for the Florida peninsula) has much in common with the rural Midwest. With the relative decline of agriculture and its increased mechanization, rural population decreased and the cities proved unable to absorb the surplus. The blacks, especially, moved north to the Atlantic Megalopolis. Grazing, forestry, and fruits increasingly replaced crops with high labor requirements. Meanwhile industry was slow to develop in the Coastal Plain. Manufactures during the last century were largely the processing of lumber, naval stores, cotton, tobacco, and fertilizers. Such industries required little labor, and that labor could be low-paid, only semiskilled labor. In recent decades, the picture has brightened: migration to Florida (and to retirement areas northward) brought in new consumers. Industrialists realized the advantages of modern, uncrowded factories on cheap land with year-round equable climates. The government established numerous military bases and scientific stations (e.g., Cape Canaveral). Consequently, dormant cities have grown, and classic Southern mansions may soon be overshadowed by skyscrapers and factories.

THE GULF SOUTH

This huge region, here called the Gulf South, has much physical resemblance to the Southeastern Plain. However, because its location is more continental, the Gulf South is more likely to suffer extreme heat in summer and severe cold spells in winter. Like the Southeastern Plain, with many swampy and marshy coastal areas the Gulf South is served by the Intracoastal Waterway and by bays which provide excellent natural harbors. Even more important is the Mississippi system, which provides a waterway unequaled in Anglo-America except by the Great Lakes–St. Lawrence Seaway. The floodplain of the Mississippi has formed a broad wedge of *alluvium* which today, as it has been for nearly two centuries, is the agricultural core of the region.

New Developments in the Gulf South

The plantation and the neoplantation
The antebellum plantation was found on relatively flat areas where large fields could be cultivated by *slave gangs*. Usually these plantations were much larger than Midwestern farms, units of over 1,000 acres being fairly common. Such large areas were scarce on the rougher surfaces of the Piedmont. After the

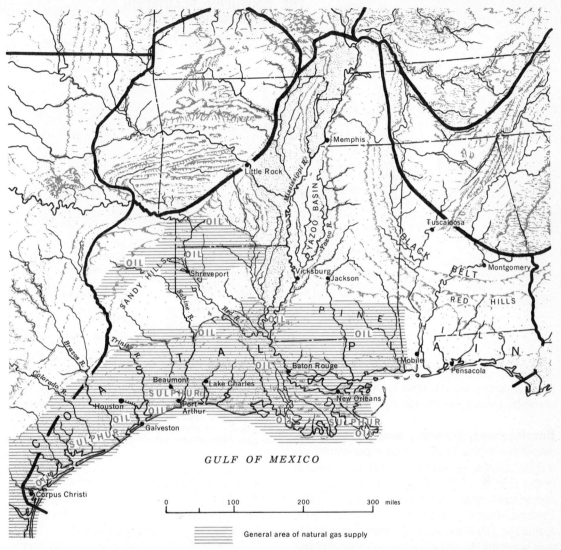

Figure on map includes labels: Memphis, Little Rock, Tuscaloosa, Montgomery, Shreveport, Vicksburg, Jackson, Baton Rouge, Mobile, Pensacola, Beaumont, Lake Charles, New Orleans, Houston, Port Arthur, Galveston, Corpus Christi. Physiographic labels: YAZOO BASIN, BLACK BELT, RED HILLS, PINE HILLS, SANDY HILLS, OIL, SULPHUR, Mississippi R., Yazoo R., Sabine R., Red R., Trinity R., Brazos R., Colorado R.

GULF OF MEXICO

0   100   200   300   miles

General area of natural gas supply

Figure 6.11 Landforms of the Gulf South. Most of this area consists of alluvium or sands deposited in what was formerly a part of the Gulf of Mexico. As in the Southeastern Plain, groundwater conditions diversify local environments. (Base map copyright by A. K. Lobeck. Reprinted with permission of The Geographical Press, Hammond, Inc.)

Civil War, the majority of the plantations were cultivated on a *sharecropper* basis (40 acres and a mule). Such a fragmented landscape was hardly suited to raising cotton with tractors and cotton-picking machinery, the introduction of which both caused and was stimulated by the out-migration of rural labor. The consequence was the development of what Merle Prunty calls the *neoplantation* (Figure 6.12), centered around a tractor station, cultivated in large fields, and emphasizing high yields with a low labor cost per unit. The cultivation is managed by one farmer; the modest supply of labor is paid cash, not a share of the crop; and crop rotation (including livestock) is the rule where soil conditions permit. The small farmer has not been entirely eliminated by the spread of the

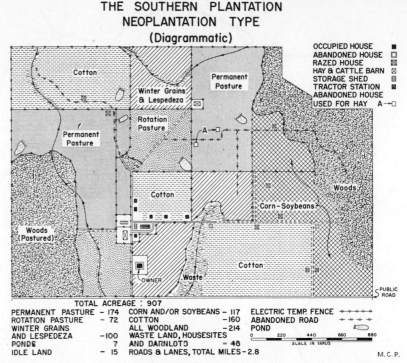

THE SOUTHERN PLANTATION
NEOPLANTATION TYPE
(Diagrammatic)

OCCUPIED HOUSE ■
ABANDONED HOUSE ☐
RAZED HOUSE ⊠
HAY & CATTLE BARN ⊠
STORAGE SHED ▤
TRACTOR STATION ▦
ABANDONED HOUSE
USED FOR HAY A→☐

TOTAL ACREAGE : 907

PERMANENT PASTURE	– 174	CORN AND/OR SOYBEANS – 117
ROTATION PASTURE	– 72	COTTON –160
WINTER GRAINS		ALL WOODLAND –214
AND LESPEDEZA	–100	WASTE LAND, HOUSESITES
PONDS	7	AND BARNLOTS – 48
IDLE LAND	– 15	ROADS & LANES, TOTAL MILES – 2.8

ELECTRIC TEMP. FENCE ∘-∘-∘-∘
ABANDONED ROAD +-+-+-+
POND ⬭

0   220   440   660   880
SCALE IN YARDS

M.C.P.

Figure 6.12 This generalized example is based on neoplantations scattered throughout the coastal plain from Virginia to Texas. Compared with the traditional Southern plantation, the few workers' homes, the tractor stations, and the crop diversification are noteworthy. (Merle C. Prunty, Jr., "The Renaissance of the Southern Plantation," *Geographical Review*, vol. 45 (1955), pp. 459–491.)

neoplantation, but commonly his small farm earnings are supplemented by city work.

Employment, income, and poverty As elsewhere in the South, income per family on a state basis is well below the national average in the Gulf South but above the national average in such cities as Memphis, Houston, New Orleans, Baton Rouge, and Beaumont–Port Arthur. In 1973 the annual income per family was estimated to be below the national average by the following percentages: Alabama 29 percent, Mississippi 25 percent, Arkansas 22 percent, Louisiana 12 percent, Texas 3 percent. The relatively better income averages for Texas and Louisiana are partly accounted for by the development of oil, gas, and sulfur and of industrial and commercial activities related to these resources. In all the Gulf South the bulk of the 1973 income came from employment concentrated in the cities: manufacturing, trade, transportation, and services and government. For example, in Louisiana 66 percent of

the population but 90 percent of the income was urban; less prosperous Mississippi was only 44 percent urban, but 76 percent of its income came from urban sources.

Poverty is not lacking in the Urban South, but the great *poverty gap* (the gap between the actual earnings of poor families and the amount considered necessary for a minimum decent standard of living) is in the Agricultural South which is characterized by high proportions of blacks and low educational levels. Many of the more ambitious have migrated to Southern cities or to the urban Central Lowland, leaving behind a large proportion of people who are too old or for other reasons are not considered part of the potential labor force. Less than one-sixth of the workers re-

Table 6.1 Population Changes in Four Gulf States and the United States, 1940–1970

	ALA.	LA.	MISS.	ARK.	U.S.
Population change, %					
1940–1950	+8.1	+13.5	−0.2	−2.0	+14.5
1950–1960	+6.7	+21.4	0.0	−6.5	+18.5
1960–1970	+5.4	+11.8	+1.8	+7.7	+13.3
Nonwhite population, %					
1940	35.1	36.1	49.0	27.7	10.2
1960	30.1	32.1	42.3	21.9	11.4
1970	26.3	36.8	36.8	18.3	12.1
Urban residents, %					
1940	26.3	30.1	20.0	24.1	56.1
1970	58.4	66.1	44.5	50.0	73.5
Net migration, thousands					
1940–1950	−271	−112	−350	−320	+1,035
1950–1960	−361	−42	−433	−430	+2,973
1960–1970	−233	−130	−267	−71	+3,020
Per capita income					
1940	$ 282	$ 363	$ 218	$ 256	$ 595
1970	3,849	3,054	2,575	2,795	3,920

SOURCES: U.S. Bureau of the Census, *Statistical Abstract of the United States;* and *County and City Data Book: 1972,* Washington, 1972, U.S. Census, 1970.

main in agriculture, forestry, mining, or other extractive industries. Three-fifths are in trade and other service industries and one-quarter in manufacturing.

Population changes and problems The changes in the Gulf South economy have had striking effects on both the economic and the social structure. Traditionally there were three groups: (1) the white planter-merchant-professional-clerical class; (2) the "poor white" class, who worked on small farms and who later supplied much of the labor for Southern manufacturing; and (3) the Negro, who worked as a domestic servant or common laborer in the city, as a farm laborer or sharecropper in the country. Some of the poor whites rose to the upper class, and some blacks rose to perform professional and commercial functions, especially for the black community, but until very recently a shift upward economically and socially was more difficult for the black in the South than in the North and West.

Table 6.1 shows some of the changes that have occurred in four Gulf South states. In general, the poor industrial mix and low rate of urbanization have been responsible for slow economic progress. More rapid development along the Gulf from Mobile to Houston is counterbalanced by the economic backwardness inland in the agricultural-forestry areas. Consequently heavy out-migration has occurred in the latter area, especially among blacks and poorly trained whites whose opportunities have been lessened by mechanization.

Mississippi Channels, Alluvium, and Cities

The Mississippi floodplains provide homes for about 3½ million people. The southern delta was used by the French for cotton and sugar culture in the mid-eighteenth century; elsewhere the plain itself had little use, but the waterway was a commercial highway—at first for furs, later for the shipment of Ohio Valley

In Assumption Parish, Louisiana, the natural levees along the Bayou La Fourche form a ridge 15 to 20 feet high and 6 to 8 miles wide, with the river flowing on the crest. Drainage is away from the river. The fields were laid out long ago by French settlers whose homesteads formed elongated villages along the river road. The fertile, fine sandy loam and silt soils are used for sugar and rice; the adjacent swamps and marshes provide muskrat and nutria habitats. (USDA)

farm products to Southern planters; the swampy plain remained in the hands of the trappers. Until 1840 when levees were built, the planters occupied the brown loess soils on and in back of the bluffs overlooking the river from the east because fear of floods kept them from permanent exploitation of the alluvial wealth.

The changing, twisting channel of the Mississippi was a challenge to skilled pilots, as has been so vividly described by Mark Twain. The development of the shallow-draft steamboat made its navigation possible, and the places where the channel cut into the eastern bluffs provided landing places for port towns such as Natchez, Vicksburg, and Memphis. When the demand for cotton grew, the planters cleared the floodplain forests, built dikes, and planted fields that in most years were safe from the river. Not all the land was cleared—even today many roads across the floodplain are largely adjoined by drainage canals beyond which are *cypress*, *tupelo*, and *gum* swamps.

Then, as today, the floodplain consisted of three kinds of soil commonly grouped together as alluvium. The broad flat basins have clay soils with poor internal drainage. The better soils for cotton are the sandy loams found on old natural levees or river channels, commonly 5 to 15 feet higher than the clay soils. The highest terraces include some loess soils. Intermediate are the silty loams usable for pasture when drained. Physically it is possible to convert most of the plain into drained lands; economically this is not at present feasible for half the potential cropland.

In terms of crops, the floodplain can be divided into three areas: (1) south of 31° latitude the climate is generally too humid for profitable cotton production; (2) north of this and separated from it by a swampy, sparsely settled area is the Delta (so-called locally), a cotton-soybean area extending north to the mouth of the Ohio; (3) west of these sections in southern Arkansas, eastern Texas, and Louisiana are heavy clay areas planted in rice, flooded during the growth period and harvested like wheat by combines. Cattle are especially common where unused rice fields supplement other pastures. West of the Mississippi, coastal prairies are widespread and alternate with forests, swamps, and marsh.

The total capital investment in protecting most of this alluvial land against most floods has been about a half billion dollars for levees and ditches; and this amount does not include investments in the TVA and other dams along the Ohio, upper Mississippi, Missouri, and their tributaries. However, flood precautions did not suffice to control the 1973 flood. Heavy additional investments are required to cultivate the land with modern techniques: thus a cotton picker may cost over $10,000. Economically this is no land for the poor small farmer who, however, still occupies it in places for social rather than economic reasons.

Memphis Few cities are so related to raw material–oriented industries as Memphis, commercial metropolis for the northern half of the floodplain and the higher parts in western Tennessee and northern Mississippi. Memphis has the largest inland cotton market in the country and also the largest hardwood lumber market. Three raw material–oriented industries—food products, lumber products, and chemicals—are noteworthy.

New Orleans and southern Louisiana
Southern Louisiana seems to have been largely built, or rebuilt, by man. Its earliest settlement by Europeans was on the natural levees: on them in 1718 the French built the infant New Orleans primarily to open the trade of the Mississippi. Even today the city and the farms seem embraced by marshes and swamps, and the bayous and drainage canals are conspicuous parts of the landscape; extensive areas, almost roadless, can be observed best by boat. The region includes the so-called Evangeline country settled by refugees from Nova Scotia whose descendants still speak a French dialect.

The countryside can be described by sectors radiating from the city. To the southeast is a largely marshy area with truck crops on much of the better-drained land. Recently this has been the state's most productive area in petroleum and sulfur and significant for natural gas. Production here is possible only because of new techniques devised to obtain the minerals first on marshy lands, later offshore. Land use in the half circle west of New Orleans alternates between swamp and sugar land but with considerable fishing from the bayou ports; there too oil and gas fields are common. The

New Orleans, once consisting of low buildings on a flat delta, now has a skyline of high-rise buildings, bridges, and elevated expressways. This photo shows the Louisiana Superdome under construction in the center of the city. (Chamber of Commerce of the New Orleans Area)

sector north and northeast is devoted mainly to truck crops, dairying, and winter strawberries; lumbering and paper are major nonagricultural activities.

New Orleans   The New Orleans SMSA had an unenviable site. The French Quarter, carefully preserved to attract tourists, is on the back slope of the natural levee; much of the more modern city is on drained land, and at high water the Mississippi flows above the street level. Hot and sticky much of the year and, until this century, often fever- and mosquito-ridden and drained by open sewers, the modern city is a prize example of what sanitary engineers can do to change the environment. The water supply, formerly obtained from cisterns, is now obtained from purified, filtered river water. Numerous pumps drain the covered canals and eject the sewage into the sea. The older buildings were necessarily low, but the newer part of the city has skyscrapers and the new expressways and bridges seem to tower over the low, older city. New Orleans is becoming a largely air-conditioned, modern city. The city is primarily a commercial and service center with manufactures related to commerce and regional consumption. Trade, finance, and commercial services account for two-fifths of all employment; industry only for one-thirteenth. The major manufacture is food processing and packing, including the processing of imported foodstuffs such as bananas and coffee. A rapidly growing industry is petroleum processing and petrochemicals, in part as a result of the recent oil and gas boom near the river mouth. Other manufactures are consumer goods for the metropolitan market and the adjacent Gulf South.

In spite of the slow river approach to the city, New Orleans has been and is among the leading American ports. In the first half of the last century, the Southern city rivaled and sometimes exceeded New York in value and quantity of goods handled. Even today New Orleans has a freight rate advantage over North Atlantic and Pacific ports in the Mississippi Valley. The city is attempting to expand and service international trade with buildings such as the 33-story International Trade Mart. At present, export and coastwise shipments are by tonnage nearly six times import and coastwise receipts.

The Eastern Coastal Plains and Gateways

East of the Mississippi, the Gulf South consists of coastal marshes fringed by offshore bars, spits, and islands; a flat, wooded area; and a sandy inland plain. Between this plain and the southwestern edge of the Piedmont is an arc of prairie endowed with a rich, black, limey soil. This "Black Belt," once an area of large cotton plantations, now specializes in beef and dairy cattle. Southwest of the Black Belt, timberland predominates, but cotton, poultry, and livestock farming are intermixed and occupy increasing parts of the land toward the Mississippi.

Eastern Mississippi and most of Alabama are drained directly into the Gulf by a number of small and moderate-sized rivers. The largest of these is the Alabama-Tombigbee system which drains about half of Alabama, including almost all the Black Belt and the extreme southwestern end of the Appalachians. On for-

mer cotton lands within this area farmers were forced to diversify because of the destruction that the boll weevil worked. Enterprise, Alabama, so pleased by the financial results of this pest-stimulated farm diversification, erected a monument to the boll weevil. Now in southern Alabama the farmer specializes in peanuts, plus some corn, cotton, cattle, and hogs. Closer to the Gulf Coast the soil is less suited for agriculture and therefore used mainly for pine forests. The sandy coast, significant mainly for fishing and resort towns, is a dismal, little-used area in midwinter.

Mobile and other gateways   A series of small ports, each on an inlet on the Gulf, includes Apalachicola, Panama City, Pensacola, Biloxi, and Gulfport; all have fishing, shipping, vacation trade, a government base or hospital, and a few simple industries: lumber, paper, chemicals, synthetic fibers, or food packing. Only Mobile, located on a deeply indented bay, shows signs of becoming a commercial-industrial metropolis. Yet two-thirds of all Mobile manufacturing employment was in nondurable goods with emphasis on food, chemicals, and paper.

Although Mobile was founded by the French in 1711, its growth occurred largely in the second quarter of the nineteenth century when American settlers, stimulated by soil exhaustion in the Southeastern Plain and by the increasing European demand for upland cotton, moved into Alabama. Carrying their household goods on wagons and driving their livestock before them, the immigrants arrived via three dirt roads, all converging on Mobile. Later the shipment of supplies and the export of cotton depended on river traffic to Mobile down the Tombigbee from Demopolis and down the Alabama from Montgomery or even further upstream. The zone within 40 miles of the Gulf proved too rainy in autumn for cotton, but Gulf ports benefited by the output of huge cotton plantations northward. Mobile was the established commercial center of Alabama long before Birmingham, now the state's leading city, was founded; while Montgomery, more centrally located in the state and at the southeastern end of the Black Belt, became the political and social capital.

Later as railroads and paved roads focused on Mobile and Montgomery, the use of inland water routes declined. Cattle displaced cotton in the Black Belt, and corn, pecans, truck crops, and livestock shared the land with cotton and forestry on the sandy soils.

West of the Mississippi Delta

Crossing the Mississippi River does not bring any abrupt change in the physical features found in the Gulf South, but there is a change in the proportion of the land each side occupies. Thus the loess bluffs which almost everywhere overlook the Mississippi from the east occupy a negligible part of eastern Arkansas and southeastern Missouri. The swampy areas are much more extensive west of the river and form broad bands along the Gulf Coast and along the rivers. The longleaf pine forest occurs in west central Louisiana and eastern Texas, and to the north, the oak-pine forest characteristic of the Southern Piedmont reappears in northern Louisiana, Arkansas, and northeastern Texas. The black soils and tall grasslands of the Black Belt are found in a marshier version in the lush coastal prairies of the Texas–western Louisiana Gulf Coast. Petroleum, natural gas, and salt deposits are much more productive here than east of the river.

Before the discovery of oil near Beaumont, Texas, in 1901, the western Gulf South was generally unprogressive, producing lumber, cotton, rice, cattle, and, in the French-speaking section, sugarcane. Large-scale rice cultivation had already been introduced, being the foundation of an industry which today uses huge combine harvesters and elaborate systems of irrigation and drainage, with seeding and pest control by plane. Muskrat trapping is a widespread but declining industry, as is the hardwood lumbering on the marshy areas and pine cutting on the sandy uplands. Lumbering could be readily established on a sustained-yield basis because of the long growing season.

Mineral wealth Mineral exploitation of the western Gulf South transformed the area, providing capital for the development of cities and industries and for pipelines, barge routes, and tanker services to ship its fuels and chemicals to the Central Lowland and the Atlantic Megalopolis. This mineral wealth is so valuable as to be hard to visualize. All the gold produced in California *since 1848* was valued at $2.4 billion, which is about half the value of the crude oil and gas produced in Louisiana in 1971. To this can be added the Louisiana production of sulfur ($89 million) and of salt ($67 million).

The value of this mineral wealth depended on the technical and market setting—it could hardly have been exploited much before the early twentieth century. Earlier demands for petroleum and natural gas were limited to household use (kerosene, gas stoves, and gaslight), and these markets were in the Northeast, difficult to reach before the development of pipelines and tankers. The techniques for exploiting marshland and continental-shelf deposits have been developed only within the last quarter century. As for sulfur, the Frasch process which permitted the extraction of molten sulfur from the deep deposits in the salt domes was not introduced commercially until 1903. Salt, which underlies much of the Gulf South, was widely available, and only in recent decades has it been worthwhile to exploit such deep deposits. The result: Today the flow of fuels and raw materials by pipeline, rail, barge, and tanker from the Gulf South northeastward represents the leading trade route by tonnage in the nation. It has created a cluster of Gulf South cities—Baton Rouge, Shreveport, New Orleans, Lake Charles, Beaumont, Galveston–Texas City, Houston, and Corpus Christi—which together form the "Petrochemical Empire." They process large quantities of raw materials, and require elaborate and often

NETWORK OF MAJOR NATURAL GAS PIPELINES

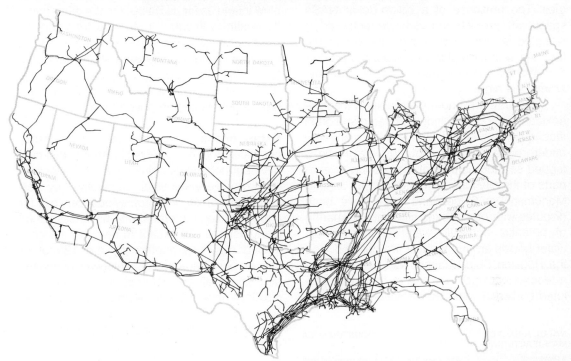

Figure 6.13 This map shows the conspicuous part played by the Gulf South in supplying the nation with natural gas. Petroleum pipelines would show a somewhat similar pattern. (Map by Federal Reserve Bank of Philadelphia)

highly automated machinery as well as complete networks of communication and transportation. Behind these production and transport activities have arisen a host of auxiliary manufacturing, business service, and professional activities.

The Houston-Galveston SMSA The economic capital of this Petrochemical Empire is Houston, at one time a commercial outlet mainly for the farms and ranches of southern Texas. In 1900 Houston was eighty-fourth in population among American cities; by 1970 it had advanced to sixth largely because of oil and aggressive business leadership. Originally it was an inland city reachable only by small boats; with the increasing size of ocean vessels, Galveston, on a long low island across the mouth of Galveston Bay, became its outport. Although Galveston rebuilt following a hurricane in 1900, protecting itself by a seawall, a 36-foot-deep channel was excavated to

Houston in 1914, wide enough for all but the largest vessels and leading to a turning basin within the city. Houston rose to second among American ports (behind only New Orleans) in tonnage shipped. Although Galveston has gained some industries, mostly petrochemical, the most rapid development has been along the ship channels in Galveston Bay and Buffalo Bayou.

The industrial economy of Houston includes every category of manufacturing represented except tobacco and leather. However, the petroleum and chemical products together account for half of the value added by manufacturing but, reflecting the high degree of automation in these industries, only one-fourth of the industrial employment. Many of the other industries supply consumer goods for local consumption or machinery for the basic industries. The presence of a billion-dollar NASA spacecraft project and defense activities is reflected in ordnance and machinery industries. As in other regional capitals, the proportion of employment in trade, service, and government is high.

Houston is a boom metropolis with paradoxical situations resulting from rapid and often inadequately planned growth. Its mammoth underground water resources have been tapped so thoroughly that the ground level of parts of the city sank—around the San Jacinto Monument by 6 feet—and there have been disputes with other Texas cities about sharing of potential domestic water supplies. Most water bodies around the city are polluted, and the Houston Ship Channel was described by a federal inspector as "one of the worst polluted bodies of water in the nation." The me-

tropolis has generated smog which at times blew inland as far as Dallas. On the other hand, its wealth is flaunted in its industries and impressive shopping centers. In contrast to the indicators of wealth, statistics show that Houston ranks 136th among all SMSAs in average per household income; one-fifth of the families have incomes on the poverty level.

Other cities   The other cities in the Petrochemical Empire resemble Houston in that they have petrochemical industries and are located on navigable waterways. Generally they perform commercial and professional services for a more limited hinterland and have less varied manufactures. All except Shreveport are connected with one another by the 12-foot or deeper Gulf Intracoastal Waterway or by the Mississippi; all are connected by oil and gas pipelines. In addition to oil and gas, many have secondary industries such as tin, zinc, and aluminum smelting based on the use of gas.

Water, Water Everywhere

The Gulf South might seem to be plentifully supplied with water; but is it good water? The streams from the north are clogged with silt, sewage, and industrial wastes; the streams from the west and northwest are being drained upstream for irrigation and domestic use, and the water returned to these streams is increasingly brackish and contaminated. Near the Texas Coast so much water is being pumped from wells that salt water is invading the aquifers. Thus, although hardly a stream lacks reservoirs and other forms of regulation, there is danger of inadequate *clean* water to serve the growing population, agriculture, forestry, and manufacturing.

The enormous water needs of productive enterprise are often overlooked: to grow a southern pine may use as much as 2 gallons per board foot; to convert this pine into newsprint requires 26,000 gallons per ton; to manufacture steel for paper machinery requires as much as 65,000 gallons per ton of machinery.

VALUE ADDED BY MANUFACTURING   **HOUSTON SMSA**

% Distribution   Location quotients: 1.0 = national average per capita

Employ-ment	Value added	SIC source	0	1.0	2.0	3.0	4.0	5.0
9.1	9.5	Food products						
NA	NA	Tobacco products	NA					
0.5	0.1	Textiles						
0.9	0.3	Apparel						
1.5	0.6	Lumber						
1.5	0.6	Furniture						
2.9	2.0	Paper products						
3.7	2.6	Printing						
13.9	28.1	Chemicals						9.3
7.1	13.6	Petro-coal products						
1.1	0.7	Rubber-plastic						
NA	NA	Leather	NA					
7.1	2.9	Stone-clay-glass						
8.9	5.4	Primary metals						
16.9	10.8	Fabricated metals						
14.2	9.7	Machinery						
3.1	7.2	Electrical machinery						
1.7	0.8	Transport equipment						
1.0	0.6	Instruments						
100.0	100.0	All categories						

Figure 6.14   Houston manufacturing is related to a few industrial categories. True or false? Defend your answer.

The CBD of Houston is clearly delineated by the skyscrapers which rise strikingly above an urbanized area elsewhere spread out on a flat plain. (Houston Chamber of Commerce)

Add to this human consumption (drinking water, bathing, laundry, toilet, etc.) of 100 to 200 gallons per capita per day, and it is understandable why there may not be adequate water for rice cultivation and other uses. Nevertheless, in this area rainfall is heavy and evaporation is low; compared to the western United States, this is a water-rich area. Can this resource be used efficiently? The solutions will involve huge capital investments and many curbs on the carelessness of the inhabitants. To change human habits is rarely easy, and Eastern Americans, especially, have been accustomed to think of water as an unlimited resource.

THE FUTURE OF THE SOUTH

The South has had three handicaps: its long, hot summers, late development of industry and decision-making services, and the racial problems inherited from the peculiar institution of slavery. Much progress has been made in solutions to each of these problems. The long, hot summers have been compensated by air conditioning, and the short, mild winters have attracted migrants from the North. In industrial development Southern factories have had an advantage of more modern design and machinery, and because of better labor conditions and equipment, Southern industry has been able to undercut the North in production costs per unit for many items. Racial problems have not been completely solved anywhere in the United States, but the South has gone far in opening opportunities to minority peoples. Finally, the development of modern metropolises in the South in the last quarter century has outpaced other regions. This does not imply that Atlanta, Houston, or Dallas will displace New York, Los Angeles, Chicago, and Detroit as decision-making central places but rather that they may be predicted to share increasingly in such national functions.

If in the next century attractive places for living become more important than fertile flatlands for farming in determining the growth of population, the Southern Uplands should have an increasing importance in providing homesites and recreational facilities. In addition to attractive scenery, the Southern Uplands offers water, fuel, and most notably forests that can be cultivated rather than merely cleared. The geographical significance of its central location between the well-populated Northeast and equally populated but less developed South should not be overlooked. A basic problem has been past mismanagement; the wealth both of human skills and of natural resources has been not only poorly exploited but often exploited for the benefit of other regions. The expanding economies of the Southern Piedmont and the Tennessee Valley should serve as growth poles from which economic and social development may spread into the adjoining hills with the mountains being preserved for recreation and forestry.

The Southeastern Plains region offers an equal challenge. The weather, except for rare hurricanes and tornadoes, is equable and the flora grows lustily in forests and swamps, plantation gardens, and productive fields. Indeed the growth of vegetation, insect life, and bacteria could overwhelm man if necessary controls are not applied. Even men need some controls: some are building monotonous rows of potential slum housing, while others design and erect pleasure palaces for resort hotels. The Florida peninsula provides countless examples of both good and bad development. One should worry whether its subtropical settings are destined to attract more people and sprawling settlements than the space and freshwater resources can support.

The Gulf South has similar problems and virtues plus huge petroleum, natural gas, salt, and sulfur resources. There the water resources, so basic to human happiness, range in some places from inadequate for industrial and domestic needs to temporarily huge surpluses during river floods. Increasingly the waters are polluted by industrial wastes and domestic sewage. The air is also contaminated with increasing inflows of industrial pollutants and automotive exhausts. Will the Gulf South repeat some of the mistakes made during the nineteenth-century industrialization of the Northeast?

The South differs from the Northeast in its traditions and in its generally mild climate with long growing seasons. As elsewhere in the humid United States, the urban patterns are largely determined by relief features, water routes, and minerals; the rural patterns are more related to soils and associated drainage conditions. The combination of these sets of patterns results in intensive development being interspersed with areas of little or no development or of rural decay—of wealthy centers such as Houston interspersed with marshy and sandy wastes with poor farmsteads housing families in unpainted shacks. Social and technological revolutions have created serious tensions, especially in the rural areas. Farming has changed from a labor-intensive cultivation of a few staple crops to highly mechanized, more diversified agriculture which has little use for semiskilled labor. Emigration northward or cityward has provided some employment for displaced rural labor but not enough.

The soil wealth needs to be conserved to provide for permanent forestry and agriculture in a region of exceptionally favorable climate for plant growth. The mineral resources, generally of a kind not easily recycled, will ultimately be depleted, but the wealth they have generated has provided capital for the development of a wide range of service and industrial activities. On the other hand, the twin dangers of air and water pollution and power scarcity could retard or even reverse the present trend toward a developing economy. In the long run the quality of human wisdom and skills developed in the South will determine whether its attractive physical settings provide good homes for mankind or a patchwork of urban and rural ghettos.

SELECTED REFERENCES

ANDERSON, JAMES R.: *Land Use and Development: Southeastern Coastal Plain,* Agricultural Information Bulletin No. 154, Washington, 1956.

ARBINGAST, STANLEY A., and LORRIN KENNAMER: *Atlas of Texas,* Bureau of Business Research, University of Texas, Austin, 1963.

ARKANSAS INDUSTRIAL DEVELOPMENT COMMISSION: *An Economic Atlas of Arkansas,* Little Rock, 1961.

BUREAU OF BUSINESS AND ECONOMIC RESEARCH: *The Carolina Economy,* University of South Carolina, Columbia, no date. One of the many pamphlets available from state agencies.

DEVORSEY, LOUIS, JR.: "Florida's Seaward Boundary: A Problem in Applied Historical Geography" *Professional Geographer,* vol. 25 (1973), pp. 214–220.

FORD, THOMAS R. (ed.): *The Southern Appalachian Region: A Survey,* University of Kentucky Press, Lexington, 1962. A comprehensive study financed by the Ford Foundation.

JORDAN, TERRY G.: "The Imprint of the Upper and Lower South on Mid-nineteenth-century Texas," *Annals,* AAG, vol. 57 (1967), pp. 667–690.

KERSTEN, EARL W. JR.: "Changing Economy and Landscape in a Missouri Ozarks Area," *Annals,* AAG, vol. 48 (1958), pp. 398–418.

KNIFFEN, FRED B.: *Louisiana, Its Land and People,* Louisiana State University Press, Baton Rouge, 1968.

KYLE, JOHN H.: *The Building of the TVA,* Louisiana State University Press, Baton Rouge, 1958.

LONSDALE, RICHARD E.: *Atlas of North Carolina,* University of North Carolina Press, Chapel Hill, 1967.

MCLAUGHLIN, GLENN E., and STEFAN ROBOCK: *Why Industry Moves South,* National Planning Association, Washington, 1950.

PADGETT, HERBERT R.: "Physical and Cultural Associations on the Louisiana Coast," *Annals,* AAG, vol. 59 (1969), pp. 481–493.

PARKINS, A. E.: *The South: Its Economic-Geographic Development,* Wiley, New York, 1938.

PRUNTY, MERLE C.: "Land Occupance in the Southeast: Landmarks and Forecasts," *Geographical Review,* vol. 42 (1952), pp. 439–461.

————: "Some Contemporary Myths and Challenges in Southern Rural Land Utilization," *Southeastern Geographer,* vol. 10 (1972); reprint, 12 pp.

————, and CHARLES S. AIKEN: "The Demise of the Piedmont Cotton Region," *Annals,* AAG, vol. 62 (1972), pp. 283–306.

RAISZ, ERWIN: *Atlas of Florida,* University of Florida Press, Gainesville, 1964.

SALTER, PAUL SANFORD: "Changing Agricultural Patterns on the South Carolina Sea Islands," *Journal of Geography,* vol. 67 (1968), pp. 223–228.

STOKES, GEORGE A.: "Lumbering and Western Louisiana Cultural Landscapes," *Annals,* AAG, vol. 47 (1957), pp. 250–266.

U.S. FOREST SERVICE: *Timber Trends in the United States,* Washington, 1965.

WELLER, JACK E.: *Yesterday's People: Life in Contemporary Appalachia,* University of Kentucky Press, Lexington, 1965.

7

THE INTERIOR WEST

No sharp boundaries form the eastern edge of the Interior West. Some scholars have chosen a fluctuating line of semiaridity between the 98th and 100th meridians, others the fringe of the short-grass high prairies, and still others the sharp Front Ranges of the Rockies. Wherever its eastern boundaries, it is a land of challenge and environmental contrast which has added a romantic note to American folklore, literature, song, movies, and television. Its resources are diverse but patchy: isolated mines, limited oases, small pastures and forests in steep mountains, and rivers winding across stark deserts. Past settlement required a gambler's fortitude and, in some parts of the Interior West, still does: a new resource, a new boom—all too often followed by decline and abandonment; sometimes growth was renewed, based on a newly discovered resource or an old resource enhanced by new technology.

Where else but in the Interior West can one find so forbiddingly extensive and rugged a mountain system that spawns most of the con-

Water is the key to Western development. However, the various uses of water do not always fit together. Hoover Dam and Lake Mead store Colorado River water which is released as power is generated for California and Nevada. Unfortunately, the seasonal needs for irrigation downstream do not always coincide with the needs for power. (Las Vegas News Bureau)

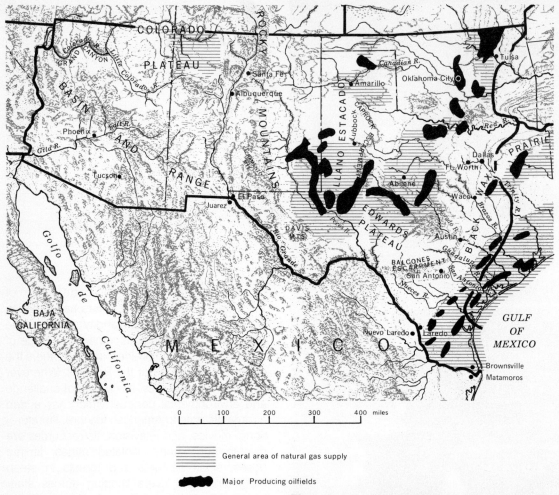

0   100   200   300   400   miles

General area of natural gas supply

Major Producing oilfields

Figure 7.1 Landforms of the Southwest. This region and the High West (Figure 7.6) constitute the Interior West, essentially a zone of transition among adjoining regions. Is this statement more true for this region than for other regions you have studied? What is the evidence in terms of landforms? Climate? Minerals? Soils? Products? Economic development? (Base map copyright by A. K. Lobeck. Reprinted with permission of The Geographical Press, Hammond, Inc.)

tinent's great rivers and yet gives grudgingly of abundant mineral wealth; a plateau so high and so broad as to be all but devoid of human settlement, but at the same time a thin scattering of cities where in some cases both a desert and a forested mountain may be found within the same metropolitan limits? The wilderness and the luxurious mansion are neighbors; even the desert itself is subdivided for homes where there is hope of getting water, the limiting factor to Western expansion.

ENVIRONMENT AND RESOURCES

A diversity of environments—some prohibitively harsh to man, others more amenable to human manipulation—characterizes the Interior West Fortunately, the region's natural resources— principally, water, timber, soil, and minerals—

are varied and in some places plentiful. On the other hand, their exploitation has involved overcoming major locational handicaps, such as relative internal inaccessibility and remoteness of external markets.

An east-west traverse of any part of the Interior West, be it near the Canadian border or a thousand miles south across southern Colorado, Utah, and Nevada, presents a succession of quite distinct physical landscapes. Sharp contrasts from high, but relatively level, plains in the east to towering mountains, lofty plateaus, and broken basin and range country in the west are apparent even to the casual cross-country traveler. These landforms have produced an equally diverse succession of climates, plant communities, and soil zones, all of which can be grouped into several distinctive physical regions.

The Higher Great Plains

Stretching for nearly 1,500 miles from Mexico to Canada this higher, western portion of the Great Plains generally consists of vast coalesced alluvial fans built out eastward for several hundred miles from the base of the Rocky Mountains. Generally the surface of the Plains appears monotonously flat to gently undulating. There are local variations such as the glaciated portions of the low-lying Missouri Plateau in Montana, the Pine Ridge escarpment of northwestern Nebraska, the basinlike Colorado Piedmont which dips eastward from the mile-high Denver area, the ancient volcanic tablelands of Raton Mesa in northeastern New Mexico, and the slightly elevated Llano Estacado (Staked Plain) and Edwards Plateau of western Texas.

Climatically, the continentality of the Higher Plains and its position in the rain shadow (lee side) of the Rockies and on the dry (west) side of the 20-inch annual precipitation line assures extremes of cold and light snow in winter and heat and scant rainfall in summer. Indrafts of warm, moist air from the

Gulf of Mexico occasionally alter this general weather pattern. Farther south and closer to the Gulf, climate is milder in winter and somewhat more humid in summer. To the residents, welcome relief during severe winters is often experienced along the base of the Rockies in the form of a dry, westerly flow of air known locally as the *chinook* (snow-eater) wind. As this air descends the eastern slopes of the Rockies, it warms by compression, sometimes causing temperatures at the foot of the mountains to rise from below zero to well above freezing in a matter of hours. These chinook winds are also common east of the Canadian Rockies in Alberta.

The distribution and type of natural vegetation and soils in the Plains are the result of the interaction of climate, landform, latitude, and continentality. The tangible expressions of semiarid climate are a seemingly unending cover of short grasses and a conspicuous lack of trees except along stream courses. The early settlers noted that the productive chestnut and brown soils of the Higher Plains owed their fertility mainly to the humus produced by the ubiquitous grasses. The combination of prolonged droughts, high winds, and poor soil management practices has created dust bowl conditions in large areas. On the other hand, irrigation, fallowing, and other soil conservation techniques have helped to reclaim some of the lost land.

Rocky Mountain System

In area and relief the Rockies are the most impressive mountain system in the United States. Composed of numerous ranges whose rugged peaks in places tower above 14,000 feet, the Rockies extend from the Sangre de Cristo of north central New Mexico northwestward to Waterton-Glacier International Peace Park. Northward in Canada the name Rocky Mountains is used for a specific range in the Cordillera and not for the whole mountain system. From eastern Wyoming's Laramie Range

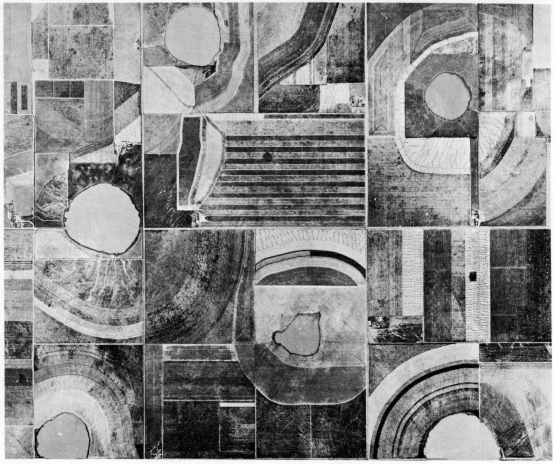

This photograph and the one on the facing page were taken at the same place—about 60 miles northwest of Lubbock, Texas. The High Plains (shown above in November, 1941) are marked by shallow depressions filled with water from recent rains. Another pattern consists of the square sections into which the land was divided by the survey. The field patterns reflect the prevalent dry-farming practices, with plowing generally following the contours as a moisture-conservation practice. (USDA)

to the Wasatch Mountains overlooking the Great Salt Lake of Utah, the Rockies exceed 300 miles in width. The Rockies presented the single, most formidable landform barrier to the Western expansion of settlement.

It may be difficult to imagine this great mountain chain rising from what was a vast sea a thousand miles wide that divided the continent some 100 million years ago. The forces that built and later began wearing down the mountains are still active, ranking the Rockies amongst the "younger" of the continent's landform regions. The Grand Tetons, for example, were uplifted for the most part in the last few million years, and only since the late Pleistocene period have alpine glaciers sculptured the jagged ridges and steep valleys that make the Tetons such a spectacular scenic attraction to tourists. In the present century the Northern Rockies, having experienced two severe earthquakes and many light tremors since 1925, have been seismically more active than the middle and southern ranges.

Climate varies considerably with altitude and exposure to wind and sun in the Rockies. Winter at higher elevations is characteristically

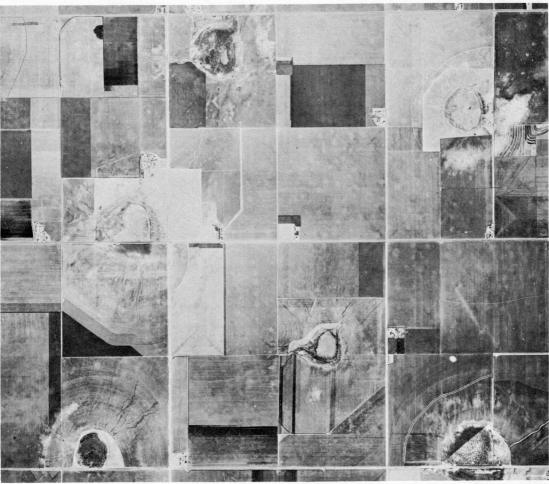

By the spring of 1953, the area shown on the facing page had been converted to pump irrigation, and cotton had become the dominant crop. The season was dry (note the lack of water in the depressions). The field patterns were mostly adjusted to straight-line irrigated farming rather than dry-farming techniques. (USDA)

harsh, especially in the northwestern ranges where snow, dropped by eastward or southward moving cold fronts, commonly accumulates to depths of 40 feet or more and temperatures plunge well below zero. Yet high grassy valleys (referred to locally as parks) behind the eastern front of the Rockies experience average winters that are a few degrees warmer than those on the windier Plains, and summers in the parks are cooler than on the Plains. Where air flowing from the northwest (westerly winds) is forced to rise over mountains and cool to the point of condensation, precipitation is greater; in general, it is greater in the northwestern ranges than in the eastern Rockies.

For instance, the Salmon River Mountains of Idaho capture more than 30 inches mean annual precipitation, whereas the Big Horn Mountains, some 350 miles due east in Wyoming, average 10 inches less each year—air masses simply contain less moisture by the time they reach the Big Horns.

Coniferous forest, the characteristic vegetation of the Rockies, is richest in the northwestern ranges. Coniferous forests extend into the Southern Rockies, but their distribution is

Zion Canyon's sheer sandstone walls have been exposed by the erosive action of the Virgin River and its tributaries. Sediments and sand dunes deposited by ancient seas and winds have been uplifted in the last several million years, thus causing the streams draining this southwestern part of the Colorado Plateau to speed up and cut deeper into their channels. The Virgin River flows southwestward, eventually meeting the Colorado River at Lake Mead. (Crane Miller)

more discontinuous and at higher elevations, and individual stands are thinner. Slope exposure influences vegetation significantly everywhere in the Rockies with shady, north-facing slopes more readily retaining soil moisture and thus supporting denser stands of trees than sunny or south-facing slopes, where shrubland may replace woodland. The distribution of the two dominant commercial species of conifers in the Rocky Mountain system also reflects differing moisture conditions; ponderosa pine has adapted to the more arid Southern Rockies and Douglas fir to the wetter northern climates. Lodgepole pine, western white pine, Engelmann spruce, and tamarack also contribute to the total annual Rocky Mountain cut of several billion board feet, almost 10 percent of the national lumber production. Mixed with the conifers are deciduous poplars (principally, the aspen), whose colored leaves in autumn splash the sea of evergreen with hues of yellow and gold. The forests provide habitats for a varied fauna, including fur-bearing mammals that in the past were essential to the livelihood of Indians and early European trappers and today provide a summer tourist attraction.

Colorado Plateau

Named from the river that drains most of its 150,000 square miles, the Colorado Plateau extends from the western edge of the Rockies in Colorado and New Mexico into southern Utah and northern Arizona. Uplifted, and perhaps still rising, the plateau is a highly elevated block generally exceeding 5,000 feet in altitude and in some places 11,000 feet. The upland is mostly covered with thick layers of almost horizontal sedimentary rocks which have been deeply dissected by the Colorado River and its tributaries. Mesa Verde in Colorado, Soda Canyon astride the Colorado–New Mexico border, and the Canyon Lands of Utah all display in diverse ways the gradational work of these streams. But the most spectacular is the Grand Canyon, where along a 5,000-foot cross section from the Colorado River up to the rim of the canyon one can view 600 million years of geological history in its sedimentary formations.

The climate of the Colorado Plateau is as unfriendly to human settlement as are its landforms. Because of its continentality and high elevation, winters are long, cold, and dry. Fortunately, the small amount of snow melts slowly into the subsoil, providing more effective moisture than does the occasional summer thundershower whose moisture runs off and evaporates rapidly. The effect of altitude is illustrated by annual precipitation of less than 10 inches in the lower center interior and more than 20 inches on the higher outer rim. Summer daytime temperatures that occasionally exceed 100 degrees are explained by nearly cloudless skies, high angle of the noontime sun's rays, high elevation, and low relative humidity.

Mountain regions are excellent places to study the response of vegetation and soils to aridity, altitude, and exposure. In the Colorado Plateau the coniferous forests, dominated by ponderosa pine and underlain by acidic and shallow residual soils, occupy the outer rim of the plateau above 7,500 feet where precipitation is highest. Ponderosa pine is a significant commercial tree in the plateau, especially on its southern edge surrounding the volcanic San Francisco Peaks of northern Arizona. Downslope, forests grade into pinyon-juniper woodlands and then into high desert shrub associations supported by gray desert soils.

Basin and Range

Aptly named for the numerous north-south fault-block mountain ranges and intervening down-dropped basins arranged *en échelon,*

the Basin and Range region is as inhospitable as any in the Interior West. The Nevada, or northern, portion of the basin and range country is commonly referred to as the Great Basin because of its numerous basins of interior drainage. The basin and range landscape is scenically dramatic, but its climate is unattractive to agricultural man. Situated in the rain shadow of the Pacific mountain systems, this is the driest part of the continent, and the hottest in summer. Much of the region receives from a trace to 10 inches precipitation annually; some areas receive no measurable precipitation for years. Precipitation is most likely to occur in winter (usually as snow), except in southern Arizona and New Mexico where summer rainfall brought in by tropical air masses from the Gulf of Mexico sometimes reaches cloudburst proportions. Daily temperatures in July and August often exceed 110 degrees, with some relief at night. Winter temperatures occasionally drop below zero at night in the higher basins and mountains, especially when high atmospheric pressure prevails.

Vegetation in the basin and range country is adapted to an arid environment. The traveler passing through this region sees a type of vegetation not found so extensively elsewhere in the United States. Plants in the Sonora, Colorado, and other southern deserts, such as cacti, store water in their thick, succulent stems. Plants in the higher, colder deserts, including all manner of woody shrubs, gather moisture from the soil by means of widely extended root systems or taproots reaching down to groundwater tables. Some plants, notably desert wildflowers, simply wait until an environmentally opportune time (usually following adequate precipitation) to appear. Trees are conspicuously absent except above 5,000 feet, where pinyon-juniper woodlands mix with Great Basin sage and other shrub communities. Still higher upslope and in favored exposure and soil situations, ponderosa pine and other coniferous forest associations are found. At timberline, bristlecone pines, unique as the world's oldest living tree (individual trees have

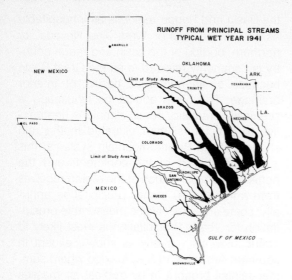

Figure 7.2 Average climatic and climate-related data are apt to be misleading; hence data are given here for extreme, rather than average, years. (*The Report of the U.S. Study Commission: Texas,* Austin, 1962.)

been dated at more than 4,000 years of age), sometimes prevail in nearly pure, but thin, stands.

Gray desert soils in the northern basin and range country differ mainly in mineral content—and therefore in color—from the red desert soils of southern Arizona and New Mexico; the former are composed of calcium minerals accumulated in the basins, the latter of iron oxides. The desert soils in both cases contain little humus because of sparse vegetation growth, and they are not suitable for cultivation unless amended and irrigated. Man has found that outer slopes of alluvial fans and river terraces and floodplains, such as along parts of the Colorado, Gila, and Rio Grande, are best suited for agriculture.

Water, the Basic Resource

The Interior West is a dry land. Yet, favorable subsurface geology and diverse topography contribute to the region's water resource potential without which permanent settlement may well have been comparatively sporadic to this day. Water-bearing sedimentary formations beneath Texas and much of the eastern Southwest (Oklahoma and southeastern New Mexico) store vast amounts of groundwater that

have proved vital to agricultural development. In the High West, the Rocky Mountain system and adjacent drainage and groundwater basins provide watersheds unmatched in Anglo-America.

Southwest groundwater The location of streams and water "holes" was of major concern to early explorers, cattlemen, and settlers. Even the presence of a river valley did not guarantee water, for many streams are dry during much of the year. Well-drilling machinery was a godsend, enabling underground water to be tapped. Yet this groundwater was, and is, not unlimited; many areas are now discovering that the water table is dropping year after year. This problem is especially serious in Texas and Oklahoma where unrestricted quantities of groundwater may be pumped by the owner of the surface land although rights to surface water use are carefully regulated (Figure 7.3).

Assuming that water may be conserved by storage reservoirs, retardation of evaporation, and efficient use, the problem of quality still remains. Some of the groundwater is saline or brackish. Much of the surface water carries a heavy load of silt which may fill up reservoirs in a century or less. Irrigated lands must be drained to remove surplus alkali; this in turn increases the salinity of the discharged water. Much more serious is contamination from municipal sewage, industrial wastes, and wastes from mining operations.

The easily available water resources of the region are already "used" except for modest supplies of brackish water which may be desalinated. Development plans for each subregion involve water; for example, an elaborate study[1] made of eight river basins in Texas presented a plan for the utilization of the bulk of all Texas water through the year 2010. This involves flood and pollution control, hydroelectric power, drainage, irrigation, and municipal and industrial water supply, at a capital cost of $3 billion for an area with an estimated 2010 population of 20 million. The recommendations, comprehensive though they are, will not cure all the major water problems; for example, the irreplaceable groundwater supply now being pumped to irrigate cotton on the High Plains will be largely used up by the year 2010.

High West drainage basins
A regional analysis largely in terms of drainage basins will indicate the importance of water resources in the High West. Be it from the Rio Grande or Colorado in the Southwest, the Snake or Missouri in the north, or the South Platte or Arkansas on the Colorado Piedmont, most of urban and agricultural America west of the Mississippi is sustained by streams emanating from the Rocky Mountain ranges. Each river originates in seasonally snow-covered high peaks, mostly in the Rockies, where the slopes are covered with an open forest; the headwaters of each are commonly impounded in water bodies, some natural but more man-made. Downstream, waters are often used for mining; for urban use; and finally for feeding of streams,

[1] *The Report of U.S. Study Commission,* Austin, March 1962.

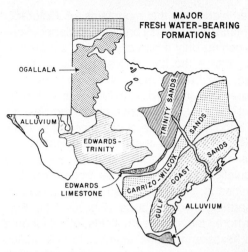

Figure 7.3 In Texas, groundwater supplements streams as a source of water supply and in many areas is the major water source. The Ogallala formation is a water reserve that is not being replenished. The areas dependent on Gulf Coast sands are expected to supplement their supplies by distilling seawater. (*The Report of the U.S. Study Commission: Texas,* Austin, 1962.)

irrigation canals, and the underground waters on the adjacent plains. Nowadays, mountain freshets deposit erosional and mining debris over good soils developed on alluvial fans, and urban sewage pollutes the waters nourishing the plains and basins. The merits of alternative water uses must be weighed: it is estimated that water needed to irrigate 1 acre will suffice for 4 to 5 urban families housing 18 people on the same area.[2] An urban acre in industrial or commercial activity can use much more water. Further, potential consumption depends on the amount of purification and recycling done in each industry.

Mineral Resources
Mineral exploitation in the Interior West, although in instances ephemeral compared to water resource development, brought with it a tide of settlement that flowed and ebbed starting in the mid-nineteenth century. Placer and lode miners stripped away fortunes in gold and

[2] M. John Loeffler, "The Population Syndromes on the Colorado Piedmont," *Annals A.A.G.,* vol. 55 (1965), p. 66.

silver hidden in the mountains of Colorado, Montana, and Nevada and then departed, leaving behind only a partially settled country. At a later time the lure of less precious metals (lead, zinc, copper, molybdenum) and recently of uranium and hydrocarbons was not sufficient to attract the "get-rich-quick" hordes, but did bring a semblance of permanency to some mining settlements that have survived to the present. But the magnitude of economic and population growth caused by metallic ore discoveries is small compared to the impact of unearthing hydrocarbons (Figure 7.4). Furthermore, the petroleum fields of Oklahoma and Texas and, more recently, the oil shales of Colorado held far greater reserves of their wealth than did the Colorado gold fields.

The example of Leadville   The Arkansas River heads in the snows on the highest of all Rocky Mountain peaks, near Leadville, Colorado. A long-established trail followed the river up to Tennessee Pass (10,240 feet) and thence down Eagle Creek to the upper Colorado Valley. Gold seekers en route to and from California by this route discovered gold near Leadville in the fall of 1859. Word of the strike spread, and by 1861 Oro City was the most populous town in Colorado. In a few years the placer gold was exhausted, the town deserted. In 1874 prospectors discovered silver-lead ore, and by 1878 the town was revived as "Leadville" and connected with supply centers at Pueblo and Denver by rail (Figure 7.6, p. 209).

Smelting was done near the mines, at first using local charcoal and thus destroying large acreages of forest. Water was essential in most mining processes, and the used water was returned to the streams, slightly contaminated. Much of the mining was underground, but mine dumps mar the surface. Although the landscape was changed by this mining activity, the area affected is so small a part of the Rockies that the scarring detracts little from the local recreational potential.

The principle that mines open and close but that the region as a whole continues to be a mining area is illustrated by the fact that the last smelter at Leadville closed in 1961, but mining continues at Climax, 12 miles northeast of Leadville. Here a rich deposit of molybdenum ore accounts for nearly one-quarter of all Colorado mineral production and nearly three-fourths of the nation's molybdenum production. Molybdenum is highly prized as a ferroalloy, imparting durability to steel.

Copper and other metals   After the California gold rush, Arizona and New Mexico were prospected with local success, for example, the silver mines at Tombstone and gold near Yuma, Wickenburg, and Prescott—all in Arizona. The greatest discovery of all in 1877, however, was the copper at Bisbee, Arizona, which has produced four-fifths of Arizona mineral wealth. Copper is the major source of income for people in Grant County in New Mexico and in Cochise, Greenleaf, and Pinal counties in Arizona. The worldwide rise in the use of electricity and electrical equipment has increased many times the demand for copper. But the copper economy of the Southwest as elsewhere is complicated because profitability depends on competition from other areas and the recovery of by-products such as silver. For

INCOME   INTERIOR WEST

% Distribution   Location quotients: 1.0 = national average per capita

Employment	Income	SIC source	0	1.0	2.0	3.0	4.0	5.0
8.5	0.7	Farms						
2.8	2.7	Mining						
5.4	4.8	Construction						
15.2	11.8	Manufacturing						
21.5	11.8	Trade						
4.6	3.2	Finance						
6.2	5.3	Transportation						
15.5	8.3	Services						
19.9	16.4	Government						
—	38.1	Other income						
100.0	100.0	Total						

Figure 7.4   Contrast the outstanding position of mining in the Interior West with the extractive industry's LQ in the Atlantic Megalopolis (Figure 1.2) or the Pacific States (Figure 1.3).

Northeast of Amarillo, Texas, hard winter wheat shares the land with "grasshoppers" (oil pumps). The latter occupy the smaller part of the area but produce the greater income. (Texas Highway Department)

example, the Jerome District, in Yavapai County, two decades ago was the seventh largest copper producer in the United States; now it is abandoned, except as a tourist attraction, while Bagdad, an isolated copper camp 60 miles to the west, is a growing producer that obtains silver and molybdenum as by-products.

Fossil fuels Although the first oil well drilled in Texas dates from 1866, the Texas-Oklahoma oil boom really began at the outset of the present century. In recent years Southwestern minerals have accounted for over one-third of the value of United States mineral production, with five-sixths of this amount coming from petroleum and natural gas; in Texas and Oklahoma over nine-tenths of the value is from petroleum and gas. Much of the economic and population growth of the Southwest in recent decades is attributable to minerals and mineral-based industries.

Oil and natural gas are widespread in Texas (in 205 out of 254 counties), Oklahoma (66 out of 77 counties), and northwestern and southeastern New Mexico (8 out of 32 counties). This vast fuel resource is not a single unit, but rather it consists of a number of large fields. Production for each region rises rapidly with new discoveries and falls with depletion. Production has also been controlled by state regulation to prevent an oversupply in the market. The earliest oil discoveries were in the eastern parts of Texas and Oklahoma. Today, the leading gas-and-oil-producing counties are mostly in the Amarillo-Lubbock-Odessa area of Texas, adjacent New Mexico, and the Oklahoma Panhandle. Obviously the future of the petroleum–natural gas industry depends on reserves, and Southwestern proved reserves are high. Although one-third of the nation's reserves (in 1971) are in Texas, this is only enough to equal about four years' current national production. Proved reserves indicate only the supplies that the industry considers certain to exist; past experience indicates that actual reserves may greatly exceed the reserves considered "proved." With American demands on oil resources increasing so greatly in the past decade, it is to be hoped that much larger reserves will be found.

The extraction of petroleum and natural gas employs only about 150,000 out of more than 5 million in the Southwestern nonagricultural labor force. However, indirect employment in petrochemical manufacturing, equipment for oil wells, oil storage, and shipment is much higher. In addition, the profit on the production of mineral fuels has yielded capital for economic growth, bringing in some industries which may continue long after the oil and gas are exhausted.

Petroleum reserves estimated at 600 billion barrels, or enough to last nearly a century at the current rate of United States consumption, lie buried in the *oil shales* of the High West. The process of heating the kerogen in crushed shale, thereby converting it to oil, having been proven possible, the federal government late in 1973 approved the leasing of some 30,000 acres in the area where Wyoming, Utah, and Colorado converge in order to test the feasibility of large-scale shale oil extraction. The high cost of producing oil from this process, however, is likely to mean much higher retail prices for petroleum products when compared with the relatively low costs of production from present wells. Because of the potential damage to flora and fauna, as a result of extensive open-pit operations, environ-

mental groups vehemently opposed the pilot project. This experimental development may trigger a new wave of mining settlement, which will further change the landscape of this nearly empty, but outstandingly scenic, area.

With increasing reliance on domestic sources of energy becoming a fact of life in the United States, coal mining in the Interior West assumed new significance. Low-grade coal is widespread in northwest and north central New Mexico and northeastern Arizona. Coal in Colfax County in New Mexico is coked for metallurgical use; elsewhere coal is mined for use in carboelectric plants. In the High West, major bituminous coal deposits in Colorado, Utah, Wyoming, and Montana are mined largely for coking coal and use in thermal electric plants. To diminish the high costs of transporting coal, the development of *coal gasification* (production of methane gas from the reaction of coal with oxygen and hydrogen from steam) plants adjacent to some strip mines is planned in the Interior West; however, gasification plants require large amounts of water, which is in meager supply near most coal fields. A major reallocation of water resources to meet this new demand could noticeably affect other economic development of the region.

THE SOUTHWEST (Figure 7.1)

In peoples as well as their physical settings the one-seventh of the United States included in the Southwest is a land of diversity. Here diverse whites met and struggled—Spanish, Southern planters, cattlemen, and shepherds; Midwestern and Southern Uplands farmers, ore and mineral prospectors—as well as varied Indian peoples as the nomadic Apaches, the sedentary Pueblo farmers, and the remnants of eastern agricultural tribes forced westward by the United States government. Other immigrants included German settlers, black slaves brought in by cotton farmers, and most recently migrants from Mexico.

Resources and Employment

In 1880 southwestern employment was based largely on resources: 70 percent was agricultural, about 1 percent mining, and only 7 percent manufacturing (mostly of agricultural and mineral products). By 1970 agricultural employment was only 7 percent, mining remained low at 3 percent, manufacturing had risen to 18 percent, and the others employed were mainly in government service activities. But this employment is unevenly distributed both in quantity and in the nature of the work and of the employees. The distinctive subregional patterns of resource exploitation and settlement are illustrated below.

The Eastern Transition Zone

The culture of the proud Texan was formed in part in a subhumid environment subject to wide fluctuations in precipitation, soil moisture, and stream flow. In the past this was a significant area for range cattle, for cotton growing and for farmers learning to adjust to conditions in the drier lands. To this earlier economy was added, in the present century, the impact of the oil fields. In terms of the physical environment this is a transition area from the Coastal Plain and Central Lowland to the Great Plains. Soils are generally fertile and neither strongly acid nor alkaline; vegetation ranges from forest to grassland and savanna. Throughout this transition zone a line of major cities—San Antonio, Austin, Waco, Dallas–Fort Worth, Oklahoma City, and Tulsa—is located where rivers from the northwest flow toward the Gulf of Mexico.

The early white settlers drove the Indians westward from most of the area except in the northeast where eastern Indian tribes were resettled in Oklahoma (then called Indian Territory).[3] Most of the Hispano (Mexican) peoples left Texas when it became independent. Three groups of whites poured into Texas: farmers

[3] In 1970 there were 98,000 Indians in Oklahoma and 18,000 in Texas.

and ranchers from the Upper South (from Missouri to Virginia), cotton planters from the Old South (with their slaves) settling in east Texas while Germans and other European immigrants moved into south central Texas. Later when Indian Territory was opened to settlers, Midwesterners raced into Oklahoma and spilled over into Texas. In southern Texas Mexicans crossed the Rio Grande and provided a cheap labor supply on ranches and farms. But the dominant group consisted of Americans of Western European descent (Anglos) in central Texas within the triangular cultural hearth enclosed approximately by lines connecting Dallas–Fort Worth, San Antonio, and Houston.

San Antonio and southern Texas The oldest and southernmost of the large cities serves a huge area of ranchland and irrigated farms extending south and west to the Rio Grande and its irrigated winter garden of citrus and winter vegetables. North of the irrigated area are several large ranches, which include the 900,000-acre King Ranch where Zebu cattle were bred with Herefords and other European breeds to produce high-grade cattle. Northward the ranch area grades into cotton-grain farms centered on San Antonio. This city was founded by the Spanish as a political capital in 1718; later it became a stockyard center, and recently military and governmental activities became dominant. Included also in the commercial hinterland of San Antonio is the moister eastern part of the Edwards Plateau, edged by the Balcones Escarpment (see Figure 7.1). Within an hour's drive from San Antonio the visitor can see the change from open cattle range to the goat and sheep ranges on the plateau and to mechanized farming on the dark soils extending northeastward. Nearly half of the people in the San Antonio hinterland are Mexican, and the old Hispanic houses, markets, and churches contrast sharply with the modern canal-centered shopping-entertainment area, the Tower of the Americas, and the tall skyscrapers.

Austin and the Blackland Prairie About 75 miles northeast of San Antonio, Austin, capital of Texas, located where the Colorado River[4] crosses the Balcones Escarpment onto the prairie, is largely supported by state institutions. Near Austin, the Blackland (Black Waxy) Prairie, named for its rich, limey soil, widens into an extensive, well-farmed area, once devoted to cotton but now highly diversified with mechanized cotton farming intermixed with dairying, beef cattle, poultry, hogs, grain, and vegetables. Waco and some other former agricultural service centers north of Austin are developing manufacturing industries, especially those using petrochemicals as raw materials (in tire production, for example).

Dallas–Fort Worth Promoters of the Dallas–Fort Worth area have expanded it to include eight counties called the Southwest Metroplex, thus acquiring a slightly larger population than the rival Houston area. Fort Worth, once a military outpost on the edge of Indian country, became a focal center for western Texan development. As such it added functions such as stockyards, meatpacking, railroad center, and oil refining. During World War II, aircraft factories were moved into the area from the Atlantic Coast to take advantage of a more defensible location. Much of the new industrial development took place between Fort Worth and Dallas.

Fort Worth was oriented westward; the older and much larger Dallas was originally oriented eastward, being more interested in Wall Street than in the livestock market. It started as a railroad junction and wholesale distributing center. Cotton, insurance, oil, and finance added to its business in turn. The city benefited from the development of the east Texas oil fields, and the nearby cotton fields stimulated the development of cotton machinery and textile and clothing industries. Dallas is a Federal Reserve Bank city serving all of Texas and southern New Mexico and Arizona. Over one hundred insurance companies and innumerable regional sales offices are located there. Its shops are considered so outstanding that recently it has been recognized as a style center for women's wear.

Oklahoma City–Tulsa The major stimulus to Oklahoma development was oil. In 1901 oil was struck near the minor farm center of Tulsa on the Arkansas River; several decades later the city with some truth claimed to be the "Oil Capital of the World." For many years, Tulsa served as a basing point from which much of the world's oil pricing was determined. Although the concentration of Oklahoma petroleum production has moved southwest and west, the city flourishes as a center of research in oil technology, oil company offices, and oil financing, oil refining, and airline servicing. Of current significance to Tulsa's continued growth is the development of a navigable waterway from near the city along the lower 500 miles of the Arkansas River to its junction with the Mississippi River.

Oklahoma City was a boomtown in 1889 when the territory was opened to settlement, but its real growth began after 1928 with the discovery of oil around the city. In addition to its political and commercial functions, the capital soon added manufacturing, especially in lines related to oil and aircraft. In both Tulsa and Oklahoma City the resource base of their hinterlands is the reason for the commerce and industries (and jobs) of the cities. Although the wells have had a longer producing life than the metal mines of the Southwest, the impermanency of an economy based on mining is well documented in the past.

The Southern Plains
The external image of the Plains has changed greatly since they were first visited by American explorers. Damned by Pike and Long as a vast desert and classified on early maps as the

---

[4] Not to be confused with the Colorado River of Colorado, Utah, and Arizona. Colorado is a Spanish word referring to a stream that is colored with reddish mud.

Wherever the land is flat, cotton is now harvested by machine. This photograph is of the High Plains of Texas where cotton is defoliated and picked clean. (USDA)

"Great American Desert," the Plains at first were an obstacle to be traversed rather than a land to be used. Later in the nineteenth century the transcontinental railroads, favored by a period of relatively rainy weather, were able to attract settlers to the fertile grasslands. Nevertheless, most settlement of the Texas-Oklahoma Plains (except for open-range grazing) was deferred to the present century. The nature of this settlement varied in each of three subregions.

The Rolling Plains West of the Cross Timbers (a narrow north-south belt of small hardwood trees between the Colorado and Canadian rivers) lies a varied section characterized by a mixture of grassland and scrub woodland. Its rainfall is barely enough for the dry farming of cotton, wheat, and sorghum, and water resources for irrigation are limited; the poorer lands are in cattle ranches. In common with other Plains areas, most of the counties are losing population while the remaining farms are growing larger.

Llano Estacado The salvation of agriculture in the Panhandle region has come from its underground water. The abrupt Cap Rock Escarpment separates the Rolling Plains from a higher, flat area to the westward underlain by a water-bearing layer of rock (an aquifer). This groundwater is being used more rapidly than it is replaced by percolation of surface water. The soil is fertile and the rainfall suffices for a turf of short grass. But surface water is scarce, and early travelers called the Llano Estacado south of the Canadian River the "Sahara of North America." The bulk of the land is still primarily ranching country. Higher incomes are obtained in those local areas producing oil, wheat, or cotton.

On the Llano Estacado west of Lubbock,

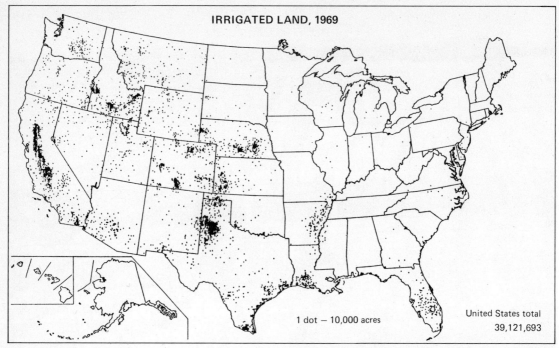

IRRIGATED LAND, 1969

1 dot — 10,000 acres

United States total
39,121,693

Figure 7.5 Irrigated acreage is obviously far more extensive west of the Mississippi than in the East, where atmospheric moisture is greater and more dependable. Outstanding in irrigated cropland in the Interior West are northwestern Texas, Colorado east of the Rockies, and southern Idaho. (U.S. Department of Commerce, Social and Economic Statistics Administration, Bureau of the Census)

a dust bowl in the 1930's, water is being pumped up several hundred feet to supplement the 20-inch rainfall. Irrigation triples the cotton yield, but this may not be a permanent technique, for it is estimated that by the year 2000 the groundwater will be barely adequate to supply the cities. The small cities of the region, Midland and Odessa, for example, grew from the exploitation of petroleum resources rather than from the scanty agricultural base.

Land use changes slightly to the north. In the northern Texas Panhandle and adjacent Oklahoma wheat and grain sorghum replace cotton; the acreage of extensive dry farming, plus a small amount of stream irrigation, is greater than the acreage irrigated by wells. Availability of water remains the limiting environmental factor. Water in the Canadian River reservoir, 10 miles north of Amarillo, is reserved mainly for urban expansion. Yet with all the potential water shortage, a number of counties are increasing in population—largely because of oil and related industries. The lead-

ing transportation, oil-refining, and air force center of the region is Amarillo.

Edwards Plateau The Llano Estacado merges southward into a vast limestone upland, composed mainly of a hilly surface which ends to the south and east at the Balcones Escarpment. Essentially it is ranch country— cattle, sheep, and goats—with some cultivated crops grown in the valleys to supply fodder. As in the Plains to the north, the underlying limestone stores water which can be recovered through wells. Also similar to the northward area, agricultural service towns are few. The cities large enough to have daily newspapers are on the edge of the area; the largest, San Angelo, has nearby oil wells and an air force base.

West from the Pecos

The Southwestern landscapes west of the Pecos River Plain to California (Figure 7.1) are familiar to most Americans, being widely displayed in Western stories on TV and in the movies. Diverse combinations of colorful rock escarpments, deep canyons, purplish mountains on the horizon, sparse grassland, sage-green shrubs, and open pine-juniper forests are all brightened by a brilliant sun shining in an intense blue sky.

Settlement Some 3 million people of diverse backgrounds are scattered throughout this generally dry but picturesque land. About 175,000 are Indians, descendants of Pueblo agriculturists or nomadic peoples such as the Navajos and the Apaches. Generally the Indians live on or near reservations in northeastern Arizona and central New Mexico, on lands too barren to have attracted white settlers. Hispanos entered the area from Mexico primarily via Chihuahua, El Paso, and the Rio Grande with a lesser stream through Nogales, Arizona. Hispanos were the majority until the Anglo influx of the last 60 years. The earliest Anglos were traders, gold seekers, and cattlemen who entered the region from east Texas. Still others entered from the Midwest along the Santa Fe Trail and, later, the Santa Fe Railroad. Mormons from Utah and Californians also immigrated, but in smaller groups. The Anglo settlement pattern focused on the two main east-west railroad lines (Santa Fe and Southern Pacific), and fewer people settled along the less important north-south connecting lines in central New Mexico and central Arizona. Branch rail lines penetrated into mineralized areas when copper, silver, and alloy metals displaced gold as the leading mineral. In the last half century, with the advent of air conditioning and the trend to migration to milder climates, Easterners flowed into the Southwest; southern Arizona became an outstanding growth area, attracting tourists, retired people, and skilled workers—all escaping from cold winters.

The upper Rio Grande Valley

Much of the population of New Mexico and trans-Pecos Texas lives within the valleys occupied by the Rio Grande and its major western tributary, the San Jose. The narrow strip of irrigation is interrupted where the Rio Grande flows in canyons. From 1822 until the completion of the Santa Fe Railroad (1880) Yankee traders hauled manufactures over the old Santa Fe Trail to be exchanged for New Mexican gold, silver, and furs in this region inhabited then by Spanish and Pueblo Indian farmers.

Today the activities of the valley are focused on two cities, Albuquerque and El Paso. The former is the commercial, transportation, and educational center of New Mexico. Its industries include the expected food and meat-packing industries based on regional agricultural resources to which have been added defense and atomic industries, an outgrowth of scientific work at the atomic center at Los Alamos, 50 miles to the north. El Paso, in extreme western Texas, is a smelting and refining center for the New Mexico–Arizona copper mines and a major port of entry from Mexico. Because the surrounding area is exceptionally barren, the irrigated areas west and east of the city stand out conspicuously when seen from the air.

International cooperation is well illustrated along this border with Mexico. In addition to El Paso other border cities include Brownsville, McAllen, Laredo, Eagle Pass, and Del Rio. Each has its Mexican counterpart, and shopping across the border is common. Wages in the Mexican towns are about one-fourth those in their American neighbors. Since 1966 the Mexican government has encouraged the opening of American-owned factories within 12 miles of the border, and both countries have relaxed tariff restrictions so that American-made parts can be assembled in Mexico and then returned to the United States. Furthermore, American-financed farms are now producing vegetables which are transported across the border to compete with farm crops in south Texas.

Basin and range country Descending westward from its source high in the mountains of southwestern New Mexico, the Gila River winds its way through 300 miles of sparsely settled basin and range country until it nears Phoenix, a mushrooming metropolis of more than 1 million people. The skyrocketing population that made Arizona a boom state in the 1960s is concentrated in Phoenix and Tucson (100 miles to the southeast of Phoenix). The Arizona boom has been attributed to the four C's: cattle, copper, cotton, and climate; the same might be said for the growth on a much smaller scale in southwestern New Mexico. To these should be added, especially for the Phoenix-Tucson area, commerce, consumer goods, and in recent decades, retirement, electronic, and aircraft industries. Cattle and copper are concentrated in the highlands of southeastern Arizona and adjacent New Mexico, and crop agriculture centers on the irrigated areas of the Gila, the Salt, and other Gila tributaries.

As in most of the West, minerals were the initial incentive for exploration and temporary settlement. Silver ores were first discovered by the Spanish in the late sixteenth century, but no major discoveries were made until the mid-nineteenth century when silver was exploited south of Tucson, and copper and gold between Tucson and the Colorado River. Larger-scale operations developed in the highland ranges after 1875 as transcontinental railroads were constructed in the area. Gradually mining shifted to copper, and since 1907 Arizona has been the leading copper-producing state in most years. Adjacent New Mexico contributes about one-fifth as much copper, but still sufficient to rank that state third among the nation's producers in 1971.

Mining is an activity which is scattered in distribution and intermittent in time. Ghost towns are common: for example, Jerome and its huge smelter at nearby Clarksdale ceased operations in 1953 after producing almost 3 billion pounds of copper, along with gold, silver, and zinc by-products. The significance of mining is partially in the employment which it gives and the towns which are created, but equally important is the capital which it creates for other development. For example, metallic ores produced since the beginning of mining are valued at nearly $2 billion in New Mexico and nearly $11 billion in Arizona—a sizable chunk of capital for other developments.

THE SPARSELY SETTLED HIGH WEST

Nature has afforded magnificent scenery to the High West: a land of spectacular mountains, colorful canyons, extensive tablelands, and gently sloping alluvial fans. Man has been less able to wrest a living from this environment than from other parts of Anglo-America. Water is scarce; exploitable minerals are in relatively small and scattered areas; and tourist income, concentrated in three months of the year, is important mainly near only a few well-known attractions. The population of this vast region is less than that of Indiana, whose area is only one-sixteenth as large. In per capita income the High West averages below that of the nation—only the Southern states have a lower average!

The population of the High West is clustered in a few places; one-third lives in the Denver and Salt Lake City SMSAs. Other people live in groups or strips in urban and irrigation settlements along the Rocky Mountain piedmonts of Colorado and Montana, the Wasatch Piedmont in Utah, and on the Snake Plains of Idaho.

The impact of government is very significant in this region. More than half the land is government owned, notwithstanding that most of the Higher Plains section is privately owned. Furthermore, government disbursements (three-fifths federal) account for one-quarter of all personal income.

Development of the Economy

The High West was settled piecemeal. Many pioneers crossed the region en route to Oregon

Figure 7.6 Note the great areal extent of the Rockies, Colorado Plateau, and Great Basin. In what ways might these high, rugged landforms still act as barriers to western expansion? How, on the other hand, might they attract development in the High West? (Base map copyright by A. K. Lobeck. Reprinted with permission of The Geographical Press, Hammond, Inc.)

or California without testing either its mineral or its agricultural potential. The first white settlers were the Mormons, who started irrigating east of Great Salt Lake in 1847. Gold was discovered near Denver in 1858 and shortly thereafter in the Colorado, Montana, and Idaho mountains. Cattle from Texas were driven into Colorado soon after, and by 1871 the first herds had reached Montana. Meanwhile in 1869 the Union Pacific bisected the region, and in 1870 several agricultural colonies

started irrigating the Colorado Piedmont. Placer mining soon exhausted the easily available gold; subsequently milling machinery and complicated metallurgical processes requiring considerable capital were introduced. With the arrival of the railroad at Denver in 1872, this became an ideal spot both to manufacture machinery and to process the ore.

The advancing rail net led to the settlement of the Higher Plains in the late 1880s, in part by ranchers who fenced their range and in part by irrigation and dry farmers. The lush pastures in the Rocky Mountain parks were already settled, and many of the interior oases had been exploited by Mormon groups. Large irrigation projects awaited the help of the federal government after about 1912. Meanwhile many gold and silver mines became exhausted, and ghost towns became a common feature; miners' attention turned to copper, lead, zinc, alloy metals, petroleum, coal, and, much later, uranium. The national parks had been available for decades by rail, but the tourist business really expanded following the universal ownership of the automobile and the development of paved highways. Thus in less than a centruy the High West had changed from a primitive area strewn with mining camps and irrigation towns to a largely empty area crossed by a network of highways and punctuated by relatively small but modern cities.

Land and Water Titles

Water rights   Many institutions which were new to settlers from the humid East originated in the High West. English common law, developed in a land of adequate water, followed the *riparian doctrine* under which the landowner has the full right to use any water flowing in or past his property, provided he does not diminish the volume of the stream. In contrast, 17 Western states use the *appropriation doctrine* under which the practice is "first come, first served." The settlers in each valley file with the state a claim to the right to use a certain amount of the water. If the claim is approved, the landlord has a perpetual right to this amount of surface water as long as he continues to use it for the purpose specified. The right of the earliest applicant has priority over that of later applicants, so that if the stream is low, the rights of the latter may have little value. The appropriation doctrine is a common practice in all the semiarid and arid West.

These different ownership regulations resulted in a different spatial and political organization of the environment. Such a system requires special organizations known as irrigation districts, conservancy districts, cooperative enterprises, water users' associations, and the like; there are also federal and state reclamation projects. All these distribute the cost of irrigation canals and reservoirs for the good of their members, and enforce the legal distribution of the available water. The administration of the use of underground water is usually different from that of surface water. The former usually belongs to the owner of the surface who by pumping at will may seriously lower the water table. For this reason, in some areas pumping is restricted.

Large land units   A second distinctive Western feature is the need for large farms, especially in grazing and dry-farming areas. The 160-acre homestead, well suited to the humid East, was quite inadequate; 40 acres of tillable land might be suitable for an irrigation farmer, but 640 acres or more were needed for dry farming and many square miles for ranching. Large acreages alone will not suffice for a ranch if well or stream water is not available. Various acts after 1873 made it possible to acquire larger holdings. Farms and ranches too small to be operated profitably were merged into larger units. Consequently the average farm or ranch in the region encompasses several square miles. Variation between states is related to environmental conditions and the carrying capacity of the land: the average farm in Idaho averages 566 acres; in Nevada 5,070 acres.

The range   The use of public range is a third distinctive Western feature, which arose from the changing use of the range. With the introduction of barbed wire, private ranches were

SEASONAL USE OF WESTERN RANGE

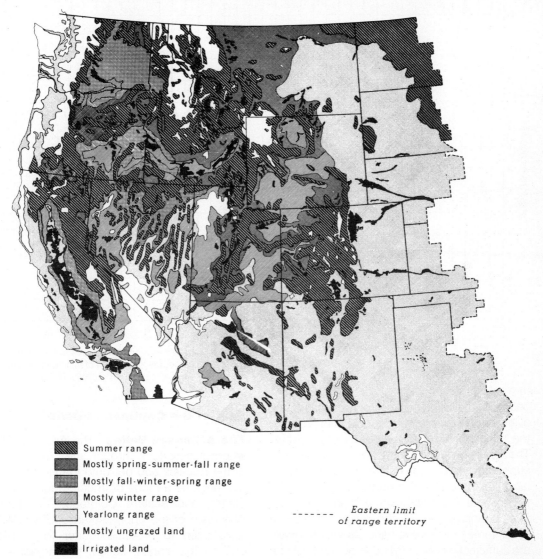

Summer range

Mostly spring-summer-fall range

Mostly fall-winter-spring range

Mostly winter range

Yearlong range

Mostly ungrazed land

Irrigated land

- - - - - - -   *Eastern limit
of range territory*

Figure 7.7 Although much of the West is commonly perceived as a vast potential ranch, there are significant differences in the quality of the range. The irrigated land provides supplementary fodder for animals inadequately nourished by the sparse natural herbage. (USDA)

fenced in, but public lands were open to unrestricted grazing. Since on poorer grazing lands a square mile sufficed to feed only one to three steers, many public lands were consistently over-grazed. The Grazing Act of 1934 reduced such damage to the range by organizing the public land into grazing districts within which grazing is now regulated by permits.

Repeating Patterns

The interconnection of mountain ranges, the plains, and linking stream valleys is a common pattern in the High West and in the western part of the Southwest. Despite this repeating pat-

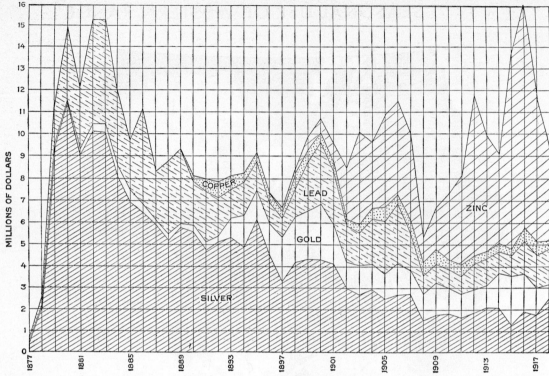

Figure 7.8 Mineral production in Lake County, Colorado, reflects the ups and downs of mining in the Leadville area. (U.S. Geological Survey Bulletin 707, p. 107.)

tern, each valley claims some individuality, based on the idiosyncrasies of the settlers, the available natural resources, local climates, and the accessibility of the valley to other areas. The mountain parks are generally semiarid or subhumid and provide pasture and some cropland while the higher mountains receive relatively greater precipitation and are forested. The igneous rocks of the ranges contain a great variety of metallic minerals which locally are sufficiently concentrated to be the basis for mining industries. In contrast, sedimentary rocks of the plains and some of the plateaus contain hydrocarbons. As the mountain streams leave their narrow valleys and cross the plains, their waters may be channeled so as to irrigate rich croplands and pastures. The larger cities are likely to be concentrated in these irrigated areas. Beyond the irrigable areas, sparse grazing and dry farming may be found with wells providing local water supply.

East of the Continental Divide

The Arkansas Valley The Arkansas River where it descends through the Front Ranges of the Rockies and out onto the Higher Plains has become a focus of irrigated agriculture in central and eastern Colorado. The narrow floodplain of the upper Arkansas River Valley is irrigated to produce fodder for livestock grazing the slopes. Salida, the largest town, has a strategic position at a junction of routes leading westward over Monarch Pass and southward to San Luis Park. The nearby San Luis Basin, well irrigated by the headwaters of the Rio Grande, was settled by Spanish-speaking farmers a century ago. Eastward the Arkansas flows across the Plains, first entrenched amid a 40-mile stretch of pasture. Beyond Pueblo the narrow but productive irrigated land yields sugar beets, fodder crops,

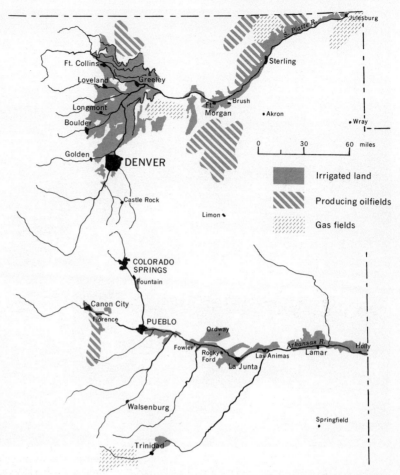

Figure 7.9 The section of Colorado east of the Rockies' Front Ranges illustrates a repeating pattern common throughout the High West: minerals; a stream for irrigation; level, irrigable farmlands; adjacent farmsteads; and modest commercial centers, a few of which have grown to have more than local importance. (After Loeffler)

vegetables, and cantaloupes. The key to both urban and irrigated development is water, and the present supply is completely utilized—at times inadequate because of the uncertain flow of the Arkansas. In order to increase the flow, water from the Frying Pan and Roaring Fork rivers, both tributaries of the Colorado, was diverted by a tunnel under the continental divide to the upper Arkansas (Figure 7.9).

Pueblo and Colorado Springs These cities, less than 40 miles apart, show how small environmental and historical differences combine to create two quite different urban milieus. Industrial Pueblo, once a fur-trading post, is now a primary-metals center around which

other functions, commercial, military, and service, have developed. The local steel industry assembles its raw materials from within the region: coking coal comes from near Trinidad 60 miles to the south, limestone from the mountains 40 miles to the west, and iron ore from eastern Wyoming and southwestern Utah.

Colorado Springs has a different history, having started as a resort center. Its light industries include food, printing, and electronics; its economy and growth are now dominated by

Denver—the Colorado capitol in the foreground, which is exactly 1 mile high—is on the western edge of the Great Plains. When the weather is clear the 150-mile Rocky Mountain skyline is visible. (© Dillon Aerial Photography, Inc.)

armed forces organizations and personnel (for example, the Air Force Academy) which account directly for a quarter of all employment and for even more of the purchasing power.

The South Platte Although minerals once attracted people to this region, its valuable product now is its water. The South Platte River receives numerous tributaries from the High Plains to the south and from the Rockies to the northwest. These source areas supply the water that irrigates the agriculturally productive northern Colorado Piedmont. The mountainous headwaters area has many ghost towns, reminders of the earlier mining days. One of these, Central City, is a tourist attraction overshadowed in fact as well as in metaphor by the adjacent spectacular Rockies. The South Platte

Valley downstream still has minerals, but these are the nonmetallics such as natural gas, petroleum, coal, sand, and gravel of the Plains.

Denver "Mile-High City," founded to serve the people of the adjacent mountains and the Plains, now serves a wider regional hinterland. The development of Denver reflects the varying eras of Colorado history—mining (1870–1900), agriculture (1900–1940), and the Era of Defense (1942–   ).[5] At first Denver supplied urban services to the nearby mines and to

[5]*Economic Growth in Colorado,* Denver Research Institute, University of Denver, 1963, pp. 7–14.

irrigated settlements which sold foodstuffs to the miners. Central to the state, it became the state capital; central to the Rocky Mountain Front, it became a regional service and supply capital for an extensive region of scattered settlement. Its tributary areas to the west were expanded by building the Moffat Tunnel and expensive highways through the highest part of the Rockies. As the city grew in population, it attracted federal and corporation offices. By the late 1960s food products ranked second only to ordnance and metal products in manufacturing employment.

The northern Colorado Piedmont The Colorado Piedmont, an extensive outwash plain north and northeast of Denver, supports a quarter million people. Because of the decline in agricultural employment, this is an area of only modest growth. Educational centers and small manufacturing in the numerous small cities, and income from petroleum and natural gas, supplement the business generated by sugar beet, alfalfa, potato, beans, and vegetable production. Similar to the water diversion for the Arkansas Valley, Colorado River water is pumped through tunnels under the continental divide into the Big Thompson, a central Platte tributary in the north Colorado Piedmont. The adjacent sparsely settled High Plains, largely lacking water for irrigation, yield an impressive tonnage of wheat and beef similar to the farm-ranch economy of western Kansas.

The North Platte and the Yellowstone The North Platte tributaries lead to several passes, about 8,000 feet in altitude, through the Rockies along the Wyoming Basin. These passes have been used for the major overland road and fastest transcontinental rail routes.

The North Platte–Yellowstone country was graphically described by a Crow chief, and it is doubtful if his description of the environment and economy of the time could be improved:

"The Crow country is a good country. The Great Spirit has put it exactly in the right place
. . . whichever way you travel you fare worse. If you go to the south you have to wander over great barren plains. . . . To the north it is cold; the winters are long and bitter and there is no grass. . . . About the forks of the Missouri is a fine country; good water, good grass, plenty of buffalo. In summer it is almost as good as Crow country, but in winter it is cold; the grass is gone and there is no salt weed for the horses.

The Crow country has snowy mountains and sunny plains, all kinds of climate and good things for every season. When the summer heats scorch the prairies, you can draw up under the mountains where the air is sweet and cool, the grass fresh, and the bright streams come tumbling out of the snowbanks. There you can hunt the elk, the deer, and the antelope when their skins are fit for dressing; there you will find plenty of grizzlies and mountain sheep.

In the autumn when your horses are fat and strong from the mountain pastures you can go down into the plains and hunt the buffalo or trap beaver on the streams. And when winter comes on you can take shelter in the woody bottoms along the rivers; there you will find buffalo meat for yourselves and cottonwood bark for your horses, or you may winter in the Wind River Valley where there is salt weed in abundance. . . . There is no country like the Crow country.[6]

Today the bison are gone, and extensive reservations of relatively poor land remain to the Crow in Big Horn County, Montana, where Custer and his men were exterminated. Much of the land of the Wyoming, Big Horn, and other basins is almost empty; narrow oases along the streams produce alfalfa, sugar beets, winter wheat, hay, potatoes, and beans. In Wyoming livestock contributes four times as much value as crops to the economy, whereas mining (largely petroleum) contributes more

[6] From an interview by Lt. James H. Bradley with Arapooish, Chief of the Crows, in *Contributions of the Historical Society of Montana,* vol. 9 (1923), pp. 306–307.

than farming and ranching together. Casper, slightly smaller than Cheyenne, the state capital and livestock market, is largely an oil-refining and wholesale center.

The landscape attractions of Yellowstone National Park are known to millions of summer visitors; the regional economy may be less observed. In Montana the Yellowstone River waters a narrow irrigated strip some 400 miles long. The surrounding sheep and cattle ranches are similar to the mediocre range of northeastern Wyoming. The commercial center for all this immense oil-ranch-oasis country is Billings, one of the leading transportation and distribution centers of the High West. Upstream from Billings the landscape is rougher, more humid, and somewhat wooded. The main valley ascends to geyser-rich Yellowstone Park, so high that its narrow roads are snow-free for tourist travel only half of the year. West of the railroad and lumbering town of Livingston an easy pass, crossed by a transcontinental highway and the Northern Pacific Railroad, separates the Yellowstone from the headwaters of the Missouri River.

The upper Missouri It is difficult to realize that a century ago steamboats leaving St. Louis each spring were considered the easy way to get to Fort Benton, Montana. The trip took 40 days. Beyond there a wagon road, completed in 1863, enabled travelers to reach Walla Walla, Washington, after several weeks of primitive travel through the Northern Rockies; only fifty-some years earlier Lewis and Clark first explored this rugged region. Today the upper Missouri is hardly recognized as a river; it is so regulated by dams that much of it consists of elongated lakes, the largest of which is the 100-mile-long Fort Peck Reservoir whose creation greatly expanded the potential irrigated area. Even without irrigation the Plains of northern Montana are humid enough in most years for dry farming of hay and wheat to supplement ranching. The rural population is sparse, and the small towns are strung along the railroads. Population densities increase to-ward the mountains; Great Falls, the second most populous SMSA in Montana, produces power for copper, zinc, and aluminum processing.

The first significant settlement in the mountain section began in 1863 with a gold rush at Virginia City. As in Colorado, placer gold was soon exhausted. In 1879 prospectors discovered copper in the Butte District, an area of 8 square miles astride the continental divide on which the city of Butte is now located. Probably $3 billion worth of copper ore has been mined there, with considerable silver, gold, lead, zinc, and some manganese as by-products. About 95 percent of the metallic ores mined in Montana still originates near Butte. The ore is smelted at Anaconda, 25 miles to the west, and also processed at Helena or at Great Falls. Within the triangle formed by Butte, Anaconda, and Great Falls are over half the population of the upper Missouri Valley in Montana. Elsewhere in Montana, agriculture, which employs directly one-sixth of the state's labor force, was the motivating force for settlement. Although oil or natural gas exploitation is widespread on the Montana Plains, the total direct employment is only a few thousand. In the last decade strip coal mining has grown in eastern Montana largely because the bituminous coal provides a desired low-sulfur fuel. Although mining now employs only one-fortieth of the labor force of Montana, there is no doubt that minerals brought settlement to the Missouri slope of the Rockies.

West of the Continental Divide

The Upper Columbia Watershed The landscapes and economy are somewhat different on the west side of the continental divide. An intricate trellis of streams separated by almost parallel ridges drains northwestern Montana and the Idaho Panhandle. The majestic Northern Rockies were generally a barrier to travel, but by following the valleys draining to the Pacific or using accessible passes, three transcontinental railroads and three major highways cross the area with little difficulty. More humid than the rest of Montana, this is a land of trees and recreation (for example, Waterton-Glacier International Peace Park). Mining is also a major occupation, notably at Coeur d'Alene, Idaho. Unlike the rest of the Rockies the lumbering industry is fully developed here. Lumbering, mining, tourism, and marginal agriculture characterize the Flathead and other valleys which have much unsettled land off the main routes.

The Snake Watershed The attractive physical setting of southern Idaho has been known for at least a century and a half, having been traversed first by fur traders and later by settlers using the Oregon Trail. Mining settlement followed gold discoveries in the mountains north of Boise in 1862, and silver in southwest Idaho. Agricultural and ranch settlement supplied local markets until the construction of the Oregon Short Line (now the Union Pacific) led to an irrigation boom in 1882. Existing cities, all modest in size, are mainly food-processing, transportation, and political centers.

A mass of granite mountains, some rising to over 12,000 feet and deeply dissected by canyons, effectively separates northern Idaho from the arid Snake Plain. Isolation was a real problem until 1927 when the two parts of Idaho were connected by a road; even today there is only one winding north-south trunk route entirely within the state. The flat Snake Plain is covered with fertile soil which has weathered from volcanic rocks. Sagebrush and bunchgrass are the natural vegetation except where irrigation is possible from water diverted from the Snake and its northern tributaries. The irrigated areas, producing famous Idaho spuds (potatoes), sugar beets, fodder crops, vegetables, fruit, and wheat, contrast with the cattle and sheep ranches on the nonirrigated lands. The Snake River exits the Plain in a northwestward direction, cutting through rugged terrain in Hells Canyon, 5,500 feet deep.

The Upper Colorado Watershed and Plateau This once isolated area is being catapulted into the modern world. A decade ago the main outside contacts were visitors to the Grand Canyon, Monument Valley, and the Four Corners country. The damming of the Colorado River at Glen Canyon opened a new recreation area on Lake Powell as well as provided a major source of power. In the last decade low-grade coal resources, discovered on Indian reservations, are now converted to thermal power; ultimately the power generated at six plants will equal the present power needs of millions of people as far away as Phoenix and even Southern California. This project is an example of the controversy which can arise over the utilization of our environment and its natural resources. From one point of view the strip mining of the coal mutilates much wilderness sacred to the Indians; air can be polluted as far as 100 miles from the plants; water used to cool the condensers has alternate uses for regional water supply. On the other side is the need for more power to be used elsewhere, some employment for local people, and royalty payments to Indian tribal councils.

The future potential of other regional mineral resources is now being considered. Oil shale and bituminous coal are widely distributed in the Upper Colorado Watershed and natural gas is available locally. San Juan County in southeastern Utah already produces most of Utah's petroleum. Iron ores, copper, lead, zinc, silver, and, especially, uranium are being exploited in the plateau and in the Rockies west of the continental divide. But present development is handicapped by isolation from major markets and lack of accessible level land.

Although Indian reservations are found in many parts of the High West, Indian population is concentrated on the Colorado Plateau. Many of the Indians work off the reservations and may be seen in towns and working on highways and other construction projects; others, in traditional Indian clothing, sell their services and handicrafts to tourists; several Indian

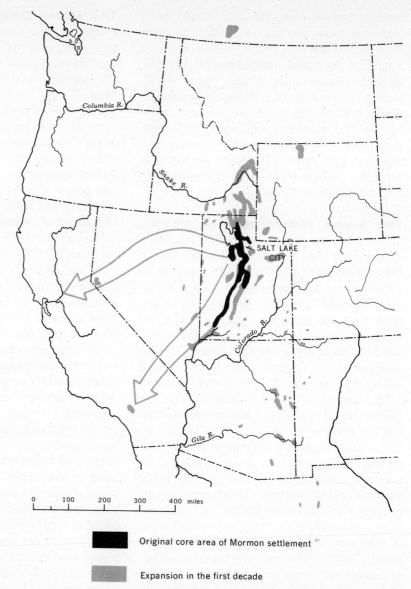

Original core area of Mormon settlement

Expansion in the first decade

Figure 7.10 The rapid expansion of a persecuted Mormon group in a region which had been despised by other settlers is part of the romance of the American West. (After Meinig)

groups have set up motels and factories; one Navajo group, for example, produces electronic parts. Because the reservation lands are held in trust by the federal government for the tribes, oil and other mineral discoveries benefit tribal treasuries. Nevertheless Indian incomes are low: in Arizona Indian incomes are about one-third the average per capita income for the state.

The Great Basin and Mormon culture region This is the West as protrayed by Hollywood; the land of great open spaces, scattered mines, ghost towns, horseback riders, widespread herds, flocks, and few oases.

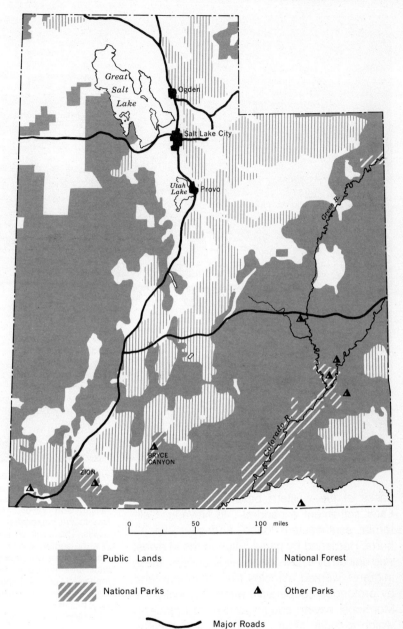

Public Lands

National Forest

National Parks

▲ Other Parks

⌒‿⌒ Major Roads

Figure 7.11 Government, especially the federal government, controls much of the land of Utah (and adjoining areas as well) largely because no one else wants it.

Few natural routes cross the Great Basin, and even the least-used route depends on traveling from water hole to water hole. The major immigrant routes followed either the modest Humboldt River across northern Nevada or a series of small streams southwestward from the foot of the Wasatch across southern Nevada to the Mojave River of California.

The Mormons From Salt Lake City, established in 1847 on the Jordan River, the Mormons spread rapidly throughout the basin, converting the small streams into a string of

This gold-mining operation west of Carlin, Nevada, was opened by the Carlin Gold Mining Company during the 1960s. The company is a subsidiary of the Newmont Mining Corporation, an investment trust which specializes in the exploitation of newly discovered mineral deposits. The open pit mine is in the upper right, the mill is in the center, and the tailings pond (which accumulates waste) in the foreground. In the center foreground, a water-treatment plant neutralizes water overflowing from the tailings pond. Although close to the Overland Trail, the first transcontinental railroad, and a transcontinental highway, this mineral resource has only recently been utilized. (Newmont Mining Corporation)

oases at the western base of the Wasatch. Later settlement expanded into Nevada, California, southeastern Idaho, and southern Alberta. Hardened by persecution in the Midwest and unified by a new-found religious faith, these migrants worked miracles from marginal land by prolonged cooperative effort. Ironically the Mormons, having sought an isolated place in which to locate their church-oriented society, soon found the Great Basin to be central amid the routes tapping the wealth of the West (Figure 7.10).

Salt Lake City remains the core of the Mormon culture region. Yet the city contains an appreciable non-Mormon population. Originally an agricultural center, Salt Lake City attracted converts to Mormonism who brought in a variety of industrial skills, but as an industrial center the city is not outstanding. Its raw material–processing industries are mainly outside the city.

Nearby minerals have aided the development of metropolitan Salt Lake City. Metals industries and defense industries have the only plants employing more than 1,000 workers each. A major copper deposit is at Bingham on the edge of the metropolis; iron ore is available 175 miles to the south, and coal and petroleum are widespread on the Colorado Plateau to the southeast. Both next to and south of Great Salt Lake, copper smelters and refineries efficiently process low-grade ores, yielding gold, silver, lead, zinc, and molybdenum as by-products. One of the few steel-processing centers in the mountainous West is located at Geneva, on Utah Lake.

The intensive irrigation agriculture on which Mormon settlement has been based is watered by a number of streams rising eastward in the Wasatch Range. This piedmont area has nearly 50 percent more precipitation than the central Great Basin. The crops range from dry-farmed wheat and barley to irrigated fruits, vegetables, and sugar beets. Dairy cattle are a common sight on most irrigated farms; beef cattle and sheep graze on adjacent dry lands. The surplus production of the region is exported to more densely populated areas.

Economically the Great Basin has more diversification than unity. The sections around Reno and Las Vegas and adjacent eastern California are tied into the economies of San Francisco and Los Angeles. These areas account for more than four-fifths of the income and employment of Nevada. On the other hand, the state of Utah, divided between the Great Basin and the Colorado Plateau, is focused on the eastern Great Basin. Although interconnections within the large region are not lacking, neither are they strong. The dividing or separating influences of mountains are still strong throughout the Great Basin, as in the rest of the High West.

LOOKING AHEAD

Potential Problems

The Interior West faces three major interlocking problems: water, minerals, and pollution. Lack of water is the most obvious problem in the Southwest, a land of low and fluctuating precipitation. Water and water rights have proved

limiting factors in both urban and rural expansion in the High West as well. Only the Colorado River appears to have much surplus water and it is highly saline. All this apparent surplus has been assigned to the Southwest and California or to diversion projects across the continental divide; there would be a shortage if all the allocated water were actually used. Water pollution, from mining wastes, sewage, and alkalies flushed from the soil, is an increasing problem, not easily solved. Competition for water, such as existed between Arizona and California or between Mexico and the United States over use of the Colorado River, is another complex problem. By living standards in other arid lands of the world the Interior West as a whole has adequate water for many times its population; by American standards of extravagant domestic and industrial use, water scarcity is current and likely to increase in the future.

It is the nature of mineral resources that sooner or later they will be exhausted. When the oil, natural gas, coal, copper, uranium, and other minerals of the Interior West are extracted and shipped elsewhere, other industries must be developed to take the place of mining if the level of economic development is to be continued. Since mining commonly involves the pollution or disruption of small sections of the local environment, its economic values must be balanced against its aesthetic impact on the landscape.

Modern technology has so far been only partially successful in coping with the pollution of air, water, and natural vegetation. Smog, impure water, and similar forms of pollution are now common in and downwind and downstream from exploited mining and industrial areas. The cost of preventing air pollution from the smelters of one mining company is estimated at $30 million. And can anything of this sort really be satisfactorily applied to prevent vast scenic landscapes from being defaced by strip mining? The Interior West holds this energy-hungry nation's greatest reserves of oil shale and much of its strippable coal: clearly, these minerals are being increasingly exploited, and in the process magnificent scenery, the chief visual attraction of the Interior West, is being despoiled.

Viable Alternatives?

The Interior West is obviously a supplier of much of the nation's natural resource needs; thus long-term solutions to its internal environmental problems to a large degree depend on national policy decisions. For instance, the United States now has a Clean Air Act, and if the clean energy sources (low-sulfur oil, natural gas, thermonuclear power, for example) were in sufficient supply to implement it, the demand for strip-mined coal from the Interior West might well diminish. Thus, the Montana cattle rancher or the Arizona sheepherder with a thousand-acre parcel of land carrying only a few dozen head of livestock might be under less pressure to sell out to a mining firm that could otherwise extract millions of tons of coal from the same land. In any case, there are no ready answers to the Interior West's environmental problems, especially if such solutions are to be national or perhaps international in scope.

Demographic Trends

The population of the Interior West is growing by percentage more rapidly than the national average, but most of the growth is concentrated in the metropolitan areas. In the 1950s, most rural counties had a net out-migration, and the trend continued through the 1960s with several of the region's states experiencing net out-migration. This is similar to rural areas elsewhere in the country which have suffered a like out-migration. Perhaps a case could be made for a western Appalachia project on a grand scale! Nevertheless it seems amazing that in areas so sparsely settled and occupied generally less than a century, more opportunities have not been found. Certainly most of the environment of the High West is attractive; the difficulties rather have been in a poor industrial mix and in the isolation of many areas from those amenities that Americans increasingly expect. Possibly with the increasing amounts of leisure and better transportation, the spectacular mountains and great open spaces will become a refuge for tens of millions of noise-and-smog-bedeviled metropolitan workers. Perhaps, too, a few wilderness areas will be saved for those who wish to tramp through the America that nature made.

SELECTED REFERENCES

CALDWELL, HARRY H. (ed.): *Idaho Economic Atlas,* Idaho Bureau of Mines, Moscow, Idaho, 1970.

CAMPBELL, CHARLES E.: "Some Environmental Effects of Rural Subdividing in an Arid Area: A Case Study in Arizona," *Journal of Geography,* vol. 71 (1972), pp. 147–154.

CROSS, JACK L. et al.: *Arizona: Its People and Resources,* University of Arizona Press, Tucson, 1960.

DUNCAN, DONALD C., and VERNON E. SWANSON: "Organic-Rich Shale of the United States and World Land Areas," *U.S. Geological Survey Circular No. 523,* 1965, 33 pp., abridged.

DURRENBERGER, ROBERT: "The Colorado Plateau," *Annals,* AAG, vol. 62 (1972), pp. 211–236.

GOLZE, ALFRED R.: *Reclamation in the United States,* Caxton, Caldwell, Idaho, 1961.

HELBURN, NICHOLAS, M. J. EDIE, and GORDON LIGHTFOOT: *Montana in Maps,* Research and Endowment Foundation, Montana State College, Missoula, 1962.

HORGAN, PAUL: *Great River: The Rio Grande in North American History,* Rinehart, New York, 1954. Volume 2 is especially valuable to the historical geographer.

HOUGHTON, JOHN G.: "Great Basin Precipitation Estimates from Short Term Records," *Professional Geographer,* vol. 26 (1974), pp. 27–33.

HUNDLEY, NORRIS, JR.: *Dividing the Waters,* University of California Press, Berkeley and Los Angeles, 1966.

HUNT, LACY H.: "Industrial Development on the Mexican Border," *Business Review,* Federal Reserve Bank of Dallas, February 1970, pp. 3–12.

JAEGER, E. C.: *The North American Deserts,* Stanford University Press, Stanford, Calif., 1957.

KRAENZEL, C. F.: *The Great Plains in Transition,* University of Oklahoma Press, Norman, 1955.

LOEFFLER, M. JOHN: "The Population Syndromes on the Colorado Piedmont," *Annals,* AAG, vol. 55 (1965), pp. 26–66.

MEINIG, D. W.: *Imperial Texas: An Interpretive Essay in Cultural Geography,* University of Texas Press, Austin, 1969.

————: *Southwest: Three Peoples in Geographical Change, 1600–1970,* Oxford University Press, New York, 1971.

MORRIS, JOHN W.: *The Southwestern United States,* Van Nostrand, New York, 1970.

OKLAHOMA STATE UNIVERSITY COLLEGE OF BUSI-NESS: *The Oklahoma Economy,* Economic Research Series No. 1, Stillwater, 1963.

QUINN, FRANK: "Water Transfers: Must the American West Be Won Again?" *Geographical Review,* vol. 58 (1968), pp. 108–132.

The Report of the U.S. Study Commission, 4 parts, Austin, March 1962; also available as 87th Cong., 2d Sess. H. Doc. 494, 1962.

U. S. DEPARTMENT OF INTERIOR: *Natural Resources of Colorado,* Washington, 1963. Similar pamphlets, available for all Western states, are especially good in portraying the work of federal agencies.

U.S. GEOLOGICAL SURVEY: *Guidebook to the Western United States:* Part A, *The Northern Pacific Route;* Bulletin 611, part B, *The Overland Route;* Bulletin 612, part E, *The Denver and Rio Grande Western Route;* Bulletin 707, Washington, 1920–1922. These well-illustrated guide-books are based on data a half century old but are invalu-able for giving an impression of the natural background and historical development of sites along transcontinental railroads.

ZIERER, CLIFFORD M. (ed.): *California and the South-west,* Wiley, New York, 1956.

8

THE PACIFIC STATES

Moderating marine influences carried landward by prevailing westerly winds have given the Pacific States distinct environmental advantages over the rest of Anglo-America. Indeed, most of the region's 28 million inhabitants live within 100 miles of the Pacific where climatic extremes rarely occur. Millions of new residents have sought out climates that south of San Francisco resemble those of the Mediterranean rivieras and that northward compare with coastal climates from France to Norway.

Although the continent's largest Indian population (north of Mexico) once flourished in the climatic "lotus land" along the Pacific, it was not favorable climate that initially attracted white settlers. Stronger incentives were needed to stimulate thousands of miles of journey from lands of earlier settlement. Religious zeal, as well as New Spain's desire to protect its northern frontiers, brought Franciscan missionaries to California. Later, generous land grants lured ranchers to its coastal valleys. Furs and missionary enterprise attracted the

This ERTS satellite image, centered on Santa Barbara, is part of the opening illustration for Chapter 1. Note the offshore Channel Islands (a seaward extension of the Transverse Ranges) and the numerous parallel mountain ranges between which are irrigated valleys. Much of the cleared area is pastureland. The upper part of the picture extends to the Central Valley of California. (NASA)

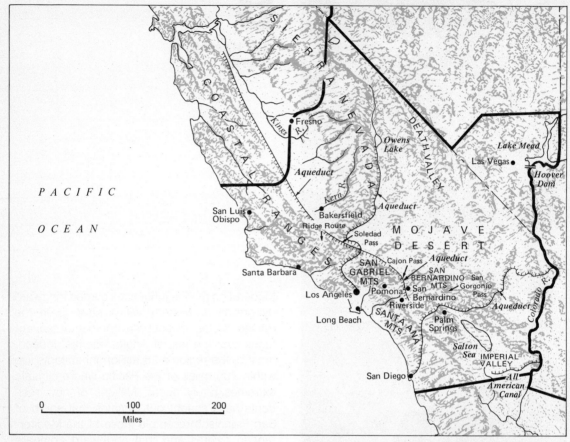

Figure 8.1 Southern California landforms. This southern portion of the Pacific States (see also Figures 8.6, 8.9, and 8.10) is no less mountainous than any other part of the region. Nevertheless it is the most populated, with settlement concentrated on or near the coast where there is a mild Mediterranean climate unmatched elsewhere in Anglo-America. (Base map by A. K. Lobeck. Reprinted with permission of The Geographical Press, Hammond, Inc.)

first Europeans to the Pacific Northwest, and later, the good farmlands of the Oregon country were discovered along with widespread forest resources. But it took the discovery of precious metals to produce the first genuine rush of new settlement. As the gold fields of California played out, many miners drifted away, but the region had earned its permanent place in the minds of men. On the heels of the gold rush came the transcontinental railroads, irrigation colonies, and oil booms that transformed California and the Northwest from a far-flung frontier to an area which was identified with the rest of the nation. In the twentieth century, the Pacific States diversified; motion-picture production and tourism became as distinctive regional industries as agriculture and lumbering. Whereas most of the region has

long since passed through the frontier stage, Alaska has not. To many people in the "lower forty-eight" Alaska still seems a distant last great frontier.

California's postwar ascendency to the position of most populous state is unprecedented in the annals of national expansion. Oregon, Washington, Alaska, and Hawaii too have grown rapidly, combining with the Golden State to produce a near doubling of the Pacific

States' population of a quarter century ago. Such rapid population increase and attendant urbanization have also produced some dubious regional distinctions, notably urban sprawl and smog in California. Fear that these ills may spread has prompted Oregon to discourage further large-scale in-migration, which may signal a regionwide tempering of the growth syndrome. It appears that the Pacific States (except Hawaii) have begun to derive greater population growth from natural increase within their boundaries than from migration as in the past.

PHYSICAL LANDSCAPES AND CLIMATES

Environmental diversity characterizes the physical geography of both the Pacific States and the Interior West. There is, however, one conspicuous difference between the two regions: the Pacific Ocean influences the climate of the former directly, but the latter only remotely. Adjacency to the rim of the Pacific basin from Southern California to the tip of the Aleutians involves degrees of instability of the earth's crust and moderation of climate unmatched in the Interior West.

Mountainous Edge of a Continent

The 3,000-mile-long Pacific shoreline is one of bold relief. From ocean-eroded headlands eastward to intermontane plateaus and basins, the mountain system averages from 100 to 300 miles in width. The upfaulted mountain ranges, downfolded valleys, and volcanic cones indicate that this is a dynamic portion of the earth's crust. For example, the San Andreas Fault zone seems to indicate a spreading of the sea floor which if carried to its conclusion millions of years from now may result in southwestern California drifting away from the North American continent. In the meantime, coastal Californians will simply adjust as best they can to the unpredictable earthquakes common to zones of crustal instability (Figure 8.6, p. 242).

Southern California mountains and basins

In the California Southland a series of diverse mountain blocks form a vast arc from Point Conception to the Mexican border 50 miles east of San Diego. These abrupt ranges also create a climatic difference between the subhumid coastal areas and the interior deserts. The faulting and folding of the past are still apparent in the present as demonstrated by the disastrous February 9, 1971 earthquake centered in northern Los Angeles County.

The highest ridges of the mountains exceed 10,000 feet in several widely separated places; however, numerous intervening passes have channeled Southland routes and settlement. For example, Cajon Pass (4,301 feet) and the Ridge Route (4,183 feet) in the Transverse Ranges serve as the major highway and railroad routes south into the Los Angeles coastal basin. Numerous ranges parallel the coastline south of Los Angeles and structurally are part of the Peninsular Ranges of Baja California. Low, but steep, palisades interspersed with marshy lagoons border the ocean southward to San Diego Bay, the only deep-water harbor south of Los Angeles–Long Beach. Eastward lies the flat floor of the down-dropped Salton Trough, which is below sea level and includes part of the irrigated Imperial Valley.

The Coast Ranges

The Coast Ranges of central and northern California, much lower but no less abrupt than the ranges on the inland edge of the Southland coastal zone, roughly parallel the shoreline. They are, however, arranged *en échelon*; that is, each range terminates as a headland projecting into the Pacific so that the river valley between the range and the next parallel range inland drains northwestward to the Coast. Each coastal valley has tended to become a separate, small agricultural region. One of the exceptions to this general pattern is at San Francisco Bay where the two great rivers of the Central Valley converge into a complex delta.

The landforms of Oregon and Washington are different. In Oregon's Coast Ranges few summits rise above 3,000 feet, and most are gently rounded by erosion. By contrast, the mountains of Washington's Olympic Peninsula approach 8,000 feet in elevation, with slopes that are long as well as steep.

Intervening lowlands   Settlement is concentrated in the lowlands and valleys and not in the surrounding mountains. Between the Coast Ranges and the higher Sierra-Cascade Ranges to the east are the well-populated Central Valley of California and the Willamette-Puget Trough of Oregon and Washington. Separated from one another by the rugged Klamath Mountains, both lowlands are filled with alluvium and glacial outwash carried down from the Sierra-Cascade Ranges. The Central Valley has been transformed by man and irrigation into the agricultural heartland of the Pacific States. The Willamette Valley, smaller than California's Central Valley, produces most of the agricultural commodities of Oregon.

The High Sierras and Cascades   The Sierra Nevada and Cascades are a thousand miles long and up to a hundred miles wide. Laced with peaks in excess of 14,000 feet throughout, the Sierra-Cascade system is a formidable landform barrier that is crossed in few places by land routes and in only one place by a river—the Columbia. The Sierras and Cascades differ markedly from one another in structure and appearance.

The Sierra Nevada is essentially a huge block mountain asymmetrically tilted to the west with an abrupt eastern scarp. Faulting has been most severe along the southeastern edge of the Sierra, the most notable recent occurrence being the 1872 earthquake near Lone Pine which vertically displaced a part of the Owens Valley surface 20 feet in a few minutes.

The Pleistocene era left a legacy in the form of photogenic alpine scenery. Large alpine glaciers scoured out jagged ridges and steep valleys along the Sierra's eastern divide and created U-shaped valleys (Yosemite, for instance) on the western slope. Today, only a few dozen tiny glaciers remain in high protected areas. But seasonal snows accumulate to such great depths that there is no reliable east-west winter passage through the Sierras from the Lake Tahoe area south to Walker Pass, a minimum detour by road of 280 miles.

In contrast the Cascades are surmounted by volcanoes and lava flows. A long string of volcanic cones extends from Mt. Lassen in northern California through Oregon and Washington to Mt. Baker just south of the British Columbia border. Individual composite cones, such as Mt. Shasta and Mt. Rainier, reach over 14,000 feet with small glaciers radiating down their slopes. As evidenced by the violent eruption of Mt. Lassen in 1914–1917, the Cascades seem as unstable as the Sierras.

The southeastern part of Oregon and all California east of the Sierra-Cascade system are part of the basin and range country described in Chapter 7. Northward, the lava-covered Columbia Plateau includes most of eastern Oregon and Washington; it averages about half the altitude of its Interior West counterpart, the Colorado Plateau. Although sub-humid and requiring irrigation for specialized crop production, its landscape is not as barren in appearance as the Colorado Plateau.

Alaska's mountains and valleys   It is not unexpected that Alaska's enormous area of 586,000 square miles would have a variety of landforms. These can be grouped into six east-west trending landform regions: (1) the sedimentary, petroleum-rich Arctic, or North Slope; (2) the 5,000- to 8,000-foot-high Brooks Range; (3) the valley of the Yukon River; (4) the Alaska Peninsula and volcanic Aleutian Islands extension; (5) the Alaska Range—with Mt. McKinley (20,320 feet), the highest mountain in Anglo-America; and (6) the mountainous and fiorded southeast and Panhandle coast.

The latter two regions are the largest single area of extensive valley glaciers in Anglo-America and possibly the most earthquake-prone part of the continent. The Anchorage area, for example, has experienced several minor temblors each year since the 1964 earthquake which displaced the earth's surface vertically as much as 50 feet. Along the coast, the fiords provide superb deep-water and protected harbors; however, this natural advantage is balanced by the constant threat of an earthquake-caused seismic sea wave. Such harbors as Valdez, the southern terminus of the Alaska Pipeline, must "live with" this potential environmental hazard.

Contrasting Mild Climates

Although the favorable climatic characteristics of the Pacific States are well publicized, the region also has climates as unattractive as any on the continent: Interior and Arctic Alaska experience long, bitterly cold winters. Windward sides of the Hawaiian Islands receive rainfall in the hundreds of inches annually. The Sierras and Cascades accumulate winter snows to record depths. And the deserts of southeastern California are as hot in summer as the Sahara. Yet of the environmental amenities that have lured millions of newcomers to the Pacific States, mild climate of the coastal strip seems to be the greatest attraction. Consequently, the majority of residents live along or near the ocean in a relatively small portion of the region's land area.

Subtropical California   The dry summer subtropical, or Mediterranean, climate of central and Southern California receives most of its precipitation in the winter and early spring months. However, differences in altitude, exposure, and distance from the sea cause great local differences in daily weather and climate. To these physical variables must be added a man-made effect—proximity to industrial and other sources of smog. The semiarid climate in the well-populated coastal lowlands receives some rain in winter, but days are warm enough for outdoor living most of the year. Relief from summer heat is usually available at the seashore and in the nearby mountains. Frosts, showers, fogs and smog, and strong winds are

often highly localized—indeed each part of each valley and slope has its individual variation from the general pattern. Even the prevailing westerly winds are occasionally reversed when high pressure builds up over the interior deserts and the strong, dry Santa Ana winds sweep down toward the coastal lowlands of Southern California.

Rarely containing any surface water, dry, gravelly streambeds are a characteristic part of the Southland coastal landscape. In many cases, their water has been diverted upstream into irrigation systems or stored and used for domestic water supplies. Flood-control reservoirs and percolation basins are usually empty, as though in anticipation of rare cloudbursts. Despite rather meager annual precipitation, averaging less than 20 inches in many populated locations, flood-control districts in some California counties maintain sophisticated and efficient flood-control systems.

The climate is much more extreme in the deserts of southeastern California where temperatures change markedly from day to night and with altitude. Winds and dust, sometimes strong enough to sandblast the paint off a car, are a common problem. In the winter the smog-free desert is commonly pleasant (50 to 75° during the day), and even during the rare cold snaps it is mild between sunrise and sunset.

In the Great Central Valley rainfall increases to the northward and up the slopes of the High Sierra; averages in the valley range from less than 10 inches to 30 inches. Eastward, the Sierra Nevada captures about two times the valley's annual precipitation, but serves a significant watershed function to the valley. The growing season is long in the Central Valley—from 300 days in the south to 200 days in the north.

California's northwest coast, often foggy and with only about 10°F seasonal range, has moderate rainfall and high relative humidity, which promote growth of the lush redwood rain forest. Inland from the coastal zone, altitude increases the rainfall and there is greater seasonal temperature range. In the rain shadow east of the Klamath Mountains and Sierra-Cascade Ranges the climate is arid and subject to seasonal extremes of temperature.

Except in the mountains, California weather interferes surprisingly little with ordinary living—the smog in some localities being the principal annoyance. Land use and housing reflect these regional and local differences in climate. Summer air conditioning is rarely needed in foggy San Francisco or along the central coast but is considered almost a necessity in interior valleys. Some lowland areas that are subject to frosts which may destroy citrus, specialize in wine grapes, vegetables, and dairy products. In fall, when the desiccating Santa Ana winds are most frequent in the suburbanized hill country around Los Angeles Basin, chaparral and other fire-prone vegetation associations are closely monitored so as to lessen the possibility of dangerous brush fires occurring.

Southern California smog Air pollution appears to be Southern California's most severe environmental handicap. Although most large industrial cities have smog problems, Los Angeles and neighboring cities possess a seemingly optimal combination of topographical, meteorological, and cultural factors that favor the concentration of air pollutants. Basin topography (for example, the Los Angeles Basin and the San Gabriel Valley) and frequent temperature inversions confine dirty air over populated areas. The various pollutants themselves are produced daily by the emissions of millions of motor vehicles and to a lesser extent by industry. Southlanders have been eminently successful in importing fresh water from far outside their region; yet the same option is obviously unavailable in the case of clean air. In short, Southern Californians must improve conditions in their existing air shed.

Marine Northwest coasts The coasts of Oregon and Washington and southeastern

Alaska have cloudy, rainy climates with few daily or seasonal temperature extremes. Precipitation occurs throughout the year, but is markedly more pronounced in winter in Oregon and Washington and in fall along the Alaska Panhandle. Maritime polar air masses originating from the Gulf of Alaska bring most of the moisture and help to promote growth of the vast forest of tall, coniferous trees. The effects of oceanic air masses are quite dramatic in the Olympic Peninsula. Here on the windward slopes of the 8,000-foot-high Olympic Mountains annual precipitation averages upwards of 150 inches. Yet only 75 miles eastward in the rain shadow of the mountains average precipitation barely reaches 20 inches a year and farmland must be irrigated. Together with a nearly year-round growing season and rich alluvial and volcanic soils, the moist atmosphere of the western Olympic Peninsula sustains the continent's lushest coniferous rain forest.

There are significant regional differences throughout the great latitudinal extent of the Northwest states. For instance, Portland and Seattle each average nearly 40 inches annual precipitation, and monthly mean temperatures in each city range from 38°F in January to the mid-60s in July. Winters in the two population centers of the Northwest are not particularly cold or snowy, but the seemingly constant rainfall and overcast skies do little to lift the human spirit. A thousand miles north of Seattle, Juneau (Alaska) is similarly wet and without sunshine; but with some 55 inches precipitation spread more evenly throughout the whole year, its climatic monotony must at times seem unending.

Tropical Hawaii If mild temperature is the climatic reputation of the Pacific States, Hawaii should serve as the region's prime attraction. Tropical heat is so moderated by the ocean that temperatures are pleasant the year around, averaging 72° in January and 79° in July in Honolulu with all-time extremes of 52° and 93°.

The high volcanic Hawaiian Islands lie directly in the path of the trade winds, forcing them to rise and drop copious amounts of rain on the northeast, windward sides of the islands. By contrast, leeward coastal lowlands are drier (and their soils quite porous) to the point of requiring irrigation where cultivated. Within Honolulu mean annual precipitation varies from 24 inches at Honolulu airport to nearly 100 inches at the higher, northern edge of the city. Rain falls on Honolulu in every month but is heaviest from December through February when the trade winds are strongest.

THE DEVELOPING SOUTHERN CALIFORNIA MEGALOPOLIS

About two-thirds of California's 22 million people reside in Southern California, a subtropical area of deserts, poor grasslands, and partly wooded, partly barren mountains which only two centuries ago barely supported some 70,000 Indians. The physical setting (Figure 8.1) is little different than in the adjacent sparsely settled Southwest except in one important respect: it is near the sea. The Pacific modifies the climate in each season. Most past settlement was concentrated in the narrow coastal zone which had the mild climate, but in recent decades settlement densities have spread inland where summers are hot and winters are mild and sunny.

Climate is not the only attraction that has brought millions to the California Southland. A succession of additions to the cultural landscape has made the region more attractive: for example, the livestock and Mediterranean crops introduced from Spain by the missionaries. Equally important were such water-management techniques as well drilling, irrigation, and the piping in of water which fell as rain or snow on mountains a thousand miles away. These additions, however, would have been of little economic significance without the railroads and highways which connect California with distant markets.

Economic History

Agricultural beginnings   The modern economy and society in the Southland are the result of past booms and transformations. About the time of the American Revolution, Spanish missionaries from Mexico established a line of missions from San Diego to Sonoma, north of San Francisco, spaced no more than a day's journey (by muleback) apart. The peaceful, primitive Indians were unusually skilled in using the nonagricultural aspects of their environment and soon learned to till European crops and tend livestock. Less happily, the Indians fell prey to European diseases, so that few of them survived. In a largely unsuccessful effort to encourage immigration to Alta (upper) California, the Spanish established small towns (pueblos) and military outposts (presidios); however, although all these settlements were slow to grow, some, notably Los Angeles, San Diego, San Francisco, and San Jose, eventually became major settlement nuclei.

During the next 70 years, the Spanish and Mexican governments assigned huge ranchos to immigrants, some from Spain and Mexico, some from the United States. The only exportable products were hides and tallow, which were sold to New England sea captains. After Mexico lost California to the United States (1848), the gold rush created a new market for beef, grain, and wine produced locally. New crops were introduced, including the navel orange from Brazil (1873), lemon (1874), Valencia orange (1880), avocado (1910), and date (1912). Broader markets were opened when rail connections to the East via San Francisco were completed in 1876 and directly eastward from Los Angeles in 1885.

At this time subtropical agricultural products were scarce in the eastern United States. Several new techniques helped California produce reach the distant markets: canning (1858), artificial dehydration (1870), and refrigerated freight cars (1880). Although the increased agricultural activity resulted in some growth in urban activities, Southern California remained agriculturally oriented until the 1920s.

The shift to industry Successive developments changed the economy of the coastal zone from agriculture to other industry. Large quantities of oil were discovered in the Los Angeles Basin between 1920 and 1924, providing a surplus product which could be shipped east through the newly opened Panama Canal. About the same time, major moving-picture studios moved to Hollywood to take advantage of abundant sunshine and the diverse landscapes available nearby. Large-scale aircraft manufacturers who could assemble their product outdoors and conduct test flights throughout the year located their plants in Santa Monica, San Diego, and other coastal cities. The automobile assembly industry also started in the 1920s, several decades before its product dominated the regional settlement pattern. All these manufacturers brought auxiliary industries to supply their needs and an even greater number of secondary and service industries to supply the homes and consumer goods required by the burgeoning population.

Between the two world wars, maturing Southern California consisted mainly of Los Angeles and San Diego and a sprinkling of small cities and towns, all connected by roads, railroads, and the Pacific Electric interurban lines. Each city spread over a large area because single-family houses predominated and even the so-called "apartments" usually rose only two or three floors. In contrast to Eastern cities, the CBDs had low buildings since maximum heights were limited to 150 feet because of earthquake danger. Thousands of acres of orange groves dotted the landscape, sharing the nonurbanized land with cattle ranches, dairy farms, vineyards, and gardens. Automobiles and industrial employment were increasing, but smog and freeways were still nonexistent.

World War II brought a new type of indus-trial growth, involving military activities, aircraft, munitions, steel, and other supplies needed for the Pacific war. After the war many scientific, aerospace, instrumental, and consumer goods industries were added. Along with these developments came a tremendous suburban expansion into areas unreached by public transport and distant from the new factories. The automobile became the accepted form of transportation. The rapid transit lines were generally deserted, and some of the first freeways were constructed along the abandoned Pacific Electric right-of-way.

Although at first there was adequate well water stored in underlying sediments, external water was obtained from an aqueduct from Owens Valley started in 1908 and completed in 1913. In 1939 additional water was pumped from the Colorado River. The need for imported water grew steadily as urban numbers increased. In the 1970s another aqueduct was completed bringing Feather River water 600 miles from the northern Sierras. Experiments with the desalting of seawater are also well advanced.

Rural land uses changed to urban uses. Orange groves and other farms were replaced with houses in exploding urbanized areas. Dairy farming was concentrated on dry feedlots which stable cows before a food trough on very valuable agricultural land—some worth more than $25,000 per acre. Agriculture has not yet disappeared completely. Some counties south of the Transverse Ranges remain among the state's top ten agricultural counties (by value of product) and continue to increase the value of agricultural output year after year despite a shrinking supply of prime land.

Income and employment Although California boasts that it leads all states in the value of agricultural products, only a small percentage of Southern California income can be attributed to agriculture. Likewise little employment is provided by its extractive industries, oil and gas; the mining of salts, stone, and iron ore; and lumbering. Over one-third of the in-

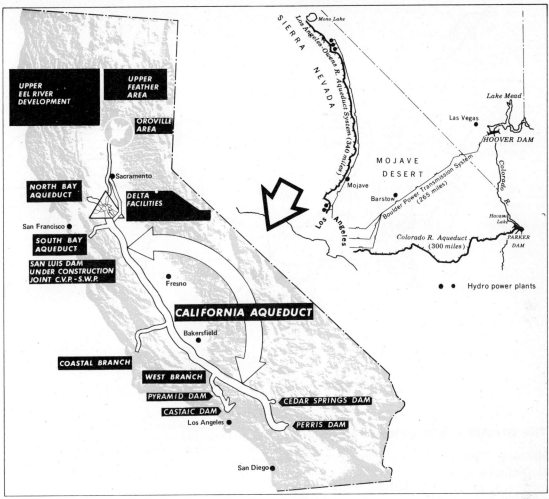

UPPER
EEL RIVER
DEVELOPMENT

UPPER
FEATHER
AREA

OROVILLE
AREA

NORTH BAY
AQUEDUCT

Sacramento

DELTA
FACILITIES

San Francisco

SOUTH BAY
AQUEDUCT

SAN LUIS DAM
UNDER CONSTRUCTION
JOINT C.V.P. - S.W.P.

Fresno

CALIFORNIA AQUEDUCT

Bakersfield

COASTAL BRANCH

WEST BRANCH

PYRAMID DAM

CASTAIC DAM

Los Angeles

CEDAR SPRINGS DAM

PERRIS DAM

San Diego

SIERRA NEVADA

Mono Lake

Los Angeles-Owens R. Aqueduct System (340 miles)

Las Vegas

Lake Mead

HOOVER DAM

MOJAVE DESERT

Mojave

Barstow

Boulder Power Transmission System (265 miles)

Colorado R.

Havasu Lake

Colorado R. Aqueduct (300 miles)

PARKER DAM

Los Angeles

● ● Hydro power plants

Figure 8.2 Southern California derived its water at first from local mountain streams and from wells driven into valley sediments. This map shows the plan now being implemented to bring northern California water southward. By mid-1974 Perris Reservoir was filled with water imported over 600 miles from Oroville Reservoir. (California Department of Water Resources)

come and employment arises from manufacturing and construction; most of the rest is in trade and services.

Who are the California workers? The basic stock was Spanish and Yankee with a minor amount of Indian blood. Orientals were added to the early population but usually did not marry outside their own group. These early settlers were overwhelmed by large numbers from Texas, the Mississippi Valley, and Western Europe, including many with rural backgrounds. Employment opportunities have brought in many Mexicans and, in recent decades, a considerable black population, as well as whites from Atlantic Coast cities. The region is more of a melting pot than the United States interior. In Los Angeles County for example, of a population of about 7 million in 1970, approximately 17 percent were Latins (Spanish surname or maiden name), about 10 percent black, and nearly 4 percent Oriental or American Indian.

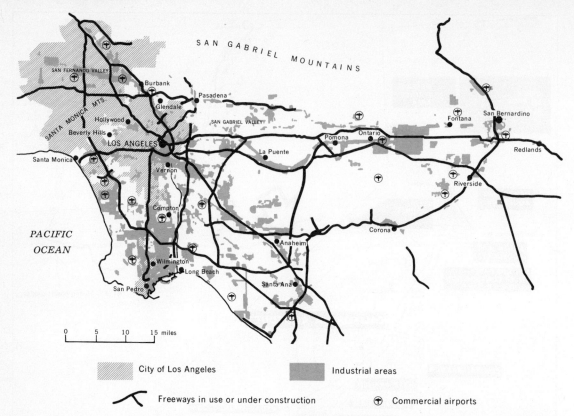

SAN GABRIEL MOUNTAINS

SAN FERNANDO VALLEY
Burbank
Pasadena
SANTA MONICA MTS.
Glendale
Hollywood
SAN GABRIEL VALLEY
Beverly Hills
Fontana
San Bernardino
LOS ANGELES
Pomona
Ontario
Redlands
Santa Monica
La Puente
Vernon
Riverside
PACIFIC
OCEAN
Compton
Corona
Anaheim
Wilmington
Long Beach
Santa Ana
San Pedro

0   5   10   15 miles

City of Los Angeles   Industrial areas

Freeways in use or under construction   Commercial airports

The Greater Los Angeles Area

History The nation's second metropolis
started as a Spanish colonial village one-half
mile west of the Los Angeles River whose
waters were used to irrigate the surrounding
fields. The location was strategic; river valleys
led upstream to the San Fernando and San
Gabriel valleys and downstream to a poorly
sheltered bay at San Pedro. Like the Indian
settlements and other early Spanish towns, Los
Angeles was located where water was available
at the edge of the hills.

With the building of the railroads and the
consequent agricultural boom in the 1880s and
1890s Los Angeles grew, its CBD extending
a mile south and southwestward while the residential district expanded to the west. In 1892
oil was discovered in the city, and oil processing was added to food processing and con-

Figure 8.3 Industrial Los Angeles is as scattered as
commercial and residential Los Angeles. At first factories
were located near railroads; later the harbor became an
important localizing factor; and in recent decades freeways, other major highways, and available space for large
factories have been major considerations.

sumer goods as a major industry. The original
manufacturing area was to the south in nearby
Vernon, but industrial zones are now common
throughout the metropolitan area, being especially concentrated along the rail lines and
freeways (Figure 8.3).

The 1920s saw the growth of residential
suburbs while the older residential part became
less desirable housing, some of which deteriorated into slums. Glendale and Pasadena to the
north and northeast became upper-class residential suburbs with the completion of Pacific
Electric tracks to the central terminal. Another
interurban line extended northwestward to

Hollywood on the slopes of the Santa Monica Mountains where the motion-picture industry constructed studios over vast areas of cheap land. Shortly, Hollywood and much of the San Fernando Valley joined Los Angeles in order to share Owens Valley water. After huge artificial harbors were constructed at San Pedro Bay, Los Angeles annexed a 20-mile "shoe-string" of land extending to San Pedro to control port facilities and related industries.

The metropolitan pattern The present period of urban expansion began during World War II. The first freeway, the winding Pasadena Freeway, was opened in 1940; other routes were laid out in the next decades. Industry and auto exhausts increasingly converted fog into smog. Fashionable suburbs were laid out above the smog zone, increasingly developing on terraced hillsides which a few decades earlier seemed destined to remain in chaparral. As a result of the residential sections spreading over a large area, there was a need for the establishment of commercial and service centers near the suburbs. Therefore business offices, financial activities, skyscrapers, theaters, and concert halls are developing in many centers away from the central city. The Los Angeles–Long Beach SMSA now has numerous commercial nuclei, and in value of retail trade these outlying centers now surpass the original central city.

A regional grouping of urban functions has grown up. Sparsely or lightly settled hilly areas still compartmentalize the lowland. The low Santa Monica Mountains separate the long-settled Hollywood–Santa Monica Plain from the new expanding San Fernando Valley subdivisions. The Baldwin Hills, partly residential and partly occupied by oil derricks, separate Hollywood from newer southwest Los Angeles with its international airport and growing industries. To the south urban land uses extend almost to the independent industrial and port city of Long Beach. Southeast of central Los Angeles the railroads to San Diego and the parallel Santa Ana Freeway serve an almost continuous urban belt into Orange County.

The harbor cities Each of the outlying cities has a distinctive history. Long Beach was a seaside resort town of less than 3,000 in 1900. Oil was discovered there in the early 1920s; the once fashionable suburb of Signal Hill attained worldwide notoriety for its forest of oil derricks—one on each city lot; the artificial Long Beach Harbor was constructed from the profits of 500 city-owned wells. The quietness of the resort-fishing city was further upset by the creation of a naval base there in 1925. Long Beach today is a major port and industrial center specializing in aircraft and automobile parts, oil refining, oil-well equipment, and seafood canning.

The development of smaller Wilmington and San Pedro is little different. Most of the San Pedro–Wilmington industries are related to the port. Between 1912 and 1914 the harbor was carved out of the marsh in time to serve the Pacific Coast trade resulting from the opening of the Panama Canal. San Pedro is California's leading fishing port, and Wilmington has had petroleum industries since 1934 when one of the most productive California oil fields was discovered there.

The San Gabriel Valley This lowland was occupied by Spanish missionaries and by Mexican ranchers on seven large estates. Intensive utilization is less than a century old. Pasadena, the principal city, was founded in 1874 by Indianapolis settlers who started growing irrigated oranges. The entire valley was converted into irrigated farms among which arose a number of commercial and residential towns. Pasadena was especially noted for its fine homes, resort hotels, and such institutions as the Huntington Library and the California Institute of Technology. After World War II, the towns in San Gabriel Valley grew together and spread up the slopes of adjacent hills. Industry, initially developed along transcontinental rail lines from

Grissom Island is one of four artificial islands constructed off Long Beach to serve as a base for offshore oil exploitation without spoiling the beauty of the coastal area. (Long Beach Promotion, Inc.)

the east, is expanding and changing the urban character of the once quiet valley.

San Fernando Valley and northward

Two cities at the mouth of the San Fernando Valley, Glendale and Burbank, were founded as agricultural centers during the railroad expansion of the 1880s; later both became commuting towns. With industrial growth first in moving pictures and later in aircraft, Burbank became an industrial city. The western two-thirds of the San Fernando Valley remained agricultural until the 1950s when, with the growth of the freeway system, the valley provided space for suburban residences and for industries such as electronics and automobile assembly. Most of its towns, still referred to by local names, have been annexed by Los Angeles. When the San Fernando Valley was mostly built up by the sixties, urbanization spilled northwestward into the Simi Valley, Westlake Village, and the Thousand Oaks–

Conejo area in southeastern Ventura County.

Future megalopolitan expansion is expected to incorporate the attractive coast and hills northward to Santa Barbara and possibly to San Luis Obispo, thus including the missile-testing facilities at Vandenberg Air Force Base. The largest of the coastal lowlands is Ventura County's Oxnard Plain, which rivals the rich Salinas Valley in value and diversity of agricultural output, yet which is also urbanizing rapidly.

Orange County

From 1960 to 1970 Orange County claimed the fastest population growth rate of any California county (102 percent to 1.42 million) as a result of having much level and rolling land available for development. Like Los Angeles County its early development was based on inland irrigation farms and coastal resort and fishing villages. The discovery of oil and later industrialization along rail lines spread the urban land uses. The exploitation of southern Orange County, however, was restricted by the 90,000-acre Irvine Ranch whose wealthy owners delayed urban development until the 1960s. The city of Irvine is exemplary of the advantages of large-scale land development by a single company. It is rapidly becoming California's premier new town, planned as a series of villages separated by greenbelts but unified by bus lines and municipal services.

A number of residential towns have grown up between Los Angeles and San Diego, but settlement has been slowed by water shortages and extensive military reservations. A sign of rapid growth along the southern littoral is the increasing number of thermonuclear and thermal electric power plants, which may lessen the impact of an energy crisis in the Southern California Megalopolis.

South Coast and Southeastern Interior

San Diego San Diego might be thought of as a smaller version of Los Angeles: Both cities started as agricultural centers; both have mammoth aircraft and military industries, suburbs connected by freeways, and a considerable retired population. Their differences are equally striking. San Diego has a fine natural harbor, but its hinterland is less extensive than that of Los Angeles and it has fewer natural resources—lacking oil, natural gas, and a high mountain watershed. Its poorer location south of the main transcontinental lines has meant that its through rail traffic is commonly routed via Los Angeles.

Modern San Diego grew after its selection as a major naval base in 1907. Much of its present industry is defense-oriented, although some, for example aircraft and electronics, produce for both civilian and government markets. Seafood canning and shipbuilding, the other sizable industries, are small compared with aerospace and ordnance.

San Bernardino–San Jacinto lowlands

The almost unsettled Santa Ana Mountains separate the semiarid San Bernardino Lowland from the urbanized coastal lowland. This interior valley is in the process of changing from rural to urban land uses, but it also contains much uninhabited desert area. Its major crop is oranges, but there are also vineyards, orchards, dairy farms, and truck gardens. The principal city, San Bernardino, was founded by the Mormons in 1851 on a broad alluvial fan, watered by streams from the San Gabriel Mountains. Routes over Cajon Pass focused on the site, and it was on or near the routes of all the railroads serving the Los Angeles area. After World War II San Bernardino acquired metal fabrication industries, aided by the proximity of Kaiser Steel, the first integrated steel

VALUE ADDED BY MANUFACTURING — **LOS ANGELES–LONG BEACH SMSA**

% Distribution — Location quotients: 1.0 = national average per capita

Employment	Value added	SIC source	Location quotient
5.9	7.6	Food products	
NA	NA	Tobacco products	NA
1.0	0.9	Textiles	
7.2	3.9	Apparel	
0.9	0.8	Lumber	
3.7	2.9	Furniture	
2.0	1.9	Paper products	
4.8	4.7	Printing	
3.7	5.9	Chemicals	
1.1	2.7	Petro-coal products	
3.3	3.1	Rubber–plastic	
NA	NA	Leather	NA
2.6	2.4	Stone–clay–glass	
3.3	3.1	Primary metals	
8.0	7.4	Fabricated metals	
10.1	8.5	Machinery	
10.8	9.8	Electrical machinery	
16.7	18.5	Transport equipment	
2.5	2.2	Instruments	
100.0	100.0	All categories	

Figure 8.4 Los Angeles County (same area as the SMSA) obviously boasts one of the most substantial and diversified manufacturing structures in Anglo-America. Compare this area with the well-diversified Philadelphia SMSA (Figure 4.14).

mill near the Pacific. Natural resources for this mill are assembled from far away: iron ore from Eagle Mountain in the southern Mojave desert, coal from Utah, and limestone from east of the San Bernardino Mountains. The other major city in the lowland is Riverside, an orange-growing, educational, and light-industrial center.

South of Riverside lies the desertlike San Jacinto Basin, whose streams rarely reach the sea. Parts of this basin remain in the hands of the Indians; small areas are intensively irrigated, as indeed most of the lowlands could be if water becomes available. Expansive residential developments such as Sun City and Rancho California portend accelerated future residential growth in the basin.

The Colorado Desert   Irrigation has transformed much of the warm Colorado Desert to productive farmland. Agriculture is most widespread in the Salton Trough, which occupies a depression extending from San Gorgonio Pass 100 miles southeast to the Mexican border. During the last century this desolate area was crossed as quickly as possible by stagecoach and later by rail. Irrigation, using water from the Colorado River, began in the below-sea-level Imperial Valley in 1901. In 1905 the river flooded (via canals) the formerly dry Salton Sea and some marginal farmland was lost. Scientific agriculture using low-cost Mexican labor proved very profitable, partly because two or more crops could be grown each year. Crops included cotton, winter vegetables, sugar beets, alfalfa, and cantaloupes. Agriculture expanded in 1910 to the Coachella Valley, northwest of Salton Sea, where artesian water was discovered and used to grow dates, grapefruit, seedless grapes, and truck crops. The climatic advantages of the region for non-agricultural purposes became apparent in the 1920s with the growth of Palm Springs as a fashionable winter resort. This urban function increased throughout the 1960s as more desert resorts were built throughout the Coachella Valley. As a result there is growing competition

for scarce water supplies between urban and agricultural needs.

The Mojave Desert

Although not ideal for agricultural settlement, urban centers have been established in the Mojave Desert. The broad basins of the Mojave, supplied by the Mojave River and other streams from adjacent high mountains, appeared less barren to early travelers than the Colorado Desert. However, irrigation has not been extensively developed in this century; agriculture is limited to the narrow Colorado Valley and to the back slopes of the San Bernardino and San Gabriel ranges. Several small towns are service centers for railways and highways, and some depend on minerals. Las Vegas is the largest city, the result of the liberal gambling laws of Nevada, making it a major recreational center for people from Southern California. Another use of large desert areas is for military maneuvers and supply depots; even empty space has its value in Southern California!

The dams which regulate the lower Colorado River are in the eastern Mojave. They distribute its waters in accord with the interstate Colorado River Compact of 1922 and with treaties with Mexico. Hoover Dam, tallest of the world's dams, created Lake Mead whose waters are used primarily to generate hydroelectric power; Parker Dam diverts water into the Colorado Aqueduct which supplies the southern coastal zone of California; Imperial Dam diverts water into the All American Canal which serves Imperial and Coachella valleys. The Colorado water situation has become critical because Southern California has been drawing more than its share of water under the interstate compact.

The Trans-Sierra and Southern Sierra Nevada

This sparsely inhabited western part of the Great Basin is linked to Southern California

This ERTS image (115 miles²) includes all of the Los Angeles SMSA. Among the more conspicuous man-made features are Long Beach–Los Angeles harbors and flood control channels draining the Los Angeles and Santa Ana basins (lower right). But despite the impact of several million people residing in this area, natural phenomena— such as the San Andreas Rift Zone (upper middle) and Garlock Fault (jutting northeastward) delineating the Mojave Desert—stand out more than do cultural features. (NASA)

because most of its water is pumped to Los Angeles (Figure 8.2). Owens Lake, Searles Lake, Death Valley, and other internally draining intermittent lakes (playas) also are mined for a variety of saline minerals. The Owens Valley, as a gateway to the eastern High Sierra and Death Valley, now depends heavily on income from tourism.

The southern Sierra Nevada is an area of present and potential recreational value east of the San Joaquin Valley. Sequoia and Kings Canyon national parks are the principal attractions, although the controversial Mineral King area (once proposed to become a major ski resort) and the extensive high back country

promise to enhance the recreation potential of the region. Although forest and water resources, along with tourism, are significant, permanent settlement is restricted to a few small towns along the gentle western slopes.

Crowley Lake and the snow-covered eastern High Sierra illustrate water resource problems and solutions in the Pacific states. Some 300 miles northeast of Los Angeles, Crowley is the largest man-made reservoir (completed in 1940) in that city's Owens River Aqueduct System. Dating from 1908, the system is the oldest major long-distance water distribution project in California and has proven indispensable to Los Angeles' growth. But Owens Valley farmers were vehemently reluctant to part with water that nourished their once verdant valley. (Crane Miller)

The Southern Central Valley

Man's use of this environment has changed greatly within a century. The central and western portion of the valley is low and flat; in the east the land is hilly and rises gradually into the Sierra Nevada foothills. This physical setting was ideal for the introduction of irrigation. Irrigation water, once obtained mainly from local wells, now is also derived from the Kings and Kern rivers.

Land use changed over the years as more remunerative crops were introduced. The subregion was settled by farmers with a cattle-and-grain economy based on large landholdings. Grapes and other subtropical fruits were introduced mainly in the present century. Irrigated cotton, grown in large fields and cultivated by machine, became the major crop in the 1920s. The dominant agricultural economy was broadened early in the century with the discovery of petroleum on the southern and western edges of the valley.

Although there are many small farms, large corporations control the majority of the land. For example, the Kern County Land Company, founded by a successful exploiter of the silver-rich Comstock lode, started as a cattle company with hundreds of thousands of acres. The company has water rights in the Kern River and now engages in irrigated agriculture, bringing in additional cattle for fattening.

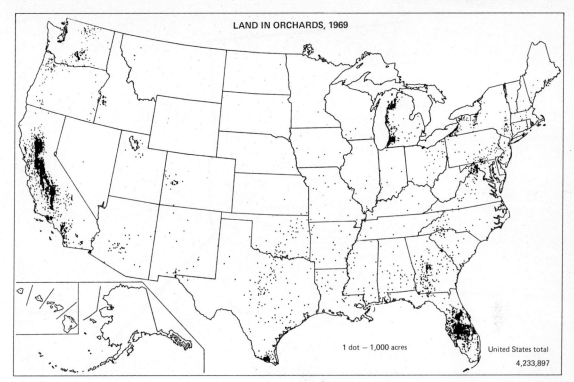

LAND IN ORCHARDS, 1969

1 dot — 1,000 acres

United States total
4,233,897

Figure 8.5 California is a national leader in the production of many irrigated deciduous and evergreen (mostly citrus) tree crops, including apricots, avocados, lemons, peaches, plums, and walnuts. Florida, however, claims leadership in orange production, largely because of its tropical environment; and Washington, with a colder climate, is the leading apple-producing state. (U.S. Department of Commerce, Social and Economic Statistics Administration, Bureau of the Census)

Fresno and Bakersfield control the trade of this region. Bakersfield at the southern entrance to the valley deals primarily in oil and cotton. The larger city of Fresno, more concerned with food processing, handles the wholesale trade of the central San Joaquin Valley. The contrast in appearance of the two cities is striking: Fresno has for decades had the more impressive skyline of high-rise buildings and more attractive downtown. Bakersfield seems spread out over the landscape in a relatively unplanned fashion.

FOCUS ON SAN FRANCISCO BAY

The geographical differences between this northern two-thirds of California and the Southland result from significant differences in resources. The most notable of these was gold, first discovered east of the site of Sacramento in 1848. This first gold rush in Anglo-American history converted the then insignificant village of San Francisco into a major port. The focus of the region became San Francisco Bay, one of the world's finest but hitherto little-used natural harbors. In contrast to the inland orientation of early Los Angeles, northern California, blessed with natural harbors from Monterey Bay to Humboldt Bay (Eureka), was linked to the sea. By 1869 San Francisco Bay became the terminus of the first transcontinental railroad and of roads from the Pacific Coast and interior valleys. Soon the Bay Area took on financial and commercial functions for most of the Far West, and, in addition, manufactured a variety of products for Western consumption.

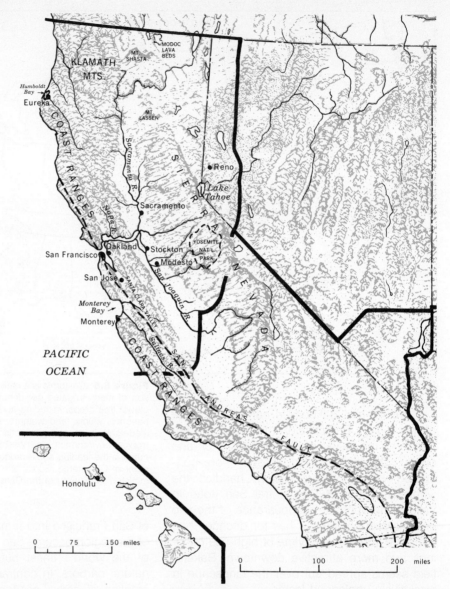

Figure 8.6 Landforms of the region that focuses commercially on San Francisco Bay. The influence of the San Francisco Federal Reserve Bank extends much further: east as far as the Rockies and north across Alaska. Note the axis of the San Andreas Fault (Rift Zone) where continental drift may be occurring. (Base map copyright by A. K. Lobeck. Reprinted with permission of The Geographical Press, Hammond, Inc.)

Settlement and Development

Spanish-Mexican settlement in central coastal California includes the same elements as in the Southland: mission agriculture and cattle ranches dotted the landscape, and the handful of presidios and pueblos were inconspicuous. Although Monterey became the capital of Alta California, Los Angeles remained the most populous pueblo. Hispanic coastal settlement ex-

tended about 30 miles north of San Francisco Bay, but ranching did not spread into the Central Valley until 1836. The gold rush of 1849, centered first east of Sacramento and later scattered throughout the Mother Lode country of the western Sierra, brought immigrants from many parts of the world, providing employment in trade, crafts, ranching, and services for those who found little or no gold. The coast north of San Francisco Bay, at first thinly settled by trappers, became a source of lumber.

After the Gold Rush

Gold was the lure that brought substantial American settlement to California; yet the gold rush lasted less than a decade. Individual prospectors moved northward to British Columbia in 1858, eastward to Nevada, and northeastward to the Rockies in the next year. Sacramento, founded as a river port for the gold fields, became the state capital in 1852.

Agricultural land use spread rapidly over the central Great Valley in the last quarter of the nineteenth century. At first dry-farmed wheat took over the extensive ranchlands. Later, irrigation farmers developed vineyards, orchards, and truck farms whose crops were marketed outside the state by both rail and ship. The favorable climate and a generous water supply made northern California outstanding for the variety, quantity, and quality of its agricultural products.

San Francisco and the Bay Area

Why the site of San Francisco?[1] When in 1914 the Federal Reserve System selected San Francisco as the location for the Twelfth District Federal Reserve Bank, it was recognizing the widely known financial and commercial dominance of this city in most of the area west of the Rockies. Why did San Francisco become the leader in the West, and why has it retained this position? The answer involves the site and locational advantages, the accidents of history, and the tendency of business to follow established channels until a change seems likely to result in outstanding economies.

The location of San Francisco on a rocky, hilly peninsula with a business section adjacent to a spacious, well-sheltered harbor seems an obvious selection of the best site in the Bay Area. However, in 1849 equally usable sites might have been developed at San Mateo, Sausalito, Oakland, Berkeley, Richmond, Pittsburg, and elsewhere on the bay. Because the warehouse function was fundamental to early San Francisco business, the direction of currents through Golden Gate and the firm bottom of Yerba Buena Cove facilitated the unloading of supply ships there. Even so, a long wharf was required to reach deep water, and the foggy site was considered a handicap by many. When the port facilities were built, small steamers started from there to ascend rivers southward into the present Fresno County and northward to Red Bluff. San Francisco became a boatman's city, and in anticipation of future port growth, land speculation became common. San Francisco became a central place to serve central California.

As city population increased, more nonbasic workers were required to serve the needs of the local population. Consequently, specialized urban land use evolved to perform services for both the regional trading area and the inhabitants of the city. The physical environment was modified by filling in tidal flatlands along the harbor to provide sites for the wholesale district. Nearby a financial district (Montgomery Street) became established on the slopes several blocks inland. As in other cities, differentiation in commercial functions became apparent; for example, a retail shopping district arose along Market Street. A light-industrial district, needing transport for raw materials and finished goods, was established on level land around the railroad terminals.

Changing land-use patterns Early routes terminated at places across the bay rather than at San Francisco and connected with the central city by ferry. As railroads took over more

[1] The following section owes much to James E. Vance, Jr., "Geography and Urban Evolution in the San Francisco Bay Area," in *The San Francisco Bay Area: Its Problems and Future,* University of California, Berkeley, 1963.

The steep streets with their cable cars, Fisherman's Wharf below, the entrance to San Francisco Bay, Alcatraz Island, and the hills north of the Bay are some of the tourist attractions of San Francisco. (Ted Needham from San Francisco Convention and Visitors Bureau)

traffic, and as navigable streams lost some of their water to irrigation projects, local water transport decreased in importance. Town sites were no longer limited to waterfronts; they sprang up along the railroads. In the late 1880s trolley-car suburbs were added to San Francisco's railroad suburbs, and retail strips arose along trolley-car routes. As suburbs sprawled out along these inland routes, San Francisco lost some of its early unity. Further decentralization occurred in the early twentieth century when business centers were established on the east side of the bay, duplicating the shopping and other functions formerly concentrated in downtown San Francisco.

As in other Anglo-American cities the automobile speeded the formation of satellite suburbs and led to a filling in of areas between rail and trolley routes. As parking within the central city became scarce, some functions moved to the suburbs. The freeway-bridge age, beginning in the 1950s, destroyed most of the remaining local water traffic. Yet the skeletons of the former land uses remained apparent in the street and railroad grids, in land uses, and in local traditions. The Bay Area consists of a number of incongruous street grids inherited from towns that have since grown together. As an old city it was inevitable that urban renewal would become necessary, and the Bay Area is preparing to rebuild to fit contemporary needs. The new patterns will not be entirely novel because the grain of the hills, the position of the water bodies, and the huge investments in structures will have a conservative influence. Industrial zones in the present city are related to transport and markets. Light industries which are consumer-oriented are mainly in San Francisco, whereas the heavier industries are located along the railroad lines, behind the docks along the western bay shore, and also along the eastern bay shore. Industry is expanding southward, displacing the intensively developed farms which cannot compete economically with industrial and residential land use. The Santa Clara Valley, for example, once noted for its orchards and vegetable gar-

dens, is gradually converting to an economy based on electronic and science-oriented industries.

A Pacific Coast New York San Francisco has been called the "New York of the Pacific Coast," and they share many cosmopolitan characteristics. Both metropolises have skyscrapers, outstanding commercial functions, and spacious harbors lined with docks, warehouses, and factories. Both at first found the enclosed waterways a major convenience for regional communication and later replaced most of the ferry services with bridges or tunnels. Both commercial centers depended on the resources of outlying rather than local hinterlands; both have important business ties overseas and in distant states. Both have compact Central Business Districts within which most high-level commercial and financial functions are performed. Both had and still have some nearby undeveloped areas of marshy and rugged lands.

The Bay Area has a smaller local market for its industries and less diversity of industrial development than the New York area. Note in Figure 8.7 how much the San Francisco–Oakland SMSA departs from the United States average in most industrial categories; recent industrial trends show that these deviations are lessening. With a larger local market and greater future industrial diversification, San Francisco is likely to grow closer to the national industrial averages. The Bay Area is not yet being integrated into a larger urban unit, as New York is now integrated into the Atlantic Megalopolis.

Planning regional growth In 1970 the population of the nine-county, 7,500 square-mile Bay Area was slightly more than 4.6 million. It has been estimated that by 1990 the area could have a population of some 7.5 million.[2] Before 1961, coordinated and cooperative planning among the area's counties and

[2] Association of Bay Area Governments, *Regional Plan 1970–1990, San Francisco Bay Region,* July 30, 1970.

cities was rare; each local government seemed bent on preserving "home rule" and determining its own future development with little regard for the regional consequences of such actions. However, during the 1960s a regional plan was prepared by the Association of Bay Area Governments (ABAG), and with its completion in 1970 a new spirit of cooperation was infused into regional planning and development. A basic concept of the plan is the "City-centered Region," which calls for accommodating future urban growth within the region in existing or new urban communities. It is hoped that extensive open space and conserved areas will remain and regional environmental quality will be improved.

Regional mass transit   As elsewhere in urban California, automobiles are by far the preferred mode of transportation in the Bay Area. The moderately successful 1972 opening of the first links of the Bay Area Rapid Transit district's (BART) system in the east bay section may signal a new era in California mass transit. A major feature of the BART system is a 4-mile transbay tube connecting Oakland and east bay suburbs with San Francisco.

A unique energy source   While the Bay Area still relies heavily on conventional sources of energy, it is the only metropolitan area in North America receiving a significant input of power generated from *geothermal* steam. In excess of 130,000 kilowatthours of electrical power are generated at the Geysers area (about 90 miles north of San Francisco) utilizing dry geothermal steam. A significant boon to geothermal resource development was a 1969 U.S. Tax Court ruling declaring geothermal steam to be a gas, and therefore eligible for the 27.5 percent tax depletion allowance. Geothermal power is considered environmentally more desirable than energy produced from burning fossil fuels or using radioactive elements, since the latter two emit harmful by-products.

Sacramento and Stockton

The dual metropolitan areas of Sacramento and Stockton provide the metropolitan focus of the Great Central Valley. Sacramento, at the junction of the American and Sacramento rivers, regularly suffered from floods until well into the twentieth century. To the north the water is now controlled for use in rice fields, and modern dams impound the headwaters of most streams. In addition to rice, the Sacramento trading area produces a wide variety of agricultural products ranging from beef cattle to walnuts. Both Sacramento and Stockton have a strong industrial base, led by food packing but also including defense-oriented industries.

Metropolitan Sacramento has expanded outward since World War II, particularly to the east toward the Sierran foothills. Low-density

VALUE ADDED BY MANUFACTURING   **SAN FRANCISCO-OAKLAND SMSA**

% Distribution   Location quotients: 1.0 = national average per capita

Employ-ment	Value added	SIC source	0	1.0	2.0	3.0	4.0	5.0
15.0	21.4	Food products						
NA	NA	Tobacco products	NA					
0.3	0.2	Textiles						
3.6	2.1	Apparel						
1.0	0.7	Lumber						
2.1	1.6	Furniture						
4.1	3.6	Paper products						
8.0	7.4	Printing						
5.0	9.1	Chemicals						
2.8	4.7	Petro-coal products						
2.1	1.8	Rubber–plastic						
NA	NA	Leather	NA					
3.9	3.4	Stone-clay-glass						
5.4	3.9	Primary metals						
9.5	8.6	Fabricated metals						
10.7	9.2	Machinery						
8.5	7.1	Electrical machinery						
5.7	7.5	Transport equipment						
1.3	1.1	Instruments						
100.0	100.0	All categories						

Figure 8.7   San Francisco–Oakland manufacturing lacks the diversity of Los Angeles–Long Beach (Figure 8.4). But, the Bay Area is well served by its large natural deep water harbor in the shipborne import of food and petroleum raw materials to be processed.

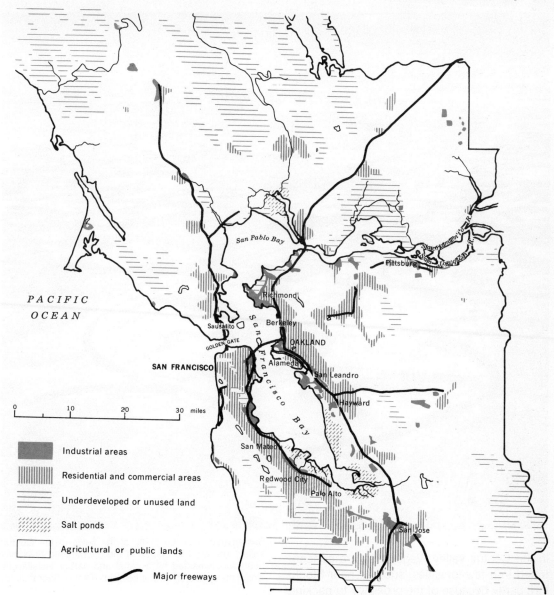

PACIFIC
OCEAN

San Pablo Bay

Pittsburg

Richmond

Sausalito

Berkeley

GOLDEN GATE

OAKLAND

SAN FRANCISCO

Alameda

San Leandro

Hayward

San Mateo

Redwood City

Palo Alto

San Jose

0   10   20   30 miles

◼ Industrial areas

▦ Residential and commercial areas

▤ Underdeveloped or unused land

▨ Salt ponds

☐ Agricultural or public lands

━ Major freeways

Figure 8.8 Compare the spatial arrangement of industry in the Bay Area with that in Los Angeles (Figure 8.3). Residential and agricultural land users compete keenly for scarce, level land in the Santa Clara Valley, south of San Jose and the Sonoma and Napa valleys north of San Pablo Bay. (After a map by the Corps of Engineers)

ranchette communities, sprawling residential tracts, and new shopping centers now abound on land that little more than a decade ago was largely agricultural. The value of a scenic setting is illustrated by the preference of Sacramento suburbanites for the oak-studded, rolling terrain in the shadow of the Sierra to the comparatively flat and treeless area west of the Sacramento River.

Agriculture in the Valleys

The Great Central Valley Intense cultivation of special crops in response to local economic or environmental conditions is apparent

Sacramento is in the midst of the fields of the Central Valley. The winding course of the Sacramento River has been supplemented by a canal and harbor installations which make Sacramento a seaport. (Port of Sacramento)

in the Central Valley. Vegetables are concentrated in a few localities, such as near Stockton, partly because of the proximity to packing plants and partly because of the highly specialized machinery used in harvesting. Alfalfa and other feed crops are widespread, but beef and dairy production concentrates near urban markets. Deciduous fruits and nuts production focuses on the northern part of the valley where cooler winters contribute to greater summer harvests from these tree crops; for example, walnuts and peaches yield best after experiencing a relatively lengthy and cool dormant (winter) period. Grape production is concentrated by type into areas of market grapes, raisin, or wine grapes; the product is greatly influenced by small differences in climate and soil. In all, California's Great Central Valley is unrivaled by any other area of comparable size in the nation in the variety and value of its agricultural output.

Significant in explaining the Central Valley's agricultural productivity is the fact that nearly one-half of the total water available from stream runoff in California drains into the valley (mostly from the Sierra Nevada). Man has augmented this natural resource with widespread drilling of wells over the last century and, more recently, with two large-scale water resource developments: the federally sponsored Central Valley Project started in the 1940s and the California State Water Project begun in the 1960s. The Central Valley Project, primarily concerned with impounding and diverting water in the Sacramento and San Joaquin river systems, is confined to the valley and its immediate environs. The State Water Project, on the other hand, not only provides irrigation, hydroelectric, recreation, and flood control services to the valley area, but also brings water from water-rich northern California to water-deficient Southern California (Figure 8.2).

Coast Range valleys Valleys to the north and south of the Bay Area also evidence crop specialization. Inland Coast Range valleys, like the Napa and Sonoma, specialize in producing varietal wine grapes; mild, but sunny, climate is the key environmental factor in the vineyard regions. Valleys fronting on the Pacific, such as the Salinas Valley, experience much fog, which enhances lettuce, artichoke, and other vegetable production. Livestock production is important in the Coast Ranges with cattle and sheep grazing both irrigated valley pastures and nonirrigated hillsides.

Land-use competition Similar to many other Anglo-American cities the competition for land is most intensive on the urban fringes. There agriculture and urban land uses compete for the limited supply of well drained, relatively flat, and otherwise environmentally and locationally well-suited land. Most urban land uses can outbid agriculture, and such land eventually converts to urban functions. Unfortunately under these circumstances land speculators may take agricultural land prematurely out of production awaiting the opportune time for its

improvement. Such leapfrogging and scattering of suburban development is well illustrated in the urban sprawl of the Santa Clara and other valleys around the Bay Area.

The conversion of farmland to nonagricultural uses may be stimulated by its assessment at potential subdivision values; consequently the farmer may see his property taxes rise to a point where it is more profitable to sell his land than his crops. To cope with this problem, several states, including California, have adopted *preferential assessment* programs whereby agricultural land is assessed on the basis of its agricultural use or income rather than on its highest and best use or market value, thus giving farmers a much needed tax break. By mid-1970, in 38 California counties comprising nearly 68 million acres, more than 6 million acres of farmland have received preferential treatment under the California Land Conservation Act of 1965.

Northwestern California
This moist tenth of California has two resources—trees and enough water to export. Most of its rivers flow, with little use, into the Pacific. Often the region has suffered from destructive floods because precipitation fluctuates widely. This is green California: trees, undergrowth, and lawns are verdant without irrigation. The landscapes appear moist and cool, in contrast to the semiarid parts of California where forest and grass fires are an ever-present danger.

There are no large cities in the northwest; Eureka with nearly 25,000 is the most populous. It does not take many workers with power saws and tractors to harvest the trees and produce lumber. Nor do the thousand small fishing vessels require large crews. There is little agriculture along the Coast, and inland much of the land is in national forest. The best-developed agriculture is in the transition zone between the northwest and the northern end of the Central Valley where grazing and orchards flourish.

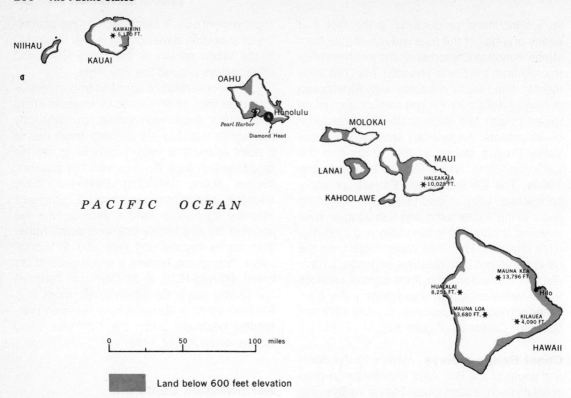

NIIHAU

KAUAI
★ KAWAIKINI
5,170 FT.

a

OAHU

Honolulu

Pearl Harbor

Diamond Head

PACIFIC   OCEAN

MOLOKAI

MAUI

LANAI

HALEAKALA
★ 10,025 FT.

KAHOOLAWE

MAUNA KEA
★ 13,796 FT.

HUALALAI
8,251 FT. ★

Hilo

MAUNA LOA
13,680 FT. ★

KILAUEA
4,090 FT. ★

HAWAII

0   50   100 miles

Land below 600 feet elevation

The Tahoe-Reno Area

Watered largely by streams from the eastern slope of the Sierra Nevada, the Nevada and California counties encompassing Lake Tahoe, Reno, and Carson City (capital of Nevada) are historically and economically tied to central California. The exploitation of precious metals was by California miners who reasoned correctly that if alluvial gold came from the Sierra Nevada, veins might also be found on the eastern slope and in adjacent mountains. In 1859 the gold and silver ores of the Comstock lode were discovered and people flocked in. Nevada's population reached a peak of 63,000 in 1880 and then declined to 43,000 in 1900. In recent years Nevada mining employs only about 4,000 people, very few of whom are in the western border counties.

Tourist trade based on gambling, floor shows, and outdoor living provides the present economic backbone of the Tahoe-Reno area. Less than 3 hours driving time from the Bay

Figure 8.9   Hawaii is a chain of volcanic islands, mostly mountainous, with each island producing several specialties. The principal specialty of Oahu is services: military, commercial, and tourist; but sugar cane and pineapple production are also significant. Kona coffee and cattle raising share the spotlight with tourism on the "Big Island."

Area, 2 hours from Sacramento-Stockton, and 1 hour from Reno–Carson City, Lake Tahoe regularly attracts multitudes for its spectacular scenery alone. Because the Tahoe Basin has the fastest population increase in the Sierra Nevada and the lake is one of the purest bodies of water in the world, the area became the subject of an intensive environmental impact study.

THE HAWAIIAN ISLANDS

These startlingly beautiful volcanic islands (Figure 8.9), the summits of a volcanic mass rising in the central Pacific, are a focus of trans-Pacific air and shipping routes. It is nearly

2,100 nautical miles (2,400 statute miles) from San Francisco to Honolulu and 2 hours change in time. Tropical climate, pleasant beaches, lush vegetation, a great variety of peoples, active and quiescent volcanoes, and a wide choice of the ultimate in tourist accommocations have made these islands one of the world's great resorts.

The people of the islands are an example of a mixed society. The original Polynesians have blended with American, Chinese, Japanese, Filipino, Portuguese, and other immigrants. The numerous racial groups and mixtures live together in a tolerant society. Outwardly most peoples seem to be highly Americanized, especially in their business activities. Despite an idyllic tropical environment the people and activities are isolated from friends and business associates in mainland America.

Agriculture contributes less than one-thirtieth of the personal income, exporting such tropical products as cane sugar, pineapples, Kona coffee, and papaya. Commercial farms are unusually large and highly mechanized and are managed by corporations. Sugar plantations are so noted for their high yields per acre and per worker that many tropical countries have sent delegations to learn the secrets of this high productivity.

Oahu Island and Honolulu

About five-sixths of the people and income are concentrated on Oahu Island, mainly within Honolulu's city limits. This island has most of the military, naval, and air force bases; the commercial and shipping facilities; the pineapple production; and the tourist activities. Government, especially federal, directly accounts for one-third of the income. Since agriculture does not support Hawaii's economy and since other occupations are dependent on tourists, governmental activity, and external transport, the islands are vulnerable to any reduction in world transport if oil becomes in short supply.

It is not surprising that Oahu with an area of only 600 square miles and a population of some 700,000 is feeling rather severe urban pressures on its cultural and physical environment. For example, the city of Honolulu seems no less plagued by urban crime and other social problems than most moderate-sized Anglo-American cities. In outlying rural areas sugar and pineapple plantations face increasing competition from suburban development for scarce level land. However, Hawaii's state-wide zoning controls have been successful in halting some subdivisions in their tracks. Even the coral reefs offshore are not immune, for their very existence is threatened wherever seawater is turned turbid by sediment-laden runoff from freshly graded shore areas and hillsides. Coral in embayments, such as Kaneohoe Bay, is especially vulnerable.

Hawaii and the Other Islands

The "Big Island" (Hawaii) and other settled islands of the state are sparsely populated compared to Oahu, but are outstanding in other respects. Hawaii boasts an area twice as large as all the other islands combined, the state's highest mountains (Mauna Loa and Mauna Kea rise more than 13,000 feet), spectacular volcanic activity, and leadership in coffee and beef production. Maui County, including the islands of Maui, Molokai, and Lanai, is second only to Oahu in pineapple production and claims an outstanding scenic attraction in Mt. Haleakala (10,000 feet) National Park in southern Maui. Kauai, the north-westernmost of the major islands, features extensive mountainous terrain which includes deeply dissected Waimea Canyon.

THE PACIFIC NORTHWEST

To three-fourths of its people living within 100 miles of the Coast, the Pacific Northwest (Figure 8.10) is a verdant land of exceptional timber and water resources, abundant fisheries, and impressively varied topography. The remainder

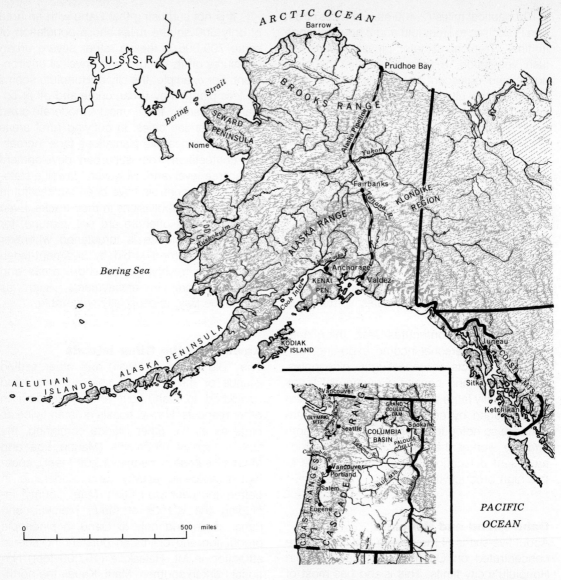

Figure 8.10 The landforms of the Pacific Northwest. Alaska, Washington, and Oregon have been placed together in this unusual way to stress the huge size of Alaska. For a larger map, see the ERTS image on the opening pages of Chapter 11. Much of the Pacific Northwest is too rugged, too dry, or too cold for intensive economic development. (Base map copyright by A. K. Lobeck. Reprinted with permission of The Geographical Press, Hammond, Inc.)

of the population residing east of the Cascades have a contrasting landscape of irrigated and dry crop farming, extensive livestock ranching, and expanses of sparsely vegetated open space. Despite the diversity of environments, a broadly based regional economy has not evolved. Within most subregions of Oregon and Washington too much industrial specialization has sometimes led to local depression.

Environment and Settlement

The Pacific side of the Cascades is a misty land of cloud-filtered sunshine, with relative freedom

Mount Hood, most conspicuous of the Oregon Cascades, provides water for this reservoir which feeds a power plant. The fir forest is being logged off in patches as part of the U.S. Forest Service sustained-yield program. (Oregon State Highway Department)

from extremes of heat in summer and cold in winter. Its climate and its rugged, tree-lined coasts are more like Scandinavia than other parts of Anglo-America. The coniferous forest is lush enough in places to be described as a "temperate rain forest." Where cleared, the soil may become leached and, on the slopes, eroded. It is a land of green pastures and meadows, with dairying, orchards, and berry patches and such truck crops as potatoes.

East of the Cascades, the landscape changes within a few miles. The forests thin out and then disappear. The sunshine can be bright, and the air is at times bitter in winter and sometimes hot and dusty in summer; the land resembles the High West with its contrasts of yellowed grasslands and wheat fields, drab-green sagebrush, dark-green orchards, and bright-green irrigated fields. Water from streams rising in the snowcapped Cascades and in the Northern Rockies makes the land habitable.

Not least among the natural resources is the scenic beauty of the land: the multicolored mesas, plateaus, and canyons of the volcanic Columbia Plateau; the cool, green forested slopes and valleys of the Cascades topped by snowcapped volcanic cones, the pastoral landscapes of the Willamette and Cowlitz lowlands terminating northward in the dark-toned embayments of Puget Sound. Westward the wooded Coast Ranges descend to a foggy, rocky Pacific Coast or end in the spectacular Olympic Mountains overlooking the Strait of Juan de Fuca.

Aboriginal settlement   Although the aboriginal Americans of the Pacific Northwest did not generally practice agriculture, theirs was a comparatively prosperous existence based on the riches of ocean and teeming river waters and productive forests. The Northwest Coast Indian cultures, stretching from northern California through the Alaska Panhandle, were eminently successful in salmon fishing, whaling, and sealing; in the construction of wooden houses and boats; and in carving and weaving. The arid land east of the Cascades was less bountiful, as was aboriginal life. Riverine fishing economies flourished along the Columbia and some of its tributaries; but away from the rivers on the Columbia Plateau and in the basin and range country of eastern Oregon hunting and gathering supported only sparse Indian populations. The groups tended to remain separate from one another as illustrated by the numerous languages and distinctive cultures that evolved in the interior.

British and American expansion   European trappers and fur traders reached the Pacific Northwest before the end of the eighteenth century. China-bound clippers from New England traded along the Coast for sea otter and other furs in demand in east Asia. During the first half of the nineteenth century, American and British fur traders came overland to establish forts from which to trade with the Indians. Later settlers came overland along the famous Oregon Trail, settling mainly in the Willamette Valley. The Cowlitz Valley and Puget Sound areas were occupied in the mid-nineteenth century as the forests were cut to supply lumber to California, Hawaii, and other lands touching the Pacific. Until the boundary issue was settled upon the 49th parallel in 1846, British interests in the Northwest, represented mainly by the Hudson's Bay Company, competed with those of the Americans.

By 1880, however, the region was still on the fringes of settlement, with only about 250,000 people. Thereafter the railroads and an expanding lumber industry spurred rapid growth. The Northern Pacific Railroad reached Puget Sound in 1883, the Great Northern in 1893, the Milwaukee in 1909. Because all three lines converged at Spokane, that interior city rose to dominance on the Columbia Plateau. Throughout the region the resource base gave employment: concomitant resource expansion occurred not only in lumber, but also in fish canning and wood products manufacturing in the western ports, fruit packing in the mountain valleys, and wheat farming in the eastern Palouse country. Heavy industry was established during World War I when shipbuilding and aircraft manufacture became significant in Seattle. Water resources were harnessed during the 1920s when hydroelectric power and related irrigation projects associated with the Columbia Basin were developed. During World War II this ample power attracted aluminum and other metals refining.

Present population and economic activity are concentrated in a narrow 250-mile-long lowland between Puget Sound and the Willamette Valley. During the 1960s growth in Oregon and Washington was moderate; population in the two states reached 5.5 million in 1970. More than 60 percent of both the regional pop-

This fire is in the Douglas fir forest of western Oregon. The area in the foreground has been recently logged and, if the fire can be kept out, will grow a thick second-growth forest of fir and hemlock. (American Forest Product Industries)

ulation and income is concentrated in six SMSAs, the only interior one being Spokane. Economic links between the "Inland Empire" east of the Cascades and the coast are not strong, and thus the interior hinterland has a minor impact upon the prosperity of Seattle and Portland.

Coastal Oregon and Washington

Lumbering Lumbering, dairying, and tourism dominate man's use of the rugged coastal lands of Oregon and Washington. More than half the lumber harvested in the Northwest is from virgin and old second-growth timber. Trees are clear-cut in patches across the hillsides, permitting the unharvested forest to reseed the cleared land. Clear-cutting is often disparaged, but in the case of Douglas fir, the dominant commercial tree of coastal and other Pacific Northwest forests, it is essential for optimim reproduction. Intolerant to shade in its

youth, Douglas fir needs the sunlight of clear-cut openings to grow.

Logging supports a scattered and relatively small population in the coastal hills and mountains; most lumber workers live in the main cities. Coos Bay, on the central Oregon Coast, is an example of a city dominated by the lumber industry. As a leading lumber shipping port it has five large lumber mills, two pulp and paper plants, one alder mill, and two myrtlewood factories—myrtlewood is a decorative hardwood unique to southwestern Oregon.

The lumbering industry has long been criticized for its wasteful practices. Optimum tree growth has been prevented by the failure to thin forests. Much small timber has been burned in huge refuse burners, other wood being unused in cleared areas. Many mature timber stands remained untouched because of lack of roads. Such wasteful practices have become rare; scrap wood is now used for hardboard or paper pulp, and pulp mills are often integrated (in location and company ownership) with sawmills. Meanwhile cleared forest lands have been converted into tree farms on much privately owned land in Oregon and Washington. Assuming that the "super-trees" are allowed to grow to full size, these farms will be ready for harvesting 40 years after planting. On this basis, the U.S. Forest Service predicts a considerable increase in allowable cut by the year 2000. With forest products accounting for nearly 70 percent of total value added by manufacturing in the state, Oregonians are justly concerned with any production declines in their major industry. Today Oregon ranks first in the nation in forest products production, followed closely by Washington.

Farming and fishing   The rainy, foggy floodplains and cleared valleys near the Coast support large herds of dairy cattle. Oregon's coastal cities, especially Reedsport and Tillamook, are famous for their fine cheeses. Ironically, some of the flatlands that require drainage in the cool season need irrigation for best results in the drier summer. The type of agriculture is a direct response to the food demands of the concentrated urban population; in addition to dairy products the farms produce consumer products such as beef and poultry. Distinctive crops include berries in coastal valleys and vegetables in scattered lowlands, notably in western Washington.

Commercial fishing along the Coast, mainly for salmon and shellfish, is a multimillion dollar industry. Some coastal settlements are entirely dependent on fish canning and freezing. Many of these ports also shelter large sport-fishing fleets.

Tourism   Wave-battered headlands, tree-lined palisades, driftwood-covered beaches, and ample fishing have attracted growing numbers of tourists to the Oregon–Washington lit-

toral. Some conception of the economic impact of tourism is illustrated by more than 100 motels with more than 1,400 rooms along one 20-mile stretch of central Oregon Coast alone. A less commercialized tourist attraction is Olympic National Park, located in part along the Pacific edge of Olympic Peninsula but in the main in the center of that wide and rugged tongue of land.

The Willamette–Puget Sound Lowlands

The Willamette Valley   The Willamette Valley is a fairly broad structural trough lying between the Coast and Cascade ranges. Fertile alluvial soils, whose parent material was transported by the Willamette River and its tributaries from the Cascades, are the basis for a thriving agriculture in the valley.

Farms in the narrow upper Willamette Valley produce cherries, walnuts, hops, and sheep. Northward near Eugene the valley broadens and much of it has been cleared, with some land suitable for every kind of middle-latitude fruit and berries, as well as dairying, nuts, flower and grass seed, and vegetables.

Industrialization is minor in the Willamette Valley. Because there is a considerable agricultural surplus for export, food packing is characteristic in the cities. Wood-products manufacturing is common in most centers. The small towns are pleasant, quiet places set amid a prosperous agriculture; their dependence on their resource hinterlands is direct.

Portland   The site and position of Portland seemed destined for a commercial city. Located where the Columbia provided a gateway through the Cascades to the Willamette Lowland and with a river entering from the south, Portland had a crossroads position. Yet tiny Portland in 1845 had rivals and handicaps. Oregon City (formerly Willamette Falls), 12 miles up the Willamette River, had both water-power and a location at the head of downstream navigation. Vancouver, Washington, on the Columbia River, was several miles closer to the Pacific. Salem was more centrally located among the Willamette Valley settlements. Portland's site had the handicaps of swamps and flood danger in the tongue of land between the Columbia and lower Willamette. Nor was Portland's river connection with the Pacific satisfactory until the channel was improved in 1877. Yet today with a 100-mile, 35-foot channel to the Pacific, with locks permitting barge traffic up the Columbia and Willamette, and with its former rivals Oregon City and Vancouver absorbed into its SMSA, Portland is outstanding as an industrial, wholesaling, shipping, and financial center for Oregon and parts of Washington and Idaho. Portland's industries are closely tied to the agricultural and forest resources of its hinterland. The city's commercial functions are almost as important as its industries, as illustrated by the variety of store and office blocks in its large downtown core and attractive shopping plazas. Portland supplies commercial services not found elsewhere on the West Coast between Seattle and San Francisco.

A future Puget Sound Megalopolis

Nearly three-quarters of the people of western Washington are in sizable cities; more than half live in the Seattle–Everett SMSA. The Puget Sound Lowland (Figure 8.12), although rough in places, and broken by peninsulas, is not yet fully occupied by urban land uses. However, commerce, factories, and dwellings occupy much of the coastal strip from Everett on the north through Seattle, and Tacoma to Olympia on the southwest. The Puget Sound region is comparable in urban functions, but not in total size, to the New York–Northeastern New Jersey Consolidated Area. The main weakness of the Puget Sound region is the lack of a densely populated hinterland. But should future trans-Pacific trade grow to equal the volume of trans-Atlantic trade, the Puget Sound region could become one of the leading American ports.

Seattle Seattle has a spectacular site, located on a low but steep ridge between Puget Sound and interior Lake Washington. The city has had an uneven history of economic growth. Lumber was the first industrial base; then canned salmon became a second resource-based industry at the end of the last century. The discovery of coal nearby gave fuel for metallurgy. Its present economy is dependent greatly on the aircraft industry.

The early spatial growth of Seattle was related to its transshipment functions. Four transcontinental railroads terminated there, and Seattle was the gateway to Alaska; but before 1940 Alaska had few people, and the flow of supplies through Seattle was a minor part of the port's activity. The original town grew on the well-drained uplands, leaving the swampy

VALUE ADDED BY MANUFACTURING — **PORTLAND SMSA**

% Distribution — Location quotients: 1.0 = national average per capita

Employment	Value added	SIC source	0	1.0	2.0	3.0	4.0	5.0
11.5	16.5	Food products						
NA	NA	Tobacco products	NA					
NA	NA	Textiles	NA					
5.5	3.7	Apparel						
9.1	7.1	Lumber						
NA	NA	Furniture	NA					
8.3	10.4	Paper products						
6.1	5.2	Printing						
2.1	4.0	Chemicals						
0.3	1.0	Petro-coal products						
NA	NA	Rubber–plastic	NA					
NA	NA	Leather	NA					
2.2	2.6	Stone-clay-glass						
8.2	10.5	Primary metals						
6.8	6.4	Fabricated metals						
8.6	10.0	Machinery						
12.2	8.7	Electrical machinery						
5.8	5.1	Transport equipment						
2.1	2.9	Instruments						
100.0	100.0	All categories						

Figure 8.11 Centered in the continent's greatest Douglas fir forests, Portland manufacturing is understandably specialized in lumber and paper products. Nevertheless, the city is industrially more diversified than might be expected.

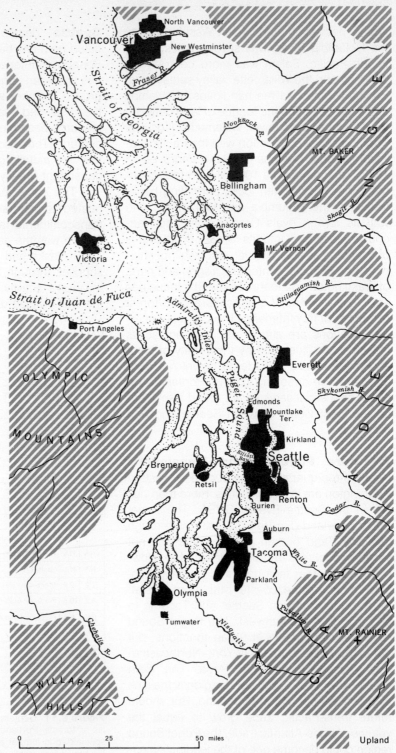

Upland

Figure 8.12 The great commercial advantage of the Puget Sound Area is its wealth of navigable channels penetrating into the land. Ferry connections between cities in the Sound and in Canada are excellent. Fishing, pleas- ure boating, shipbuilding, and hydroelectric power genera- tion are further indications of people's strong orientation to the water and its use.

lowlands for railroad tracks connecting with the docks on Elliott Bay (see Figure 8.12). Similar to growth in the San Francisco Bay Area, the Seattle SMSA expanded areally by means of a network of ferries and bridges; its residential and business sections reflect the ability of bulldozers to level hills and fill valleys.

The relative unimportance of raw materials in the ultimate growth of large cities has been noted in preceding chapters. If lumber, berries, salmon, and Alaskan gold were the sole basis of Seattle growth, it might have had a population of less than 200,000 instead of more than 1 million. The rise of Seattle's industrial giant, the Boeing Company, is one of the main reasons for the city's growth. This colossus, the greatest industrial employer in the Northwest with a labor force in the tens of thousands, owes its presence to a wealthy young Seattleite named William Boeing who became interested in flying. His repair shop on Lake Union by 1916 developed into a small plant for airplane manufacture. The United States Army began buying planes from him for the First World War; thereafter, with the exception of a brief hiatus following the war, Boeing has been turning out airplanes continuously. Through the 1960s Boeing's production and labor force increased dramatically, in part from the development of jet airliners such as the jumbo 747. But by the early seventies, with the local economy increasingly dependent on the one large company, the nationwide aerospace cutbacks hit Seattle's economy especially hard.

Tacoma Tacoma is a smaller Seattle without an aircraft industry. Tacoma, when it became the first terminal of the Northern Pacific Railroad, was a rival of Seattle; now it is noted for its copper and aluminum refining and related chemical industries, its wood- and paper-products industries, and its food packing. Its port lacks the quantity and variety of facilities and installations of the Seattle waterfront. An additional handicap, suffered by Tacoma and other cities with air-contaminating industries of necessity located on west-facing waterfronts,

is the blowing of smoke eastward over residential areas by onshore breezes.

The Cascade Range

The Cascades serve both as an orographic barrier to atmospheric moisture which would otherwise reach the Inland Empire and as a watershed for the western lowlands. Rainfall differences are illustrated by the lush Douglas fir forests on the windward (western) slopes of the range in contrast to drier ponderosa and lodgepole forests on the lee side. Tourism and recreation together with lumbering are the economic mainstays of the mountainous region.

Unique national parks Although scenic and recreation possibilities abound everywhere in the Cascades, Crater Lake, Mount Rainier, and North Cascades national parks provide the principal attractions. Because Crater Lake is unique in Anglo-America in terms of its volcanic origin, great depth, and unmatched purity, it is a significant drawing card in Oregon's half-billion dollar a year tourist industry. The scenic lure alone seems to obviate conditions of poor fishing and prohibition of boating and skiing in the park. Northward in Washington's Mount Rainier National Park, however, skiing and winter sports facilities are among the best on the continent. Cooling glaciers, lush forests on the lower slopes, and rustic campgrounds regularly attract summer visitors to Mount Rainier. Farther north, just below the British Columbia border, the North Cascades is one of the nation's newest, most rugged, and least trammeled national parks.

The Willamette: A unique national forest Stretching for 110 miles along the western slope of Oregon's Cascade Ranges, the Willamette is representative of multipurpose national forests in the Pacific Northwest. Yet it is unique as the leading timber producer among all national forests. Willamette National Forest annually produces more than 650 million board feet, or about 10 percent of all timber cut in national forests. The reforestation program of the U.S. Forest Service is exemplified in the Willamette by the annual planting, by hand, of more than 2 million seedling trees in clear-cut areas. Additional land is reforested by aerial broadcasting of seed from helicopters.

The Inland Empire

The Columbia bond The Columbia River links the economies of the Pacific Northwest. In pioneer days it provided an easy route through the mountains; more recently it has provided irrigation water for the farms of the interior and power for the cities. Its tributaries drain the eastern slopes of the Cascades, the Northern Rockies, and southeastern British Columbia.

The Inland Empire is a term used locally to describe the region east of the Cascades. It is not a lush land, but its physical environment is more livable than that of the deserts of the Great Basin and the Southwest. The inland region was settled in part from the Coast after routes had been established across it. Later the Inland Empire provided power, foods, and raw materials which stimulated further coastal urban growth.

Diverse environments To the traveler the Inland Empire seems to have everything, but one's general impression will vary according to the route. For example, a traverse from Idaho across northern Oregon crosses subhumid to semiarid districts with extensive pine-clad mountains and rolling prairies. In contrast, a route across southeastern Oregon encounters sagebrush and water scarcity. A northern traverse from Spokane across central Washington crosses grasslands and grain farms reminiscent of the prairies of North Dakota. Near the Canadian border grassland is found only in the narrow valleys, and open pine forests of the Rockies extend into the eastern slope forest of the Cascades. The story of the Inland Empire is mainly the story of water resource development.

The Spokane area Spokane, located at a falls on the Spokane River, was a good site for sawing the lumber being cut a few miles to the east; but its growth was the result of a focus for rail routes emanating from passes in the Northern Rockies. Spokane is primarily a commercial center for the agricultural and forest economies of the Inland Empire; its industries are based on power and regional raw materials. In 1974 the city hosted Expo '74 on a refurbished 100-acre riverside site which seemed well suited to the World's Fair theme of "celebrating tomorrow's fresh new environment."

To the south in the late nineteenth century the Palouse country, originally used for ranchland, was found to possess a soil able to grow grain and dried peas for the lumbermen and the miners in the nearby mountains. Later, the soils proved adaptable to highly mechanized agriculture. West of the Palouse near Richland, Washington, is the Atomic Energy Commission's large Hanford Works facility. Radioactive wastes stored there pose a potentially serious hazard should they seep into the water table and thence into the adjacent Columbia River.

Eastern Oregon The desert of southeastern Oregon has a few irrigated patches as in other parts of the Great Basin. Northeastern Oregon has a different landscape which includes the forested Blue Mountains as well as dry areas suited for dry farming, irrigation, grazing, and tourist viewing. In contrast to these dry sections the eastern slopes of the Cascades in both Oregon and Washington have forests of tall ponderosa and other pines. The interior valleys such as the Hood River, Yakima, Wenatchee, and Okanogan produce apples, fodder crops, cattle, and vegetables—all mainly consumed within the Pacific Northwest.

The Columbia as a water resource Most of the irrigated areas noted above are on tributaries of the Columbia and not on the main stream which has been harnessed for waterpower. The complex decisions related to the multiuse of a river and its water are well illus-

The Grand Coulee Dam blocks the Columbia River and generates power, part of which is used to pump water into the Grand Coulee (background) from which water is supplied to irrigated fields to the south. (U.S. Department of Interior)

trated in the development of the Columbia. For example, the decision to dam the river meant the possibility of destroying a valuable fishing industry. Although Bonneville Dam, completed in 1938 in the Columbia gorge east of Portland, provided fish ladders so that salmon could jump from pool to pool upstream, few salmon now spawn in the Columbia River tributaries. Bonneville was primarily built for power, whereas dams farther upstream were dual-purpose: power and irrigation. A milestone in the river's development was reached in 1964 when the Columbia River Treaty was signed by the United States and Canada. This treaty provided for the building of dams north of the international border (see Chapter 10).

Grand Coulee The Grand Coulee, a trough 1½ to 4 miles wide, is a former drainage channel of the Columbia River across an arid volcanic plateau. During the last Ice Age, a glacier blocked the present channel of the Columbia River, forcing it to carve another valley eastward. After the ice retreated, the Columbia returned to its former channel but left behind a high level valley (coulee) including a "dry falls." In the 1930s the Columbia was dammed just below the head of Grand Coulee, diverting some of its waters through the Coulee to a fertile million-acre irrigable section. The major crops are grain, dry beans, and cattle fodder. The relatively high density of farm settlement in the irrigated sections contrasts with the sparse population of the adjoining grasslands. Then the largest dam in the world, Grand Coulee had an installed capacity of nearly 2 million kilowatts. Part of this power is used to pump water into the Grand Coulee and connecting irrigation canals; the remainder is transmitted into power grids which supply cities in the Pacific Northwest.

Southeastern Alaska has little level land so that many small settlements are better reached by seaplane taxi than by overland routes. Note the low level of the snow line. (Alaska Travel Division)

ALASKA

It is difficult to appreciate the immensity and emptiness of Alaska; it is more than twice the size of Texas with 3 percent the number of people. From the tip of southeastern Alaska to Bering Strait is several hundred miles farther than from Seattle to Los Angeles. Although its 1960–1970 population increased rapidly at a percentage growth rate approximating that of Florida, it still has a low population density— only 0.6 per square mile. The state holds only 350,000 inhabitants, most of whom are urban dwellers living in or near Anchorage, Juneau, Sitka, or Ketchikan. The majority of the remainder live within 100 miles of Fairbanks in the interior (Figure 8.10).

A Permanent frontier?

Isolation from mainland United States can be measured by the high cost of living because of the high freight costs for everything shipped in. Goods and people reach Alaska by coastal ship or plane or via the gravel-surfaced Alaska Highway. It has been suggested that Alaska provides the United States with a permanent frontier; after more than a century of ownership only a small fraction of the land has been settled. Several resources, including gold, coal, petroleum, lumber, furs, and fish, have been found and exploited; yet, in 1971, of the 95,000 employed, 37,000 were in armed forces or public administration and 6,000 in construction. Although coastal southeastern Alaska resembles southwestern Norway, which is much more fully settled, and the Anchorage–Fairbanks area is climatically similar to well-populated parts of Finland, the parallels have not resulted in similar settlement histories.

Southeastern Alaska

The earliest development was in the southeastern Panhandle, a region with a narrow mountainous mainland with extensive valley glaciers, large offshore islands, and numerous inland passages. The southeast, an area as large as New England, has been a major fishing area, the site of the Juneau gold rush, and a gateway to the Klondike gold fields. Today mining is insignificant; the economy is based on fish, lumber, and tourism. Fishing for salmon, in part operated with Indian labor, employs less than a thousand people seasonally, plus an equal number in seafood packing. The large forest reserves on the slopes of the Coast mountains and islands are beginning to be used. For example, a pulp mill now operates at Ketchikan. Although the temperatures of this southeastern area are mild, heavy precipitation and the scarcity of flat or gently sloping land inhibit settlement.

The Seward-Anchorage-Fairbanks Axis

More rapid economic growth has occurred along the government-owned Alaska Railroad and the Seward-Anchorage-Fairbanks Highway. South of the Alaska Range, mild summers with moderate precipitation are adequate for the farms which supply local markets. North of the mountains, climate is less attractive for agriculture: January temperatures average below zero, and at Fairbanks the average first killing fall frost occurs in late August; the average last spring frost is in late May.

The few major cities do not depend greatly on regional resource development. Anchorage, the largest city in Alaska, with a good harbor and large airport, owes its rapid growth to military activities, as does the much smaller Fairbanks on the Tanana tributary of the Yukon River. These two cities are the commercial centers for an immense area of which only that portion east of the Alaska Railroad has land accessibility by a few roads, including the Alaska Highway connecting with Alberta, Canada. The central portion is accessible in summer by navigation of the Yukon-Tanana waterways.

Resource Potential?

What is there to develop, and how much of it is worth developing in this rigorous, isolated setting? Only valuable minerals, particularly those which can be readily transported to distant markets, have economic potential. At present oil (with associated natural gas) accounts for 40 percent of the mineral production. The petroleum-rich North Slope will provide an impetus to Alaska's economic growth when a pipeline is constructed across Alaska to Valdez (Figure 8.10). This pipeline was long delayed by concern for the negative impact upon the Alaskan physical environment. There were fears of possible oil spills from an earthquake-ruptured pipeline or a tsunami sweeping through Valdez. There were also objections from some people in British Columbia who do not want to see large tankers carrying oil along the dangerous reef-dotted Canadian coast to Puget Sound refineries. However, the Alaska Pipeline gained final approval late in 1973, and construction commenced with the spring thaw in 1974. Completion is scheduled for 1977, but in the meantime West Coast refinery capability needs to be expanded lest much of the Alaska crude go to Japan or elsewhere for refining.

Forest products, especially lumber, pulpwood, and furs, offer other possibilities for resource expansion. Fur trapping is likely to remain a small industry, but fur farming offers greater possibilities. Forest reserves are ample, but much of the forest is not presently economically accessible. Transportation is not likely to be provided to develop forest resources alone because the harvested forest would not regenerate itself in a century. Could the cleared land be used later for agriculture? This hardly seems likely, with the surplus of better agricultural land available in the continental United States. Such possible agricultural produce would be competitive only in the small local markets.

Hydroelectric power is a major resource, with an estimated potential of 15 million kilowatts under the most adverse conditions. But there is no nearby market for even a fraction of this much hydroelectric energy, nor is one foreseen in the near future.

REGIONAL PROSPECT: DECELERATING GROWTH

Most coastal counties in the five Pacific States are still growing in population. With the exception of San Francisco County, which experienced a slight drop in population during the sixties, the few counties showing a net out-migration are in the more rugged areas. This widespread growth reflects the continued tendency of people and industries to seek milder climates for home and employment. Foodstuffs and raw materials, once the major attraction of this region, still play a significant part in the total economy, but if the forecasts for the San Francisco Bay Area are correct, they will play a decreasing role both as raw materials and as a base for industry. Both California and Hawaii are investing heavily in education aimed at supporting a society based on technology and automation rather than on animate energy and raw materials. The former handicap of distance from markets has been overcome by transport technology and by the accelerating growth of mammoth markets in the Pacific World.

The population of California is about 22 million, and already highways, campsites, and tourist attractions are jammed literally bumper to bumper on weekends. What will it be like when there are 29 million Californians, as predicted in the mid-1970s for the year 2000? One humorist has predicted that in a century every acre of California will be used for one of four categories: business, residential, roads, or parking. Fortunately, California's population growth is noticeably slackening its pace—population projections of the 1960s called for

at least 40 million Californians by the turn of the century. Furthermore, much of California is simply too rugged for intensive use. Actually very little of the Sierra is now being used for recreation, and all but a few thousand people keep to within some hundred yards of the highways. The less-used mountains are not unattractive: the most modest peak would be a major tourist attraction if located near Chicago or New Orleans. The problem is how to pay for the roads in order to make the California mountains accessible to weak-legged urbanites. Furthermore, some environmentalists have mounted formidable opposition to further mountain highway building.

The problem of water is also serious (although northwestern California still possesses little-used reserves). To what extent will, or can, the state build more extensive distribution systems? Already legislation has been adopted curtailing further dam and reservoir building on certain northwestern California "wild rivers." Can desalted seawater and reclaimed sewage add to the water supply? Will increased urban densities lead to a limitation on irrigation agriculture? The answers to these questions may be politically rather than geographically motivated.

Indian California and Polynesian Hawaii have in a century been greatly altered and in many ways improved by the dynamism of an exotic Anglo-Saxon culture. Will the California environment remain attractive, or will its natural beauties be overwhelmed by smog, noise, and urban sprawl? There is also a cultural and social problem, for some of the populace seems unable to fit into a technological, highly automated society because of lack of education, lack of ability, or prejudice. Will the services and markets of an increased population lead to improvements in living standards or to congestion and chaos?

Compared with California and Arizona, the recent population and economic growth of the Pacific Northwest has been modest. In each settled area there is a high degree of local specialization and a consequent vulnerability to economic fluctuations. Lumber, fish, wheat, livestock, gold, aircraft, irrigation projects, hydroelectric power, shipbuilding, and military bases have played major parts but have not led to well-integrated local economies. A withdrawal of government or airline contracts, a closing of military bases, the exhaustion of forests, a change in reclamation policy—any one of these could be catastrophic to certain parts of the region.

If it is assumed that a desirable environment for living rather than the mere presence of raw materials will influence the population distribution of the next century, the Pacific Northwest has a promising future. Its climates include those in which Western Europeans have flourished; its scenery is attractive; and except for northern Alaska, the region is accessible to world trade. Waterpower is available, along with oil and gas from western Canada and Alaska; the forests and fisheries could be exploited as permanent resources. But above all, it offers fine sites for a Pacific urban civilization to benefit from the anticipated increased trade and human interaction among the Pacific rim countries.

Selected References

ASCHMANN, HOMER: "Purpose in the Southern California Landscape," *Journal of Geography,* vol. 66 (1967), pp. 311–317.

ASSOCIATION OF BAY AREA GOVERNMENTS: *Regional Plan 1970–1990, San Francisco Bay Region, 1970.* This is one among a number of studies produced by ABAG, a nongovernmental regional planning association comprised of Bay Area counties and cities. The Southern California Association of Governments (SCAG) serves a similar role for several southern California counties.

BROWN, RALPH C.: "The Proposed Trans-Alaska Pipeline System: Potential Highway to the North American Arctic," *Professional Geographer,* vol. 23 (1971), pp. 15–18.

DICKEN, SAMUEL N.: *Oregon Geography,* 4th ed., University of Oregon Cooperative Bookstore, Eugene, 1965.

DURRENBERGER, R. W.: *Patterns on the Land,* National Press Books, Palo Alto, California, 1972. An interesting and informative atlas.

FLEMING, DOUGLAS K. (ed.): *Views of Washington State,* Association of American Geographers, Washington, D. C., 1974.

GREGOR, H. F.: "The Plantation in California," *Professional Geographer,* vol. 14 (March 1962), pp. 1–4.

GRIFFIN, PAUL F., and RONALD L. CHATHAM: "Urban Impact on Agriculture in Santa Clara County, California," *Annals,* AAG, vol. 48 (1958), pp. 195–208.

HARRIES, KEITH D.: "Ethnic Variations in Los Angeles Business Patterns," *Annals,* AAG, vol. 61 (1971), pp. 736–743.

HIGHSMITH, RICHARD M., JR.: *Atlas of the Pacific Northwest Resources and Development,* Oregon State University Press, Corvallis, Oregon, 1968.

LANTIS, D. W., R. STEINER, and A. E. KARINEN: *California: Land of Contrast,* Kendall-Hunt, Dubuque, Iowa, 1973. A detailed regional geography for use in California colleges.

MACHINKO, G.: "The Columbia Basin Project," *Geographical Review,* vol. 53 (1963), pp. 185–199.

MARTS, M. E., and W. R. D. SEWELL: "The Conflict between Fish and Power Resources in the Pacific Northwest," *Annals,* AAG, vol. 50 (1960), pp. 42–50.

MEINIG, D. W.: *The Great Columbia Plain—A Historical Geography 1805–1910,* University of Washington Press, Seattle, 1968.

ROGERS, GEORGE W.: *The Future of Alaska,* published for Resources for the Future, Inc., Johns Hopkins, Baltimore, 1962.

SECURITY PACIFIC NATIONAL BANK: *The Southern California Report,* prepared by the Economic Research Division of the Bank, Los Angeles, 1970. A study of growth and economic statures of the ten Southern California counties.

STORER, TRACY I., and ROBERT L. USINGER: *Sierra Nevada Natural History,* University of California Press, Berkeley and Los Angeles, 1963. A somewhat technical, but thorough and useful, handbook for those frequenting the Sierra Nevada.

THOMAS, WILLIAM L., JR. (ed.): "Man, Time, and Space in Southern California," *Annals,* AAG, vol. 49, no. 3 (September 1959), supplement. A superb overview stressing the historical approach.

THROWER, NORMAN J. W.: "California Population: Distribution in 1960," *Annals,* AAG, vol. 56, no. 2, 1966, map supplement. A detailed dot map on a physiographic base. A 1970 multicolor version sponsored by the California Atlas Project of the California Council on Geographic Education was made available in 1974.

U.S. DEPARTMENT OF COMMERCE, OFFICE OF AREA DEVELOPMENT: *Future Development of the San Francisco Bay Area: 1960–2020,* U.S. Army Engineer District, San Francisco Corps of Engineers, Washington, 1959.

VANCE, JAMES E., JR.: "California and the Search for the Ideal," *Annals,* AAG, vol. 62 (1972), pp. 185–210.

WEAVER, SAMUEL P.: *Hawaii, U.S.A.,* Pageant Press, New York, 1959.

WIRTH, THEODORE J., and ASSOCIATES: *Lake Tahoe—An Environmental Impact Statement,* Billings, Mont., and Chevy Chase, Md., 1972.

9

EASTERN CANADA

CANADA AS A SEPARATE NATION

Canada, particularly in its southern parts, has many social, economic, and geographical characteristics which are similar to those of the United States. The economies of the two countries differ mainly in scale rather than in type; there are in fact many across-the-border linkages. Most of the people of the two nations come from the same ethnic and national origins in Europe. Despite the many similarities, however, Canadians feel that they are different from Americans and are sometimes overly sensitive to these poorly defined differences.

The assumption that Canada is culturally distinctive from the United States—an assumption which lies at the heart of Canadian nationhood, historically and today—is a large and nebulous subject, notoriously difficult to specify and delineate. The differences of tastes, preferences, attitudes, and institutions within the various regions of Canada seem to be larger than those between Canada and the contiguous areas of the United States. . . . If there is such a thing as a distinctive Canadian

Fogo Island, Newfoundland, a characteristic small "outpost" settlement. Note the low, rocky hills barren of trees. Houses are dispersed around the harbor and are connected by one winding road. There are many small family docks but no large port facilities. (National Film Board of Canada, photo by G. Hunter)

way of life it has yet to be crystallized sufficiently to be clearly identified.[1]

Although there are many common elements in the two Anglo-American environments, there are differences in the proportions in which the diverse ingredients are combined. These different areal patterns result in distinctive geographies of the United States and Canada. Thus Canada has:

1 A much larger proportion of both barren and forested land than has the United States. It is unlikely that much of the land will have future agricultural settlement but it does have a recreation potential.

2 Larger areas than the United States in which long periods of cold winter weather handicap outdoor activity.

3 A more resource-oriented economy than the United States, in which many raw materials are exported in only semiprocessed form.

4 Greater dependence than the United States on distant markets, both domestic and foreign, and on transportation to these markets.

5 Four major population clusters which are more separated from each other than from adjacent population clusters in the United States.

6 Most important, only one-tenth the population and one-twelfth the personal income of the United States.

7 Most of its population spreads across the southern part of the country within 200 miles of the United States border; thus Canadians are generally familiar with American culture, whereas many Americans live far from Canada and have little reason to think about that country.

As in the United States, most Canadian employment is in urban places. (The Canadian census defines an "urban place" as any incorporated place with more than 1,000 persons.) About 80 percent of Canadians live in such urban centers. Even primary production, such as mines or sawmills, not usually thought of as urban activities, often takes place in small settlements not defined officially as urban. Primary production, however, accounts for a declining proportion of Canadian employment, constituting less than 10 percent of the gross domestic product in 1971. Complex manufacturing now takes place in the larger cities. In 1971 Canada had 24 metropolitan centers, each with a population larger than 100,000 persons, and these cities together held more than half of the Canadian population. In 1971 the three largest cities—Toronto, Montreal, and Vancouver—accounted for one-third of Canadians' personal taxable income. Canada can therefore be considered in these chapters as an urban-oriented people and economy, as has been done in preceding chapters on the United States.

Canada is a manufacturing and industrial nation similar to the United States but on a different scale. About one-third of all value added by manufacturing in Canada comes from the first-stage processing of materials; much of this is accounted for by food processing; concentrating of mineral ores; and processing of wood, wood pulp, and paper products. Agricultural, forest, and mineral products are therefore important in Canadian manufacturing. Raw or semiprocessed materials constitute more than one-third of Canadian export values; items such as wheat, wood pulp, iron ore, and petroleum are leaders. This high level of exports, amounting to about one-fifth of the gross domestic product, enables Canada to import foodstuffs and raw materials not available internally (e.g., coffee, cotton, bauxite) and also certain manufactures which cannot at present be produced economically.

The trade ties between Canada and the United States are strong and many. About 65 to 70 percent of Canadian exports go to the United States and about the same proportion of Canadian imports come from its southern neighbor. Although some Americans may think of Canada mainly as a source of needed raw

[1] G. W. Wilson et al., *Canada: An Appraisal of Its Needs and Resources,* Twentieth Century Fund, New York, 1965, p. 401.

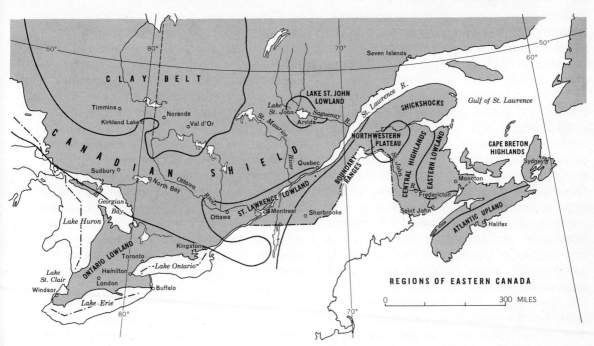

Figure 9.1 Much of the population of eastern Canada is in two lowlands, each of which has a sparsely populated area to the north. (Otis W. Freeman and John W. Morris, *World Geography,* McGraw-Hill, New York, 1965, p. 143. Used with permission of McGraw-Hill Book Company.)

materials, the character of Canadian exports to the United States changed greatly during the 1960s; manufactured goods (mainly automotive parts) constituted 50 percent of exports in the early 1970s.

Landform Regions and Natural Resources

One method of introducing Canada's environment and natural resources to the reader is to survey the country on the basis of its landform regions. Several of these Canadian landform regions are continuations of those of the northern United States. In eastern Canada the Appalachians arc across southeastern Quebec and form the hilly backbones of the Atlantic Provinces. Because these low, glaciated ranges were cut by the water highway of the Gulf of St. Lawrence, they were less of a barrier to inland movement in the nineteenth century than were the American Appalachians. As a result the coastal provinces were bypassed by ships that could reach Quebec, and the prov-

inces never attained the population densities or industrial development of New England. The natural resources of the Appalachian region include excellent coniferous forests with some hardwoods; a few minerals such as coal and asbestos; productive fisheries; and several valleys with soils suitable for agriculture. But from the time of early settlement the Atlantic Provinces had few people, and these were dispersed and constituted a small local market.

The most favorable environmental area of Canada is the narrow St. Lawrence–Great Lakes Lowland, a northeastern extension of the much larger Central Lowland of the United States. Within the provinces of Quebec and Ontario this flat-to-rolling, glacial-deposited lowland supports most of their agriculture and holds most of their people. Within the lowland region the natural resources of minerals, forests, and waterpower are minor. It is, however, the urban and industrial ''Heartland'' of

Canada, having more than half its population, producing about 75 percent of the value added by manufacturing, and dominated by 52 of the 91 Canadian cities with more than 30,000 population in 1971.

North and northwest of the St. Lawrence Lowland and extending halfway across Canada is the Canadian Shield. No comparable large landform or geological region is found in the United States; the Shield, with its advantages and disadvantages, is distinct within Canada. These glacier-scoured, old rocks—the "roots" of ancient mountains now eroded down to a rolling upland—have been called the "mineral storehouse" of Canada. The Shield also has vast pulpwood forests stretching across its southern half. Within the forest innumerable small sections of bare rock, swamps, muskegs, and lakes and a short frost-free season severely limit the possibility of agriculture. Abundant hydroelectric power has been available to run machinery in the pulp and paper mills and in the mines as well as to supply electricity to the cities south of the Shield. Settlement has been mainly urban and most of it in this century has been based on resource-oriented and transport activities.

To the west of the Canadian Shield, the Central Lowland and Great Plains of the United States extend northward and are known in Canada as the Interior Plains. These plains, about 800 miles wide at the 49th parallel international boundary, narrow to the north in the Mackenzie Valley of the Northwest Territories. Natural grassland covering the more settled, southern part of the Interior Plains gave its name to the three political units which are known collectively as the Prairie Provinces. Large grain and livestock farms occupy these prairie grasslands, but to the north extensive forests are similar to those eastward on the Canadian Shield. The Interior Plains are underlain by most of Canada's petroleum, natural gas, and potash as well as by enormous coal reserves.

The Cordillera of western North America extends northward through mountainous Brit-ish Columbia and the Yukon Territory. On the east the Rockies rise abruptly above the Interior Plains and on the west the Coast Mountains are the northward continuation of the Cascades. The Canadian part of the Cordillera is more compressed than its American equivalent; from Calgary to Vancouver is only half the distance from Denver to San Francisco. The Canadian section has more forests, water-power, and minerals, but has much less tillable land than the American Cordillera. But these resources have been far from markets in eastern Anglo-America and Europe in the past, and the region has a small local consuming population. These far western resources are now, however, close to the markets in Japan and east Asia, and therefore development has accelerated.

North of the Canadian mainland a group of large, barren islands juts northward into the Arctic Ocean. The wide straits between these Arctic Islands are ice-bound for most of the year; the southern straits are open for navigation for about two to four months in late summer. Only a few whites and Eskimo live on some of these islands; natural resources seem to be few, except for reserves of natural gas and perhaps petroleum.

These preceding six geographical regions of Canada are often used within Canada in the study of its diverse geographical patterns, but these subdivisions may be too many for a study of a large area like Anglo-America. The authors have therefore divided Canada into two large regions—the older, more populated, more industrial east, and the newer economies of the west.

EASTERN CANADA

This part of Canada consists of six provinces. Ontario and Quebec are the largest in area and the most populated, and in 1971 their residents reported 68 percent of Canadians' taxable income. The Atlantic Provinces consist of Newfoundland (which includes Labrador on the mainland), Nova Scotia, New Brunswick, and

ATLANTIC
OCEAN

Figure 9.2 Landforms of the Atlantic Gateways. Compare with Figure 9.1, which names regions based largely on these landforms. (Base map copyright by A. K. Lobeck. Reprinted with permission of The Geographical Press, Hammond, Inc.)

tiny Prince Edward Island.[2] Within Canada the eastern part of the country is usually considered in three geographical regions.[3] The

Atlantic Provinces have a resource-based economy and share similar internal problems of agricultural and fishing poverty in certain areas. Ontario and Quebec can be divided into two regions: the lowland of the southern part

[2] Newfoundland voted to join Canada in 1949. A possible political union of the three Maritime Provinces—Nova Scotia, New Brunswick, and Prince Edward Island—has been discussed with the two aims of reducing the duplication of provincial government expenditures and enabling the region to speak with a common voice in federal matters.
[3] J. Lewis Robinson, "Regional Geography of Canada," *Canada Year Book,* Ottawa, 1972, pp. 1–26.

is the Canadian Heartland—mainly urban and industrial; the Shield to the north supplies the natural resources and raw materials and is the recreational hinterland of the urban lowland.

THE ATLANTIC PROVINCES

In landforms, population, and economic development the Atlantic Provinces are similar to American Appalachia or parts of northern New England. Their slow economic growth has been a contrast to the development in southern Ontario and Quebec. The Atlantic Provinces experienced a net out-migration of people until the 1970s and have average income below the rest of Canada. Each province specialized in one or more of the primary industries of agriculture, fishing, mining, or forestry—all of which have experienced declining employment because of mechanization. Just as Appalachia's relatively empty areas attract people from American coastal cities for recreation, so too the vacationlands of the Atlantic Provinces bring in a seasonal income; but this scenery competes for the American market with similar landscapes in New England which are closer to the Atlantic Megalopolis.

The port cities of the Atlantic Provinces have not supplied gateways into the interior of Canada to the same degree as American East Coast ports. In the past the ports of Halifax and Saint John were the usual winter outlets for rail traffic from interior Canada when the St. Lawrence River was frozen; but the use of icebreakers in the St. Lawrence Gateway now permits ships to penetrate as far inland as Quebec City regularly in winter and sometimes to Montreal.

As in Appalachia, the few growth centers in the Atlantic Provinces have been inadequate to bring the region up to national economic levels. More manufacturing is needed in the cities if they are to absorb the outflowing rural population; but the region is peripheral to the main Canadian markets, and its local market is too small and scattered. Although west coast British Columbia and the east coast

Atlantic Provinces are similar in terms of their rugged landforms, resource-based economies, and populations of about 2 million each, an essential difference is that half of the people of British Columbia are concentrated into the small area of Vancouver, whereas the scattered urban population of the Atlantic Provinces provides no large urban market in one place. This population distribution is also a major difference between New England (having Metropolitan Boston) and the Atlantic Provinces (Figure 9.3).

Cities

Five cities dominate the economic life of the Atlantic Provinces, but they are not as significant in the regional economy as are the cities of the Heartland in southern Ontario and Quebec. Three of these urban centers are the focus of industrial activity in each of three provinces—Halifax in Nova Scotia, St. John's in Newfoundland, and Saint John in New Brunswick. With the addition of Moncton and Sydney the five largest cities hold only 27 percent of the regional population—a figure which emphasizes the lack of any concentrated urban markets.

Halifax   Halifax (population 225,000 in 1971) is the main industrial, commercial, government, and service center of Nova Scotia and the largest urban concentration in the Atlantic Provinces. It has the usual variety of consumer goods manufacturing found in most Anglo-American cities of this size. Some of the industries are the result of its spacious inner harbor, one of the largest in the world, and are based on imports such as petroleum, textiles, auto assembly, and cacao. Because Halifax is the most easterly major port on the Great Circle shipping route from Europe to Anglo-America, it is used as a container terminal from which ocean vessels may unload directly onto railways to serve interior cities in both Canada and the United States. As the main commercial city of the Atlantic Provinces, Halifax has the head

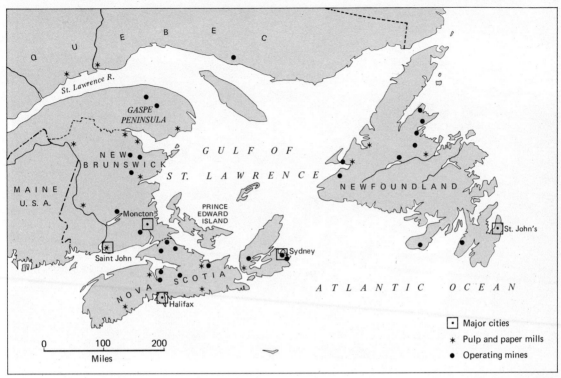

Figure 9.3 The Atlantic Provinces: The urban population is concentrated into five major cities, plus a large number of small resource-based towns. Many of these pulp and paper mill towns and mining communities are one-industry towns.

offices of most firms operating in the region and is the regional headquarters for national firms from Ontario and Quebec. In addition to the provincial government occupations as the capital, Halifax also has federal government offices such as the Navy, hydrographic service, and oceanography research. The federal government, in attempting to raise incomes and economic levels in the Atlantic Provinces, chose Halifax as a major growth point and has given financial incentives for industrial firms to locate there. If the creation of a future major urban concentration changes the geographical patterns, it will certainly affect the regional economy.

Sydney The steel manufacturing city of Sydney, along with the nearby coal-mining towns of Glace Bay and New Waterford (125,000 population in total), is the only other major population cluster in Nova Scotia. It faced serious economic difficulties during the 1960s.

Coal mining, as elsewhere in the Appalachians, has been a declining industry, despite government incentives and assistance in recent decades. In addition, the steel industry, despite access to nearby raw materials, is poorly located with relation to the consuming markets in central Canada. In an attempt to save the industry and maintain local jobs the provincial government bought out the steel company in Sydney; under this new management profits began to be made. Perhaps solutions to some of the problems of marginal coal mining and marginal agriculture of American Appalachia may be found in small-scale experiments in problem areas in the Atlantic Provinces.

Saint John and Moncton Saint John (110,000), the largest urban center in New

The origins of Halifax date back to the eighteenth century when the British established a fort and administrative center at the Citadel. The modern city core, lying between the Citadel and the harbor, is being redeveloped into high-rise office buildings. The main harbor and naval facilities are located to the left—not shown in this photograph. (Nova Scotia government)

Brunswick, is half the size of metropolitan Halifax, but many of its industries are similar. Some of Saint John's manufactures are based on imported raw materials; other industries such as food processing and pulp and paper mills obtain their supplies from the St. John River hinterland. Its harbor used to be an important winter outlet for Canada, but this function has declined as St. Lawrence winter navigation increased. Whereas Halifax dominates the economy of Nova Scotia, Saint John has grown slowly because its hinterland is served by two competing urban centers—Moncton and Fredericton. Moncton (70,000) has central position in the region and is a focus of road, rail, and air routes which converge on the isthmus of Chignecto which connects Nova Scotia and New Brunswick. It is a growing supply center for the area between the direct hinterlands of Halifax and Saint John.

St. John's   St. John's (130,000), Newfoundland, was one of the first places to be settled, in 1593, on the eastern coast of Anglo-America. It has always been the major city in Newfoundland; but with about 22 percent of the provincial population in 1971, the city does not dominate as much as it did in 1901 when 70 percent of the island's recorded population lived there. Whereas the other small towns in Newfoundland are mainly one-industry places based on fisheries or forestry, St. John's has a variety of small manufactures, much of the provincial commercial establishments, and, of course, the government functions. Its harbor facilities were rebuilt by the federal government in the 1960s, making it a more attractive and efficient port; many fishing ships of several European nations use St. John's as a supply center and a shelter while fishing on the nearby

Grand Banks. St. John's has traditionally looked toward the Atlantic and Europe, but now, as part of Canada, westward links are being created. New cities such as Corner Brook are arising in western Newfoundland Island, and in western Labrador new mining towns such as Labrador City have appeared. These new centers may further decrease the dominance of St. John's in the province.

The rest of the population of the Atlantic Provinces is dispersed around the coasts in small fishing villages or small farming communities in coastal or interior valleys, or in one-industry pulp and paper towns or a few mining communities. But changes are occurring in the geographical patterns of these resource-based settlements and in the regional economy.

Fishing

The sheltered bays and offshore banks of Newfoundland and Nova Scotia have been used by fishermen since the sixteenth century. English fishermen first used the bays and headlands on the east and northeast coasts of Newfoundland Island as summer bases for drying codfish caught on the offshore banks. Gradually more and more people began to winter there, establishing small and dispersed villages. St. John's, one of the harbors closest to England, grew as an administrative town and a supply and collecting center for the "outport" villages. French fishermen had rights to the south and west coasts of Newfoundland, but these shores were never fully occupied. Newfoundland was not attractive for settlers looking for agricultural land: the eastern coasts are hilly, rocky, and cool; level land is limited in area; soils are thin or lacking on the headlands and islands; the cool water of the Labrador current alongshore keeps summer temperatures low and promotes offshore fogs. The few people who came to the island obtained a meager living from the resources of the sea.

The geographical patterns of the fishing industry are much different in the 1970s than they were early in the century. Prior to 1940 fish products were of low quality, mainly dried or salted cod, obtained along the northeast or east coasts. Small groups fished close to shore from small boats, or they stretched nets off the many headlands or islands. After about 1950 more fish-freezing and -filleting plants were built, often with government loans, to produce a higher-quality product. The federal government gave loans to fishermen to buy modern trawlers and draggers, permitting them to fish offshore on the banks in international waters. Fishermen were encouraged to move from the many villages which lacked social services and urban amenities to larger towns where they could supply the fish-processing plants. As a result, by the early 1970s more than half of the Newfoundland catch was obtained from offshore banks. Larger ships meant fewer men, and therefore by 1971 fishermen, constituting less than 10 percent of Newfoundland's working population, numbered only about 10,000 persons.

On a smaller scale, changes have also appeared in the economy of Labrador. Prior to 1940 the scanty population lived in small fishing villages along the south coast; along the north coast about 1,000 Eskimo depended on sea resources, mainly seals. In the 1960s large reserves of medium-quality iron ore were discovered in western Labrador; by the 1970s the interior mining towns of Labrador City and Wabush, near the Quebec border, with their curved streets, stylish bungalows, and modern shopping plazas, became the largest settlements in Labrador.

Changes in coastal settlements have also occurred in Nova Scotia but have been delayed in northeastern New Brunswick. The fishing plants in Nova Scotia are larger than those in Newfoundland, partly because of the type of capital investment from large fishing companies. The Nova Scotia fish plants have the advantage of location near the market for fish products in the eastern United States. The centralization of the fishing population in the Atlantic Provinces is similar to the movement of farm workers to the cities elsewhere in Anglo-America.

Agriculture

One reason for average low incomes of workers in the Atlantic Provinces is the very low incomes of farming people in particular areas. There is a "geography of poverty" in the region, and this poverty is mainly rural—in farming and fishing areas. The governments have identified agricultural poverty in certain areas which contrast with other areas of prosperous commercial farming. The poverty problem is therefore not a characteristic of the whole Atlantic Provinces region but is localized in specific subregions where remedial measures can be planned.

In the nineteenth century Nova Scotia had a more habitable environment than Newfoundland for European and British settlers coming to Canada for agricultural land. Many Scottish Highlanders found the mediocre soils and chilly climate of Nova Scotia not inferior to their homelands. As in New England, many of the subsistence farms cleared on the rocky hills and thin soils of interior Nova Scotia were abandoned when better lands became available for settlement in central and western Canada. From the air the province appears mostly forest-covered; farms, generally small, are dispersed along the main roads. The largest areas of prosperous agriculture are in the livestock region of Chignecto Isthmus and the apple-growing Annapolis Valley. After the apple growers lost their export market in Britain during World War II, they turned to apple processing for the eastern Canadian market. They also diversified their farms, so that poultry, dairy products, and livestock for the nearby Halifax market became significant.

Rural settlement in New Brunswick is mainly peripheral—along the east coast, near but not on the south coast, and along the St. John River Valley. Farmers in New Brunswick have some of the same problems as those in Nova Scotia. Except in the St. John Valley and

the low plateau of the northwest, soils are not particularly fertile, are heavily leached, or are stoney. Many farms are too small to be economic units and have a surplus of labor; local markets are not large. Frequently wholesalers in the Maritime cities import food from central Canada's well-organized agriculture even though the same crop might be grown within the local region. Most of the commercial farmers carry on dairying in the lower St. John Valley and near Moncton, or operate large potato farms on the northwestern plateau. In the poverty areas along the east coast are part-time or subsistence farmers who obtain additional income by working in the logging camps in winter or by fishing in summer.

Diversification is coming to these poor areas of northeastern New Brunswick with the discovery of lead, zinc, and copper near Bathurst in the 1960s. The subsistence farms and poorly equipped fisheries also received government assistance which is attempting to raise the level of income in several poor rural parts across Canada. It is believed that rural poverty can be reduced by moving the surplus farm population to Maritime towns where industries are receiving government encouragement to locate or expand.

In contrast to the other Atlantic Provinces, French-Canadians form a distinctive cultural distribution pattern in northern and eastern New Brunswick. The forefathers of some of these settlers migrated to northern New Brunswick from Quebec in the last century, but others are descendants of the original "Acadians" who settled near Moncton. French-Canadians occupy most of the farms in the north and east, but they also constitute much of the labor in the forestry and fishing industries of New Brunswick.

Tiny Prince Edward Island (about the area of the state of Delaware) is known as the "Garden Province," not only because it is small in size, but because its land is used mainly for agriculture. There is no mining, virtually no forest cutting except for fuel from farm woodlots, and only a little fishing, mainly for lobsters close to the coast. Perhaps owing to past physical separation and a higher level of agricultural prosperity, the "Islanders" have a pride and culture which sets them off as a distinctive group within the Atlantic Provinces. The slightly rolling landscape is a pleasant picture of green during the summer—pasture and grain are the major land uses—with splashes of red from road cuts in the distinctive reddish soils. The major sources of farm income are livestock products, including dairy products, and potatoes. Much of the food is exported from the island; the livestock products go partly to food-deficient Newfoundland, and excellent seed potatoes are sent to the southern United States and the Caribbean countries.

The total population of Prince Edward Island has changed very little throughout this century. The land is fully occupied under present agricultural practices, and the only city and capital, Charlottetown, remains small. The surplus farm population has moved to other parts of Canada. Communication and transport to the mainland of Canada are maintained by ferries which break the ice of Northumberland Strait during the winter. From time to time proposals for building a causeway across the strait have been put forward—some observers note with malice that such proposals have often preceded federal elections!

Forestry

Primary forest activities are significant in the resource-based economies in all Atlantic Provinces except Prince Edward Island. This industry has its greatest development in New Brunswick where excellent forests cover 80 percent of the province. The pulp and paper industry is the main forest utilization. Some of the pulp and paper mills are located at river mouths on the northeast coast from whence the manufactured products can be exported directly into ocean vessels. The rivers give access to the interior forests and were used to transport pulp logs in spring and summer until land transport became the more common type of transport.

The paper mills in south central New Brunswick make greater use of roads and trucks to assemble their logs and also use railways to export newsprint to the eastern United States.

Several pulp and paper mills line the coast of Nova Scotia, but compared with the New Brunswick mills each has a smaller hinterland of interior forests and shorter rivers for access. Forestry became significant to Newfoundland in the 1920s. People began to look differently at the environment away from the coasts. The coniferous trees of the northern and western interior discouraged agriculture but were suitable for pulpwood. When a few rivers were harnessed to produce hydroelectric power, the result was pulp and paper mills at Corner Brook on the west coast and at Grand Falls on the Exploits River near the northeast coast. By the 1930s pulp and paper export values were sometimes exceeding fish exports.

Summary Much of the area of the Atlantic Provinces is used for an exploitive economy, mainly forestry; agricultural land is in small strips and pockets except on Prince Edward Island. Most settlements are small, and are often based on only one industry such as a pulp and paper mill, a fish cannery, or a mine. There is no very large urban center which can be a market for local resources, and therefore some of the products of the region are exported in competition with similar Canadian and world products. Five major urban places serve as a focus for the regional economy, each tending to have a limited local hinterland. Because the region is on the periphery of Canada and has distinct geographical patterns which do not favor major urban concentrations, economic levels of production and income are below Canadian averages. However, by the early 1970s the net out-migration of people had ceased. To many residents of the region, the slower economic pace, the still uncluttered natural environment, and the comfortable feeling of having cultural "roots" in a long-settled land make the Atlantic Provinces one of the attractive places in which to live.

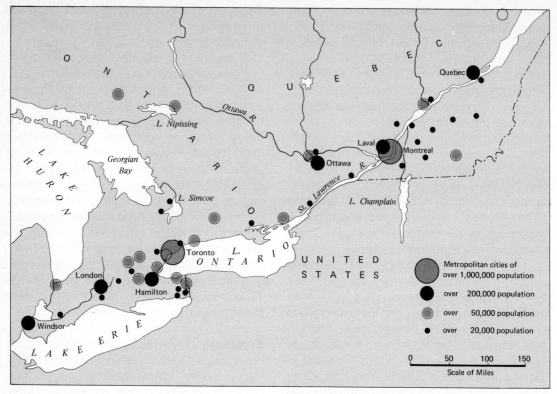

Figure 9.4 Urban centers of the St. Lawrence Lowland: A hierarchy of urban places is apparent in the distribution pattern of cities; the smaller cities are somewhat evenly spaced between the larger cities. Note the line of cities between Quebec, Montreal, Toronto, and Windsor.

THE HEARTLAND OF CANADA

South of the rocky hills of the Canadian Shield, along the St. Lawrence River and partly enclosed by the lower Great Lakes, is the lowland on which live more than half of the Canadians. It has the most valuable agricultural land in Canada, and this land is favored by relatively mild winters and warm to hot summers. This Heartland of Canada, in southern Ontario and Quebec, is similar in many ways to the American Midwest across the Great Lakes. It has the highest densities of urban, industrial, and agricultural uses in Canada. This small region has more than half of the large cities of Canada, and these produce about 75 percent of the value of Canadian manufacturing. And like the nearby American regions, the Heartland is beginning to experience the problems of congestion, pollution, and overuse in some sections.

The Heartland is dominated by the two largest metropolitan centers in Canada—Montreal in Quebec, and Toronto in Ontario. Each of these metropolitan regions is made up of several cities with different names but collectively known as Montreal and Toronto.[4] Each metropolitan area holds about 2,700,000 people, more than one-tenth of the population of Canada. Whereas Montreal stands alone in Quebec as the only very large city—having half of the population of the province—Toronto is the largest city in a cluster of coalescing urban areas at the western end of Lake Ontario (Figure 9.4).

[4] The city of Montreal has only half the population of metropolitan Montreal; metropolitan Toronto consists of the city of Toronto, with one-third of the total metropolitan population, plus the five boroughs of Etobicoke, York, East York, North York, and Scarborough.

Two Cultures

Although the Heartland is treated here as one region because of its internal similarities in landforms, agriculture, and industrialization, there are major differences in culture and language between the Quebec and Ontario parts. About 80 percent of the people of Quebec are French-speaking and they maintain a pride in their past as the original *Canadiens*; they try to preserve as much as they can of their language, laws, and religion. The other residents of Quebec who speak only English live mainly in Montreal. In contrast, most Ontario residents are English-speaking, including the many national groups who have emigrated there from Europe. In these ethnic and national backgrounds Ontario residents are the result of a "melting pot" as in the central United States. The small French-speaking minority in Ontario lives mainly in the eastern section, along the Ottawa and St. Lawrence rivers adjoining the French core in Quebec, and in northeastern Ontario. These cultural differences between the French- and English-speaking peoples can be seen in the landscape: the distinctive long-lot farms in Quebec contrast with the rectangular pattern of farms in Ontario; and the Quebec village dominated by its large central church and often with no commercial core differs from the Ontario small town with its "main street."

The people and landscapes of Quebec form a distinct geographical and cultural entity in Canada and in Anglo-America. The present French-speaking population is descended from about 60,000 settlers who lived along the St. Lawrence River when the area was conquered by the British in 1763. With very little further immigration the *Canadiens* multiplied within the confines of southern Quebec, retreated into relative cultural isolation there, and occupied most of the suitable agricultural land. As densities increased in the central core, the French-Canadians began to move outward. They occupied the farmlands in the Appalachian hills to the southeast, once settled by British loyalists from the United States, and pushed into northern New England and northern New Brunswick. Smaller colonies of French-speaking settlers migrated northward into pockets of level land within the Canadian Shield, and others left the homeland core to form linguistic minority groups dispersed across western Canada.

This dual cultural origin, French and British, gives variety to Canadian society, but it also poses political problems for Canadian parliamentary leaders who must give consideration to the rights of the large French-speaking minority. Within Quebec many of the English-speaking minority occupy important positions in the upper levels of management and business in Montreal; one of the resentments in Quebec is that promotion in business has seemed to be easier for those of Anglo-Saxon background. Some *Canadiens* object because French-Canadians need to become bilingual to advance economically in Canada, whereas many English-speaking Canadians show no overwhelming desire to use French to communicate with the large cultural minority. The vocal nationalistic expressions of some French-Canadians in Quebec in the 1960s were partially a defensive reaction to the increasing penetration of English-speaking influences from surrounding Canada and the United States.

Quebec

Metropolitan Montreal   Montreal and Toronto are rivals for Canadian commercial and industrial leadership. Montreal's industrial development is the result of the convergence of transport routes. Its early beginnings during the fur-trade days of the eighteenth century were partially due to its position at the junction of two river routes, the Ottawa and St. Lawrence, used by the fur brigades. When railways were built in the mid-nineteenth century, Montreal was an eastern terminal and the transfer point to ocean transport. Montreal became Canada's leading seaport—its collection and distribution port functions being comparable to those of New York to the American hinterland.

The central business district of Montreal is dominated by high-rise office buildings. The St. Lawrence River and the site of the World's Fair of 1967 lie to the southeast of the city core. Part of the campus of McGill University is in the left foreground. Most of the financial decisions in Quebec are made in these downtown buildings. (City of Montreal)

Dock facilities extended all along the east side of Montreal Island, and behind them grew a warehousing and industrial zone. And near these "work places" came rows and rows of rather poor housing of the industrial workers, particularly near the Lachine Canal. However, two factors affecting Montreal's geographical position as a port have changed: whereas the harbor used to be closed by ice for three months of the winter, greater use of icebreakers in the river and in the Gulf of St. Lawrence is permitting more winter accessibility by ocean shipping; an opposite influence was the opening of the St. Lawrence Seaway west of Montreal in 1958—the city is no longer the only inland head of navigation for ocean ships of medium draft.

By some definitions of a metropolitan area, Montreal is Canada's leading industrial city. However, a slightly greater value of manufacturing is produced in the group of cities around the western end of Lake Ontario. Not only does

Montreal have a large local market for consumer goods such as food products and household equipment, but it sends manufactures to a consuming hinterland westward in the Prairie Provinces and eastward in the Maritime Provinces. Some Montreal manufactures are based on imported raw materials such as petroleum, sugar, leather, and cotton; other processors such as flour mills, meat packing and metallurgical plants are supplied by excellent railway connections from Canadian resource areas to the north and west. Other manufactured products such as transportation equipment and a variety of machinery and chemicals supply Canada's national economy.

Montreal became Canada's leading financial and commercial city early in this century, partly as a result of its early start, but also because of its central position in eastern Canada. Many of Canada's large firms have their head offices in Montreal; the tall, glass-walled office towers of the central core are similar to such buildings in other large Anglo-American cities. However, Montreal's future growth in this function is questionable because the trend in the past decade is to establish more head offices in Toronto.

Montreal's land-use patterns are related to its island site and the establishment of transport lines. Its island setting and the significance of bridges show many parallels in the land-use patterns and problems between Montreal and New York. Montreal's first industrial areas grew up along the St. Lawrence River and inland along the Lachine Canal across the southern part of Montreal Island. The main commercial core spread north and west of this transport and industry area to the base of an old volcanic hill, Mount Royal, which rose about 600 feet above the lowland. Several blocks of the central commercial core are now linked together by underground shopping plazas and connector tunnels, permitting shoppers and business-men to move in comfort during the cold winters. On the view slopes of Mount Royal, a first-class residential area maintained separate political status as the enclave city of West-mount. Postwar suburban Montreal expanded outward, like other Anglo-American cities: the dairy and vegetable farms of western and northern Montreal Island have nearly disappeared under the waves of modern ranch-style houses; new industrial zones with low, sprawling factories and ample employee parking stretch outward along the railways and highways; large suburban shopping centers are dispersed through the suburbs; new bridges plus improvements to the old bridges have permitted urban activities to expand across the St. Lawrence River to the so-called South Shore—a parallel to the expansion of New York to the Jersey shore. Whereas the narrow streets of parts of old downtown Montreal and some old residential sections have a "European" appearance which gives character

to Montreal, the new sprawling suburbs look much the same as most other Anglo-American cities.

Montreal dominates the economy of the Quebec Lowland; there are no other large cities nearby. Some of the small cities of the surrounding plain manufacture yarn or textiles and send their products to the clothing factories in Montreal. The immediate hinterland of Montreal is an excellent dairy region from which most of the forest has been removed by two centuries of farming. These farms are not the picturesque "habitant" farms of the nineteenth century, but are modern, well-equipped dairy farms which supply fresh milk to the urban population.

Metropolitan Quebec Quebec City, the provincial capital (population 480,000), is the only large urban area in the eastern St. Lawrence Lowland.[5] "Lower Town" of Quebec, with its picturesque narrow streets, crowned by the ancient stone walls of the Citadel rising over the rock cliffs above the St. Lawrence River, is a well-known tourist attraction. There are many parallels between Quebec and Victoria, British Columbia, both provincial capitals and cultural centers, in their historical competition with their counterparts, the larger industrial cities of Montreal and Vancouver. In both cases the older city near the coast lost out to the interior city. Many ships bypass Quebec to travel farther inland to the larger urban markets and transport facilities at Montreal. Manufacturing employment in Quebec is relatively less significant than in Montreal; more people are engaged in government and service occupations. Unlike Montreal, there are very few wholly English-speaking persons in Quebec City; most business and government activities are carried on in French.

Some of the city's industrial and commercial functions depend on imports and exports, others on its geographical position related to

[5]Although officially Québec, it is known as Quebec City to differentiate it from the province name; the city itself holds about 50 percent of the metropolitan population.

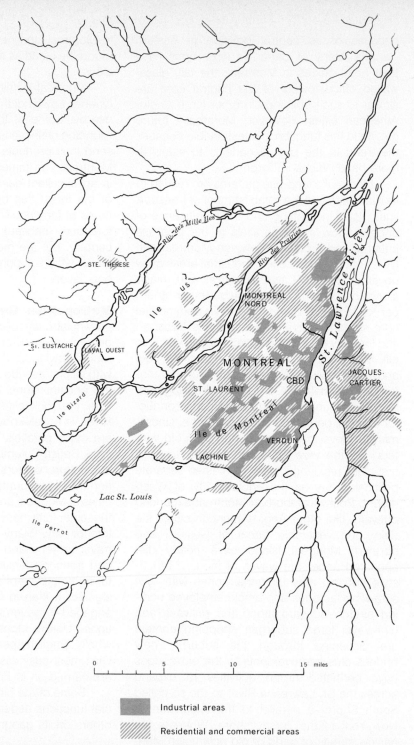

Riv.-des Mille Iles

STE. THERESE

Ile

us

Riv. des Prairies

MONTREAL
NORD

St. Lawrence River

ST. EUSTACHE

LAVAL OUEST

MONTREAL

CBD

JACQUES-
CARTIER

Ile Bizard

ST. LAURENT

Ile de Montreal

VERDUN

LACHINE

Lac St. Louis

Ile Perrot

0   5   10   15   miles

Industrial areas

Residential and commercial areas

Figure 9.5 Land use in the Montreal area. The areas without symbols are mainly agricultural. The main industrial zones are along the harbor and the railways. Most of Montreal Island is occupied by residences, but there are still farmlands in the western section. Suburban growth is beginning on the south and east sides of the St. Lawrence River. North of the city, much of the land is still in forest, despite its favorable location near the large urban market.

the resources of its hinterland. The chief industrial section is along the banks of the St. Charles River, north of the Citadel and the old commercial core. These factories produce clothing, boots and shoes, chemicals, pulp and paper for the national market, and the usual range of food and consumer goods for the local population. Grain elevators are a dominant feature of Quebec's harbor, similar to other lower river ports.

The rural Quebec Lowland   Between Quebec City and Montreal the distinctive long, narrow farms—a result of the original French-Canadian land subdivision system—are still obvious features in the rural landscape. The old farmhouses are close together along the rivers and roads; each narrow farm stretches several hundred yards at right angles to the transport line. Small villages, dominated by a large Catholic church, are spaced at fairly regular intervals along these roads, often at a crossroads junction. This type of linear rural settlement is

Rural settlement along the south shore of the estuary of the St. Lawrence. The farmhouses are close together along the road and near the large church; the narrow fields are at right-angles to the road. In the distance, the marine terrace above the river has been fully cleared for long-lot farms, but the poor, sandy soils of former beach-lines are still a forested area. (Quebec Department of Tourism)

less characteristic of the sections close to the United States border which were settled by United Empire loyalists who had a different land subdivision system.

This latter region of original English-speaking settlement, known as the Eastern Townships, has a different landscape because it has squarish farms and because it has more forest mixed with pasture on the linear hills. Within this century most of the English-speaking settlers have moved from rural south-eastern Quebec, being replaced by French-speaking people from the surplus farm population of the Lowland core. In the Eastern Townships many features are similar to rural New England south and east of it; some of the

Iroquois lock and control dam in the St. Lawrence Seaway, west of Cornwall, looking downstream. The lowland of Ontario, to the left, is more forested in this area than in southwestern Ontario. Medium-draft oceangoing ships may pass through the Iroquois lock in the left foreground. (Ontario Hydro)

small towns have pulp and paper mills or textile mills like New England towns. Sherbrooke (85,000) is the main supply-distribution center for this part of Quebec. It processes local agricultural products, but also has a textile industry and local wholesale businesses.

Ontario

The Ontario part of the Heartland was settled later than the Quebec section. The first British settlers were loyalists (called Tories by the Americans), some of whom settled along the Niagara River in 1780 while others founded Kingston in 1783. In the early nineteenth century southern Ontario was occupied by agricultural settlers in much the same way that the Ohio Basin was settled at about that same time. The heavy stands of deciduous forest were cut down slowly by primitive clearing methods; sometimes the trees were burned to obtain a "cash crop," potash, from the ashes. British immigrants poured into the sparsely occupied region. By 1851 Ontario had surpassed Quebec in population. Shallow canals were built to bypass the rapids in the St. Lawrence River west of Montreal, and the Welland Canal provided a water route around Niagara Falls; thereafter Ontario farm and forest products began to move outward to American and British markets. By 1881 most of the farmland of southern Ontario had been occupied and much of the original forest was removed. Small service and supply towns grew up along the land transport lines in the same manner as in the Midwestern states south of the Great Lakes. Toronto, the provincial capital and a lake port, became the largest city. Its growth was related to its central position as the focus of railways leading westward into the United States and northward into the Canadian Shield.

Industrial development   The largest industrial region in Canada developed around the west end of Lake Ontario and includes cities westward to the Grand River Valley and beyond to London (see Figure 9.6). This region of high urban incomes, known as the "Golden Horseshoe," is equivalent to some of the industrial zones in the United States. Many of the locating factors which favored the development of industry at particular places south of the Great Lakes (see Chapter 6) also applied to the siting and growth of industry in Ontario. Ontario's industrial expansion was most rapid during and after World War II. Almost the complete range of manufactured products made in the cities of the American Midwest are also produced in the Ontario industrial cities. The factories look the same, the brand names are similar, and many of the company names are those familiar to Americans. To the tourist driving across the good highways of southern Ontario the landscape is a dominantly rural one, as it is in the Corn Belt of the United States, but most of the people and the productive wealth of the province are in the cities.

American capital assisted economic development in southern Ontario, but it has also caused political uneasiness. The "geography of ownership" and the flow of products across the international boundary are interesting subjects for further study in the Great Lakes region. In the first half of this century, either through purchase of Canadian companies or by setting up subsidiaries, the number of American-controlled factories increased in southern Ontario, principally in metropolitan Toronto. More than half of American branch plant operations is in or near Toronto, reflecting

not only the importance of that city in Ontario manufacturing but also its proximity and accessibility to Chicago, Cleveland, Buffalo, and other large American cities. Like Toronto, Windsor, Ontario, is located near a large American industrial city and has a number of American-controlled companies. Windsor grew up as a small edition of industrial Detroit, across the half-mile-wide Detroit River. The Ford and Chrysler corporations located their Canadian companies in Windsor early in this century, and many other Detroit firms placed their branch plants there. The free flow of technology, skills, inventions, and management across the international border has been of great benefit to Ontario's industrial production, but Canadians have a nagging uneasiness when some American-controlled firms make business decisions which are contrary to Canadian political and economic policies. The "domination" of certain Canadian industries by American capital and management often enters internal Canadian political discussions.

The St. Lawrence Seaway   The recent industrial and urban growth of southern Ontario has been aided by the completion of the St. Lawrence Seaway. It is probable, however, that the seaway had a greater impact upon the trade and industries of American cities on the south side of the Great Lakes than upon Ontario cities. The latter have always been more dependent on railways (and lately on trucks and highways) for the movement of raw materials and manufactured products than on water transport. One can contrast the lack of ports and cities on the Ontario side of Lake Erie compared with the many south shore American cities. Oceangoing ships come directly to Toronto or Hamilton, but few foreign ships go beyond Lake Ontario to other Ontario ports; only a few grain ships penetrate into Lake Superior to Thunder Bay. On the other hand the seaway aided the internal movement of Canadian wheat by permitting the long, narrow lake freighters to proceed without need of transshipment down the Great Lakes to Montreal

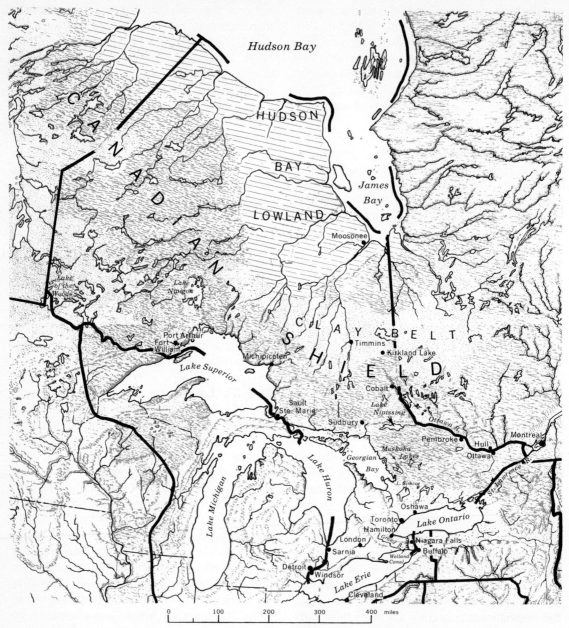

Figure 9.6 Landforms of Ontario. Ontario is centrally positioned between the southern Quebec Lowland to the east and the Canadian Interior Plains to the northwest. It adjoins the productive Great Lakes region of the United States to the south. Note the small extent of the densely occupied part of the southern Ontario Lowland between lakes Huron, Erie, and Ontario. (Base map by A. K. Lobeck. Reprinted with permission of The Geographical Press, Hammond, Inc.)

The federal parliament buildings in Canada's capital, Ottawa, above the steep bank of the Ottawa River. Pulp wood is being sorted into sizes for the pulp and paper mill on the opposite side of the river in Hull. (National Film Board of Canada photo by Malak.)

and beyond to new grain elevators on the lower St. Lawrence River. Some of the geographical patterns of interaction in central Anglo-America are determined by the seasonal use of the Great Lakes and St. Lawrence River.

Metropolitan Toronto The site of Toronto, on a natural harbor within a sandy hook, was used by the Indians as the beginning of a portage route from Lake Ontario to Georgian Bay. Toronto was chosen as the capital of Upper Canada (now Ontario) in 1793, partly because its site was thought to be a safe distance from the Americans at the Niagara River boundary. Local environmental conditions, almost unnoticed by modern urban inhabitants, were important in the early growth of the city. The original settlement occupied a narrow sand-and-clay plain deposited near the shores of former glacial Lake Iroquois. Two small rivers, the Don and Humber, were the eastern and

western boundaries to the early settlement. To the north the sharp, low bluff on the former glacial lake beachline was a minor topographic barrier which discouraged inland residential and street growth. In the mid-nineteenth century the main business district was established north of the railway lines which edged the harbor; commercial land uses spread northward toward the parklike setting of the provincial parliament buildings and the university.

Much of Toronto's commercial and industrial growth can be attributed to the advantages of its central position in southern Ontario; the city is well linked to its hinterland by a network of railways and roads. It is probable that about 30 percent of the Canadian consuming market is within 100 miles of Toronto. The original

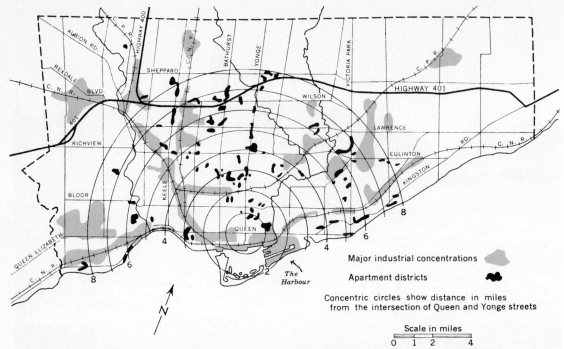

Major industrial concentrations

Apartment districts

Concentric circles show distance in miles
from the intersection of Queen and Yonge streets

Scale in miles
0   1   2   4

Figure 9.7 Distribution of two important urban elements in metropolitan Toronto: The older industrial regions are near the harbor or along the rail lines built in the nineteenth century; new industrial regions are on the outer edges of the city and often on highways. High- and medium-rise apartments near the CBD have helped to counterbalance the outward areal spread of residential areas. (After Kerr and Spelt, *The Changing Face of Toronto,* pp. 116, 131.)

industrial zone adjoined the harbor and paralleled the railways. Much of the cargo which is shipped through Toronto's port is classed as general cargo, indicating the wide range of its manufactures. One of the heaviest import items is bituminous coal for the large thermal power plants. The significance of the harbor increased during the 1960s when the St. Lawrence Seaway made Toronto accessible to ocean shipping. However, there is much more inbound freight than outbound, a reminder of the continuing importance of rail and roads in the distribution of Toronto's manufactured products.

As in other large Anglo-American cities, industry and commerce have decentralized, and along with them residential sprawl has expanded outward, converting former farms into miles of suburban housing. Some of the new industrial zones in the outer part of the city are located on highways rather than railroads. The large suburban shopping plazas look like those in American cities and have the same types of stores. The outward spread of

suburban housing has increased the distance for commuting to the downtown financial and business core; this commuting has been assisted by a subway transport system from suburban bus lines and by the building of "Los Angeles-type" freeways such as that along the green strip of the Don Valley. The centrifugal movement has been partly balanced by central growth as a result of removing old houses near the core and replacing them with high-rise apartments (Figure 9.7).

Toronto's older industries were mainly consumer goods products for the local market. As transportation improved, raw materials were imported from farther away, some from the Canadian Shield. After the large iron and steel mill was established at nearby Hamilton, many steel products were manufactured in factories in Toronto. At present the metropolitan area produces virtually the complete range of manufactures found in most large Anglo-American cities: for example, metal products, machine tools, agricultural implements, and also items such as clothing and books. Specialty production is located in some of the nearby cities, such as Oshawa (General Motors automobiles), Oakville (Ford Motor Company), and Port Credit (oil refineries and chemical plants). But behind all the obvious industrial activity is the financial and business organization and manipulation which takes place in the high-rise office buildings. Many of the head offices of Canadian companies, and American branch plants, are in Toronto where other business connections and exchanges are facilitated.[6]

Will Toronto replace Montreal as Canada's leading city? The answer to this depends partly on one's definition of Toronto and on what one means by "leading." Already the concentration of urban and industrial activities around the western end of Lake Ontario—the Oshawa-Toronto-Hamilton region—has a greater number of people and value added by manufacturing than metropolitan Montreal. The rivalry and competition for growth between Montreal and Toronto can be compared with that between New York and Chicago—the seaport and the inland city. In Canada, the hinterlands of these two major cities overlap because they are only about 250 miles apart, whereas New York and Chicago have grown by duplicating functions as a result of their distant separation. Part of the future growth of both Toronto and Chicago may be related to their use of the St. Lawrence Seaway and to whether or not these cities become ports of world importance. Toronto's growth is also dependent upon future Canadian-American political and economic cooperation. Much of Toronto's industrial expansion was the result of inflows of American capital, and many of its markets are now in the United States. In the Canadian economy Toronto's commercial and financial place in competition with Montreal may also be influenced favorably by the subtleties of confidence which businessmen may feel about future "separatist" tendencies in the province of Quebec.

Niagara Peninsula–Grand River region

This area west and southwest of Lake Ontario has urban characteristics similar to metropolitan Toronto, except that the growing urban centers are still separated from one another by prosperous farmlands. In a hierarchial arrangement of urban regions Hamilton could be considered either as a part of metropolitan Toronto or as the largest city in Niagara Peninsula–Grand River region.

Hamilton (population 500,000 in 1971) is an industrial city. Three-quarters of its industrial workers manufacture durable goods, particularly steel and its products, whereas less than half of Toronto's manufactures are in these durable goods categories. Hamilton's triangular harbor is larger than Toronto's, but much of the south side is already occupied by Canada's largest iron and steel plant. The southward expansion of its urban area was curtailed in the past by the 200- to 300-foot Niagara Escarpment. When the engineering problems related to this topographic feature were solved in the 1950s, suburban housing and commercial strips spread across the plain above the older city.

The steel plant at Hamilton has neither iron ore nor coal nearby. Formerly iron ore was imported by lake vessels from company-owned mines in the Mesabi region west of Lake Superior, and American coal moved across Lake Erie. In the 1960s the steel plant obtained most of its iron ore from several mines in the Canadian Shield including the Labrador City–Wabush ore fields. This latter movement was a direct result of the opening of the St. Lawrence Seaway.

The narrow lowland strip extending east of Hamilton to the Niagara River and north of the

[6] Donald Kerr, "Some Aspects of the Geography of Finance in Canada," *Canadian Geographer*, vol. 9, no. 4 (1965), pp. 175–192.

steep Niagara Escarpment is one of the most intensive horticulture regions in Canada. As the urban buildings of the Golden Horseshoe spread east of Hamilton, conflicts in land use became more acute between urban uses and the valuable agriculture lands, particularly on those soils which were best suited for peach trees. The lacustrine soils of the Niagara Peninsula produce most of Canada's grapes and much of its peaches, pears, cherries, and plums. Much of the production of the small farms goes to fresh fruit markets in Ontario during the summer, but processing, such as in wineries and canneries, is also an important source of employment in the small towns and cities.

Niagara Falls (population 70,000) lies at the eastern end of the Niagara Peninsula, but the industrial zone extends farther eastward across the international boundary to Buffalo. Niagara Falls, still a famous tourist attraction, is also a major industrial city. North of the city near the base of the Niagara Escarpment, Ontario's largest hydroelectric power plant can generate more than 2 million horsepower for the industries of south central Ontario. Several chemical and metallurgical plants and pulp and paper mills were originally built near the falls because of the available electric power early in this century. When it became apparent in the 1950s that the hydropower of the Niagara region could not supply the growing needs of southern Ontario manufacturing and cities, the Ontario government turned to thermal plants based on imported fuel, to nuclear power plants, and to the waterpower of the Shield rivers to the north.

West of Hamilton a line of merging industrial cities occupies the Grand River Valley. Cities such as Brantford, Paris, Cambridge, Guelph, and Kitchener-Waterloo have many similarities in their industrial production although there is some local specialization related to particular companies. This industrial belt produces a wide range of metal and electrical products, textiles, clothing, and rubber and leather goods. Although the urban areas are still separate political entities, they are connected by good highways along which extend ribbon commercial developments. In turn, the Grand River cities have many supply, financial, and market linkages with the Hamilton-Toronto industrial region. As the industrial and urban land uses of these two regions merge, a "Canadian Megalopolis" will emerge west of Lake Ontario. Planners say that about 5 million urban people might occupy the Lake Ontario–Grand River region by about 1980 if present trends continue. Having noted the current problems of urban congestion in New York, Chicago, and Los Angeles, Canadians in this urban complex have an opportunity for planning in order to avoid the past mistakes made during the growth of large American cities. Citizens may even urge a restriction on urban

VALUE ADDED BY MANUFACTURING   **ONTARIO**

% Distribution   Location quotients: 1.0 = national average per capita

Employment	Value added	SIC source	0	1.0	2.0	3.0	4.0	5.0
9.3	11.0	Food products						
0.4	0.9	Tobacco products						
5.2	3.2	Textiles						
5.0	1.4	Apparel						
2.9	1.5	Lumber						
2.7	1.8	Furniture						
5.9	5.9	Paper products						
4.3	5.0	Printing						
3.7	7.9	Chemicals						
0.4	1.0	Petro-coal products						
2.0	2.3	Rubber-plastic						
2.1	0.9	Leather						
3.3	3.7	Stone-clay-glass						
9.6	9.0	Primary metals						
9.7	9.5	Fabricated metals						
5.5	6.1	Machinery						
9.0	8.0	Electrical machinery						
13.0	16.2	Transport equipment						
6.0	5.0	Instruments						
100.0	100.0	All categories						

Totals do not add to 100 percent because of rounding off and omission of several minor industries.

Figure 9.8 The location quotients on the two Canadian charts are based on comparisons with the data for all Canada. Account for the industries which have location quotients over 1.5.

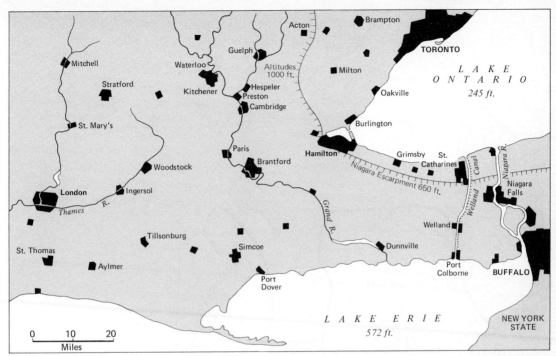

Figure 9.9 The area west of Lake Ontario and the Niagara Peninsula has the main concentration of urban centers in Canada and is also the chief industrial region. Businesses and industries are functionally interconnected in this region. As the cities of the Grand River Valley merge together, the greater the need will be for regional planning.

growth if they are convinced that being "big" does not necessarily mean pleasant living conditions.

Southwestern Ontario Another line of large urban centers, sometimes called the "Ontario Corridor," extends west of Lake Ontario through London, Chatham, Sarnia, and Windsor. The cities along it were originally linked by railways and now also by highways. The rural landscape of the southwestern peninsula differs from that around the western end of Lake Ontario mainly in the larger areas of farmland between the cities. The well-kept farmhouses, large cattle barns, and lush green summer pastures indicate that this is a major dairy region. A great deal of corn is grown, and some farmers specialize in soybeans, tobacco, or early maturing vegetables. An American visitor sees little in the rural landscape that is different from that of western Ohio or central Illinois.

Most of the manufactures of the south-western cities are similar to those of the Niagara–Grand River region. London (population 290,000), with a central position amid the most productive agricultural counties in Canada, has large food-processing industries as well as metal goods, textiles, and electrical goods. Sarnia has a large concentration of oil refineries and an allied petrochemical industry along its waterfront, south of its commercial core. The refineries are now supplied by oil pipeline from the Prairie Provinces, but in the 1930s depended on imported American oil—hence their location on the American border.

Windsor (population 260,000) is Canada's most southerly large city and lies *south* of Detroit with which it is functionally closely connected (see photo, p. 293). These two cities are an excellent example of economic and social interaction between urban units which

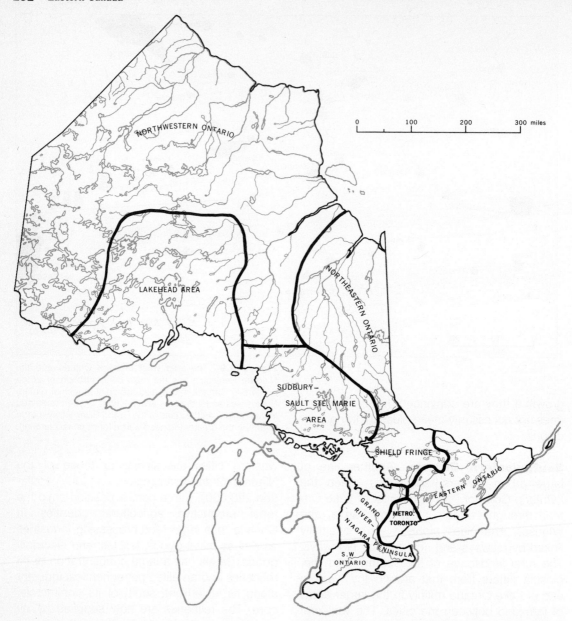

Figure 9.10 Regions of Ontario. The most populated areas, including rural-agricultural and urban-industrial, are south of the Canadian Shield fringe. Northern Ontario has a large populated area but only a few major population clusters.

are separated by an international boundary. In the 1930s plants in Windsor assembled nearly all of the Ford and Chrysler cars sold in Canada; the city called itself the "Automobile Capital of the British Commonwealth." Other American companies such as those producing pharmaceuticals and chemicals located branch plants across the border in Windsor; previ-

ously, many Windsor residents used to carry border-crossing permits and work in Detroit. Some Detroit businessmen are closer to their offices in downtown Detroit if they live in

The linear commercial core of Windsor contrasts with the much larger central city of Detroit to the north across the Detroit River. In many ways these two cities function together as an international city. Note that the commercial core of most Canadian cities can be outlined from the air by the lack of trees. An abundance of trees, in turn, is characteristic of older residential areas. (Lockwood Survey Corp. photo)

suburban Windsor rather than in the faraway urban fringes of Detroit. Many summer cottages along the Canadian shore of Lake St. Clair and the northwestern side of Lake Erie are owned by Americans; long, bumper-to-bumper lines of American cars return from these cottages through Windsor on Sunday nights, inching toward the bottleneck crossings by a bridge and a tunnel.

Eastern Ontario   This region has less industry and urban development than in central and southwestern Ontario. Ottawa, Canada's capital (population 600,000), has attracted a high proportion of professional and university-trained people, similar to Washington, D.C. In the 1850–1870 period Ottawa was a center of the lumber industry in the Ottawa Valley, but now there are few industries in the city. Most of the population is employed by the federal government or is in commercial or service occupations which provide for these civil servants. The city of Hull, across the Ottawa River in the province of Quebec, is functionally part of the Ottawa urban region; it has some manufacturing as well as government offices. The beautiful driveways, parks, and gardens maintained by the federal government for the cities of Ottawa and Hull are well known to tourists.

Agriculture on the eastern Ontario Plain

supplies milk to the urban population of Montreal and Ottawa. Although originally settled by British stock, mainly Irish, several of the counties along the lower Ottawa River now have 60 to 80 percent of their population recorded as of French-Canadian origin. The rural landscape of eastern Ontario, as illustrated by the rectangular field patterns and the styles of farmhouse architecture, is different from that of southern Quebec, but culturally and economically eastern Ontario is part of the Montreal hinterland.

Summary   The urban and industrial Heartland of Canada occupies the small lowland of southern Ontario and southwestern Quebec. The cities, industries, and rural landscapes are generally similar to those of the adjoining parts of the United States. The region has two focal points, metropolitan Montreal and Toronto; they dominate their nearby hinterlands and control much of the economic life of Canada. Within the region there are cultural and language differences between the French-speaking people of southern Quebec and the English-speaking people of southern Ontario.

THE CANADIAN SHIELD

North of the industrial and urban heartland of Canada, and stretching in a huge semicircle around Hudson Bay, lies an enormous area of ancient Precambrian rock known as the Canadian Shield. It is a major source of many natural resource raw materials for the industries and processors in the cities of southern Ontario and Quebec. It is the source of much of the metallic mineral wealth of Canada; it produces much of Canada's pulpwood and some lumber, and within the area are most of Canada's pulp and paper mills. Most of Canada's hydroelectric power is produced by Shield rivers, and it is transported to the cities and industries of the adjoining heartland. Agricultural land is limited in area and quality, and farming is a rapidly declining occupation.[7] The landscape of the

[7] J. Lewis Robinson, *Resources of the Canadian Shield*, Methuen Publishers, Toronto, 1969, 136 pp.

Canadian Shield is dominated by natural features—low hills, rocky outcrops, glacial lakes and marshes, turbulent rivers, and coniferous forests. It is to this environment that the urban residents of the lowland flee for recreation and holidays.

The Shield is a landform and geological region; its southern edge is a notable escarpment of several hundred feet elevation which rises sharply above the agricultural lowland of Quebec. In Ontario between the Ottawa River and Georgian Bay the low, rocky hills of the Shield edge are less noticeable in the landscape, but from the air the land-use contrast between the agricultural lowland and the forested Shield is very clear. The Canadian Shield extends northwestward across northern Manitoba and Saskatchewan, where it has similar environmental characteristics but less development (this will be discussed in Chapter 10).

The 2 million residents of the Shield are mainly urban people, many of them living in new, planned towns created to develop the local natural resources. This population is dispersed in dots and small clusters across the map of "middle" Canada. This frontier region of new resource development is not "northern" Canada—there are vast Subarctic and Arctic areas with few people and little resource development north of it. Because it supplements the economy of "southern" Canada which adjoins it, the southern Shield is often known as middle Canada. Since most of the regional links are now north-south with the Heartland, a counter-concept has been promoted by some in Canada, suggesting that new east-west connections—a "Mid-Canada Corridor"—would improve and diversify the Canadian economy and change the spatial arrangement of it.

The Quebec Shield

Forestry   Much of the resource development in the Shield takes place near its southern edge; there is decreasing intensity of use to the east and north in Quebec. One of these important natural resources is the vast coniferous

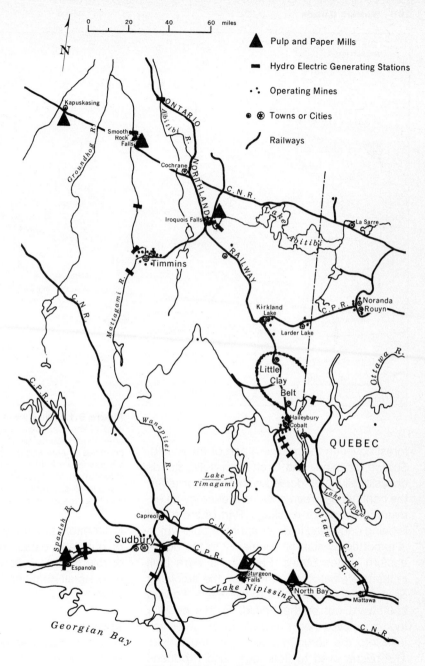

Figure 9.11 Northeastern Ontario. An integrated, extractive economy is united by roads and railways. Pulp and paper mills are located in the spruce forests of the Great Clay Belt on northward-flowing rivers and in the mixed forests on rivers flowing southward from the Shield to the Georgian Bay. Mines, both large and small, cluster around Timmins, Kirkland Lake, Cobalt, and Sudbury. Hydro-electric plants are dispersed throughout the region. Much of the Little Clay Belt has been cleared for agriculture.

NORTHWEST
TERRITORIES

H U D S O N

B A Y

MANITOBA

Churchill

Lynn
Lake

Thompson

Flin
Flon

The
Pas

Grand Rapids

L.
WINNIPEG

ONTARIO

Pickle
Lake

Red Lake

Pine Falls

Winnipeg

Steep
Rock

Thunder
Bay

L.
SUPERIOR

Manitouwadge

Marathon

Wawa

Timmins

Elliot
Lake

North
Bay

L.
HURON

Moosonee

Matagami

Amos

Noranda

Chibougamau

Lebel-sur-
Quevillon

Ottawa

Montreal
Ottawa

Poste-sur-
le-Baleine

Fort George
Fort George

QUEBEC

Rupert

Labrieville

Forestville

Arvida

Quebec

LABRADOR

Schefferville

Goose
Bay
Churchill
Churchill
Falls

Labrador City

Fermont
Gagnon

Lac
Allard

Sept Iles
Port Cartier

Baie
Comeau Murdochville

NEW
BRUNSWICK

U. S. A.

Northern railways

0   100   200
Miles

Figure 9.12 New towns and new place names dot the map of the Canadian Shield. Most of these places are one-industry towns, which are economically based mainly on mines or pulp and paper mills. Miles of forest separate the towns since there is very little agricultural settlement in the Shield. Most places have air connections to southern Canada to supplement the several rail lines penetrating into this "resource frontier."

forest covering the southern part of the Shield. Spruce, fir, pine, and larch form solid stands occasionally interspersed with poplar or alder; the continuous green cover is broken by lakes, rivers, swamps, or muskegs. Part of the forest is being converted into newsprint or pulp which is exported by ship or rail mainly to the northeastern United States. Paper mills were built in the late nineteenth century on the adjoining St. Lawrence Lowland on the rivers flowing southward out of the Shield. In this century logging moved northward along the river valleys into the spruce-fir forests of the Shield. The rivers, used to float logs, also produced hydroelectric power for the pulp and paper mills. The largest group of mills were concentrated in the Lake St. John–Saguenay Valley, with another cluster at Trois Rivières and northward along the St. Maurice Valley. In a zone along the southern edge of the Shield, from Baie Comeau on the east to Hull on the west,

is probably the world's greatest concentration of pulp and paper mills. The locating factors of raw materials, power, transport, labor, and markets all combine in optimum values in this zone.

Mining The iron ore on the Quebec-Labrador boundary had been known since the beginning of the century but was then too isolated to be developed profitably. Its geographical position in Anglo-America changed, however, with the approaching depletion of high-quality hematite ore in the Lake Superior region, and with the opening of the St. Lawrence Seaway. In the 1950s it became economical to transport the good-quality Labrador-Ungava iron ore to blast furnaces in the Lake Erie region. New port facilities were built at Sept Iles on the Gulf of St. Lawrence; a 360-mile railway was constructed across the rocky, lake-dotted Shield; and miners were housed and supplied in the new, planned town of Schefferville (population 4,000 in 1971). This procedure of discovery, technological and market assessment, new rail lines, and new towns was repeated again in the 1960s nearby in Labrador at the adjoining cities of Wabush and Labrador City and westward in Quebec at Gagnon and Fermont. In these latter cases, as a result of changes in market demands, the ores were pelletized at the site before shipment to the Lake Erie steel centers.

The towns represented by these new place names on the map of Canada have little resemblance to boomtowns on the mining frontier in the last century. Few people will move into the wilderness without the urban facilities and conveniences of southern Canadian cities. The new resource-oriented towns are planned and well organized; their curving, paved residential streets and gaily painted houses are supplied by modern supermarkets and recreation facilities. All are served by air transport, as well as railways, so that the attractions of big-city life are only a few hours away.

Although the mining frontier is now in the eastern parts of the Quebec-Labrador Shield, it was preceded by mineral discoveries in the western Quebec Shield in the 1930s. These prewar mines produced gold or copper in a zone between Noranda-Rouyn and Val d'Or. This mining zone was an eastward extension of a major mining region in northeastern Ontario. After 1950 this mining core was extended outward to the northeast with new discoveries of copper and other base metals at Chibougamau and Matagami. New northern railroads pushed into previously unoccupied territory and brought these ores to smelters at Noranda or Montreal.

Power The numerous rapids and falls of the Shield rivers not only supplied power to the internal markets of the mines and pulp and paper mills, but also served as a needed source of power for the growing industries and homes in the lowland cities. As the technology of power generation and transmission improved, southern Quebec was able to bring power from farther and farther away in the Shield. The original hydroelectric power sites, developed at the turn of the century, were on the St. Maurice River; these dams and turbines supplied part of the electric power needs of Montreal. By the 1920s the power generated from the Saguenay River, farther east, could be transmitted to Quebec City. In the 1950s some of the tributaries of the Saguenay River were harnessed; the 4 million horsepower generated at that time from several plants in the Saguenay Basin was more than was produced by any other Canadian river system. In the late 1950s another 2 million horsepower was obtained still farther east from the Bersimis River and transmitted into the grid which serves southern Quebec. In the 1960s the Manicouagan-Outardes rivers were dammed, and by the mid-1970s this was the major power-producing area in Canada, producing about 5 million horsepower for expanding Quebec industries. And near the eastern end of the Shield the enormous power of Churchill (formerly Grand) Falls on the Churchill (formerly Hamilton) River in Labrador began flowing to southern Quebec in the early 1970s. There are no other major rivers available for power development in the eastern part of the Quebec Shield; future power needs may have to be supplied by rivers dropping down to James Bay in the western part of Quebec—a controversial proposal which involves arguments over Indian rights to the land that may be flooded by power dams.

The changing geography of resources development in the Canadian Shield is illustrated by these outward-moving concentric patterns from the core area along the St. Lawrence. Mining towns and northern railroads are penetrating farther north into the mineral-rich Shield; pulp and paper companies are making more intensive use of the southern Shield forests and are pushing logging roads into areas where there is no other settlement. The geographical patterns of settlement are changing in the southern part of the Quebec Shield; but the northern section, beyond the tree line and near Hudson Strait and Hudson Bay, remains little used and is occupied by only about 2,000 Eskimo.

The Ontario Shield

The Shield of northern Ontario contrasts with rolling lowlands of southern Ontario in forest and lake cover, landforms, agricultural land use, population density, and natural resource development. The functional links between the resources of the Ontario Shield and the urban centers on the lowland are similar to those in Quebec. The development of the natural resources of the Shield stimulated the growth of cities in the Ontario Lowland and helped to funnel capital and business into Toronto.

The southern Shield edge By about 1870 the lumbering frontier had moved into the southern Shield in the upper Ottawa River Valley and east of Georgian Bay. Lumbermen hacked into the forests to help build the cities of the American Midwest. Within about 20 or 30 years most of the good white pine had been cut and the lumber industry declined in importance. Farmers had moved into pockets of level land on the Shield edge about this same time, but most found that the soils were thin and rocky—a poor reward for many years of slowly clearing the forest to establish a farm. Farm abandonment was therefore already characteristic of this region by the turn of the century.

The cutover, forested area between Georgian Bay and the upper Ottawa River was little used until the modern development of the tourist, camping, and recreation industry. The lakes and cool forests became havens for the crowded residents of the hot cities. Summer cottages became "a way of life" for many people in Toronto, and their numbers increased as roads improved. A variety of short-term ac-

commodation extends across the southern Shield from the famous Muskoka Lakes near Georgian Bay, through Algonquin Provincial Park north of Peterborough, to the upper Ottawa Valley. This region is the recreational hinterland of Toronto, in the same way that the Laurentian Hills serve Montreal and the Catskill Mountains are used by New Yorkers (Figure 9.10).

Northeastern Ontario North of the Lake Nipissing Trough—a historical, and modern, transit route between the upper Ottawa Valley and upper Great Lakes—the economy is different. People are mainly urban dwellers, living in dispersed towns and cities which are concerned with extraction, processing, or transportation of the natural resources of the Shield. The gateway to this region is North Bay (population 50,000), through which funnel people and products for the northeast region. To the west, cities are scattered along the three transcontinental railways which cross the Ontario Shield.

Northeastern Ontario, sometimes known as the "Clay Belt," has higher population densities, the beginnings of a road network, and a wider range of integrated resource use than other parts of northern Ontario. Agricultural settlers occupied the narrow lacustrine lowlands near Lake Timiskaming in the 1880s, following the loggers and lumbermen. The catalyst, however, was the discovery of some of the world's richest silver mines at Cobalt in 1903–1905. From this mining town prospectors fanned outward over the Precambrian hills, and by 1914 Canada's largest gold mines had been discovered at Timmins-Porcupine and Kirkland Lake–Larder Lake. Railways were built to bring in supplies; they were used later to ship out pulp and newsprint. The mines required electric power, and nearby rivers were dammed for that purpose. The miners needed food, and therefore agriculture expanded across the small glacial lake plain of the "Little Clay Belt" on the north side of Lake Timiskaming. Roads were build to connect the growing towns. By 1940, as a result of this development process, the region had become a functional economic unit on the northern frontier of Ontario.

Large numbers cleared farms in the Clay Belt of both Ontario and adjoining Quebec during the depression years of the 1930s when the provincial governments attempted to take people off relief payments in the cities and put them "back on the land." The misnaming of the region in so far as soils were concerned became apparent; many of the soils were sandy rather than clay, and they contained much peat. Following 1950 agriculture declined rapidly in the Ontario Clay Belt; marginal and subsistence farms were abandoned as farmers and their sons moved to better-paying jobs in Canadian cities. All across eastern Canada the "north" is a resource frontier of urban peoples; it is not an agricultural frontier of rural settlers. This abandonment and decline in the 1960s is not as characteristic in the Quebec section of the Clay Belt where low-income rural life around the parish church has been accepted as a traditional way of life. But even this culture and economy is now being questioned by young people of the region.

Although the Clay Belt region as a whole has a variety of resource developments, most of the towns and cities are dependent on one particular product. Kapuskasing and Iroquois Falls, for example, are one-industry towns, dependent entirely on their pulp and paper mills. Timmins (population 40,000) is the commercial and supply center for several nearby gold, copper, and some very large base metals mines. Several of the gold mines at Kirkland Lake were finally depleted after a half century of production, but iron ore pellets are now being produced nearby and the city has maintained its supply and commercial functions.

Sudbury–Sault Ste. Marie   When the Canadian Pacific transcontinental railway was being constructed west of North Bay in the 1880s, large deposits of copper-nickel ore were discovered by chance in a cut into the Precambrian rocks. By the turn of the century the city of Sudbury had arisen out of the rock and forest; its smelter processed the ores of several mines in the nearby elliptical geological basin; its growing commercial core was the largest between North Bay and Sault Ste. Marie. The Sudbury mines became the world's largest source of nickel and platinum, and also one of Canada's major copper producers. The modern city (population 150,000) has been rebuilt in the commercial core and has little similarity to the rough commercial establishments of the last century. The surrounding vegetation, once destroyed in order to supply the old wood-burning smelters and later destroyed by smelter fumes, is beginning to come back to life. The people and industries are proving that life in an old mining town need not be primitive and bleak.

West of Sudbury large deposits of uranium were discovered in the early 1950s, and the planned city of Elliot Lake was created 40 miles from the nearest railway. With its brightly painted cottages, curving streets, and modern shopping centers, the city showed that a mining town could be attractive. But the "boom and bust" of mining history in Anglo-America was almost repeated here—in a much more beautiful setting. Within a decade the United States found its own sources of uranium, and the Elliot Lake producers lost much of this market. Many of the comfortable homes in the city became empty during the 1960s, but the uses of uranium for peace and power hold out hopes for the survival of the town and the use of its ores.

Sault Ste. Marie (population 80,000) arose near the early canals on the St. Mary River, its industrial activity being dominated by three basic activities—transport, pulp and paper, and a steel mill. Many persons in the "Soo" are engaged in transportation activities—water traffic, railways, and the Trans-Canada Highway. In this century the locks and short canals around the rapids were gradually improved and deepened, particularly on the American side. They were capable of handling

Elliot Lake in northern Ontario is typical of most of the new towns arising on Canada's northern ''resources frontier.'' Its curving streets and neat houses are served by modern shopping centers. The city is surrounded by heavy coniferous forest. (Ontario Department of Mines)

ocean vessels with 30 feet draft during the 1940s, but they had to wait until the St. Lawrence Seaway opened the bottleneck in the lower Lakes. North of Sault Ste. Marie, the Trans-Canada Highway, the first paved road north of Lake Superior, opened up new territory in the 1960s for tourists, and the city became an important center for tourist accommodation and outfitting.

One of the first pulp and paper mills within the Canadian Shield was built at the Soo at the end of the nineteenth century. Forest concessions from the Ontario government, careful woods management, and export to United States markets allowed the mill to prosper for more than 70 years. The major industry of the Soo is one of Canada's three primary iron and steel mills. Iron ore is brought by rail from Wawa (Michipicoten) to the north; coal is imported by water from the United States, limestone comes from Lake Huron shores; local hydroelectric power is available. However, the steel mill, better located than that at Hamilton

with respect to raw materials, is handicapped by distance from the Canadian Heartland market.

Lakehead and the Northwest The activities of northwestern Ontario focus on Thunder Bay (population 110,000), a city formed by the amalgamation of Port Arthur and Fort William. Its transshipment site on the northwest side of Lake Superior has been significant for a century.[8] The large grain-storage elevators there are used for the transfer of Prairie Province wheat and other grains from rail to water transport. Steep Rock iron ore and pellets are loaded directly into lake freighters for shipment to lower Great Lakes steel centers. Thunder

[8] *The Lakehead University Review,* ''Thunder Bay,'' vol. 6, no. 1 (1973); a special issue on the geography of Thunder Bay and northwestern Ontario, edited by I. G. Davies.

Bay, like the small towns along the north shore of Lake Superior, is a major pulp and paper producer which ships newsprint to the central United States.

The other settlements of northwestern Ontario are mainly one-industry towns—having pulp and paper mills, mines, or power plants; there is a little agriculture near Thunder Bay and Dryden. The recreation resources are used more by Americans than by the relatively few Canadians in the region.

Summary Much of the Canadian Shield is uninhabited. The flat, poorly drained lowland west of James Bay and south of Hudson Bay is almost completely empty, and only a few hundred Indians live inland in the Shield forests north of the railway lines across northern Ontario. Even larger areas of rock and scrub forest are virtually unoccupied in northwestern Quebec.

Most of the settlements and resource developments are in the southern sections of the Shield, adjoining and linked to the urban-industrial Great Lakes–St. Lawrence Lowland. More than 125 metal mines are spread across the southern part of the Shield, nearly all served by railways which are helping to "open

up" the land to further exploration. This area is already one of the major mining regions in the world, and the well-mineralized Precambrian rocks are expected to yield even greater wealth as other accessible world mineral resources are exhausted. The vast coniferous forests of the southern Shield, combined with the hydropower of outward-flowing rivers, are being cut to supply the world's greatest concentration of pulp and paper mills, which, in particular, produces newsprint for American newspapers. In addition, these rivers and their falls at the southern edge of the Shield produce ample hydropower for the growing industrial economy and urban dwellers of the Canadian Heartland.

The Canadian Shield is Canada's "resources frontier." New and attractive cities are rising out of the former wilderness; new railroads and roads are penetrating northward into the land of lakes, rocks, and forests; new cottages, lodges, and motels are supplying accommodation and services for Canadians and Americans of the Great Lakes region who wish to escape from the growing congestion of central Anglo-America. A new geography is being created in the Shield region, and it is changing every year!

SELECTED REFERENCES

A wide range of geographical, economic, and resource-development information is available on request from each of the provincial governments; for example, the large and excellent *Atlas of Ontario* (1968).

Maps of Canada and areas within Canada may be obtained from the Map Distribution Office, Dept. of Energy, Mines and Resources, Ottawa. Index maps will be sent upon request.

BIRD, J. BRIAN: *The Natural Landscape of Canada,* Wiley, Toronto, 1972.

CANADIAN ASSOCIATION OF GEOGRAPHERS: *Studies in Canadian Geography,* University of Toronto Press, Toronto, 1972. Six paperback volumes dealing with six political regions of Canada, written for the Canadian Committee of the International Geographical Union.

CLARK, ANDREW H.: *Acadia: The Geography of Early Nova Scotia,* University of Wisconsin Press, Madison, 1968.

————: *Three Centuries and the Island,* University of Toronto Press, Toronto, 1954.

GENTILCORE, R. LOUIS (ed.): *Canada's Changing Geography,* Prentice Hall, Scarborough, Ontario, 1974.

IRVING, R. H. (ed.): *Readings in Canadian Geography,* Holt, Toronto, 1972.

KERR, DONALD, and JACOB SPELT: *The Changing Face of Toronto,* Geographical Branch, Department of Mines and Technical Surveys, memoir 11, The Queen's Printer, Ottawa, 1965.

QUEBEC DEPARTMENT OF INDUSTRY AND COMMERCE ECONOMIC RESEARCH BUREAU: *Atlas of Quebec Agriculture,* 47 maps, 1966.

RAYMOND, C. W., J. B. MCCLELLAN, and J. A. RAYBURN: *Land Utilization in Prince Edward Island,* Geographical Branch, Department of Energy, Mines and Resources, memoir 8, Ottawa, 1963.

ROBINSON, J. LEWIS: *Resources of the Canadian Shield,* Methuen, Toronto, 1969.

WARKENTIN, JOHN (ed.): *Canada: A Geographical Interpretation,* Methuen, Toronto, 1968. Prepared by 22 Canadian geographers for Canada's Centennial in 1967.

10

WESTERN CANADA AND THE NORTHLANDS

In contrast to parts of eastern Canada, sections of western Canada and the Northlands have been settled within the last hundred years. In many areas the development process is still going on. Geographical patterns continue to change as people make adjustments to environments which were different from those they knew in eastern Canada. The Canadian West is defined here as the four western provinces of Manitoba, Saskatchewan, Alberta, and British Columbia, and the Canadian North includes the two northern territories, Yukon and Northwest. These provinces and territories together constitute 68 percent of the land area of Canada but have only 27 percent of the Canadian population—a little less than 6 million persons in total in 1971.

As in the United States, the smaller population in the west is partially related to the lateness and direction of settlement; western Canada was settled by people who came from, or moved through, eastern Canada. Settlement was delayed by some environmental limita-

The variety of landscapes in the foothills region of southwestern Alberta. The small town of Pincher Creek is in the foreground; strip farming, with alternate strips of grain and fallow, and widely dispersed farmhouses are in the center; the forested, low foothills lie at the base of the abrupt wall of the Rocky Mountains in the distance. (National Film Board of Canada photo by G. Hunter)

tions: large areas were too dry, too cold, or too mountainous for agricultural settlement early in this century. In addition to low population in general, the Canadian West lacks a major concentration of people, industries, and markets similar to that on the Great Lakes–St. Lawrence Lowland of eastern Canada.

Comparison with the American West

The Canadian West resembles the American West in several environmental and cultural characteristics. There are only a few differences in the landscape north or south of the border: the grassy plains with their dark soils continue northward, as do the forested mountains of the western Cordillera; the rectangular survey system, the railroads financed by land grants, the food in the restaurants, and the goods in the stores seem similar. The visual political changes at the 49th parallel are minor: a different flag, a similar but different currency, a customs and immigration barrier. The people have the same physical appearance as Americans and generally wear the same styles of clothing. These similarities are noticeable to the American tourist who has the pleasure of being in a foreign land without any cultural discomfort.

Closer examination shows several significant differences.

More northward. The Interior Plains are covered more frequently with cold air masses from the north. A shorter frost-free season limits the kind and variety of crops that can be grown; but coolness reduces evaporation, and as a result the forest has been able to establish itself across the northern and central parts of the Prairie Provinces. Northern latitude brings long periods of summer daylight which, if combined with warm air masses, provides suitable growing conditions for grain in some areas.

Less mountainous. Some of the mountain ranges of the Canadian Cordillera are higher than the American ranges, but the main difference is that they do not cover as much area

as in the American West. The mountain system is about 400 miles wide across British Columbia in comparison with the 1,000 miles from Denver to the Pacific. The broad intermontane plateaus of the American mountains are lacking or are relatively narrow in Canada. But on the other hand, the mountains of interior British Columbia are more forested, and useful for lumber, than are the dry interior ranges of the western United States.

More isolated. The Canadian West is separated from the Canadian Heartland by 700 to 1,000 miles of the forested, rocky, and little-settled Canadian Shield, whereas the American West adjoins the urban and industrial Midwest. Whereas the American Southwest is not far from ocean access to the Gulf of Mexico, the northern end of the Canadian Plains at the Arctic Ocean is closed by ice for nine months of the year.

Part of a less-populated country. Because Canada has a population only one-tenth that of the United States, it has a smaller local market for its staple products. Although western Canadian wheat production, for example, averages about two-thirds that of the United States, Canada consumes only about one-quarter of its annual production and the rest must be disposed of in the world market. Similarly, although the lumber cut in British Columbia is about half that of Washington and Oregon, much of the British Columbia cut is exported, whereas most American production stays within the country.

Later economic development. The Canadian West was occupied 20 or more years later than the corresponding American areas. The first transcontinental railway, for example, crossed western Canada 17 years after the first rail line penetrated across the American Cordillera. North Dakota had its rapid population growth in the 1880s, whereas the waves of agricultural settlement moved into Manitoba and Saskatchewan in the early 1900s. Although most of the unirrigated agricultural land was occupied in the American West by about

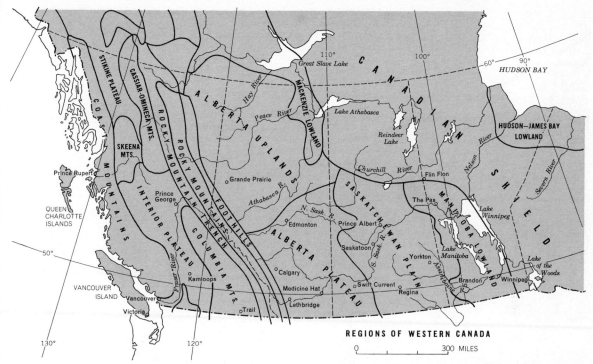

REGIONS OF WESTERN CANADA

0   300 MILES

Figure 10.1 Landform regions of western Canada. Compare the widths of the Canadian regions with those of the regions 100 miles south of the Canadian border. (Otis W. Freeman and John W. Morris, *World Geography,* McGraw-Hill, New York, 1965. Used with permission of McGraw-Hill Book Company)

1900, pioneer settlement was still going on in the Canadian Plains during the 1930s.

Ethnic-group settlement. Early in the twentieth century, Central Europeans and French-Canadians moved into the Canadian West and settled in rather homogeneous ethnic groups. These ethnic concentrations are still part of the cultural patterns. No such ethnic mosaic is found in the American West.

THE PRAIRIE PROVINCES

Only a small part of the region known as the "Prairie" Provinces is covered with prairie grassland. However, these grasslands extend across the southern part of the provinces and were the areas first occupied by agricultural settlers. Hence the region became known by the environmental characteristic most obvious to the settlers. Similarly misleading is the belief that the landform characteristics of the Interior Plains may be dismissed with the one word, "flat."

Physical Regions

The landform regions of the Interior Plains consist of four south-north trending levels which are related to the underlying rock (Figure 10.2). Above the geological-landform regions the vegetation and climate zones have a generally concentric pattern of semicircles.

The Canadian Shield, discussed more fully in Chapter 9, occupies the northeastern part of the Prairie Provinces and has a different landscape than that of the Interior Plains.[1] Similar to the Shield sections of Ontario and Quebec, the western Shield has coniferous forests, low knobby rock hills, irregular-shaped lakes, and rushing rivers. In north central Manitoba,

[1] See the *Atlas of the Prairie Provinces,* edited by T. R. Weir, Oxford University Press, Toronto, 1971, 31 pp.

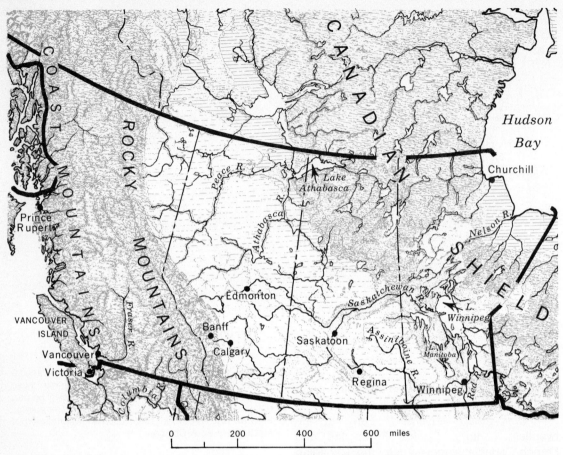

Figure 10.2 Landforms of western Canada. Compare with Figure 10.1. The Interior Plains narrow to the north between the Canadian Shield and Cordillera. (Base map copyright by A. K. Lobeck. Reprinted with permission of The Geographical Press, Hammond, Inc.)

however, these characteristics are more sub-dued because of the mantle of lake and marine deposition of the Glacial Age. Unfortunately, this relatively level land on the Manitoba Shield has a harsh climate and large areas of poor drainage. As a result there was no settlement, because land on the plains to the south was more attractive to agricultural settlers.

The Manitoba Lowland This is the flat bottom of former glacial Lake Agassiz, of which present lakes Winnipeg, Winnipegosis, and Manitoba are the remnants. The fine-grained deposits laid down in the bottom of the old glacial lake are now the thick, fertile soils of the flat Red River Plain around Winnipeg. They support prosperous grain and livestock farms—partly because of their favorable envi-

ronmental characteristics but also because of their proximity to the market and service facilities of Winnipeg. To the north, in the section known as the "Interlake" area, the soils are thinner, contain more lime, and have many stones; these poorer soils and forest environment are marginal for agricultural settlement.

The Saskatchewan Plain A geological escarpment extends north-south across southwestern Manitoba, forming the eastern boundary of the Saskatchewan Plain. In west central Manitoba the eroded, forested escarpment is an environmental attraction which has been set aside as Riding Mountain National Park. Although the hills of the escarpment are hardly "mountains" when viewed from the plain west of them, they were notable topographic features to the settlers of the flat Manitoba Lowland. The Saskatchewan Plain is about 2,000 feet above sea level; occasional flat-topped hills, erosional remnants of harder rock, rise a few hundred feet above it.

The Alberta Plateau The low geological escarpment marking the eastern boundary of the Alberta Plateau is less of a landform feature on the plains than are the steep, eroded banks of some of the entrenched rivers or the several flat-topped hills.

The Alberta Uplands The northern half of Alberta is a rougher area of hills and flat-topped uplands compared with the southern plains. The land slopes down to the northeast where the south end of the Mackenzie River Lowland is about the same altitude as the Manitoba.

The preceding landform regions are minor features in the vast area of the Prairie Provinces, but they illustrate that the Interior Plains of Canada (and also of the United States) are not uniform and level. The environmental factors which were of more significance to man were climate, vegetation, and soils.

Climate, Vegetation, Soils

The grasslands, which indicate the subhumid climate of the region, cover the southern part of the provinces. The driest area, with short-grass vegetation, is along the United States border in southeastern Alberta and southwestern Saskatchewan. Outward from this area annual precipitation increases to the west, north, and east; as a result vegetation changes from short grass to tall prairie grass and merges into a "parkland" of deciduous trees and grass. Forests cover the foothills west of Calgary and the plains west of Edmonton. The little-populated coniferous forest stretches for un-

broken miles north of the North Saskatchewan River and across the Interlake area of southern Manitoba (endpaper at back of book).

The soil zones, with a similar semicircular pattern, were mirrored in the former agricultural regions. The driest area with short-grass vegetation has brown soils and was used mainly for ranching. The tall prairie grass, which receives more precipitation, has dark-brown soils and was used mainly for wheat. The Parkland Belt has some of the best soils in the west—the black soils (chernozems); they coincided closely with the mixed-farming region which has both livestock farms and grain farms. Farther north gray forest soils, with lower inherent fertility, underlie the mixed-forest region; agriculture pushed into this zone with difficulty and is now retreating. The agricultural regions have changed in the past two decades and have become more complex as a result of changes in technology and markets (Figure 10.3).

Settlement

Prior to white penetration the Interior Plains were occupied by Indian tribes who lived on the vast herds of buffalo which roamed the grasslands. In the early nineteenth century the international border was of no significance to these herds or to the migratory Indians. White man's occupation of the Canadian Plains was not characterized by Indian wars or by rancher-farmer feuds as in the American Plains. The minor skirmishes of the only "war," the Riel Rebellion of 1885, involved only a few thousand Indians and Metis (half-breeds). Thus Canada never had a "Wild West"—and lacks this basis for a Hollywood-style movie and TV industry!

Fur traders The Canadian West was partially explored in the late eighteenth century by fur traders of the Hudson's Bay Company and the North West Company. Chains of forts (trading posts), connected by canoe routes, were established to bring furs to either the Great

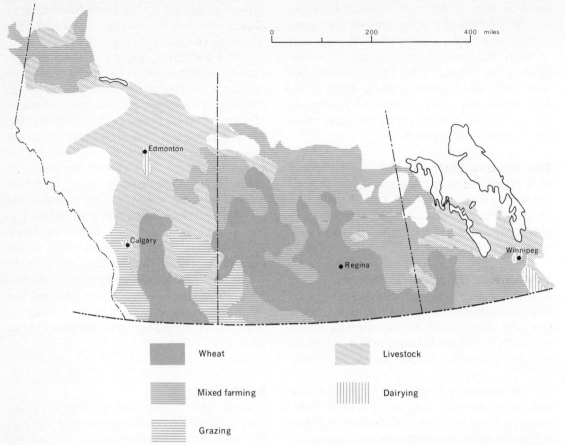

Wheat

Mixed farming

Grazing

Livestock

Dairying

Figure 10.3 Agricultural regions, southern Prairie Provinces. Agricultural patterns have diversified in the past two decades. On most of the former grasslands, wheat and other grains are now grown and livestock is raised, but the combinations of these crops and rural activities vary from region to region. The areas shown as "mixed farming" grow mixed grains, including wheat, and place about equal emphasis on livestock. The small, but valuable, areas of irrigated crops in southern Alberta are not shown on the map. (Adapted by J. L. Robinson from the map of *Agricultural Regions of Canada,* Ottawa, 1961.)

Lakes or Hudson Bay. The fur traders maintained friendly relations with Indian tribes and established a two-way flow of furs and trade goods across the continent. The rivalry between the two companies ended when the Hudson's Bay Company absorbed the North West Company in 1821, nearly a half century before agricultural settlers began to arrive in significant numbers. In 1870 the new Dominion of Canada purchased the enormous "trapping grounds" from the historic Hudson's Bay Company; the area became the Northwest Territories, except for the colony of British Columbia in the far west and the tiny (then) province of Manitoba created in that same year in the Red River Valley.

The farmers   Farms were established in the Red River Lowland long before the rest of the Canadian Plains was settled. In 1811 a small group of British settlers raised crops near Fort Garry, at the junction of the Red and Assiniboine rivers (now the city of Winnipeg). The farms barely survived, however, until shallow-draft steamers began to use the Red River later, giving access to growing American settlements in the Dakotas and Minnesota. When railways reached southern Manitoba from the United States in the 1870s, and later from eastern Canada, agricultural settlement expanded.

Settlers of European background came into an entirely different physical environment from that which they knew in eastern Canada. The grasslands were plowed up for wheat, as they had been a decade or more previously on the American Plains to the southward. By about 1900 the flat area of southern Manitoba, with fertile black soils and a slightly higher average rainfall than the plains to the west, was settled with a reasonable rural population density. Later settlers continued westward to take up homestead land in southern Saskatchewan and Alberta. A survey system, almost the same as that of the township-range system of the United States, was established at this time.

The first quarter of the twentieth century was the period of most rapid agricultural settlement. A second transcontinental rail line was built across the northern prairies with one of its western terminals at Prince Rupert, close to the Alaska Panhandle. A growing network of branch railways covered the southern plains; trains brought in immigrant settlers and took out crops of wheat and other grains. Small service towns with their characteristic tall grain elevators appeared on the rural landscape. Winnipeg grew as the gateway to the west and the main supply and distribution center. As more land was occupied, the provinces of Saskatchewan and Alberta were created in 1905.

The orderly and methodical agricultural settlement of the Canadian Plains was promoted and encouraged by the federal government, which opened immigration offices in Britain and Europe, and settlement was greatly directed by the railway companies. Sometimes the railways, with their land grants, preceded settlement and then sold land to incoming immigrants; in other places settlers took up homesteads beyond the end of branch railways

and then the lines were extended to them to carry out their wheat. For example, about a half million people came to southern Saskatchewan in the period 1900–1914 and occupied most of the available, suitable farmland. By the 1930s large rectangular fields of wheat, other grains, pasture, and fallow made checkerboard patterns across the southern Interior Plains. Roads and railroads followed straight lines for many miles.

Northward penetration The northward movement of the agricultural frontier was slower and more difficult. In the 1920s settlement followed trails and crude roads into the forest north of the North Saskatchewan River and into the Peace River block on the British Columbia–Alberta border. Removal of the forest was slow; it might have required 20 years to clear a marginally economic farm unit of about 100 acres. During this time a family could, however, obtain additional food from the fish in the lakes and game in the forest. Although precipitation on the northern frontier was more reliable than on the southern grasslands, the frost-free season was a little shorter. The northward agricultural migration reached its peak in the early 1930s when farmers had to abandon the drought-stricken southern grasslands, particularly in southwest Saskatchewan. Life on the northern frontier was not easy; but many eked out a living on subsistence or livestock farms.

By about 1940 the northern limits of agricultural expansion had been reached. The line extended northwest from the Interlake area of southern Manitoba passing just north of Prince Albert, in Saskatchewan, and Edmonton, in Alberta, to the Peace River area of northeastern British Columbia (Figure 10.4). This latter area, in latitude 55–56°N, is the same latitude as Moscow, Soviet Union. Many of the Peace River farms were settled after World War I as the "last large area of available homestead land in Canada." Their grain and livestock products were taken out to Edmonton by rail. Small serv-

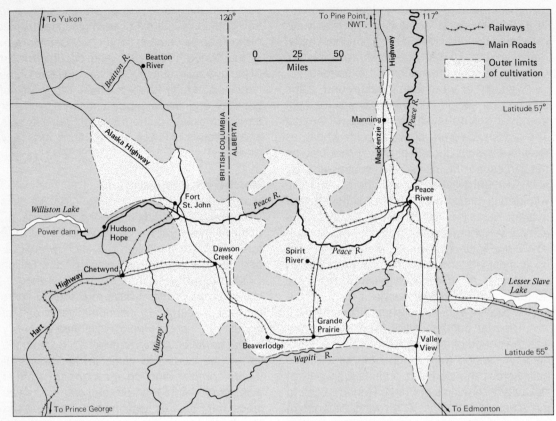

Figure 10.4 The Peace River area: Shared by Alberta and British Columbia, this area is the farthest north section of extensively cleared agricultural land in Canada. Cleared land is shown within the dotted lines; other potential agricultural land, now forested, is available. The region also produces petroleum and natural gas and has ample hydroelectric power. The area is separated from other settled centers of Canada, but connected by good transport lines.

ice-supply towns, such as Grande Prairie and Dawson Creek, served the rural areas. After 1950 accessibility improved when a second main road and a railway came into the region from Prince George to the southwest. Vancouver and Edmonton now compete for the flow of products from the Peace River area.

In the 1950s farm consolidation and farm abandonment resulted in a rapidly decreasing farm population within the forested area, similar to the decrease in the grassland region. Any further northern extension of agricultural settlement is now doubtful: the forest environment with its mediocre soils is difficult for farming; the "pioneering spirit" has virtually disappeared; and new farmland is unnecessary when southern farms are producing a surplus.

Growth of urban centers A geometric pattern of small towns and villages emerged.

These settlements were strung along the rail lines because one of their original commercial functions was to store the grain of the surrounding rural area until the railway carried it away. As road transport improved, grain could be carried farther to central places; many of the small villages are no longer needed for this grain-collection function, and many branch railways have been abandoned as uneconomic. The distribution pattern of small towns is changing.

Rural villages are quite similar across the Canadian Plains and are like those of the

A typical main street of a small Prairie Province town. Stores have false fronts; the hotel and theater are the only "large" commercial buildings. The road is wide—dusty in summer and muddy after spring rains. This is High Prairie, Alberta. (Alberta government photo)

American Midwest. The commercial cores of these small towns often have a block or two of false-fronted stores, either parallel to the railway or at right angles to it. The grain elevator is usually the highest building in the town; as one approaches a town, the number of elevators appearing on the horizon is often a good indication of the size of the commercial and residential areas.

Although farm population is decreasing across the southern Prairie Provinces, the total population is increasing because of city growth. One can distinguish a hierarchy of cities which is related to size and functions (see Figure 10.5). The three largest cities have grown mainly because of their position rather than any particular advantages of their local sites. Winnipeg is central to all Canada; east-west transport lines funnel through Winnipeg and the narrow zone between Lake Winnipeg and the international border. Edmonton is the gateway to the north, supplying the vast Mac-

kenzie Valley and the southern Yukon, and also serving a prosperous livestock and oil-well hinterland in central Alberta. Calgary is the gateway to the Rockies and is the primate city for people living nearby in a variety of environments ranging from grassland plains to scenic forested mountains. Somewhat smaller cities are Saskatoon, halfway between Winnipeg and Edmonton, and Regina, halfway between Winnipeg and Calgary. Other cities, not quite as large, service smaller local hinterlands between the above-noted large cities. For example, Brandon lies midway between Winnipeg and Regina; Medicine Hat and Lethbridge serve the area between Regina and Calgary; Red Deer, between Calgary and Edmonton, is too close to these big cities to have many urban functions of its own; Lloydminster and North Battle-

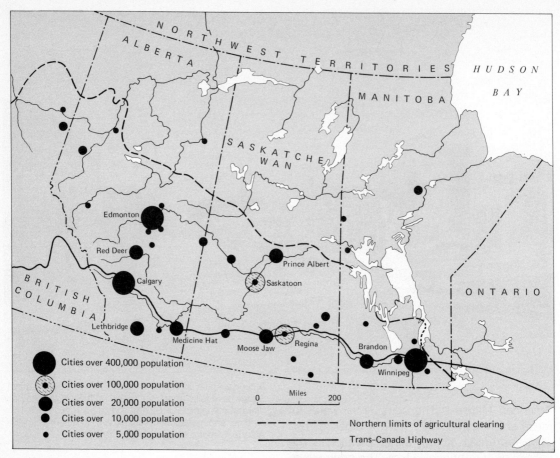

Map labels: NORTHWEST TERRITORIES, ALBERTA, SASKATCHEWAN, MANITOBA, HUDSON BAY, BRITISH COLUMBIA, ONTARIO

Edmonton, Red Deer, Calgary, Lethbridge, Medicine Hat, Moose Jaw, Prince Albert, Saskatoon, Regina, Brandon, Winnipeg

Cities over 400,000 population
Cities over 100,000 population
Cities over 20,000 population
Cities over 10,000 population
Cities over 5,000 population

0   Miles   200

——— — ——— Northern limits of agricultural clearing
———————— Trans-Canada Highway

Figure 10.5 The urban hierarchy of the Prairie Provinces: The manufacturing economy and income of the Interior Plains of Canada are concentrated in three large cities; the next largest cities are halfway between the largest cities; smaller cities are about equidistant from larger cities. Not shown on the map are the small agricultural service centers dispersed across the agricultural area (south of the dotted line).

ford vie for urban importance as the chief central place between Saskatoon and Edmonton.

Winnipeg

As the gateway to the west Winnipeg became the main supply, distribution, and transport center as the western plains were occupied by farms. Although its position of transport convergence has been compared to that of Chicago, an important difference is that the latter city is part of the industrial and agricultural Midwest whereas Winnipeg has the sparsely occupied Canadian Shield east of it. Winnipeg also grew as the main service center for the narrow strip of habitable agricultural land across southern Manitoba; by 1971 the city had 550,000 persons, more than half the population of the province. Although Winnipeg is the largest city in the Prairie Provinces, its recent rate of population growth has not been as fast as that of Edmonton and Calgary, its rivals to the west.

As population increased on the Interior Plains early in the century, that market could be supplied by some manufactures from Winnipeg, such as clothing and agricultural machinery. Many industries were based on its agricul-

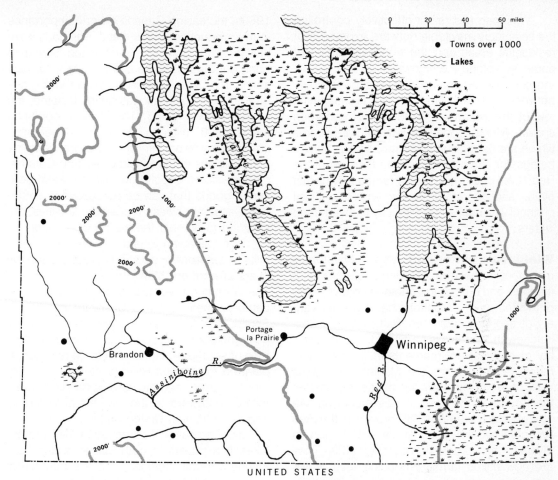

Figure 10.6 The southern Manitoba Lowland. This fertile lowland is bordered to the north and east by thinly populated forest areas, westward by a higher level of prairie (note the 2,000-foot contour), and southward by the international boundary. The original site of Winnipeg, in the center of the lowland, was at a river junction; now the city is a focus of railway and highway routes.

tural hinterland—flour and feed mills, vegetable canneries, a beet sugar refinery, and meat-packing plants. Most of these are located along the railway tracks because the raw materials were originally brought in only by rail from the agricultural hinterland. As in the American Corn Belt, some beef cattle from the western plains are brought to southern Manitoba feed-grain farms for fattening before slaughtering in Winnipeg, but others are transported through Winnipeg to feeder lots nearer the markets in southern Ontario. The large stockyards in St. Boniface, a separate political entity within Greater Winnipeg, are therefore comparable in function to the stockyards in St. Paul or Kansas City.

Winnipeg has a large number of ethnic groups. The sons and daughters of European immigrants have moved from Prairie farms into the cities; Winnipeg thus has ethnic diversity similar to some of the industrial cities of southern Ontario. The largest group of French-Canadians in the west lives on the north side of St. Boniface, where they are trying to maintain their French language amid other ethnic groups who now accept English as their language.

Winnipeg has rather effectively controlled the seemingly inevitable outward expansion of residential areas and the ribbonlike strips of commerce along the highways. As in all growing cities on the Interior Plains, the boundary between urban and rural activities is sharp, with few of the intermixed structures of suburban sprawl. Winnipeg faces a few natural hazards which are as difficult to control as are human beings: for example, the spring flooding of the Red River could not be contained on the flat plain, and therefore an expensive artificial channel was built around the city to divert flood waters.

Winnipeg's hinterland   Most of Manitoba's resources funnel through Winnipeg en route to markets, and offices in Winnipeg control much of this movement. Manitoba has a greater variety of economic activities than adjoining Saskatchewan, and this is partially due to the variety of physical environments in the province. Farms stretch across the Manitoba lowlands west of Winnipeg; they are noticeably smaller than those to the west in Saskatchewan. Although some wheat is still grown in the Red River Valley, the grain farms had begun to diversify their production by the 1930s. They are now mixed farms, producing feed grains and legumes for livestock as well as specialty crops such as sunflowers, rapeseed, flaxseed, and sugar beets.

Eastern and northern Manitoba are underlain by the Precambrian rocks of the Canadian Shield. The area is a source of metallic ores, waterpower, pulpwood, and recreation, but these are less developed than in the eastern Shield. Several settlements in both northern Manitoba and Saskatchewan depend solely on mines. Prior to 1940 the only major mines produced copper, zinc, and gold near Flin Flon, on the southern geological boundary of the Shield. The mining boom which opened up the eastern Shield after World War II also penetrated into the western Shield. For example, nickel was discovered at Lynn Lake, Manitoba, in the early 1950s and at Thompson in the

1960s, increasing Canada's world importance in the production of this metal. Railroads were built in the previously uninhabited Shield to bring out the nickel ore and to supply the new towns. By 1971 Thompson was a thriving city of 20,000 people, but was nearly isolated, the nearest town being The Pas (population 6,000), 200 miles to the south. These new northern towns are similar in appearance to the mining towns in the Shield of eastern Canada; modern stores supply most of the usual consumer goods that can be purchased in southern Canadian cities; recreation facilities are supplied to combat the feeling of isolation.

The Canadian Shield has enormous supplies of waterpower awaiting utilization, and the rivers of northern Manitoba are no exception. The Winnipeg River was dammed early in this century where it drops westward out of the Shield; it supplies electric power to a nearby pulp and paper mill and to the cities and industries of southern Manitoba. A large new power plant on the Nelson River produces electricity for Thompson, and the surplus power is transmitted southward to the markets of Winnipeg and the adjoining United States.

The recreational attraction of the northern lakes and forests in both Manitoba and Saskatchewan will increase, but the number of potential "consumers" of this scenic resource living south of the western Shield is much less than that south of the eastern Shield.

Regina and Saskatoon

These cities, each about 130,000 persons, are the only large cities in southern Saskatchewan. Regina was established in 1882 on a small creek in the midst of the flat plain as the capital of the (then) Northwest Territories. The Canadian Pacific Railway soon reached it en route to the west, and the city expanded its commercial and supply functions for the grain and cattle farms that were established across the semiarid plains. As the capital of Saskatchewan after 1905 Regina added various government occupations. Its growth was moderate, however, amid the dominant rural economy of the early part of this century; there were only 35,000 people in the city in 1921. Postwar population growth has been related to industrial expansion: the usual food-processing industries such as flour and feed mills and meat packing have been supplemented by oil refineries, a small steel mill (using scrap), and a cement plant. It is not likely, however, that Regina's industrial and commercial growth can equal that of Winnipeg or Calgary which produce a wider variety of consumer goods for larger local and regional populations.

The urban growth of Saskatoon is similar to that of Regina. The early settlement grew up on both sides of a convenient crossing of the South Saskatchewan River, used later by the main line of the Canadian National Railway to Edmonton and the West Coast. Saskatoon supplies services to the surrounding rural population, and its industries are mainly related to food processing. Like Regina, Saskatoon's population more than doubled in the period 1951–1971, as both cities absorbed part of the decreasing farm population. By 1971, these two largest cities together had almost 30 percent of Saskatchewan's population, compared with only 11 percent in 1931.

The hinterland of Regina and Saskatoon   The Saskatchewan Plain is the main wheat-producing area of Canada. Farms are large, averaging a square mile (640 acres) in the south, and nearly all are now larger than the original 160-acre homestead. As on the American Plains, more and more farms are being worked during the summer by a few men and many machines while the families live in the growing towns and cities where better education and urban amenities are available.

The farmer still has to contend with hazards in the natural environment before he obtains a crop. Precipitation is barely adequate for wheat production across southern Saskatchewan, and probably many grain farms should have remained in grassland as cattle ranches. Annual precipitation averages only about 10 to 14 inches, but fortunately about 60 percent falls during the four summer months. Other natural problems include frost, hail, grasshoppers, and plant diseases; the effects of these natural hazards are apparent in the fluctuating totals of wheat production. Although wheat acreage varies a little from year to year depending on expected markets (about 22 million to 25 million acres in the three Prairie Provinces), the annual wheat crop may range from about 500 million to 800 million bushels.

Because the consuming population of the Prairie Provinces is small, most of the wheat must be transported out of the region. The consumption of wheat products in eastern Canada is only about 150 million bushels; therefore Canada has to sell about 400 million to 600 million bushels of wheat in the world market each year. In the past much of the wheat moved eastward by rail through Winnipeg to Thunder Bay and thence via the Great Lakes to eastern ports. Small amounts moved northward along the Hudson Bay railroad to the port of Churchill. The Great Lakes are closed by ice for three or four months of the year and Hudson Bay is icebound for eight or nine months. Vancouver became a western grain port, particularly for southern Alberta, after the Panama Canal was opened in 1914. In recent years, as a result of the increased market for wheat in the countries of the western Pacific, Vancouver became the leading Canadian wheat-exporting port.

Although Saskatchewan is still known as the "wheat province" of Canada, its economy is diversifying. The oil fields, better known in Alberta, cross the provincial border into western Saskatchewan, and the Williston Basin oil field of North Dakota extends into southeastern Saskatchewan. The words of enthusiasts who claim that there are now "more oil derricks than grain elevators" in Saskatchewan reflect the changing economy—although they may have counted neither phenomenon accurately! Further wealth from beneath the soil became available in the 1960s when mining technology found a way to obtain the deep and rich potash

The headframe, circular storage bins, and other buildings of a potash mine near Esterhazy, Saskatchewan. Parkland vegetation and rectangular grain farms are in the background. (National Film Board of Canada)

deposits. This potash production ranks second in Anglo-America to southeastern New Mexico, and brought new prosperity and new occupations to several agricultural villages in central and eastern Saskatchewan.

Edmonton and Calgary

By 1951 Alberta's population became more urban than rural, and by 1971 the two largest cities of Edmonton and Calgary had 55 percent of the provincial population. These two rapidly growing cities are friendly rivals. Their urban growth rates in percent have sometimes been the highest in Canada, but this is partly a reflection of their small beginning figures. Edmonton, for example, increased in population from 80,000 in 1931 to 500,000 in 1971. In both cities local planning authorities have been

relatively successful in controlling and directing areal expansion. "Neighbourhood units," with a good mix of residential, commercial, and institutional needs, were planned and built in successive blocks on the expanding outer edges of both cities.

The cities have many similarities in their origins, functions, and manufacturing types. A fur-trading post was built near the present site of Edmonton early in the nineteenth century, and this was its main function until a branch rail line from Calgary reached it in 1891. Edmonton was chosen over Calgary as the capital of Alberta in 1905 partly because of its central position in the province. Prior to 1940 the growth of both cities was related mainly to the production of their agricultural hinterlands. Cattle from ranches on the Calgary grasslands and from farms in the Edmonton mixed-grain area came to the stockyards of both cities either to be transported eastward or to be slaughtered at local meat-packing plants. Calgary's origin as a "cow town" is still commemorated in its publicized tourist attraction, the Calgary Stampede.

Although 180 miles apart, Calgary and Edmonton operate as one "single," dispersed city in the petroleum industry.[2] Calgary has most of the head offices of the oil companies and such allied businesses as finance, land agents, consultants, and data processors; Edmonton has most of the companies concerned with operations such as drilling firms, repair companies, engineering companies, and refineries. Most companies that have head offices in one of the cities also have branch offices in the other. These functional interconnections and linkages generate a great deal of intercity traffic.

Calgary   This city, with a population of 400,000 in 1971, has a geographical position which may be compared with that of Denver, Colorado. Calgary is on the northwestern edge of a large irrigation district, and is the transportation gateway to recreation areas such as Banff National Park westward in the Rocky Mountains. For many products and services Calgary's hinterland extends into southeastern British Columbia. The city experienced a minor oil boom during the 1930s, and this brought many oil companies; they remained there when oil was discovered elsewhere in Alberta in later decades. One of the results of the business activities related to petroleum is that Calgary is reported to have the highest percentage of former American residents of any Canadian city.

[2]G. H. Zieber, "The Dispersed City Hypothesis with Reference to Calgary and Edmonton," *The Albertan Geographer*, no. 9 (1973), pp. 4–13.

Edmonton   Edmonton began to grow during World War II as the gateway to the north. The activities in the Yukon Territory, such as the building of the Alaska Highway and the postwar development of northern resources, had their southern focus on Edmonton. Wholesale firms, equipment suppliers, and transport companies all benefited from increased northern activities.

The oil boom came after 1947—a smaller replica of the effects of the Texas and Oklahoma discoveries early in the century. First the Leduc field was discovered south of the city, then the Redwater field to the northeast, and later the vast Pembina field west of Edmonton. Because petroleum reserves were greater than could be used in Alberta, the government authorized the building of pipelines to carry the petroleum—and later equally large amounts of natural gas—to urban markets in southern Ontario, the Upper Midwest, and the Canadian and American Pacific coasts. At the same time, petroleum refineries were built on the eastern edge of Edmonton and in other prairie cities; by 1972, however, the smaller refineries were closed, and processing was concentrated in Edmonton, which had over 90 percent of Alberta's refinery capacity. The beginnings of a petrochemical industry were also established at Edmonton, which has access to other raw materials such as sulfur and salt. This raw material base is therefore like that of the Gulf Coast of Texas; and like the latter, Edmonton lacks a large local market and it is far away from the chemical industries of the Canadian Heartland. Edmonton's other manufactures are mainly consumer goods for the local market, as are found in most large cities. For example, the city has a small steel mill, fed on local scrap, which produces a variety of metal goods for the petroleum and agricultural implement industries.

Alberta Resource Development

The discovery and development of petroleum and natural gas changed the base of Alberta's economy. Grain and livestock production are still important in the environmentally suitable

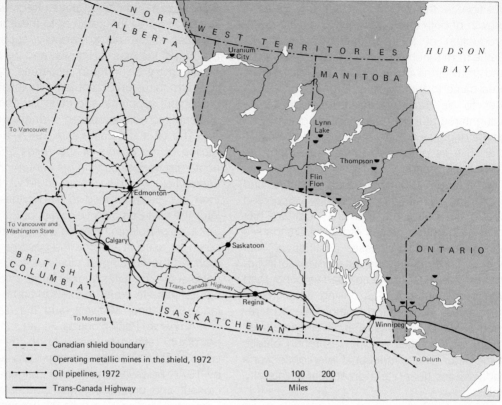

Figure 10.7 Mineral resources of the Prairie Provinces: Mining is modifying the agricultural economy of the Interior Plains of Canada. A variety of metallic mines are the basis of the main settlements in the old, hardrock area of the Shield in the northeast. A network of oil pipelines (plus natural gas pipelines not shown on the map) assembles petroleum from many oil fields for export outside of the region.

lands across the southern half of the province, but fuel resources have become equal in value of production. In the 1960s new oil and gas fields were found to the northwest—in the Swan Hills of Alberta, for example, and as far north as Fort Nelson on the Alaska Highway in northeastern British Columbia. In northeastern Alberta the Bituminous, or Tar, Sands have been known for a long time. Depending upon the extraction method, the petroleum reserves are estimated as 200 billion to 400 billion barrels—comparable to the world's known reserves of "liquid" petroleum (i.e., excluding other tar sands or oil shales). Production has been minor because of high extraction costs and a provincial quota system, but high demand for petroleum products in Anglo-America indicate that this huge reserve must be used in the near future. Throughout Alberta new revenues from petroleum brought a new level of prosperity to

many people ranging from farmers to businessmen. But whether the product is wheat, potash, or petroleum, the people of the Interior Plains remember that their prosperity depends on the external world economy.

Alberta has other natural resources, such as coal and forests, which are not seriously needed in Canada or the world at present. About half of Canada's bituminous coal reserves—an enormous 50 billion tons—underlays western Alberta, and another 25 billion tons are estimated to be under southern Saskatchewan. This coal is presently too far away, in terms of transport costs, to be used in the industries of southern Ontario, and locally it competes poorly with petroleum and natural gas. Coal production increased in the 1970s as a result of the efficiencies of long, unit coal trains which made some western Alberta fields competitive for export to Japan.

The agricultural base of Alberta's economy remains strong; the trend toward increased livestock production has accelerated. Wheat and other grains such as oats, barley, rapeseed, or flax are the usual crops. Rapeseed, for example, increased remarkably across the northern sections of farmland in Saskatchewan and Alberta in the early 1970s and ranked third in total acreage behind wheat and barley in the Prairie Provinces. On some farms the crops are grown for cash sale, but on other farms the large livestock barns indicate that the grains are eaten on the farm and livestock products are sold. There are some differences in the rural landscapes of southern Alberta compared with agriculture on the plains to the east. On the semiarid lands and in the foothills near the Rocky Mountains there are more cattle, and some sheep, ranches. Some of these grasslands are used for dry farming with narrow strips of wheat alternating with dark-brown strips of fallow; other areas are irrigated, looking from the air much like the irrigated lands northeast of Denver, Colorado. These irrigated farms, which total about 1 million acres, produce sugar beets, alfalfa, vegetables, and wheat. The growing city of Lethbridge (population 42,000) is the major supply and distribution center for the irrigation region. Lethbridge is also developing food-processing industries—a measure of the intensity of food production in its nearby hinterland.

BRITISH COLUMBIA

Most of Canada's westernmost province is occupied by the mountainous Cordillera which extends the length of western North America. In area, British Columbia is larger than California, Oregon, and Washington together. It is a land of spectacular mountain scenery: deep, narrow valleys; broad, forested interior plateaus; and an indented, fiorded coast. In population it is the extreme example of the urbanization which characterizes the rest of Canada. Less than 5 percent of the people of British Columbia live on farms; about 75 percent have homes in the southwestern corner, near the shores of Georgia Strait or on the long delta of the Fraser River. Greater Vancouver, with more than 1 million population, has 50 percent of the people of British Columbia. This coastal concentration and these urban characteristics are similar to those of the Pacific Coast states to the south.

Settlement

The Pacific Coast was explored by Spanish and British ship captains in the late eighteenth century. The interior of British Columbia was partly explored early in the nineteenth century and first settled from the east by fur traders who encouraged the interior Indians to trap. In 1843 the Hudson's Bay Company moved its Pacific headquarters north from the Columbia River in Oregon Territory to Victoria on Vancouver Island in expectation of a northward relocation of the United States boundary. Until 1858 the area which was to become British Columbia remained part of the vast fur empire of the Hudson's Bay Company. Then alluvial gold was discovered in the riverbed gravels of the Fraser River. Victoria controlled water access to the Fraser River and became the port of entry and supply center for the interior gold fields. Its gateway function resembled that of San Francisco a decade earlier. By 1862 about 15,000 miners and associated service, commercial, and transport personnel were concentrated in or near Barkerville, about 400 miles inland from the mouth of the Fraser in the Cariboo Mountains. Barkerville, now a restored Historic Site "ghost town," was then the largest British settlement west of the Great Lakes.

Within a few years the gold rush was over, settlements declined, and the interior of British Columbia had very little development for several decades. Lumbering was started on the south coast, but the technology of the time was not adequate for handling the large trees. By 1871 the colony of British Columbia was in poor financial condition and agreed to join the newly formed Dominion of Canada in return for a promise to build a transcontinental railway to the West Coast. The new province was to wait rather impatiently for 15 years before the Canadian Pacific Railway built its thin line of steel across the rocky Canadian Shield, over the grassy plains, and through the twisting valleys of the Cordillera. The city of Vancouver was born in 1887 as its western terminal. Within 24 years, in the census of 1911, Canada's new, and only, western port had a population of 121,000. The port function of Vancouver, however, remained rather minor early in the century because Pacific trade was not well developed.[3]

The Natural Resource Base

The fundamental resource base of the West Coast economy was well established early in this century. The tall coniferous trees of the Coast Forest were gradually logged on the coastal lowlands and lower mountain slopes. The logs were towed to sawmills scattered around the shores of Georgia Strait—especially those on the east coast of Vancouver Island, in Vancouver, and along the channels of the Fraser Delta. The period of great forestry expansion came after World War I when the Panama Canal permitted British Columbia lumber to be exported by ship to Europe and the eastern United States. As transportation and logging technology improved, lumbering extended northward along the coast, but the processing remained in the southwestern cities where there was reliable transport to foreign markets.

Fish canneries began operations at the mouth of the Fraser River, and at other coastal

[3] J. Lewis Robinson and Walter G. Hardwick, *British Columbia: 100 Years of Geographical Change*, Talonbooks, Vancouver, 1973, 63 pp.

rivers, where the salmon collected in late summer en route to interior spawning grounds. Farms were cleared on the fertile alluvial soils of the Fraser Delta and to a lesser extent on the lowland of eastern Vancouver Island. Most of the population was clustered around Georgia Strait, in the southwestern corner, and only a few logging camps and fish canneries dotted the central and northern coast.

Prior to 1940 settlement remained sparse in interior British Columbia, and the northern half of the province was virtually unoccupied. A mining boom of 1890–1910 brought transport lines to mines and smelters in the Kootenay region of southeastern British Columbia; the expansion of irrigation in the Okanagan Valley in the 1920s resulted in the only strip of agricultural settlement in the southern interior. British Columbia was not an agricultural province. Its people were urban—whether "urban" meant logging camps, fish canneries, or mining towns; and the commercial control of these raw materials and their transport to foreign markets centered in Vancouver.

Metropolitan Vancouver

Vancouver's urban growth resembled that of Seattle and Los Angeles in that it was greater than was warranted by the moderate exploitation of its hinterland resources. The city itself became its own best market. People flocked to Vancouver for many of the same reasons that they moved across the United States to Pacific Coast cities. To the young and adventurous it was a "faraway" part of Canada where a new life could be started amid a magnificent physical setting; to the old, the mildest winters in Canada and cool summers were desirable for retirement. To businessmen and industrialists the untapped resources of forest, fish, land, minerals, and power awaited their capital and technology. Within about two decades Vancouver became Canada's third largest city in population.

An industrial belt spread along the railway which occupied the south shore of Burrard

The scenic attraction of Vancouver is enhanced by the Coast Mountains which rise to 4,000 feet north of the harbor. The high-rise office buildings of the commercial core are to the right of center, and high-rise apartment buildings bring a very high residential density to the "West End" adjoining the core. Compare with Figure 10.8. (Vancouver Tourist Bureau)

Inlet. In addition to the wharves for ocean vessels, harbor facilities included grain elevators, a sugar refinery, oil refineries, ship-repairing firms, chemical plants, and much warehousing. Sawmills gradually gave up the valuable harbor land and moved outside of Vancouver, principally along the Fraser River. The main commercial core of Vancouver grew up south of the rail terminal and harbor facilities (Figure 10.8). In the industrial expansion after World War II many of the assembly plants of eastern Canadian businesses, warehouses, and consumer goods plants located along an interior industrial zone which extended east into adjoining Burnaby. A third industrial belt, occupied mainly by sawmills and other wood-processing plants, spread along the south side of the city, on the Fraser River. Many of the resources of western Canada now flow through the various Metropolitan Vancouver ports on their way to world markets: grain and potash from the Prairie Provinces; coal from the Rocky Mountains; and ores, lumber, and pulp from interior British Columbia.

Vancouver has become a large-enough consuming market for secondary manufacturing to develop, and has some "protection" from eastern Canadian manufacturers as a result of transport costs from the east. New industry is locating outside of Vancouver itself, whereas the city is increasing its commercial, business, and service functions. The companies which operate the resource developments throughout the province have their head offices in Vancouver. Tall new office buildings of "black" glass rise in downtown Vancouver and are similar to office towers in Toronto and Montreal. Few natural resources of British Columbia now come to Vancouver for processing,

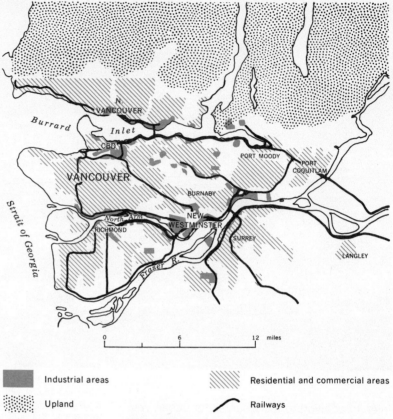

| Industrial areas | | Residential and commercial areas |
| Upland | | Railways |

Figure 10.8   Metropolitan Vancouver. The original site of the city was on the south side of Burrard Inlet, east of the protected, narrow entrance to the inner harbor. The present city has spread southward over the delta islands and lowlands of the Fraser River.

but the financial control of these industries is probably in Vancouver's CBD (Figure 10.9).

The separate cities of North and West Vancouver, on the north shore of Burrard Inlet, were mainly residential. They were connected by ferry to the Vancouver commercial core until 1938 when a bridge was built across the entrance to the inner harbor. The parallel with the building of a bridge across the San Francisco harbor can be drawn. Residences then spread rapidly up the lower slopes of the North Shore mountains. The same type of harbor facilities and industries as found on the Vancouver side spread to the North Vancouver waterfront.

Postwar suburban expansion also spread south of the Fraser River; prosperous dairy farms on the Fraser Delta were subdivided into residential plots. By the 1970s much of the western end of the Fraser Delta had been con-

verted into miles of middle-class housing and suburban shopping areas; very little agricultural land remains between Vancouver and the United States border.

The lands around the Georgia Strait of southwestern British Columbia form an integrated, functional region similar to the urban complexes at the southeastern end of Puget Sound or around San Francisco Bay. Hourly ferry service between Victoria and Vancouver and between Vancouver and Nanaimo moves people and products continuously. Barges full of pulpwood chips from the Fraser River lumber mills dot the strait as they move toward nearby pulp and paper mills. Ships may call at several of the ports around the strait in assembling a mixed cargo. Dairy products and vegetables from lower Fraser Valley farms feed Victoria as well as the several cities of metropolitan Vancouver.

Victoria

Although the capital of the province and the main port of entry prior to 1890, Victoria was separated from the resource developments on the mainland and lost its dominance to the rail terminal of Vancouver. The city is mainly an administrative center; government occupations, both provincial and federal, are the chief nonmanufacturing employment (the metropolitan population was 200,000 in 1971). Local industries are concerned with wood processing and shipbuilding. Victoria and the small towns north of it on Vancouver Island are still popular places for Canadians' retirement because of the mild climate. The city attempts to maintain some sections of its urban landscape as ''a little bit of olde [*sic*] England,'' an attraction for American tourists.

The West Coast

North of the Georgia Strait urban and industrial region, the coast is sparsely occupied. Spectacular views are presented to tourists on the coastal steamers—high mountains of 8,000 to 12,000 feet rising steeply above densely forested lower slopes to snowcapped peaks; an indented, fiorded, island-fringed coast of everchanging landscapes. In winter, however, the rain comes down almost continuously and heavy clouds block out the mountain views.

This west coast is part of the resources hinterland of the Georgia Strait region; products flow toward the industrial cities. All the fish canneries along the central coast are now closed because modern fish-packing vessels carry the salmon, caught off river mouths, directly to large canneries at Prince Rupert or near Vancouver, where export transportation is available. Although logging camps still dot the coast, the huge logs are transported by modern self-dumping log barges or flat log booms to the processing plants around Georgia Strait. The pulp and paper industry of British Columbia was entirely coastal prior to 1960. There it was integrated into the lumber industry; pulp mills often adjoined large lumber and plywood mills, using waste wood from the sawmills and smaller logs not suitable for plywood. Mining revived on Vancouver Island and on the Queen Charlotte Islands in the 1950s. However, the small copper and iron deposits have little direct effect upon British Columbia industry since the concentrates are shipped directly to Japan.

Two ports, Prince Rupert (16,000 population) and Kitimat (12,000), provide urban services for the northern coast, near the Alaska Panhandle. Prince Rupert was created prior to

VALUE ADDED BY MANUFACTURING — **BRITISH COLUMBIA**

% Distribution — Location quotients: 1.0 = national average per capita

Employ-ment	Value added	SIC source	0	1.0	2.0	3.0	4.0	5.0
1.2	1.4	Food products						
N.A.	N.A.	Tobacco products						
.9	0.8	Textiles						
2.0	0.9	Apparel						5.3
37.8	31.6	Lumber						
1.9	1.6	Furniture						
12.3	19.4	Paper products						
3.4	4.5	Printing						
1.8	3.5	Chemicals						
N.A.	N.A.	Petro-coal products						
N.A.	N.A.	Rubber-plastic						
.2	0.2	Leather						
2.2	3.0	Stone-clay-glass						
6.3	8.8	Primary metals						
6.2	7.0	Fabricated metals						
2.2	2.9	Machinery						
1.6	1.9	Electrical machinery						
4.3	5.9	Transport equipment						
1.7	2.2	Instruments						
100.0	100.0	All categories						

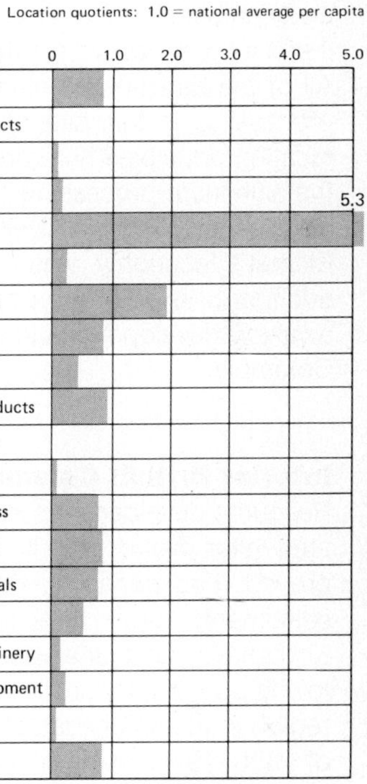

Totals do not add to 100 percent because of rounding off and omission of several minor industries.

Figure 10.9 Compare this chart with Figure 9.8 and account for the major differences. Also compare it with the following American charts: Figures 8.6, 6.7, and 6.14.

World War I as a planned town; as the northwestern terminal of the Canadian National Railway it was expected to compete with Vancouver for the Pacific trade. Its growth did not materialize; the city did not have a developing resource hinterland nor the advantages of the established services of the Georgia Strait region. Although Prince Rupert was closer to the ports of east Asia, most of British Columbia trade prior to 1940 was southward and via the Panama Canal to the North Atlantic region. Prince Rupert has fish canneries and freezing plants and a cellulose mill—and hopes that its port may yet become a "doorway to the Orient" as trans-Pacific trade increases.

Kitimat is another modern planned city. In the early 1950s an imaginative power project dammed the interior Nechako River, and led the water through a long tunnel under the Coast Mountains to a huge power plant carved into the rock base of the mountains. Fifty miles away an aluminum smelter was built, and near it arose the attractive residential city of Kitimat. All of the bauxite and alumina is imported for processing at this site of cheap power. The location principles here are similar to those of the aluminum-processing plants in Washington State using Columbia River power. In the 1970s Kitimat's economy was broadened with the addition of a pulp and paper mill—part of the awaking developments in northwestern British Columbia.

Interior British Columbia

Resource developments in the interior accelerated after World War II, encouraged by improved road transport. Prior to 1940 interior settlements were in three separate pockets: the Kootenays, Okanagan Valley, and dispersed towns on the Interior Plateau. In the Kootenay region in the southeast, after the mining boom of 1890–1910, many of the mines closed, but the large ore body at Kimberley remained as Canada's major producer of lead, zinc, and silver. The ore is smelted and refined 150 miles away at Trail, on the Columbia River near the

United States border. As the only metals refinery in western Canada, Trail processes the ores of southeastern British Columbia and also those from as far away as Keno Hill in the Yukon and Pine Point in the Northwest Territories. Forestry, aided by two new pulp and paper mills, broadened the economy of the Kootenay region in the 1960s.

Agricultural settlement is scanty in the narrow and dry valleys of the southern interior. British settlers started irrigation prior to 1914 on the narrow terraces of the northern Okanagan Valley and apples did well; the irrigated acreage spread southward in the interwar period. The Okanagan Valley is now the leading apple producer of Canada, supplying the western Canadian market and having a surplus for export. The orchards also produce cherries, peaches, pears, plums, and Canada's only apricots. This irrigated orchard region competes in Canada with the Niagara Peninsula of Ontario and is similar to the Wenatchee-Yakima fruit area nearby in interior Washington State.

The Interior Plateau of central British Columbia is well forested. Because the valuable Douglas fir of the Coast Forest was in danger of depletion, the forest was put under government-regulated cutting after World War II; lumbermen then turned to the under-used interior forests in the 1950s. Exploitation was aided by the provincially owned British Columbia Railway running from North Vancouver through Prince George, with extensions into northeastern and north central British Columbia. By the early 1960s the interior forests were supplying almost half of the lumber cut in British Columbia. Pulp and paper mills at Kamloops, Quesnel, and Prince George, for example, have increased the value of interior forestry production. Functional and corporate integration took place in the interior forest industry during the 1960s, similar to that which developed on the coast earlier, resulting in more efficient use of wood resources.

A great deal of water is unused in British Columbia. Clear water is a valuable commodity

Producing Mines

Pulp and Paper Mills

Planned Pulp and Paper Mills

Figure 10.10 Mines and pulp and paper mills in British Columbia. Mines are concentrated in three zones—in the southeast near the Trail smelter, near the few transport lines of the central interior, and along the coast for export (mainly) to Japan. All pulp and paper mills were located on the coast until 1962, but by 1966 the interior forests were being used for pulp (as well as lumber).

and the Canadian Cordillera has a surplus. Prior to 1940 the major hydropower developments were on the short coastal rivers in the southwest, to supply industries and other urban uses in metropolitan Vancouver; the main interior power plants were on tributaries of the Columbia River chiefly for the large Trail smelter and refinery. The mighty Fraser River, an enormous potential source of power, remained unharnessed because the provincial

government wanted no interference with the valuable salmon runs of the Fraser River Basin.

By the 1970s two power projects were completed in the interior to meet the expected

This dry interior Okanagan valley in south central British Columbia extends southward across the international border. On both sides of the border, irrigation has changed the landscape into one of intensive orcharding. Apricots are produced on the Canadian side of the valley—although this area is near the northern climatic limits for this fruit—because they cannot be grown elsewhere in Canada. Southward, in the United States part of this valley, apricots are not grown because they yield better in California. (British Columbia Government)

demands for electric power in British Columbia and to produce a surplus for the adjoining northwestern states. The Columbia River was already well developed for power production in the United States, but one-third of the river's volume came from its headwaters in Canada. In order to use this water more efficiently, three flood-control dams were built in Canada to control the water going through the power plants downstream in the United States. This is an example of international cooperation in the use of needed power resources.

Believing that the Columbia River power would not be sufficient for future needs, the provincial government built another major power dam on the Peace River, where it tumbled eastward out of the Rocky Mountains. Electric power should therefore be ample in northwestern Anglo-America for any industrial expansion in the next decade, and can be supplemented by thermal or nuclear power if needed.

Summary In the Canadian West the level lands and rural economy of the Interior Plains contrast with the rugged, forested landscapes and urban centers of the Cordillera. In both regions changes are occurring in the areal distribution of economic activities. Diversification is apparent on the Canadian prairies; although grains and cattle are still important, resource-oriented and urban activities are also increasing. In British Columbia metropolitan Vancouver still dominates the economy, but resource developments are increasing in the interior. With 6 million people in an area of about 1 million square miles, western Canada has a small and dispersed local market. Its manufactures are still small in volume and value, particularly when compared with those of Ontario, and are concerned mainly with partial processing of local natural resources. Throughout the Canadian West the people and their occupations are maintained greatly through the export of surplus raw materials; wheat, other grains, cattle, petroleum, natural gas, and potash flow out of the prairies; lumber, plywood, pulp and paper, apples, fish, coal, and several metallic ores are exported from the Cordillera.

As in eastern Canada, only a small part of the four western provinces is effectively occupied. Similar to north central Quebec and northwestern Ontario, many thousands of square miles of the northern Prairie Provinces and British Columbia have no land transport and virtually no resident people. Despite the increasing population of Anglo-America, and the world, it is doubtful if these northern areas will ever be well populated. Their potential value as agricultural land is not related so much to the hazards of the natural environment—and there are many—as to the Anglo-American surplus of better land closer to markets. Their mineral and forest resources are now in demand elsewhere, but the small dots on the map representing urban people in these exploitive occupations are minor concentrations amid the vast wilderness.

THE NORTHLANDS

The northern quarter of Anglo-America differs from the lands to the south in many ways. Its vast spaces are almost empty of population, and its known natural resources either are scanty or cannot compete with similar resources located closer to markets. In the Northlands there seem to be few resources to attract large groups of people into a variety of occupations, and the problem of cold is one which discourages many people. Only a few

thousand pioneers have ventured into the region to try to win a livelihood from the natural environment. Whereas one must learn about the process of settlement in the rest of Anglo-America by reading textbooks, one can read about the present northern pioneers in our newspapers and popular periodicals and get some idea of the difficulties faced by our forefathers a century or more ago.

For about two centuries Anglo-Americans have been moving west across the continent; a number of phrases, such as "Go west, young man" or "Westward the course of Empire," illustrate these themes in the settlement history of the United States. The same westward movement filled in the agricultural lands of western Canada in the early part of this century. After World War II some Canadians tried to create a northern image with slogans such as "Canada's destiny is in the North" and "Canada is a northern nation." Despite a definite increase in the number of people moving into the two northern territories, the northern flow is but a trickle compared with the people that are concentrating into southern Canadian cities; and recent northern resource development is really minor compared with developments in the "Near North" or "middle Canada." The Yukon Territory, for example, increased in population from 5,000 in 1941 to 19,000 in 1971. This impressive *percentage* increase does indicate that something is happening in the north—but the total numerical increase of about 14,000 people in 30 years is less than the *annual* increase in population in a large Canadian city.

The Northlands cover a large area. The Canadian Northland—the Yukon and the Northwest Territories—plus Greenland totals about 2,300,000 square miles; this area is three times the size of Mexico, four times the area of Quebec, or eight times that of Texas. In east-west extent, in the latitude of 60 to 65°, the region stretches about one-third of the way around the world. Distances are therefore great in the Northlands; one has to adopt new scales

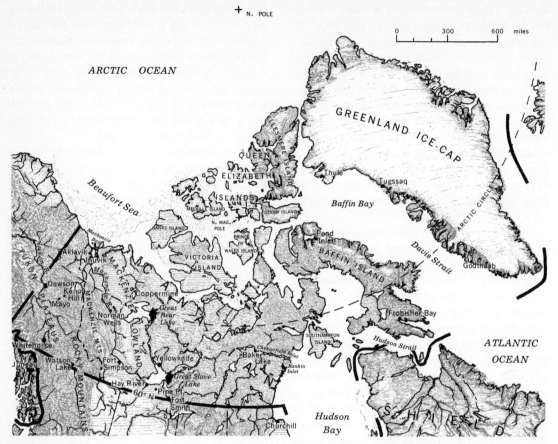

Figure 10.11 Landforms of northern Canada and Greenland. Yukon Territory is part of the complex mountains of the Cordillera; the Mackenzie Valley, which has the most resource development in the Northwest Territories, is a narrow strip west of the Canadian Shield. Only the edges of Greenland are not covered by a large icecap. (Base map copyright by A. K. Lobeck. Reprinted with permission of The Geographical Press, Hammond, Inc.)

of description and comparison, in contrast to the relatively small urban and farm areas discussed in preceding chapters.

Perception of the North

"North" is a relative term to Canadians, most of whom live in a narrow strip across the southern part of their country. To the people of Quebec and Ontario, north is the southern Canadian Shield; there the exciting resource expansion of the past 20 years has brought middle Canada into the functioning economy of eastern Canada (see Chapter 9). In the west, "northern" development means the northern parts of the provinces, and the phrase seldom refers to the Mackenzie River Valley or the valleys of the Yukon Territory. The Canadian

Northlands as defined here have two distinctly different subregions: the Subarctic northwest has most of the white population and some resource potential, whereas the Arctic northeast is the land of the Eskimo with few known natural resources.

As congestion and decreasing natural resources become apparent in the densely occupied parts of Anglo-America (and elsewhere in the world), one has to reassess the resource potential of these relatively empty northern lands. Can the Northlands offer opportunities to modern pioneers comparable to those offered by the Canadian West during the last century? Do the Northlands have a resource potential which will attract any significant exploitation and which will supply raw materials to the growing urban centers to the south? Can modern technology overcome major environmental handicaps? This assessment must look carefully at the physical environment which differs radically from the rest of the continent. The adaptations and adjustments which man has made in using his environment in settling Anglo-America have to be different in the north; the relationships between man and the natural environment are closer and more obvious than in urban-dominated southern Anglo-America.

Northern Physical Environment

In the enormous Yukon and Northwest Territories (1,512,000 square miles), one could expect a variety of physical environments. Baffin Island, for example, is larger than California or the Atlantic Megalopolis.

Landforms Northern landforms are continuations of major features in the structure of the rest of Anglo-America. The mountainous Cordillera extends through the Yukon Territory and arcs westward into Alaska; the Interior Plains narrow to the north where they become the Mackenzie Valley; the Canadian Shield broadens northward to the Arctic coast of mainland Canada—in fact, the ancient Precambrian rocks of the Shield extend into the northeastern islands such as Baffin and Ellesmere. The Arctic Islands, lying north of the mainland, have no topographic uniformity: the eastern islands are high and rugged, with long twisting fiords facing Davis Strait and Baffin Bay; in contrast some of the central islands are flat, lake-covered plains which have only recently (measured in geological time) risen from the sea, following the removal of the weight of the continental ice cap. The straits between the Arctic Islands are generally wide and most are deep; they are covered by sea ice for 9 to 11

NATURAL VEGETATION

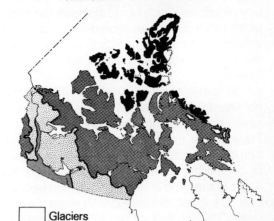

Glaciers

Rock desert

Tundra

Forest-tundra

Boreal forest

Figure 10.12 Natural vegetation of the Northwest Territories. The tundra region coincides closely with the area of Arctic climate. The northern sections of the Arctic area have virtually no vegetation and are classed as rock desert. (From *The Northwest Territories Today,* Ottawa, 1965.)

months of the year, however, and are then generally impassable for ship navigation.

Climate and vegetation There are major contrasts in climate and vegetation between the northwest and northeast. The Subarctic summers in the valleys of the northwest are warm; in contrast, the Arctic climate of the northeast has cool summers. July mean temperatures in the west central Yukon and the southern Mackenzie Valley average a little above 60°, and daily temperatures in July may sometimes rise into the 80s. As a result, coniferous forests have been able to grow during the warm summers in the northwest valleys and some hardy crops are raised for local food. Although the whole region experiences the long duration of early summer daylight in these northern latitudes, this does not necessarily mean warmth everywhere. Equal hours of daylight in southern Baffin Island and southern Greenland, for example, do not give the same warm temperatures as recorded in the same latitude of the southern Yukon. Other factors are involved, such as the temperatures of air masses.

In contrast to the modest warmth of some northwest valleys, average July mean temperatures in the Arctic northeast are less than 50°. Trees do not grow there, and normal agriculture is impossible. Owing partly to the presence of cold water in the channels between the Arctic Islands and in Hudson Bay, summers are cool. The Arctic climate extends along the east side of Hudson Bay as far as 600 miles *south* of the Arctic Circle. This wide southern penetration of the Arctic climate—and the resulting characteristics of scanty vegetation, negligible agricultural potential, and summer ice conditions—contrasts with the narrow strip of Arctic climate across the northern Soviet Union, and explains some of the differences in northern development between Canada and the Soviet Union. For 10 or 11 months of the year the northern Arctic Islands, joined together by ice, can be considered as one large "land" mass. Travel from island to island by dog team or modern tracked vehicles is therefore possible almost everywhere in winter. But the open season is a very short one for the less expensive water transport now used to supply weather stations or to investigate mineral possibilities.

Permafrost Another environmental hazard, called permafrost, is not experienced in southern Canada. When the continental ice cap covered northern Canada, the land and rock beneath it became permanently frozen to depths of at least several hundred feet. Most of this ice cap melted away 6,000 to 8,000 years ago, but a large remnant still occupies most of Greenland. During the summer, when daily temperatures are above 32° nearly everywhere in the north, the land thaws to a depth of only a few inches or a few feet. If the surface consists of unconsolidated materials, the land may become a soggy, spongy mass over which

travel by foot or by wheeled vehicles becomes almost impossible. Because there is very little underground drainage into the frozen material during the summer, water collects on the surface forming innumerable irregular-shaped lakes, swamps, or muskegs. Overland travel is therefore much easier during the winter on a frozen surface. The designing of suitable foundations for buildings erected in Arctic areas with permafrost is a serious construction problem in the Northlands.

Exploration and Settlement

The northern parts of Anglo-America may have been the first sections to be inhabited. It is likely that Asiatic peoples—the prehistoric ancestors of American Indians—migrated across the Bering Strait to Alaska many thousand years ago. Archaeologists have yet to discover enough signs to prove the exact times and routes which these people followed—they probably came through the valleys of the Yukon Territory or along the southern Alaskan coast—to reach the central parts of the continent. The Eskimo were likely a later wave of migrants; they probably moved along the northern Alaskan coast in search of land game and sea mammals about 3,000 to 5,000 years ago. Eskimos spread thinly across Arctic Canada and reached western Greenland about A.D. 1000—about the same time that the Norse were "discovering" North America for Europeans.

The exploration of the Northlands holds a place of interest in Canadian history similar to the exploration of the West in American history. Early exploration by Europeans was part of the futile search for a Northwest Passage—a water route through Anglo-America to east Asia. The eastern Arctic was entered from the North Atlantic during the sixteenth and seventeenth centuries. These voyages during the brief summers charted many of the Arctic Islands and the shores of Hudson Bay; the sea captains reported on the unfavorable ice conditions and the barren landscapes. The interior rivers were explored as part of the search for new fur-trapping areas; the Mackenzie Valley was occupied in the early 1800s by a string of fur-trading posts along the river. Fur traders did not penetrate into the less accessible Yukon valleys, however, until the middle of the nineteenth century. The fur trade was essentially the only resource utilization in the northwest during the nineteenth century. Because fur-bearing animals lived in the northwestern forests and were scanty in the treeless northeast, the latter region had few European settlements until early in the twentieth century.

Minerals "opened" the Northlands in this century. The story of the gold rush of 1898 to the Klondike area of the Yukon Territory has been told many times—and over the decades facts and colorful inaccuracies have become intermixed! Because many Americans took part in the Yukon gold rush, departing from Seattle and San Francisco, many Americans believed then that the Yukon was politically part of Alaska. Canada had to bring the North West Mounted Police into the region to maintain control and sovereignty. The boom city of Dawson arose at the junction of the Yukon and Klondike rivers, and about 25,000 people were in the area by the turn of the century. A transportation system evolved which brought supplies and equipment to the miners and to the service and commercial establishments of Dawson. A narrow-gauge railway was built from Skagway through the mountain passes to Whitehorse where there were rapids in the Yukon River. North of Whitehorse large flat-bottomed, paddle-wheeled river steamers carried freight and passengers downstream to Dawson. For about 40 years after 1900 the economy of the Yukon evolved about three small towns, and their water transportation links in the Yukon River Basin. During this time the Yukon lapsed into economic stagnation and its population decreased to less than 5,000 persons.

Mining awakened the Mackenzie Valley of the Northwest Territories in the 1930s. Pitch-blende, a source of valuable radium and later of uranium, was discovered on the eastern shores of Great Bear Lake, and gold was found on the northeast side of Great Slave Lake. Petroleum reserves, which had been known previously, were then brought into production to supply these northern mines. These same petroleum resources became of strategic value during World War II when they were the only nearby source of petroleum products for military bases in Alaska. During this war the engineering feat of carving the Alaska Highway through the little-known northwestern area brought this vast region more directly into the expanding economy of Anglo-America.

World War II also brought Europeans into the Canadian Arctic in large numbers for the first time. Airfields were constructed across the short polar route through northeastern Canada and Greenland; weather stations dispersed through the Arctic Islands warned flyers of the movement of the air masses which originated there. Americans entered the Canadian Arctic in significant numbers during the cold war of the 1950s when the United States received permission from Canada to construct three lines of radar stations across Canada. The most northern of these, the DEW (Distant Early Warning) line, extended along the Alaskan coast and the mainland coast of Arctic Canada in about latitude 65°. After 1950 Canadian government personnel became more numerous in hospitals, schools, and welfare offices; government research employees such as meteorologists and transport specialists also came north. Most of these southern Canadians stayed for only a few years and then were returned by their employers to southern positions.

The Eskimo

The impact of this externally stimulated activity upon the native Eskimo was obvious. For centuries these few thousand people lived an almost primitive life of hunting, in which the close adjustments between man and his environment changed with the seasons. Starvation was undoubtedly frequent when caribou failed to appear or seals were scarce; there were few other resources of the land or sea upon which the Eskimo could depend for a living. This close relationship of the Eskimo to his environment is described in numerous elementary school textbooks, often as a happy example of a primitive economy. Although there were happy and peaceful moments for a people ignorant of the problems of the rest of the world, theirs was in reality a hard life. The fact that 1 million square miles of Canadian Arctic supported only about 9,000 Eskimos in 1940 suggests how the scarcity of food had prevented a numerical increase. The one exploited resource of the region was the trapping of white foxes.

After 1940 the construction activity related to air bases, weather stations, and social facilities gave wider employment opportunities to the Eskimo. Although the external demand for white foxes declined, this was balanced by increased markets for Eskimo handicrafts such as carvings and paintings. These latter activities, mostly initiated by the white man from "outside," were established in particular places, and thus the Eskimo moved to these centers of economic and government activity. Their migratory way of life, using skin tents in summer and snow houses in winter, rapidly disappeared and was replaced by "urban" living in wooden houses imported in precut form from the south (photo, p. 336). On a much smaller scale, therefore, the migration of "rural" people to urban places is taking place in the Canadian Arctic as it is in other parts of Anglo-America. And for the Eskimo, the problems of adjusting to a harsh natural environment (not unlike the adjustments which farming peoples made to their environments in the last century) are being replaced by new social problems, similar to the problems of urban people in the rest of Anglo-America.

Territorial Economies

Yukon Territory   Mining has been the major primary occupation of people in the Yukon throughout this century, and transportation is the other main source of employment. The wartime building of the Alaska Highway across the unoccupied southern Yukon opened up a new transport route. Whitehorse was sited at the junction of this new east-west route and the old north-south river route; it became the gateway to the Yukon and the transport, commercial, and service center for the Territory. The territorial capital was moved in the mid-1950s from Dawson to Whitehorse. Similar to the population distribution patterns in southern Canada, about 65 percent of the people of the Yukon live in Whitehorse and its suburbs (population 12,000). This example of Whitehorse indicates that urban concentration is occurring, on a much smaller scale, in the north as in other parts of Anglo-America.

Except for minerals, the other natural resources of the Yukon are in little demand in Canada or in the world. Although thousands of arable acres in narrow strips in the river valleys could produce feed-grains or pasture, there is very little present agricultural production; more food was produced locally at the turn of the century than in the 1970s. Forests grow on the lower slopes of the valleys, but only a few small sawmills operate for the local market; the scattered and marginal forest resource cannot compete with the larger and better-located trees southward in British Columbia. Fur resources supported the few thousand Indians in the quiet period of 1910–1940, but the value of the Yukon fur catch is now less than 1 percent of the average annual value of Canadian fur production. One of the potential resources of the Yukon is its "unspoiled" natural environment; as transportation improves, thousands of visitors are bringing income into the Territory and take back nothing more than the satisfaction of seeing lakes, mountains, forests, and historic sites.

The development of mineral resources has both caused and been the result of changes in transportation patterns and facilities. After about 1950 the Canadian government built new roads in the Yukon, feeding traffic toward Whitehorse and to the Alaska Highway leading

DISTRIBUTION OF POPULATION BY COMMUNITIES OF 50 PERSONS AND OVER

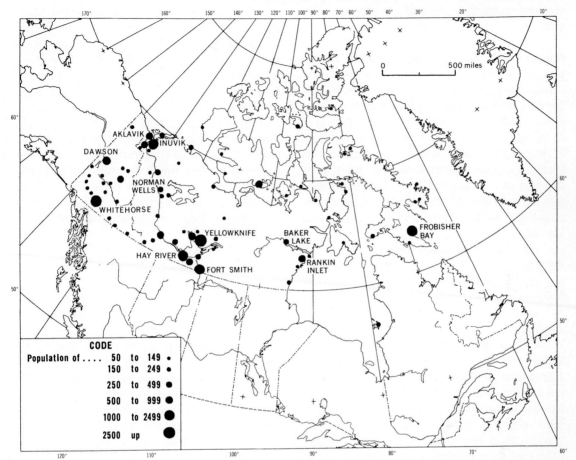

Figure 10.13 Population distribution in the Northwest Territories. The largest settlements are in the Mackenzie Valley, particularly around Great Slave Lake. Nearly all Arctic settlements are coastal, and large areas of the interior are unoccupied for most of the year. Why was there a large settlement at Frobisher Bay? (From *The Northwest Territories Today,* Ottawa, 1965.)

to Edmonton. The river steamers ceased operations when they could no longer compete with road and air traffic. The alluvial gold of the Klondike was depleted by 1966, but Dawson residents have attempted to keep the town alive by attracting tourists to the scene of the Klondike gold rush. The ores from the lead-zinc-silver mine at Keno Hill and the asbestos from Clinton Creek, west of Dawson, are taken out by truck. In the southeastern Yukon, base metal discoveries resulted in the planned town of Faro, created to house the miners and their families; it is similar to other new mining towns in the Canadian Shield. Because there are no

smelters in the Territory or nearby, all concentrates are shipped out of the region.

Just as the 1900 economy was functionally linked by water transport, so the mining development of the 1970s is functionally connected by roads. The present economy of the Yukon, as in the past, is dependent on external markets for its future development. The Canadian government and mining companies have two questions when considering the future:

Can Yukon minerals compete with those more accessible to world markets? Should the government subsidize mineral development in order to maintain northern settlement?

Mackenzie Valley, Northwest Territories Although the economy of the Mackenzie Valley is much like that of the Yukon Territory, the physical character of the valley is much different. Whereas the Yukon River and its tributaries cut down into a plateau and flow in deep valleys with gentle upper slopes, the Mackenzie River is entrenched into the glacial deposits of a broad, flat plain. Between these two main valleys of northwestern Canada lie about 300 miles of the rugged, inaccessible Mackenzie Mountains.

For about 130 years after exploration in the late eighteenth century the fur trade was the only resource-oriented activity along the Mackenzie River. The trading posts were linked by water transport using paddle-wheeled steamers.

Mineral resources brought the Mackenzie Valley into the Canadian economy in the 1930s. The pitchblende ores from Great Bear Lake were the source of uranium for the world's first atom bombs. This mine closed in 1961 when its reserves were depleted. The gold mines at Yellowknife on Great Slave Lake produced more ounces of gold per ton of ore than any other gold mine in Canada; this high quality balanced the high transport costs of supplies and equipment. The third mineral to be developed was petroleum; but exploration at Norman Wells proved that the oil field was a small one. The hopes that large oil deposits like those of the Interior Plains of Alberta or the Prudhoe Bay field of Arctic Alaska would also be found in the northern Mackenzie Valley had not been fulfilled by the mid-1970s. Much of the local flurry of activity in the 1970s was the result of proposals to build an oil and/or natural gas pipeline along the Mackenzie Valley. A side effect of this proposal was an increase in northern research because of the lack of basic environmental information upon which to base route and construction decisions.

The basic mining economy of the Mackenzie Valley changed little during the period 1935–1970. During this time there was more talk than action in Canada about developing minerals on the "northern frontier"; persons writing in comfort in southern Canadian cities exhorted others to move northward! The European (nonnative) population of the Mackenzie Valley increased from about 4,000 in 1941 to about 21,000 in 1971, comparable to the same increase for the Yukon Territory noted previously. The only large new mine that opened in the mid-1960s produced high-quality lead-zinc at Pine Point on the south side of Great Slave Lake. This mine brought the first railroad into the Northwest Territories in 1966 in order to transport the concentrates to faraway Trail, British Columbia.

The other natural resources of the Mackenzie Valley are like those of the Yukon in their paucity, except for fish in Great Slave Lake. The cold and clear water of this large lake yields high-quality lake trout and whitefish which are transported by refrigerated trucks or railway from Hay River to markets in the American Midwest. Fur resources are scarce and are harvested mainly by the scanty Indian population. Trees are small, but a little lumber is cut for local construction. The land and climate permit the growing of hardy grain crops and vegetables, but local demand is small.

The transportation system of the Mackenzie Valley has not changed as completely as that of the Yukon. A road network has not yet evolved. The first road into the Northwest Territories, started in the late 1940s to Hay River on the south side of Great Slave Lake, was extended to Yellowknife about 1960, decreasing the cost of importing food and supplies to this largest town in the Territories. Otherwise, the small settlements along the Mackenzie River, and the planned town of Inuvik on the east side of the Mackenzie Delta, are serviced by aircraft or by small diesel tugs pushing shallow-draft barges.

Yellowknife is a modern city arising amid the low, rocky hills of the Canadian Shield, on the shores of Great Slave Lake. Modern bungalows and apartment houses ring the central core which has government offices and businesses. One of the gold mines lies at a distance to the center. (Northwest Territories Tourist Service)

Yellowknife, the service-supply center for a few gold mines, had about 7,000 residents in 1971. In 1967 its functions were expanded when it was chosen as the first capital of the Northwest Territories. Unlike Whitehorse in the Yukon, Yellowknife has no crossroads position in the Mackenzie Valley, nor is it a supply center for a growing mining hinterland. But within a few years of becoming the territorial capital, the town had a high-rise apartment building, a multistory office building, and a modern hotel—an indication that the government bureaucracy formerly in Ottawa was being transplanted northward in comfort!

The Arctic mainland and the Arctic Islands The northeastern and northern parts of the Northwest Territories do not have the resource potential nor even the small-scale economic development of the Canadian Northwest. The northern tree line, which can be used as the boundary between the Arctic and Subarctic climates, is also a cultural line; Indians live south of this line and Eskimo north of it.

The treeless Arctic land of the Eskimo has few natural resources—either for the local population or for the external market. It is now apparent that even the scanty game resources on the land or in the sea cannot support the Northwest Territories Eskimo population of 10,000 (plus 3,700 Eskimo in Arctic Quebec).

Rankin Inlet, an Eskimo settlement on the west side of Hudson Bay. These prefabricated houses are brought in from southern Canada and placed on piles above the permanently frozen ground. The Eskimos who live here are employed mainly in the production of handicrafts. (Photo by Michel Bouchard, Department of Northern Affairs, Ottawa)

Normal agriculture is not possible—due as much to lack of soils as to the cool summer climate. Fish are scarce in the enormous area of Hudson Bay, but a few thousand Arctic char (a type of salmon) are exported as a ''luxury crop'' from some Arctic rivers. The introduction of guns several decades ago resulted in the rapid depletion of the caribou on the mainland, and these animals were never plentiful on the Arctic Islands. Similarly, walrus and musk oxen were almost exterminated in the Arctic, although they are now legally protected. The widespread killing of seals in the international waters of the northwest Atlantic has adversely affected this important food resource of the Canadian Eskimo.

As in the Northwest, mineral resources are the hope for the future economic development of the Arctic. The ancient Precambrian rocks extend northward through Baffin Island; scattered mineralization has been reported, the richest find being a large iron deposit inland on northern Baffin Island. The short ice-free season there of about three months increases costs of production in comparison with iron ore fields elsewhere. The Arctic sections of the Canadian Shield west of Hudson Bay have not been thoroughly prospected, but areas of volcanic rocks, similar to those of the mineralized southern Shield, have been mapped by government geologists. The younger sedimentary rocks of the northwestern Arctic Islands may contain petroleum, and it is known that there are large quantities of natural gas; transport to outside markets would seem to demand new techniques and ingenuity.

Although modern technology could employ under-ice submarines, powerful icebreakers, and even enclosed giant domes to house workers, the problems of ice and cold are just as real to modern northern pioneers, businessmen, or adventurers as they were to the sea captains and explorers in their tiny ships of the nineteenth century. The natural environment simply has little to offer in the way of potential natural resources; modern technology may be able to benefit more people by expending its energies in more southern regions. Perhaps the Arctic landscape may some day be of more value to Anglo-Americans for its characteristic of being "unoccupied."

Greenland

After 1953 the former Danish colony of Greenland became an integral part of Denmark. Its military, commercial, and political relations with Anglo-America are so close, however, that it can be considered as a part of it. Most of its 50,000 inhabitants are descended from Eskimo who migrated there from the Canadian Arctic in the eighth to tenth centuries. Danes, who were not allowed to move freely to Greenland until 1951, now number about 2,000. Americans have permission from the Danish government to occupy the large air base and Arctic research station at Thule in northwestern Greenland.

Greenland was so named to attract settlers who might have been repelled had its name more accurately described the ice-covered island. Greenland is geologically similar to the Canadian Shield, and its high coastal mountains look like nearby Baffin Island. Its interior is covered with an ice cap estimated to be 6,000 to 10,000 feet thick, and occupying about nine-tenths of the island's area. The ice-free land, mainly a strip along the southwest, has tundra vegetation with predominantly North American plants.

Most Greenlanders live in the more favorable environment of the southwest coast where Godthaab, the capital, and other small fishing villages are located. This coast is often ice-free throughout the winter because of a warm ocean current from the North Atlantic; thus water transport is possible most of the year in contrast to the short navigation season off Baffin Island on the opposite side of Davis Strait. Some of the villages at the heads of fiords have some level land and arable soil where it is possible to raise vegetables; sheep are kept on the rough pastures. Most Greenlanders are now engaged in fishing and use modern fishing vessels along the southwest coast and in the Atlantic south of Greenland. One of the few industries is the packing of seafood for export.

Like other Arctic areas, Greenland is highly subsidized by Denmark; its deficit increased in recent decades as a result of attempts to modernize the economy and government. With a scattered and small population it seems unlikely that Greenlanders themselves can pay for these modern facilities. Imports, largely from Denmark, greatly exceed exports. The latter include cryolite and fish products, both shipped mainly to the United States. Lead, zinc, and coal have been mined from time to time, but mining is economically marginal. In Greenland, as in the Canadian North and Alaska, the federal government puts more money into the north than it receives back in revenues or taxes. This investment may be for political or military reasons; for the purpose of extending the "occupied" area of the country; or for humanitarian reasons of improving the social conditions of the native people. These are costs which the peoples in the southern parts of the three nations seem willing to pay.

Summary

The number of Northlands people who benefit from the investment of southern capital is small. One can ask whether this same amount of investment in the settled areas of Canada or the United States would not benefit more people. Would it, for example, be more economical to recover more scrap metal from within our cities than to try to mine iron ore on northern Baffin Island? Even if we do find future demands for the scanty resources of the North-lands, few people need live there to extract the raw materials to be consumed by southern industries. And what is our social responsibility to these sparsely settled parts of the world? This question must be faced by residents of the densely populated parts of Anglo-America at local, regional, national, and international scales.

Perhaps our urban society will soon need these "empty" places. Just as the Appalach-ians provide recreation for the Atlantic Mega-lopolis, and the desert and mountains relieve the congestion pressures of California urban-ites, and the lakes and forests of the Shield attract the people of Montreal and Toronto, so may the Northlands be a welcome change of environment for urban residents of Canada and the adjoining United States. Area and space in themselves will become a resource in demand from the future crowded residents of Anglo-American cities. A different environment—no matter how harsh or unattractive for permanent settlement—will provide an appealing change and a place to visit. If Ellesmere or Melville islands ever become crowded with visitors, then the geographical patterns of Anglo-America will be different than they are now!

SELECTED REFERENCES

Current geographical articles appear in the following periodicals: the *Canadian Geographer* and the *Canadian Geographical Journal.* Articles by geographers on Quebec (about two-thirds of them in French) appear in the *Cahiers* of Laval University and the *Revue* of the University of Montreal.

Atlas of the Northwest Territories, Canada, prepared for the Advisory Commission on Government, Ottawa, 1966.

BAIRD, PATRICK D.: *The Polar World,* Wiley, New York, 1964.

British Columbia Geographical Series: An annual periodical, starting in 1960, of geographical articles about British Columbia. Published by Department of Geography, University of British Columbia, Vancouver, for the British Columbia Division, Canadian Association of Geographers.

CHAPMAN, JOHN D., and A. L. FARLEY (eds.): *Atlas of British Columbia Resources,* British Columbia Natural Resources Conference, Victoria, 1956.

Geographical Branch, Department of Energy, Mines and Resources, Ottawa, has published a number of geographical memoirs on particular Arctic areas, such as: *Mackenzie Delta, Southampton Island, Bathurst Inlet, Queen Elizabeth Islands.*

HARDY, W. G. (ed.): *Alberta: A Natural History,* The Patrons, Edmonton, 1967. An engrossing, nontechnical account of the natural history of this vast and varied landlocked province complemented by a wealth of photographs, maps, and diagrams.

Information about local geographical studies and reports may be obtained from the Geography Departments at any of the Canadian universities. For example, there are regional geographical periodicals such as the *Albertan Geographer* and *B. C. Geographical Series.*

Information about northern Canada may be obtained from the Department of Northern Affairs in Ottawa, or by making specific requests to the territorial capitals in Whitehorse and Yellowknife. A large number of geographical booklets, many of them on northern Canada, were prepared by the former Geographical Branch in Ottawa; lists of these may be obtained from the Department of Energy, Mines and Resources, Ottawa.

MACDONALD, R. ST. J. (ed.): *The Arctic Frontier,* University of Toronto Press, Toronto, 1966.

MACKINTOSH, W. A., and W. L. G. JOERG (eds.): *Canadian Frontiers of Settlement,* in 9 vols.; note vol. 2, *History of Prairie Settlement and Dominion Lands Policy,* Macmillan, Toronto, 1938.

Many articles on northern Canada have been published in the *Canadian Geographical Journal,* Ottawa, and *The Beaver Magazine,* Hudson's Bay House, Winnipeg. A wide range of scientific reports are published in *Arctic,* issued by the Arctic Institute of North America, Montreal. A number of physical geography studies have appeared in the *Geographical Bulletin.*

MCCOURT, EDWARD: *Saskatchewan,* Macmillan, Toronto, 1968.

METEOROLOGICAL BRANCH, AIR SERVICES, DEPARTMENT OF TRANSPORT: *The Climate of the Canadian Arctic,* Toronto, reprinted from the *Canada Year Book: 1967.*

PHILLIPS, R. A. J.: *Canada's North,* Macmillan, Toronto, 1967. An excellent summary of past and current developments in the Yukon and Northwest Territories.

Proceedings of British Columbia Natural Resources Conferences, Victoria, B.C. Annual volumes, starting in 1951, on trends in resource developments; special inventory volumes were published in 1956 and 1964.

ROBINSON, J. LEWIS: "The Northern Extension of the Pioneer Fringe of Agriculture on the Great Plains of Canada," *Proceedings of 8th General Assembly, International Geographical Union,* Washington, 1952, pp. 657–662.

———, and WALTER G. HARDWICK: *British Columbia: One Hundred Years of Geographical Change,* Talonbooks, Vancouver, 1973.

WEIR, THOMAS R.: *Economic Atlas of Manitoba,* Manitoba Department of Industry and Commerce, Winnipeg, 1960.

WONDERS, WILLIAM C. (ed.): *Canada's Changing North,* McClelland and Stewart, Toronto, 1971.

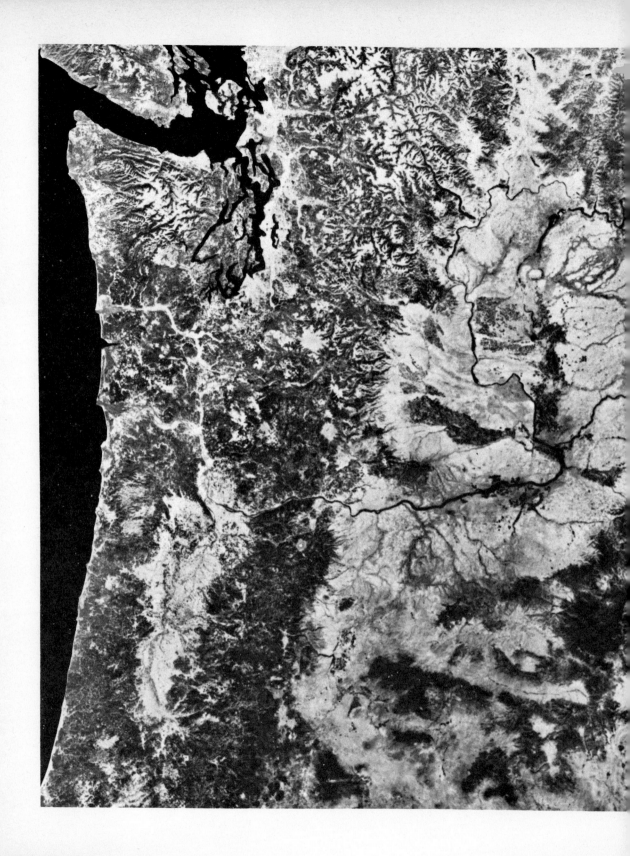

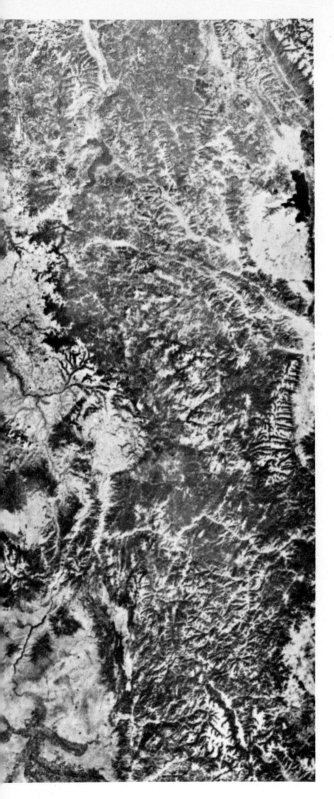

11

THE FUTURE
OF ANGLO-AMERICA

For many millennia, aboriginal man in Anglo-America lived in harmony with his environment, doing little to exploit it. In sharp contrast, in less than four centuries, European settlers and their descendants developed an economy in Anglo-America that far surpasses that of their homelands. Furs, lumber, farmlands, gold, iron, coal, and petroleum contributed to this economic growth, but these resources would have been valueless without the ingenuity provided by daring, tireless, and innovative men.

The rapidity with which Anglo-America was settled by Europeans has brought wealth to many, and at least an adequate standard of living to most of its people. It is barely two centuries since the waves of settlement crossed the Appalachians to open up a vast new land and barely a century since Canada and the United States completed their territorial claims to a 7.5 million square mile continent. Rapid exploitation of new lands, apparently inexhaustible raw materials, and new technologies encouraged belief that unlimited growth was both possible and desirable. Indeed great numbers of Anglo-American fortunes were

An ERTS mosaic of the Pacific Northwest. Compare this photograph with Figures 8.10 and 8.12. Try to identify water bodies, cities, forests, grasslands, irrigated areas. (NASA)

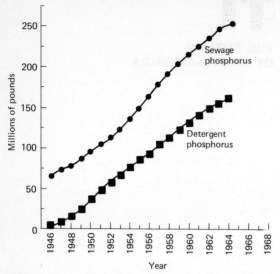

Figure 11.1 Nearly all the increase in sewage phosphorus is accounted for by the phosphorus content of household detergents. Phosphate pollution stimulates heavy overgrowths of algae in water bodies and thus uses up oxygen needed to sustain fish life. (From The Commission on Population Growth, *Report,* Washington, 1972, vol. III, p. 354)

based on the growth of land values, the expanding sales of consumers goods and services, and the exploitation of technological innovations.

The success of the Anglo-American dream of affluence, partly as the result of rapid growth, caused many to overlook the problems of disadvantaged Anglo-Americans who did not share in the rising standards of living. The accepted belief of most Anglo-Americans was that those who worked hard and intelligently would share in the growing affluence. This philosophy overlooked the fact that many were in poverty through no fault of their own because of changes in business conditions, technological unemployment, poor health, mental and/or educational inadequacies, and racial or other discrimination. Although civil rights legislation, welfare measures, and propaganda campaigns have brought some opportunities to many disadvantaged people, in the early 1970s about one-tenth of United States families had incomes below the minimum standard for de-

cent living. These low incomes varied in relation to racial origins or descent; less than 9 percent of persons of British origins were economically disadvantaged in contrast to 24 percent of Spanish origins and 32 percent of Negro and other minority groups. Likewise unemployment percentages were twice or more as great for minority racial groups than for whites. Among the major causes of poverty and unemployment has been the replacement of workers by machines in agriculture, forestry, mining, and some factories; this loss of jobs in farm and raw material–producing areas has caused cityward migrations of workers, many of whom are poorly trained for urban work and urban living. This situation, plus discrimination, has created ghetto conditions in many central cities, while the more affluent urban workers have moved to the suburbs or to luxurious apartments in the central city.

GROWTH PROBLEMS IN A FINITE WORLD

In the last decade, perceptive Anglo-Americans have become aware that broader problems have developed from the impact of growth on land use. Continued population increase accompanied by a rise in the standard of living threatens to exhaust many Anglo-American resources; at the same time the use of these resources pollutes the environment to such an extent that production may be reduced and a healthful life may become impossible in thickly settled areas. These problems have been known to geographers, ecologists, and conservationists since early in the present century, but a rash of recent events has made most Anglo-Americans more aware of them. Smog, once an urban annoyance, is now recognized as a health danger, and the automobile has been pinpointed as the principal culprit. Heavy industries, once a source of pride, have been blamed for stream, air, noise, and visual pollution. Rachel Carson's *Silent Spring* indicated that DDT and other chemical remedies for natural ills were capable of doing more ecological harm than good. More recently the Club of Rome study, *The Limits to Growth,* forecast catastrophe if man did not radically change his growth patterns. To Anglo-Americans so dependent on energy in business, household, and pleasure, the energy crisis of early 1974 hit home. It seemed impossible to conceive a modern life without adequate electricity, natural gas, oil, and gasoline, but Anglo-American cities have recently experienced this condition.

Exponential Growth

Although for analysis the problem of Anglo-American growth can be subdivided, each of its parts reacts on all others. Thus in an automobile-dependent society, more people mean more cars. These are manufactured with scarce resources and consume scarce fuels. Both the automobile factories and the operation of the cars create additional pollution. At the same time each of these factories and resource-consuming activities supplies thousands of jobs and gives consumer income to many, many people.

Each part of the growth problem grows exponentially, in the same way that interest on a savings account increases through compounding even though no additional funds are deposited. The curves on Figures 3.2 to 3.5 illustrate exponential growth.

Population Growth and the Quality of Life

Long-range population estimates are based on certain assumptions which may or may not prove to be correct. For the United States the Census Bureau has produced a variety of projections which differ mainly in the assumed fertility rate among women of childbearing age. Even if that fertility rate declines from what it was in the 1960s, the United States population could approach 300 million in 2000 and be 400 million in 2020. The Bureau of the Census estimates that if fertility continues to decline

slowly, a stable population (zero population growth) may be reached by 2037. Whether these figures are realized depends on variables such as the use of birth control measures, the desire for small families, the decline or increase of death rates, the desire of women for careers, and the net migration into or from the United States.

Projections of Canadian population increase show the same problems of assessing the many variables which interact to cause increased numbers. In Canada, however, population increase has been more strongly influenced by immigration and emigration figures. After World War II Canada opened its doors to immigrants from all parts of the world, but particularly from Europe. In the past decade there has been a strong northward flow from the United States. Canada's population increased from 12 million in 1945 to 22 million in 1972—a rapid percentage increase, but still small in total numbers compared with the larger population in the United States. Incoming population supplied labor in the resource-producing industries and services in the cities, and they also became consumers for Canadian-produced goods. But this flood of immigration declined in the early 1970s, partly as a result of a stricter government control over the type of person who could enter the country. With much of the country less habitable than the United States, Canada may reach population "saturation" at the turn of this century with about 30 million people. Having the advantage of proximity, Canadians have been able to see the problems of excessive population and wanton resource use in the United States, and many Canadians are working politically to prevent a population of even 30 million being reached.

It seems possible that the population will double during the working life of most students who read this book. The pressures of this doubled population on goods and living space, on increased withdrawals of irreplaceable resources, and on the pollution of the environment may be overwhelming *if our present lifestyles are not altered.*

Table 11.1 Regional Summary

REGIONS AND SUBREGIONS	LAND AREA (THOUSAND SQ. MI.)	POPULATION 1960 1970 (MILLIONS)		ESTIMATED POPULATION 2000
ATLANTIC MEGALOPOLIS AND ADJACENT NORTHEAST	156	45.2	52.2	74.0
New York Gateway	48	19.4	22.8	34.0
New England Gateway	64	9.9	10.9	17.0
Delaware-Chesapeake gateways	44	15.9	18.4	23.0
CENTRAL LOWLAND	831	61.4	67.1	135.0
Ohio Basin	152	18.3	20.1	24.0
Great Lakes region	145	25.4	28.2	85.0
The Midwest	535	17.7	18.8	26.0
THE SOUTH	487	35.5	40.0	60.0
Southern Uplands	148	13.5	14.0	19.0
Southeastern Plain	127	9.7	12.6	20.0
Gulf South	212	12.3	14.3	21.0
INTERIOR WEST	1,134	15.6	18.1	22.0
Southwest	533	11.3	13.0	15.0
High West	601	4.3	5.1	7.0
PACIFIC STATES	919	21.4	26.5	44.0
Southern California Megalopolis	65	9.7	12.9	22.0
Focus on San Francisco Bay	115	6.8	7.2	12.0
Hawaiian Islands	6	0.6	0.8	1.2
Pacific Northwest	148	4.7	6.1	9.0
Alaska	571	0.1	0.3	0.5
EASTERN CANADA	1,215	13.4	15.8	22.0
Atlantic Provinces	95	1.9	2.0	3.0
Heartland of Canada	100	10.0	12.0	16.0
Canadian Shield (including the part outside Eastern Canada)	1,630	1.7	2.0	3.0
WESTERN CANADA AND THE NORTHLANDS	2,636	4.8	5.8	8.0
Prairie Provinces	758	3.1	3.5	4.5
British Columbia	366	1.6	2.2	3.5
Northlands	1,512	0.03	0.05	0.1
UNITED STATES	3,549	178.0	203.0	307.0
CANADA	3,560	18.0	22.0	30.0
GREENLAND	840	.03	0.05	0.08
ANGLO-AMERICA	7,949	196.0	225.1	338

The sums of the columns may not equal the totals because of rounding. The estimates for the year 2000 are based on *1972 Obers Projections, Regional Economic Activity in the United States,* U.S. Government Printing Office, Washington, 1972, and on similar Canadian data. More recent estimates based on a lifetime birthrate of 1,800 per 1,000 women suggest the possibility that the rate of natural increase (excluding immigrants) is close to zero. Past experience has indicated that natural rates of increase are subject to change with cultural conditions so that all projections are likely to include a considerable margin of error. The predictions above are probably more significant for showing the expected relative growth of regional populations than for showing national projections.

Increased Living Standards

The U.S. Department of Commerce estimates that the average United States per capita income will increase from $3,400 in 1969 to the equivalent of $8,300 (assuming a 1967 price level) in the year 2000. If this increased income is spent on more and larger automobiles, larger houses, and increased consumption of other material goods, the results could cause catastrophic resource exhaustion and pollution. If, on the other hand, the goods manufactured are more durable and if much more is spent on services, increased living standards are feasible.

Department of Commerce forecasts also suggest that per capita income will become more evenly distributed over the country. In 1929 per capita income was 74 percent above the national average in the New York City area but 62 percent below in southwestern Louisiana. In 1969 the New York figure was 30 percent above, the Louisiana figure 31 percent below—a narrowing of the gap. For 2000 the predicted figures are for New York 19 percent above and for Louisiana 25 percent below the national average. These estimates do not allow for the higher cost of living in the New York area.

With improved transportation and communication and with personal income less dependent on local raw materials and more dependent on services, probably more people will be attracted to areas with mild climates and scenic settings. This trend is already noticeable in Florida, California, the Southwest, and the Georgia Strait area of Canada. There is a similar trend toward moving to small cities, many of which are suburbs of the large metropolitan centers. Some city planners have suggested that cities be designed on a "human" scale so that people will not feel submerged by the millions in large metropolitan areas. Many planned communities in the last decade have been subdivided into villages clustered around central offices and stores which offer a variety of services. If these villages are restricted in size to several thousand each, most people will feel that they know the local leaders and can have a significant voice in determining the pattern of village life. Unfortunately there is little likelihood that the thousands of poor residents in the inner cities of places such as New York, Cleveland, or Chicago will achieve the peaceful life in a quiet suburban village.

Raw Material Exhaustion and the Use of Marginal Resources

The rate of resource exhaustion varies greatly with the per capita demand for resources, the possibility of recycling resources economically, and the possibility of obtaining more plentiful substitutes for some uses of a given resource. All these factors change with new discoveries in technology, with the habits and whims of consumers, and with changes in production costs. Many deposits of potential resources are submarginal, costing more to produce than they would bring in the market. Anglo-America still has unoccupied land available for agriculture, but much of this land would yield little or no profit under our present economic systems. Vast forests remain untapped across Middle Canada, but the trees are too small to be harvested economically in competition with forests of larger trees. Enormous supplies of petroleum may be obtained from oil shales, coal conversion, or bituminous sands, but the development of these sources may not be economical until the price of gasoline exceeds $1 per gallon.

Improved efficiency in production or increased demands (and prices) for such resources may make the deposits economically exploitable. For example, primitive man exploited copper only where almost pure metal occurred in a natural state. About 5,000 years ago men in the Middle East discovered that copper ores could be smelted in a charcoal fire to obtain metal. With the progress of metallurgy, copper deposits containing progressively smaller percentages of metal could be profitably exploited. In the western United States, ores with less than one-half of 1 percent copper are used; in most mines by-products

The city swallows up even the best farmland as is illustrated by these two photos of Santa Clara County, California. The photo on the left was taken in January 1950 near San Jose; the one on the right was taken in June 1956. (USDA)

such as gold, silver, lead, and zinc contribute to the cost of concentrating and smelting the ore. Such low-grade ore could not be used if the price of copper were not maintained by the huge demands of the electrical and other industries.

Fuel and power limitations The danger of resource exhaustion in Anglo-America is most critical in the fuels. Until recently it was assumed that coal reserves would last thousands of years, but most Appalachian coals have such a high sulfur content that their use *with present technologies* would contribute to

air pollution. Consequently, fields east of the Rockies are being exploited although these are much farther from the major markets for power. A similar problem has arisen with oil which Anglo-America is importing in great quantities. Many of the available oils are not desirable because of their high sulfur content. Oil is known to be available on the continental shelf and in the Alaskan and Canadian Arctic, but environmental considerations have slowed the

exploitation of some potential oil fields. However, the consumption of oil is so huge that Anglo-American reserves might last only a decade or two if not supplemented by imports. There is a comparable potential shortage of natural gas, and huge ships are being built to bring in liquefied gas from overseas.

Ten years ago it appeared that nuclear power would solve the anticipated energy crisis. Although supplies of uranium fuel were known to be limited and might become exhausted in a half century, the breeder reactor (not yet perfected on a large scale) had the capability of producing much more atomic fuel than it consumed. Although nuclear power plants have operated successfully for two decades, the fear of atomic explosion and the problem of disposing of polluting by-product waste have slowed the construction of further nuclear plants. Eventually atomic technology may be able to control these problems, but at present there seems to be little agreement among atomic scientists about when this can be achieved.

Other sources of power may be made economically feasible. Relatively small amounts have been spent on research with geothermal or tidal power, the use of solar energy in the deserts, the use of oil shales in Colorado and of tar sands in the northern Prairie Provinces, and the conversion of coal into gas which could be piped long distances. All these solutions to the energy shortage have potential for success, but tremendous investments of time and money in technological innovations are needed before conventional fuels can be replaced. Because the energy crisis has arrived in the United States, pressure is building to risk more environmental pollution as a stopgap measure.

Recyclable materials Until recently Anglo-Americans have been so impressed with their abundant resources that they have tended to save labor rather than physical resources. Actually most metals, lumber, paper, cloth, glass, brick, and stone, and even motor oil, can be recycled almost indefinitely. The problem is partly a question of cost and partly a problem of altering human habits. Most recyclable materials are not fully used, but they may be dissipated into such minute quantities that their recovery is uneconomical. Thus rusted iron, broken bricks, scraps of paper, and cloth are rarely worth recovering. Chemicals which play such an important part in contemporary society

are a double problem: they are so diluted in use as to be unrecoverable, and their nondegradable residues contribute greatly to air and water pollution.

The advantages of organic products
Most plants and animals provide industrial raw materials which can be regrown by natural processes. Plants absorb certain pollutants from the air and release oxygen to the atmosphere. For example, many parts of Anglo-America could be replanted in well-managed forests using new seedlings which produce lumber two or three times faster than in self-procreating forests. Another example, the soybean, introduced to Anglo-America after the beginning of this century, is now a major crop. Its products include hay, feed, oil, and raw materials for paints, plastics, fibers, and adhesives. The soybean is also a nitrogen-producer which helps replenish soils depleted by corn cultivation.

More food Anglo-America seems to have adequate soil and water resources to provide food for twice or more its present population. If necessary, more food could be made available by diverting to food use foodstuffs used as industrial raw materials. A prime example is the soybean, which is gaining wide use as a protein supplement to a variety of foods. Anglo-Americans are the leading per capita consumers of meat. If meat consumption were reduced, much more grain would be available for direct human consumption since 6 to 10 pounds of grain are required to produce 1 pound of meat. Until recently the United States government has followed the policy of paying farmers to keep productive land out of production; recent world shortages of grain and other foods have led to a change in the policy of restricting production. If the above possibilities were put into practice, it is likely that Anglo-America could provide food surpluses for more crowded parts of the world.

Supertrees, 40 years old   "Natural" trees, 40 years old

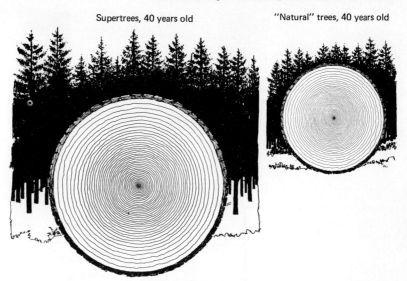

Figure 11.2 The breeding of varieties of supertrees multiplies the productivity of lumber on an acre of forest land. The Georgia-Pacific Corporation has been developing supertree seed orchards since 1952: Douglas fir orchards in California and Oregon and southern pine in Louisiana and Georgia. (Georgia-Pacific Corporation)

Time, Cost, and Habit as Limiting Factors

Many of the possibilities suggested above are difficult to put into practice. It takes time to build the factories and machinery to employ new processes. Huge investments are required for such new industries, and the desirable goods may be more expensive to produce than the products they are replacing. The most serious problem may be that of changing human habits, for most Anglo-Americans find it easier to follow established methods. Crisis may be the catalyst that changes old habits. History has shown that people respond to emergencies such as war, epidemics, and drought with innovations and ingenuity.

LAND SHORTAGE— NATIONALLY AND REGIONALLY?

In terms of total area, Anglo-America seems uncrowded. The United States and Canada have over 5 billion acres, or about 20 acres of land for each person of 1971 population. The urban student may best visualize this amount of land as 20 football fields per person. About half of this land is worthless by present economic and technological standards, but there still remains 10 acres per person of usable land. If the Anglo-American population could be stabilized at 500 million, each person would have 4 acres, the equivalent of a square of 417 feet on each side. This density of 120 people per square mile is moderate compared to the present populations of Japan (728 per square mile), China (210 per square mile), or West Germany (624 per square mile).

Most contemporary Anglo-Americans have little desire to live permanently in the tundra, in the northern forests of Canada and Alaska, in the more barren parts of the desert, or in marshlands. Resources which may be found in such areas will probably be exploited by task forces which will work there for weeks, months, or a few years as necessary. It seems inevitable that the bulk of the Anglo-American population will live in metropolitan cities and in suburban satellites. With the increased mobility of manufacturing and service industries, these activities are likely to become relatively more important in areas attractive for residential purposes.

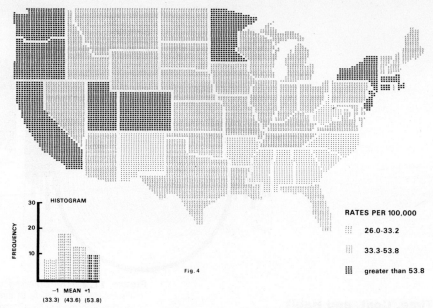

Fig. 4

RATES PER 100,000

26.0-33.2

33.3-53.8

greater than 53.8

Figure 11.3 The computer can be programmed to draw maps such as this one showing the number of dentists per 100,000 people in each state. How would you explain the distribution of states in each category? (Gary W. Shannon and G. E. Alan Dever, *Health Care Delivery, Spatial Perspectives,* McGraw-Hill, New York, 1974, p. 42. Used with permission of McGraw-Hill Book Company)

Some of this urban growth will continue to occupy good agricultural land, but if a stabilized population is achieved, land used for urban purposes should be a small fraction of the usable land, possibly one-fortieth of the whole. With the above trends in mind (and with the knowledge that unforeseeable changes in human objectives, productivity, and technology may alter or upset the best of forecasts), let us consider the future by major regions. In doing so, remember that present geographic patterns are based on huge investments of human wealth and effort and that these vested interests in the land will not easily be discarded.

The Atlantic Megalopolis

With the increasing demands for services and decision making, this relatively old area of Anglo-American settlement should continue to grow. Basic problems will be the scarcity of unpolluted water supplies and urban renewal in the old cities. Equally necessary will be the provision of parks and playgrounds within the cities and of vacation areas outside the thickly settled areas. Increasingly, functions now performed in the central cities will be relegated to suburban satellites, and the dilemma of how to rebuild, redesign, or reuse the old city cores must be resolved. Agricultural land use near the cities will decrease as urban uses expand, but the remaining farmland will be used more intensively for garden and special crops. Forest acreage should expand but primarily for recreation rather than for lumber. Local fuels and raw materials will supply an even smaller percentage of local needs than they do today. The political structure will require simplification into a single megalopolitan government to deal with water supply, pollution, public transport, and other problems.

The huge and diverse populations of this region have brought about major political, economic, and sociological problems. Adequate housing, education, recreation, and health care for all may require investments of

There is no reason why people must stay indoors when the weather is fine. Pittsburgh's civic auditorium has a retractable dome which can be closed in 2½ minutes. This building is in an extensive urban-renewal project in downtown Pittsburgh. (Robert E. Dick Studios from Chamber of Commerce of Pittsburgh)

social capital perhaps beyond the ability of the local governments to fund them.

Eastern Canada

This huge region has functions which are similar to both the Atlantic Megalopolis and the eastern half of the Central Lowland. The smaller population of the Canadian region generates a correspondingly smaller market. The Canadian region has certain advantages such as a larger resource base and control of much of the St. Lawrence–Great Lakes Seaway. In the Heartland cities such as metropolitan Toronto and Montreal both the advantages and disadvantages of high urban densities and industrialization are now apparent, and it may not be too late to plan and direct future growth to obtain greater social benefits. Although political union with the United States does not seem

likely, some sort of common market, perhaps foreshadowed by free trade arrangements in the automotive industries, would seem advantageous to both nations.

The Central Lowland

Aside from severe seasonal and daily changes in weather, this region seems to have much that is needed for good living, including adequate food resources; excellent waterways; and a dense network of good highways, rail routes, and pipelines. The quality of the land for both rural and urban production ranks among the best large areas in the world, and

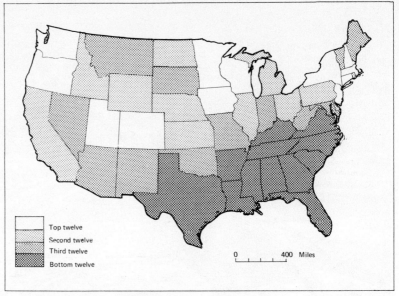

this land is centered in relation to present and potential Anglo-American markets. This productive region, with its Canadian extension to the north and northeast, is truly the Anglo-American Heartland. Many of its social and economic problems have arisen from its rapid change from a farm-based economy to an industrial-commercial economy. Along with this economic transformation has come the cityward migration of displaced workers from the increasingly mechanized farm and raw material industries. The central core of this region, around the lower Great Lakes, is developing into a Great Lakes Megalopolis.

The South

The mild subtropical climate with a long growing season is well suited for both outdoor living and the raising of fresh foods. While discomfort results from short cold spells and from hot, humid summers, the introduction of the heat pump and air conditioning can keep indoor temperatures pleasant. The region has a wide range of accessible natural resources, and their dispersal has permitted population to re-

Figure 11.4 This map rates the 48 states on the basis of six criteria of social well-being: I. Income, wealth, and employment; II. Housing; III. Health; IV. Education; V. Social Disorganization; VI. Alienation and Participation. All of these except criterion V correlate strongly with general social well-being, for example, the correlation of criterion I is .88. Standard scores were worked out for each state for each criterion and combined in a composite indicator. Massachusetts rated highest with 1.24 and Mississippi lowest with −2.64. The map divides the states into four equal classes. (For a detailed explanation, see David M. Smith, *The Geography of Social Well-Being in the United States,* McGraw-Hill, New York, 1973. Chapter 7. Map used with permission of McGraw-Hill Book Company)

main fairly evenly dispersed. With many attractive sites in towns and small cities available, the South may prove ideal for those who prefer the suburban type of life to the giant megalopolis. A major problem is the regulation of water supply, for certain parts of the South have suffered from floods, drought, and inadequate domestic water supplies. The latter handicap is especially serious in the Florida peninsula and Texas where the demand for fresh water already exceeds the local supply at times. Desalinization of ocean water with atomic power and the better storage of temporary water surpluses in reservoirs may ensure a dependable supply.

The Interior West

This largely semiarid region, interspersed with deserts and moisture-collecting mountains, also contains vast scenic resources and huge mineral deposits. In recent decades the value of oil and gas has overshadowed the mining of ores. The need for the huge oil deposits locked in Colorado oil shale suggests that fuels will continue to dominate the economy. Meanwhile parts of the Interior West are attracting permanent residents who like the combination of semiarid climate and spectacular landscapes. It is to be expected, however, that this part of the United States will continue to support low densities of population and depend on an extractive economy.

The Pacific States

The areas near the Pacific have a marine climate resembling that found in the same latitudes in Western Europe. In the southern half of California especially, water shortages, air pollution, and the slowdown of industrial expansion have at least temporarily slowed inmigration. Assuming that Americans obtain a shorter working week and desire a climate for outdoor living, who can deny the lure of the Pacific Coast? If trans-Pacific trade develops to anything like that across the North Atlantic in the first half of this century, then the Pacific State cities will see new economic growth.

Western Canada and the Northlands

The Canadian West has a surplus of many of the raw materials needed elsewhere in Anglo-America and the world. The land is not overcrowded and produces export surpluses of grain, meat, oil, gas, metallic minerals, fertilizers, and lumber. The Prairie Provinces have disadvantages of a severe winter climate, but the coastal strip in British Columbia has similar climatic attractions to the adjoining Pacific states.

Except in a few small areas, Western Canada still has ample fresh air and fresh water, and markets for its surpluses should not be hard to secure. In the Subarctic and Arctic, open and empty space is plentiful, but natural resources are few and the climate repels most people. Production costs are high for any product that may be used. Alaska is American politically, but for most of the area its problems are similar to those of the Northlands. If Alaska reaches the population forecast of 628,000 by 2020, these people will probably be in the coastal areas. Almost any other part of Anglo-America could be made habitable for considerable numbers with much less effort than in the Northlands.

THE CLOUDED CRYSTAL BALL

Forecasting the future is not an exact science! The authors are confident of only one prediction: in the twenty-first century Anglo-America will be different from contemporary Anglo-America in ways that none of us can imagine. The physical environment will be much the same as it is today over large areas. The big changes will depend on what man does to the landscapes. Will man limit his demands on available resources? Will planners devise solutions to land-use problems before those problems reach the crisis stage?

The energy shortage in certain areas is far from hopeless, but men need time and equipment to harness other sources of power.[1] The amounts that governments have spent on this critical energy problem are minute compared with those spent for military and space exploration. The harnessing of solar energy can create more than enough power for all foreseeable human needs, but a million-kilowatt plant would require a sunny square area measuring 60 miles on each side. Such a solar-powered plant, with contemporary technology, would cost five or ten times as much as a

[1] The facts and conclusions are derived mainly from David J. Rose "Energy Policy in the U.S.," *Scientific American,* vol. 230, no. 1 (January 1974), pp. 20–29.

nuclear or coal-fueled plant. The cost of obtaining petroleum from oil shales or coal is equally high and may require at least a decade of technological experimentation. The Canadians are better off for energy supplies mainly because their national resources are more adequate in relation to their population.

Anglo-Americans are discovering rather painfully that a frontier has been reached. That new frontier is more technological that geographical. Since it takes time to construct new power sources and to test new technologies, a gap has developed between Anglo-American demands for power and the supply immediately available. Reduced consumption, perhaps for a decade, seems the only answer.

Thus a realization of the limits to growth should be coming to Anglo-America. Its citizens have 8 million square miles of the earth to utilize. If and when the resources of that land are exhausted, the environmental pantry will be empty. Foreign sources of fuels and raw materials will cease to be available as underdeveloped lands approach Anglo-American levels of living and demand more material goods for themselves. Future social and economic growth must be in the form of better services and more efficient use of the resources we have. Perhaps environmental thrift may become a new Anglo-American ethic.

Quantity or Quality?

Our crystal ball suggests that Anglo-American society should change its objectives. Most economists and engineers agree that our affluent society has the ability to produce enough for the reasonable needs of its citizens. The major problems are distribution and incentives rather than production. The increase in material goods has not guaranteed happiness—indeed many of the wealthy seem beset with unsolvable problems. Life, liberty, and the pursuit of happiness seem as difficult to achieve now as in 1776. The by-products of an industrial society seem increasingly to pollute the land, the oceans, and the atmosphere.

What Anglo-America becomes will depend primarily on what Anglo-Americans become. Our examination of Anglo-America has indicated that while the characteristics of physical landscapes are important, these are converted into resources only when the inhabitants have the ability and incentives to utilize them, and in some cases, conserve them. Technology, skill, cultural habits, and psychological drives, as well as leaders, innovators, and tireless workers, create civilizations.

If one may dream of a utopian Anglo-America, one could visualize a land in which there are opportunities for a variety of life styles in the diverse environments available. Most people probably will prefer to live where the greatest population density exists today; many will live in megalopolitan areas, and, it is hoped, these can be constructed (or reconstructed) without ghettos, noise, pollution, and overcrowding. But population growth may occur increasingly in physically attractive environments with mild climates and interesting landscapes.

Megalopolitan growth will be modest, but an almost continuous urban and suburban landscape seems likely in an area bounded approximately by lines connecting Norfolk, Boston, Montreal, Minneapolis, Kansas City, Louisville, and back to Norfolk. Other megalopolitan complexes may expand along the Florida and Gulf South coasts, in the Southern Piedmont, and along the Pacific Coast. Within the remaining settled areas a sprinkling of cities and villages will offer a variety of settings: urban, suburban, and rural for a variety of tastes. Each of these diverse settlements might develop an individual character and culture of its own suited to aims and objectives of local groups and reflecting local creativity. Craftsmanship and the joy of working at an interesting job, as well as adequate material goods, could become the birthright of all Anglo-Americans. Such a redevelopment of the Anglo-American Realm might fit the "land for living" rather than for merely "making a living."

A Wealthy Region in a Poor World

Anglo-Americans account for about one-sixteenth of the world's population but receive about one-third of the world's income.[2] The Anglo-American consumption of physical goods is estimated to be between two-fifths and one-half of the world's total (in terms of value). Anglo-America, and most European countries, Japan, Australia, New Zealand, and a few other prosperous areas, comprise one-third of the world's more affluent people. Some of the less affluent areas sell fuels and raw materials to more developed and affluent nations, but the huge sums received in this trade commonly bring substantial benefit to only a small fraction of their peoples. Thus a sharp gap remains between the generally well-fed, well-clothed, and well-housed peoples of the developed nations and the poorer two-thirds of the world's population. Poverty exists in Anglo-America too and scars the lives of millions of Anglo-Americans; but, materially at least, these poor are much better off than the great majority of people in the underdeveloped world, for example, in countries such as India, Bangladesh, Haiti, and the famine-stricken areas of Africa.

The affluent countries have sent substantial amounts of aid to the underdeveloped and poverty-stricken nations, but the gap between the rich and poor areas remains great. There are still many areas where the per capita annual income averages less that $100. These inequalities are made even more painful by increasing communications. The well-fed Anglo-American can watch on TV the starving peoples of Bangladesh or Sub-Saharan Africa. The world's poor can see the life of middle- and upper-class Anglo-Americans portrayed in moving pictures or acted out by tourist groups housed in Hilton hotels.

The increasing need for the resources of the poor lands to enable the affluent nations to maintain their high and often extravagant level of consumption has been underlined by the 1973 energy crisis. Perhaps this is only the first of such world resource crises. We Anglo-Americans have consumed our natural resources at a rate unparalleled in human history so that the United States now imports many commodities that were important exports less than a century ago.

The Commission on Population Growth and the American Future points out that we can solve the problems of resource adequacy and control of pollutants if we wish. Ronald Ridker states:

For the poorer two-thirds of the world, at least, this formulation of the problem is the height of luxury. Not only are the social options exceedingly narrow in contrast to those of the United States, but in many of these countries, even concerns about toxic pollutants must be given low priority compared to problems of food and resource adequacy. Short of dramatic technological breakthroughs, rapid declines in birthrates, or massive transfers of resources from richer countries, their relative position, if not their absolute position as well, is likely to deteriorate further during the next 30 to 50 years. The turmoil caused by this poverty and inequality in the distribution of the world's wealth can only grow worse with time. One can be sanguine about America's long-term future only by ignoring this problem.[3]

---

[2] Anglo-Americans receive two-fifths of the reported world income but the smaller fraction has been used to allow for Communist countries for which comparable data are not available.

[3] The Commission on Population Growth and the American Future, *Population, Resources, and the Environment*, Ronald G. Ridker (ed.), vol. III of Commission Research reports, Government Printing Office, 1972, pp. 31–32.

SELECTED REFERENCES

CHASE, STUART: *The Most Probable World,* Penguin Books, Baltimore, 1969.

COMMITTEE ON MERCHANT MARINE AND FISHERIES, HOUSE OF REPRESENTATIVES: 93rd Congress, *Hearing with Appendix: Growth and Its Implications for the Future, Part 1,* Government Printing Office, Washington, 1973.

All the publications of Resources for the Future, Inc. (published by Johns Hopkins, Baltimore) are pertinent and to be recommended. Especially relevant are:

CLAWSON, MARION: *America's Land and Its Use,* 1972.

CLAWSON, MARION, R. BURNELL HELD, and CHARLES H. STODDARD: *Land for the Future,* 1960.

HANSEN, NILES M.: *Rural Poverty and the Urban Crisis: A Strategy for Regional Development,* Indiana University Press, Bloomington, 1970.

LANDSBERG, HANS H., LEONARD L. FISCHMAN, and JOSEPH L. FISHER: *Resources in America's Future,* 1963. An abstract of this book is also available as a Johns Hopkins paperback: Hans H. Landsberg, *Natural Resources for U.S. Growth,* 1964.

LOWENTHAL, DAVID: "The American Scene," *Geographical Review,* vol. 58 (1968) pp. 61–88.

MEADOWS, D. H., D. L. MEADOWS, JORGEN RANDERS, WILLIAM W. BEHRENS III: *The Limits to Growth,* Universe Books, New York, 1972.

U.S. COMMISSION ON POPULATION GROWTH AND THE AMERICAN FUTURE: *Demographic and Social Aspects of Population Growth,* Charles F. Westoff and Robert Parke, Jr. (eds.), vol. I of Commission research reports, Government Printing Office, Washington, 1972. Vols. II–VII cover other aspects of population growth.

————: *Population, Resources, and the Environment,* Ronald G. Ridker (ed.), vol. III of Commission research reports, Government Printing Office, Washington, 1972.

U.S. DEPARTMENT OF COMMERCE: *Obers Projections—Regional Economic Activity in the United States,* 5 volumes, prepared for U.S. Water Resources Council, Washington, 1972. Historical and projected data are for the period 1929–2020.

U.S. DEPARTMENT OF THE INTERIOR: *Conservation Yearbook* (annual since 1965), Washington.

WILSON, GEORGE W., SCOTT GORDON, and JUDEK STANISLAW: *Canada: An Appraisal of Its Needs and Resources,* Twentieth Century Fund, New York, 1965; University of Toronto Press, Toronto, 1965.

INDEX

INDEX

INDEX

Page numbers in *italic* indicate figures or photographs.

Agribusiness, 141, 240
Agriculture (*see* Farming)
Air conditioning, 156, 182
Aircraft, 120, 150, 166, 204, 208, 232, 236, 237
Akron, Ohio, 129
Alabama, 178, 179
Alaska, *34, 252,* 262–264, 353
Alaska Highway, 262
Alaska Pipeline, 229
Albany, New York, 78
Alberta, 303, 307, 310, 317–319
Albuquerque, New Mexico, 207
Allegheny Plateau, *11, 73, 97, 113,* 157
Allentown, Pennsylvania, 75
Alluvial areas, 27, 28, 35, 156, *169,* 176, *177*
Alluvial fans, 193
Aluminum, 124, 164, 259
Amarillo, Texas, 202, 206
Anaconda, Montana, 216
Anchorage, Alaska, 228, 262, 263
Annapolis, Maryland, 102
Annapolis Valley, 276
Appalachia, *160,* 162–164
Appalachian Mountains, 29, 30–31, 34, 101, 158–164
Appalachian Regional Development Act, 162

Appropriation doctrine, 210
Arctic Islands, 270, 329, 330, 335
Arkansas Valley, 167, 200, 204, 212–213
Aroostook County, Maine, 87, 95
Artesian wells, 149
Asheville, North Carolina, 164
Atlanta, Georgia, 155, 156, 165–167
Atlantic Provinces, 272–277
Attleboro, Massachusetts, 94
Augusta, Georgia, 169, 175
Austin, Texas, 203, 204
Automobile, 54, 62, 112, 123, 130–132, 166, 235, 245, 342

Bakersfield, California, 24
Balcones Escarpment, *192,* 203, 206
Baltimore, Maryland, 74, 102, *103*
Bangor, Maine, 95
Basin and range, *192,* 197–198, 208, *209*
Baton Rouge, Louisiana, 184
Beaumont, Texas, 184
Beaver, 43, 215
Berkshire Hills, 74, 95
Bethlehem, Pennsylvania, 75
Big Horn Country, 195, 215
Bingham, Utah, 218

Binghamton, New York, 79
Billings, Montana, 216
Birmingham, Alabama, 164
Bisbee, Arizona, 200
Bison, 36–37, 215
Black Belt, 31, 157
Black Hills, South Dakota, 139, 150
Black Waxy Prairie (Blackland), *192,* 204
Blacks, 77, *83,* 96, 112, 115, 164, 171, 174, 178, 202, 233, 342
Blue Grass region, *113,* 122–123
Blue Ridge, *158,* 163, 164
Boll weevil, 183
Bonneville Dam, 261
Boston, Massachusetts, 70, *71,* 77, 87, 89–93
Bourbon County, Kentucky, 123
Breeder reactor, 348
Breweries, 136, 143
Bridgeport, Connecticut, 85, 130
British Columbia, *47,* 57, 319–327
Brooklyn, New York, 14, 84
Brownsville, Texas, 207
Buffalo, New York, 70, 128
Butte District, Montana, 216

Cajon Pass, 227, 237
Calgary, Alberta, 311, 317
California, 32, 49, 225–249
California Water Project, *233,* 249
Calumet area, Indiana, 136
Camden, New Jersey, 99, *100*
Canadian Shield, 57, 270, 292, 294–301, 305, 314, 318, 336
Cape Cod, 80, 87, 93
Cascades, 228, 252, *253,* 259–260
Casper, Wyoming, 216
Cattle, 37–38, 141–143, 149, 151, 170, 208
Cedar Rapids, Iowa, 143
Cement, 75
Central Business District (CBD), 53, *68–69,* 80–83, 91, 98, 104, *117,* 131, 135, 148, *187*
Central City, Colorado, 214
Central Valley, California, *225,* 227, 229, 240–241, 247–249

Chaparral, 230
Charleston, South Carolina, 155, 172, 175
Charleston, West Virginia, 119
Charlotte, North Carolina, 155, 165
Charlottetown, Prince Edward Island, 277
Chattanooga, Tennessee, 159, 163–164
Chemical industry, 101, 119, 120, 128, 132, 181, 348
Chernozem soil, 37
Chesapeake and Delaware Canal, 103
Chesapeake Bay, 70, *71,* 96–97
Cheyenne, Wyoming, 216
Chicago, Illinois, 13, *108–109,* 124, *125, 127,* 133–137, 156
Chicanos, 3–4, 207, 233
Chinook wind, 193
Cigar industry, 174
Cincinnati, Ohio, 32, 70, 120, *121*
Cities (*see under* Urban)
City-centered region, 246
Clay Belt, Ontario, 24, 295, 298, 299
Clean Air Act, 222
Clear cutting, *253,* 255
Cleveland, Ohio, 128–130
Climate, 23, *25,* 72, 111, 155–156, 197, 227–231, 329–330
Climax, Colorado, 200
Clothing industry, 82, 91, 93, 94, 132
Coachella Valley, California, 238
Coal, 75, 115, 119, 130, 136, 144, 162, 202, 213, 318–319
Coal gasification, 202
Coast Ranges, 227–228, 254
Coastal Plain, 31, 73–74, 101, 104, 156, 167–176
Coeur d' Alene, Idaho, *209,* 217
Colorado Aqueduct, 238
Colorado Desert, 197, 238
Colorado Piedmont, 193, 208, *213*–216
Colorado Plateau, *192,* 196–197, 209, 217–218
Colorado River (Texas), *192,* 204
Colorado River Compact, 238
Colorado Springs, Colorado, 213–214
Columbia, Maryland, *65,* 103
Columbia, South Carolina, 168, 175

Columbia Plateau, 228, 254
Columbia River, 228, 260–261, 326
Columbia River Treaty, 261, 326
Columbus, Georgia, 169, 175
Columbus, Ohio, 120
Commuting, 83
Computer, 14, *350*
Computer industries, 100
Comstock lode, 240, 250
Connecticut Lowland, 28, 87, 89, 94–95
Consumer goods, 101, 123, 147
Continental drift, 227, *242*
Continental shelf, 184
Contour farming, *98*
Coos Bay, Oregon, 255
Copper, *55,* 57, 133, 164, 200–201, 208, 216, 259
Cordillera, 270, 319
Core, 13, 80–84, *139,* 352
Corn Belt, 12, *13, 54,* 74, 123, *139*
Correlation, 14, *352*
Cotton, *54,* 153, 172, 176, 181, 204, *205,* 208, 240
Council Bluffs, Iowa, 144
County seats, 120, 123
Cranberries, 87
Crop rotation, 177
Cross Timbers, 205
Cuban refugees, 172, 174
Cultural hearth, 69, 203
Cumberland Gap, 29, 111
Cumberland Plateau, *113, 157, 158,* 162
Cumberland Road, 102, 115
Cypress, 27, 156

Dairy Belt (Region), *13, 139,* 141, 145–146
Dairying, 133, 137, 145–146, 150, 232, 255
Dallas-Fort Worth, Texas SMSAs, 14, 203, 204
Dawson, Yukon, 331, 333
Dayton, Ohio, 120, *121*
Death Valley, 239
Decision making, 76, *77n.,* 131, 187
Delaware-Chesapeake Gateways, *71,* 96–107
Delaware River, *64,* 70, 98, 100–101

Dentists, U.S., *350*
Denver, Colorado, 41, 200, 208, 209, 213–215
Desalinization of water, 199, 264, 352
Desert, 41–44, 197, 198, 349
Des Moines, Iowa, 142
Destructive exploitation, 7–8, 133, 137–138
Detroit, Michigan, 60–65, 131–132
District of Columbia, 104
Douglas fir, 196, 254, *255, 349*
Doxiadis, Constantinos, 60–65
Drainage, 97, 130, 143, 155–157, 198
Drought, 149
Dry farming, 39, 149, 216, 319
Duluth-Superior SMSA, 133
Durable goods, 115, 132
Dust bowl, 193, 206

Earth Resources Technology Satellite (ERTS), 3, 9–10, *152–153, 224–225, 239, 340–341*
Earthquakes, 194, 227, 228
Eastern Townships, Quebec, 283
Eastern Transition zone, Texas, 203–204
Eastern Woodlands, *20,* 26–32
Edmonton, Alberta, 311, 316–317
Edwards Plateau, *192,* 203, 206
Electronics, 92, 93, 100, 165
Elliot Lake, Ontario, 299, *300*
El Paso, Texas, 207
Employment, *53,* 92, 115, 140, 144, 154, 182, 202, 203, 233, 342, *352*
Environmental impact study, 250
Erie Canal, 29, 75, 78, 128
Eskimo, 3–4, 21, 26, 298, 330, 331, 335–337
Eureka, California, 249
Evansville, Indiana, 124
Everglades, *153,* 170, 174

Fairbanks, Alaska, 262, 263
Fairfield County, Connecticut, 86
Fall line, 74, *97,* 106, 166–167
Fall River, Massachusetts, 94
Farm machinery, *51,* 131, 140, 141, *142,* 150, 172, 176, *205*

Farming, 53, 87, 115, 138–151, 162, 178, 240, 247–249
Federal Reserve Banks, 78, 106, *146*, 204
Feed-grain livestock farm, *140*, 141–143
Fencing, 39, 143
Fertilizer, 141–142, 156, 174, 175
Fire, forest, 230, *255*
Fishing, 23, 33–34, 87–88, 92, 93, 96, 249, 256, 263, 275
Flatwoods, 170
Flint, Michigan, 132
Flint Hills, Kansas, *139*, 151
Floods, 114, 117, 188, 229
Florida Peninsula, *152–153*, 170–176, 188, 352, 354
Flour milling, 39, 99, 128, 147–148
Fodder crops, 145, 212
Folded Appalachians, 74–75
Food, *22*, 348
Food processing, 96, 123, 143, 150, 175, 231, 246
Forest, 23, 26–27, 32–33, 156, 161, 196, 253–254, *349*
Fort Lauderdale, Florida, 172
Fort Peck Reservoir, 216
Fraser River, 41, 319, 320, 325
Free-trade zone, 130
French Canadians, 3–4, 58, 276, 279, 294, 305, 313
Fresno, California, 241
Frontier, 23, 26, 28, *30*, 41, *42*, 44–45, 109, 262, 294, 296, 297, 299, 301, 309, 334, 354
Fruit, 128, 132, *241*
Functional organization, areal, *126*, *127*
Fur traders, *24*, 26, 131, 133, 143, 331, 332
Furniture manufactures, 132, 165

Galveston, Texas, 185
Garment district, New York, *81–82*
Gary, Indiana, 136
General cargo, 102, 125, 130
General farming region, *139*, 143
Georgia, 156

Georgia Strait region, 322–323
Geothermal power, 246, 348
Germans, 112, 136, 203
Ghetto, 61–62, 66, 82, 96, 104
Ghost towns, 41, *43*, 208
Gila River, 198, 208
Glaciation, 31, 79, 87, *110*, 111, 134, 143, 194, 228, 294
Glass industry, 119, 123, 130
Glen Canyon Dam, 217
Gloucester, Massachusetts, 89, 92
Goats, 206
Gogebic Range, 133
Gold, 41, 150, 208, 216, 217, 247, 262
Government activity, 96, 103–105, 120, 208, 221, 262
Grand Banks, 275
Grand Canyon, 197, 217
Grand Coulee, 261
Grand Rapids, Michigan, 34, 132
Grand River Valley, Ontario, 290, 291
Grasslands, 32–*41*, 149–151
Grazing, 176, 205, 210–211
"Great American Desert," 35, 205
Great Basin, 197, *209*, 218
Great Falls, Montana, 216
Great Lakes, 49, 111, 124, 136–137
Great Lakes Megalopolis, 127–128, 352
Great Lakes region, *110*, 113, 124–138
Great Lakes-St. Lawrence Seaway, 124–125, 137, 285–287
Great Plains, 39, 193, 204–206, *209*, 212, *214*–216
Great Smokies, 157, *158–159*, 163
Great Valley, 30, 111, 157, *158*, 160, *163*, 164
Green Mountains, Vermont, 74, 95
Greenland, 3–4, 337
Greensboro-High Point-Winston-Salem SMSA, 165
Greenville, South Carolina, 165
Gross national product (GNP), 5–6
Groundwater, 177, 198, *199*, 205
Growing season, 155, 169, 352
Growth problems, 7–9, 264, 342–349, 354
Gulf Coast, 31, 354
Gulf of Mexico, *177*, 193, 197

Halifax, Nova Scotia, 272, 274
Hamilton, Ontario, 289
Hampton Roads, Virginia, 102–106, 175
Harlem, New York City, *83*
Harrisburg, Pennsylvania, 74
Hartford, Connecticut, 70, 95
Hawaiian Islands, 230–231, 250–251
Helena, Montana, 216
Hematite, 133
High (Higher) Plains, *139,* 193–*195,* 208,
    212–217
High West, 208–219, *209*
Hinterland, 78–79, 102, *147,* 175
Hispano peoples, 203, 207
Hogs, 141, 143
Hollywood, California, 232
Holyoke, Massachusetts, 94
Home rule, 246
Homestead Act, 147
Honolulu, Hawaii, 230–231, 251
Hoover Dam, *191,* 238
Horses, 123
Housing, 160, 350, 352
    (*See also* Ghetto; Slum; Urban planning
    and renewal)
Houston, Texas, 185–187, 204
Hudson Bay, 26, 40, 315, 330, 336
Hudson County, New Jersey, 84
Hudson-Mohawk Valley, 29, 78–81, 99, 111
Hudson's Bay Company, 57, 254, 308
Humboldt River, 218
Humid continental climate, 28
Humid subtropical climate, 28, 155
Hydroelectric power, 114, 160–161, 254,
    261, 264

Illinois River, 134
Illth, 7–8
Immigration, 48, 77, 93, 112
Imperial Valley, 227
Income, 5–6, *15,* 89, 102, 115, 124, 125, 162,
    166, 175, 176, 178, *200,* 218, 232, *352*
Indianapolis, Indiana, 34, 123
Indians, 21, *22,* 24, 27, 28, 33, *34,* 36–37,
    43, *44,* 51, 215, 217, 231, 254, 297, 307

Inland Empire, 255, 260–261
Inner city, 132
Inner ring, *80,* 84
Insurance industry, 95
Intensive land use, 172
Interior Plains, 270, 304, 305
Intracoastal Waterway, 176, 186
Iowa, 141–143
Iron, 55
    (*See also* Steel)
Iron ore, 57, 133, 164, 213, 238
Irrigation, 40, 45, 97, 149, *206,* 209, *213,* 217,
    231, 238
Irvine, California, 65, 237

Jacksonville, Florida, 175
James River, 104, 106
Jerome, Chauncey, 95
Jerome, Arizona, 201, 208
Jewelry, 94
Juneau, Alaska, 230, 262

Kansas, 150
Kansas City, Missouri-Kansas, 144, 151
Kenosha, Wisconsin, 130, 136
Kern County Land Company, 240
Ketchikan, Alaska, 262
Kettering, Charles F., 120
Keweenaw Peninsula, Michigan, 133
Key West, Florida, 174
King Ranch, Texas, 203
Kitimat, British Columbia, 324
Knoxville, Tennessee, 159, *163,* 164

Labrador, 275, 297
Lake Erie, 124–132
Lake Mead, *191,* 238
Lake Michigan, 134
Lake Okeechobee, 170, 174
Lake Superior, 133
Lake Tahoe, 250
Lakehead area, 300
Lamprey, sea, 138

Lancaster County, Pennsylvania, *98, 99*
Land grants, 225
Land shortage, 349–353
Land titles, 210
Land use, 45, 210, 249, 251
Lansing, Michigan, 63
Laredo, Texas, 207
Large-scale farming, 141–142, 210
Las Vegas, Nevada, 218, 238
Lead, 216
Leadville, Colorado, 200, *212*
Levees, 156, *180*
Lewis and Clark expedition, 216
Lexington, Kentucky, 123
Limestone, 74, 123, 136, 157, 158, 170
Little Rock, Arkansas, 167
Livestock, 141–151, 204
Llano Estacado, 192, 205–206
Location quotient graphs, 14–*16, 82, 92, 101,
    119, 136, 166, 186, 200, 237, 246, 257,
    290, 323*
Loess, 27
Loft industries, 82, 135
London, Ontario, 291
Long Beach, California, 235
Long Island, New York, 14, 78, 84, 85
Lorain, Ohio, *129*
Los Angeles area, California, 230, 232, 234–
    237, *239*
Louisiana, 178, 179
Louisville, Kentucky, 122–123
Lowell, Massachusetts, 93
Lower Ohio Plateaus, *113,* 122–124
Lubbock, Texas, 202, 205
Lumbering, *19,* 26–27, 32–35, 95, 131, 147,
    150, 169–170, 249, 255–256, 262, 277,
    320, 349
Lynn, Massachusetts, 89, 92

Machinery, 92, 95, 120, 123, 140
Mackenzie Valley, 331, 333, 334
Macon, Georgia, 169, 175
Manchester, New Hampshire, 93
Manganese, 216
Manhattan (Island), New York, 68–69, 80–84,
    135

Manitoba, 306, 308–309, 313, 314
Manufacturing, 48–51, *53,* 57, 82–83, 89, 115,
    118–119, 135–136, *137,* 143, 176, 204, 232,
    254, 280, 288–293, 321
Marine West Coast climate, 33
Marion, Ohio, 120
Maritime provinces, 57, 272–277
Mason-Dixon line, 96
Massachusetts, *352*
Meat consumption, 348
Meat packing, 150, 204
Mechanization, 48, *51,* 112, 162, 342
Mediterranean climate, *226, 229*
Megalopolis, 59
Memphis, Tennessee, 181
Meriden, Connecticut, *94*
Merrimack Valley, 89
Mesa Verde, 43, 197
Mesabi Range, 133
Mesquite, *41,* 42
Metal manufactures, 95, 116, 120
Metis, 307
Mexican border, 207
Mexicans, 202–203, 233
Miami-Palm Beach Megalopolis, *153,* 173–
    174
Miami Valley, Ohio, 119–120
Michigan, 60–65, 130–132
Michigan City, Indiana, *134*
Midland, Texas, 202, 206
Midland Hearth, 70
Midwest, 11–12, 49, 50, 87, *110,* 113, 138–
    151
Migration, 67, 115, 149, 187, 342
Milling-in-bond, 128
Milwaukee, Wisconsin, 70, 136–137
Mining, 40–41, *42–43, 53,* 199–200, *212,* 216,
    295–297, 320
Minneapolis-St. Paul SMSAs, 65, 146–148
Minority peoples, 187, 251, 342
    (*See also* Blacks; Chicanos; Indians; Ori-
    entals)
Mississippi, 178, 179, 182, *352*
Mississippi "Delta," 181
Mississippi River, 26, 31, 49, 179–181
Missouri Plateau, 193
Missouri River, 144–*145,* 215–216

Mobile, Alabama, 183–184
Model, 75
Mohawk Valley, 78
Mojave Desert, 238, *239*
Molybdenum, 200
Moncton, New Brunswick, 274
Montana, 215–216
Montgomery, Alabama, 169
Montreal, Quebec, 58, 279–282, 289, 351
Mormons, 44, 207, 209, 218–219, 237
Mount Hood, *253*
Mount McKinley, 228
Mount Rainier, 259
Moving pictures, 232
Multiple-use region, 114
Muncie, Indiana, 123
Muscle Shoals, Alabama, 159
Muskeg, 24

Nantucket, Massachusetts, 93
Napa Valley, *247, 249*
Narragansett Basin, 87, 89, 93–94
Nashville Basin, Tennessee, 113, 123
Natchez, Mississippi, 181
Natural gas, 123, *180,* 184–186, *192,* 201–202, 262, 353
Natural resources, 87–89, 132, 136–137, 188, 342, 351
Navajos, 207, 218
Naval stores, 34, 169
Neoplantation, 177, *178*
Nevada, 218
New Bedford, Massachusetts, 93
New Brunswick, 276, 277
New England, 28, 49, 70, *71,* 86–97
New Haven, Connecticut, *94,* 95
New Jersey, 84–85
New Orleans, Louisiana, 157, 181–183
New York Gateway, 77–86
New York City, New York, 14, *68–69,* 75, *76,* 79–86, 99, 104, 183, 245
New York State Barge Canal, 78
Newark, New Jersey, 84
Newfoundland, 275, 277
Newport, Rhode Island, 94
Newport News-Hampton SMSA, Virginia, 106

Niagara Falls, 128, 290
Nickel, 57, 299
Nodal region, 13
Norfolk, Virginia, 104–106
North Carolina, 170
North Platte valley, 215
North Slope, Alaska, 228
Northern Rockies, 194, 216
Northern Woodlands, 20, 23–26
Northwest Territories, 308, 331, 334–336
Northwestern California, 249–250
Nova Scotia, 275, 276
Nuclear power, 114, 161, 237

Oakland, California, 246
Odessa, Texas, 202, 206
Ohio Basin, 109, *110,* 113–124
Ohio Valley, 29, 31, 113, 114
Oil shale, 200, 202, 217, 353
Okanagan Valley, British Columbia, 320, 324, *326*
Oklahoma, 138, 201
Oklahoma City, Oklahoma, 204
Olympic Mountains, 228, 230
Omaha, Nebraska, 144–145
Ontario, 57, 62, 284–294, 298–301
Orange County, California, 236
Oranges, 170–174, 231
Orchards, *241,* 248–249
Oregon City, Oregon, 256
Oregon Trail, 217, 254
Orientals, 233
Organic products, 348
Orlando, Florida, 174–175
Ottawa, Ontario, 287, 293
Ottawa River, 298
Ouachita Mountains, *158,* 166
Out-migration, 54, 124, 139–141, 151, 154, 162, 222
Owens Valley, 232, *233,* 239, *240*
Oxnard Plain (Ventura County, California), 236
Ozark Plateau, 143, 144, *158,* 166–167

Palm Beach, Florida, 174

Palm Springs, California, 238
Palouse country, 254
Paper and pulp manufactures, 147, *273*, 277, *325*
Parkland, 36, 307
Parks, 195
Pasadena, California, 234–235
Patterns, *10–12*, 31, 59–66, 87, 111–113, 117, 128, 157, 169, 188, *194–195*, 211–212, 245
Peace River, 309–311
Pecos River Valley, 207
Pennsylvania Dutch, 29, 75, *98*
Pennsylvania Railroad, 99
Penobscot Valley, 95
Peoria, Illinois, 143
Perception, 21, 47, 328
Permafrost, 24, 330
Petrochemical Empire, 185–187, 204
Petrochemicals, 183–186
Petroleum, *11, 177,* 181–182, *185, 192,* 201–202, 232, 262, 353, 354
Pharmaceuticals, 123, 132
Philadelphia, Pennsylvania, *8, 63–64,* 77, 96, 98–102
Phoenix, Arizona, 208
Phosphate, 174, *342*
Photographic equipment, 78
Piedmont, 74, *98,* 100, 164–167, 176
Pineapples, 250
Pines, 156, 186, 196, 197, *349*
Pioneering, 23, 45
Pipelines, *185,* 229, 262
Pittsburgh, Pennsylvania, 111, 115–119
Plantation system, 152, 176–177
Planter aristocracy, 29–31, 96, 102, 115, 171, 179
Platte River, 151
Pollution, 6, 9, 45, 64, 66, 86, 128, 136–137, 138, 140, 186, 221, 230, 264, *342,* 346–348
Pontiac, Michigan, 132
"Poor whites," 29–31, 179
Population, 7, *56,* 58–59, 115, 119, 124, 139–140, 179, 342–344, 349
Port Alberni, British Columbia, *46–47*
Portland, Maine, 96
Portland, Oregon, 230, 256–257

Ports, 157, 172
　(*See also* specific ports)
Potatoes, *56,* 95, 133, 217, 277
Poverty, 14, 154, 176, 178–179, 342
Prairie, the, 35–40, 110
Prairie Provinces, 39, 40, 57, 305–319
Preferential assessment, 249
Primary industries, 56
Prince Edward Island, 57, 276–277
Providence, Rhode Island, 93–94
Publishing industry, *82,* 83
Pueblo, Colorado, 200, 212–213
Puget Sound, Lowlands, 254, 257–259

Quarrying, 88
Quebec, 26, 57, 279–284, 294–298
Quebec City, Quebec, 272, 281

Railroads, 31, 39, 49, 130, 134–136, 158, 164–166
Rainfall, 193, 197, 205, 230
Ranching, 149, 210, 217
Range, Western, 210–*211*
Raw materials, 51–52, *55,* 96–97, 101, 124, 128
Recreation, 63, 84, 95, 115, *159,* 350
Rectangular survey, 11, 31, 63, 111–113, 157, 309
Recycling, 188, 199, 345, 348
Red River (of the North), 40, 149
Reforestation, 161, 260
Regina, Saskatchewan, 314
Regional concept, 12–17, 49, 59, 106, 138, *139,* 344
Regional planning, 60–66, 245–246
　(*See also* Urban planning and renewal)
Regional specialization, 48, 70, 252
Remote sensing, 3, 9–10
Reno, Nevada, 218, 250
Resorts, 95, 172–175
Retirement areas, 155, 173, 174
Rice, 181, 246
Richmond, Virginia, 74, 102, 107
Ridge and Valley Province, 74–75

Rio Grande, 198, 203, 207, 212
Riparian doctrine, 210
Riverside, California, 238
Roanoke, Virginia, 162
Rochester, New York, 78
Rocky Mountains, 41, 43, *192–196*, 199, *209,* 212, 306, 319
Root, Elisha, 95
Routes, 24, 26, 78–79, 99, 157, 158, 164, 166
Runoff, *198*
Rural New England, 95–96
Rural population, *56,* 150

Sacramento, California, 65, 241, 246
Sagebrush, 43, 217
Saguenay Valley, 297
Saint John, New Brunswick, 57, 272, 273
St. John's Newfoundland, 274
St. Lawrence Lowland, 58, 269, 278
St. Lawrence River, 26, 34, 40, 272, 279, 281
St. Lawrence Seaway, 280, *284,* 285, 288, 300
St. Louis, Missouri, 70, 135, 143–144
St. Paul, Minnesota, 146–147
St. Petersburg, Florida, 174
Salinas Valley, 249
Salmon, 138, 254, 261
Salt Lake City, Utah, 208, 218
Salt River, 208
Salton Sea, 227
San Andreas Fault, 227, *239, 242*
San Antonio, Texas, 203–204
San Bernardino, California, 237
San Diego, California, 227, 237
San Francisco Bay area, 227, 230, 241–247
San Gabriel Valley, 234–236
San Jacinto Basin, 238
Sand Hills, Nebraska, *139,* 151
Santa Ana winds, 229, 230
Santa Barbara, California, *225,* 236
Santa Clara Valley, 245, *247,* 346–347
Santa Fe Trail, 207
Sarnia, Ontario, 291
Saskatachewan, 307, 309, 315, 316
Saskatoon, Saskatchewan, 315
Sault Ste. Marie, Ontario, 299

Savannah, Georgia, 172, 175
Schefferville, Quebec, 297
Schenectady, New York, 78
Schuylkill River, 98–99
Scotch-Irish, 29, 75
Scranton, Pennsylvania, 75
Seattle, Washington, 230, 254, 257–259
Secondary industries, 56
Sequoia National Park, 238
Service industies, *52,* 83, 89, 141
Settlement, *30,* 35–45, *58,* 111–113, 134, 171–173, 176, 207, 252–255, 307
Sewage disposal, 54, 117, *342*
Sheep, 207, 249
Shipbuilding, 87, 107
Shreveport, Louisiana, 186
Shrublands, 40–44
Sidewalk farming, 149
Sierra Nevada, 228, 239–*240,* 250
Silver, 200, 208, 216, 217
Sioux Falls, South Dakota, 150
Site, 12
Sitka, Alaska, 262
Situation, 13
Slate, 75
Slaves, Negro, 22, 29–30, 153, 176
Slum, *8,* 66, 82
Smog, 117, 186, 227, 229, 342
Snake Plains, Idaho, 208, 217
Soil erosion, 156, *165*
Soils, 24, 27, 37, 44, 74, 109–111, 123, 145, 157, *165,* 169, 181, 188, 197, 307, 348
Solar energy, 348, 353–354
Sonoma Valley, *247,* 249
Soo canals, 114, 133, 299
Sorghum, 149, 205
South Bend, Indiana, 130
South Dakota, 139, 150
South Platte Valley, *213–215*
Southeastern Plain, *154–155,* 167–176, 188
Southern Pacific Railroad, 207
Southern Piedmont, *158,* 164–166, 188, 354
Southern (Great) Plains, 204–206
Southern Rockies, 195–196, 209
Southwestern Ohio Megalopis, *113,* 119–122
Soybeans, 143, 181, 348

Spanish, 202–203, 233, 342
Spokane, Washington, 254, 260
Spring Wheat Belt, *139,* 149–150
Springfield, Massachusetts, *94,* 95
Standard of living, 6, 342
Standard Metropolitan Statistical Areas (SMSAs), 14
Steamboat traffic, 144–147, 180–181
Steel, *60,* 75, 116, 128, 136, 164, 186
Steppes, the, 35, 37, 39, *40–41*
Stockton, California, 246
Strip cropping, *98,* 149
Strip mining, 162, 216, 222
Suburbs, 61, 62, 135–136, 244, 349, 352
Sudbury, Ontario, 299
Sugar beets, 150, 212, 215, 217
Sugar cane, 171, 181, *250*
Suitcase farming, 149
Sulfur, *55,* 177, 181, 184
Susquehanna River Valley, 99
Sydney, Nova Scotia, 273
Syracuse, New York, 78
Systems, regional, 15–16

Tacoma, Washington, 259
Taconite, 133
Tampa-St. Petersburg SMSA, 174
Taylor Grazing Act, 211
Tennessee River, 156, *161–162,* 188
Tennessee Valley Authority (TVA), 114, 157, 159–161, *163*
Tertiary industries, 56
Texas, 38, *40–41,* 49, 138, 178, 201, 205–206
Textile industry, 75, 93, 165
Thunder Bay, Ontario, 285, 300
Tidal power, 348
Tidewater, 29–30, 96, 104
Timmins, Ontario, 299
Tobacco, 28*n.,* 74, 87, 97, 104, 106, 123, 165, 169, 176
Toledo, Ohio, *62,* 63, 129–130
Toronto, Ontario, 285, 287–289, 298, 351
Tourism, *86,* 156, 256
Towns, New England, 89*n.,* 95
Township, 111, *112*

Township-range survey, 11, 31, 111–113
Trail, British Columbia, 234
Trans-Sierra, 238–239
Transverse Range, *225,* 227
Transportation equipment, 128, 143, 166
Trans-shipment, 76–77, 122, 125
Tree farming, 155, 256
Trenton, New Jersey, 74, 100–101
Troy, New York, 78
Truck gardening, *172*
Tucson, Arizona, 208
Tulsa, Oklahoma, 204
Tundra, 26, 329, 337, 349

Uniform region, 12–13
Union Pacific Railroad, 39, 209
Upper (Great) Lakes, *125,* 133
Upper Ohio Plateaus, *113,* 115–119
Uranium, 200
Urban hierarchies, 59, 111–113, *126–127, 146–147, 312*
Urban planning and renewal, *8,* 62, 66, 99, 103, 104, 117–118, *121,* 128, 132, 147–148, 237, 350, *351*
Urban revolution, 48
Urbanization, 8–9, 47–66
Urbanized areas, 14, 124
Utah, 218, *221*

Valdez, Alaska, 229, 262
Vancouver, British Columbia, 315, 319–322
Vancouver Island, 320
Vegetables, 203, 213
Vegetation, 21, 155–156
Vermillion Range, 133
Vicksburg, Mississippi, 31, 181
Victoria, British Columbia, 319, 323
Vineyards, 237, 248–250
Virginia City, Montana, 216

Wabash-Lower Ohio Valley, *113,* 123–124
Waco, Texas, 203–204
Wasatch Range, 194, 208, 218

Washington, District of Columbia, 102–104
Water, 114–115, 134, 149, 156–157, 182, 186–187, 199, 212, 219–220, 350, 352
Water rights, 210–211
Waterbury, Connecticut, *94*
Waterpower, 94
Waterton-Glacier International Peace Park, 193, 217
Wealth, 4–6
Well drilling, 39
Welland Canal, Ontario, *291*
Wheat, *54*, 57, 149–151, 205, 206, *308*
White Mountains, 74
Whitehorse, Yukon, 331, 332
Whiting, Indiana, 136
Whitney, Eli, 95
Wichita, Kansas, 150
Wilkes-Barre, Pennsylvania, 75
Willamette National Forest, 259–260
Willamette Valley, 228, 254, 256
Williamsburg, Virginia, 104
Wilmington, Delaware, 74, 101
Wilmington, North Carolina, 177
Windsor, Ontario, 61, 285, 291–293

Winnipeg, Manitoba, 306, 309, 311–314
Winter Wheat Belt, *138*, 150–151
Wisconsin, *32*, 136–137
Wood pulp, 95, 133, 170, 256, 277, 294–296, 323–325
Wooded Midwest, 31–32
Worcester, Massachusetts, *72*, 94
Wyoming, *19*
Wyoming Basin, *209*, 215

Yakima Valley, 260
Yellowknife, Northwest Territories, 334, 335
Yellowstone Park, 216
Yellowstone Valley, 215–216
Yosemite National Park, 228
Youngstown, Ohio, 119
Yukon River, 228, 263
Yukon Territory, 327, 331–334

Zinc, 208, 216
Zion Canyon, *196*